To Daphne,

On her birthday

Peace, Love, & Friendship

Angie   9-2-8P

Jessica Savitch

and

the Selling

of Television News

Gwenda Blair

Almost

Golden

SIMON AND SCHUSTER

NEW YORK · LONDON · TORONTO · SYDNEY · TOKYO

SIMON AND SCHUSTER
*Simon & Schuster Building
Rockefeller Center
1230 Avenue of the Americas
New York, New York 10020*

*Copyright © 1988 by Gwenda Blair
All rights reserved
including the right of reproduction
in whole or in part in any form.
Published by the Simon & Schuster Trade Division
SIMON AND SCHUSTER and colophon are
registered trademarks of Simon & Schuster Inc.
Designed by Edith Fowler
Manufactured in the United States of America*

10   9   8   7   6   5   4   3

Library of Congress Cataloging in Publication Data

*Blair, Gwenda.
  Almost golden.*

  *Includes index.
    1. Savitch, Jessica.   2. Journalists—United
States—Biography.   3. Television broadcasting
of news—Social aspects—United States.   I. Title.
PN4874.S297B5   1988   070'.92'4   [B]
88-11425
ISBN 0-671-63285-X*

Acknowledgments

This book is based almost entirely on personal interviews with more than 350 people, including those who knew Jessica Savitch personally, professionally, or both, and those who did not know her but were involved in or knowledgeable about broadcasting. I am grateful for their time and, in many cases, the considerable effort they devoted to this project. More than half of the interviews were conducted in person; because of time and travel constraints, the rest were by telephone. Most of those I spoke with are included in the following list, but a small number are omitted because they felt too vulnerable to allow their names to be published.

I would like to thank the following: Betsy Aaron, Cliff Abromats, Dee Adamczyk, David Adams, Bill Adler, Don Alhart, Bob Allen, Diane Allen, Jennifer Allen, Steve Altman, Anne Amico, Bob Asman, Wally Athey, Win Baker, Max Barber, Joe Bartelme, Randall Barton, Peter Basil, Francie Barnard, David Beddow, Marsha Bemko, Alan J. Bell, Carol Bell, Leslie Bennetts, Don Benskin, Richard Berman, Paul Bissonette, Harriet Blacker, Craig Bland, Neil Bobrick, Don Bowers, Wayne Boyer, Tom Brokaw, John Bowen, Doug Brown, Milton Burris, Tony Busch, Gary Calderwood, Liz Callan, Marrie Campbell, Candy Carell, Lee Chiaramonte, Cindy Chock, Connie Chung, Lillian Ciarrochi, Leslie Cockburn, Roseanne Colletti, Chet Collier, Blair Clark, John Clement, Barbara Cohen, John Colle, Nancy Collins, Ann Compton, Steve Conn, Frank Costa,

Bill Cran, Patricia Creaghan, Mort Crim, Les Crystal, Jim Cusick, Joe DalCorso, John Charles Daly, Mahdu Damania, Robert Davies, Joel Davis, Sid Davis, Jered Dawaliby, Joe Deane, Nancy Dickerson, Marvin Diskin, Grace Diekhaus, Sam Donaldson, Linda Doserets, June Douglas, Paul Dowie, Herb Dudnick, Joe Duncan, Susan Dutcher, Richard Edelman, Renee Edelman, Steve Edwards, Mike Elliott, Ellen Ehrlich, Linda Ellerbee, Jay Emmett, Martha Emmett, Bob Eolin, Susan Erenburg, Don Fair, David Fanning, Eileen Farrington, Frances Farenthold, Don Farmer, Sid Feders, Julius Fischbein, Reisel Fischbein, Barbara Fischel, Ed Fischel, Dick Fischer, Don Fitzpatrick, Steven Flax, Debi Fortune Farnham, Diane Feinberg, Jack Fentress, Reuven Frank, Ray Freeman, Dwayne Friedel, Marvin H. Friedman, Steve Friedman, George Gaines, Dyanne Garner, Stephen Gary, Dean Gaskill, Alfred Geller, Bill Gilliant, Judith Girard, Norm Glen, Dave Glodt, Linda Goff, Eleanor Sonnenschein Gochenaur, Fred Graham, Howard Green, Jeff Greenhawt, Greer Griffith, Doris Haber, Marty Haig, David Halberstam, Bruce Halford, Dr. Jake Hammond, Suzanne Hansberry, Deborah Harbin, Rev. John Harper, Joe C. Harris, John Hart, Jake Haselkorn, Harvey Hauptman, Walt Hawver, Ken Headrick, Judith Hennessee, Jack Hewitt, Larry Hoffner, Fred Hofheinz, John Holland, Ron Hollander, Bob Hosking, Dick Hunt, Roy Hyman, Al Ittleson, John Irvin, Peter Jacobus, Bob Jamieson, Dick John, Phil Jones, Ed Joyce, Larry Kane, Stephanie Kaplan, Bob Kasmire, Louis Katz, Joe Keating, Sr., Kitty Kelley, Ann Kemp, Art Kent, Ron Kershaw, Bob Kieve, Douglas Kiker, Ed Kilgore, Mike Kirk, Mary Klette, George Koehler, Allen Kohler, Mel Korn, Walter Kravitz, Tom Kreneck, Charla Krupp, Bob Kur, Bill Kuster, Eve Krzyzanowski, Tom LaMaine, John Lane, Esq., Shelley Laurence, Tom Leahy, Jim Lee, Vince Leonard, Sue Levitt, Mark Levy, Vincent Lopopolo, Don Lovett, Olivia Lovett, Mike Ludlam, Dotty Lynch, Robin Mackintosh, Robert MacNeil, Michael Mallowe, Scott Malone, Vince Manzi, Frank Marciante, Mary Pangalos Manilla, Dave Marash, Marjorie Margolies, Howard Marks, Nelson Martinez, Kati Marton, Sue Mascio, Barbara Matusow, Lee McCarthy, Donald McClellan, Ida McGuinness, Jud McIlvain, Don Meaney, Al Meltzer, Tony Messuri, Gary Merkin, Bern Meyer, Ray Miller, Gilbert Millstein, Andrea Mitchell, Bill Monroe, Mauri Moore, Gersh Morgenstern, Jo Moring, April Morris, Cliff Morrison, Roger Mudd, Bob Mulholland, Walt Murphy, Brooke Myers, Dave Neal, Barry Nemcoff, Bob Nicholas, Rusty Nicholl, Ron Nicosin, Nick Nickson, Shad Northshield, Jack Olender, Esq., Charles Osgood, Gene Packard, Harold J. Pannepacker, Jane Pauley, Sue Percival, Bob Pierpoint, Jim Pilkington, Wally Pfister, Alan Pingally, Malcolm Poindexter, Jerry Polikoff, Pat Polillo, Sandy Polillo, Jan Porembski, Katherine Powers, Eleanor Prescott, David Price, Al

6

Primo, Dick Pyle, Charles Quinn, Matt Quinn, Jo Rand, Martin Rand, Rita Rappaport, Sidney Resnick, Leona Resnick, Pam Ridder, Gloria Rivera, Ann Rogers, Bill Rubens, Bud Rukeyser, Ed Safdie, Dick Salant, David Salzman, Cindy Samuels, Marlene Sanders, Dorothy Savitch, Bill Schechner, Danny Schechter, Ray Scherer, Steve Schiffman, Max Schindler, Herb Schlosser, Jim Schmidt, Dr. Lawrence B. Schreiber, Larry Schultz, Marilyn Schultz, Jordan Schwartz, Steve Schwartz, Bill Schwing, Louise Schwing, Larry Shainman, John Shaw, Bill Sheehan, Sheldon Silverstein, Bill Slatter, Bill Small, Martha Smilgas, Jack Smith, Jeanne Smith, Rose Smith, Sally Bedell Smith, Steve Smith, Deedee Snibbee, Sandy Socolow, Gerry Solomon, Herb Squires, Alan Statsky, Dave Stewart, Ricki Stofsky, Ron Stone, Martha Stonequist, Peter Sturdivant, Bob Sutton, Don Swaim, Barry Swartz, Pauline Swartz, Helene Swertlow, Eleanor Tinsley, Ken Tiven, Ed Tivnan, Jim Thompson, Ray Timothy, Ron Tindiglia, Ian Todhunter, Jim Topping, John Torrenzio, John Travieso, Pat Trese, Richard Valeriani, Joe Vandergast, Sander Vanocur, Frank Virgilio, Mike Verno, Jaroslav Vodehnal, Barbara Vogt, John Von Soosten, Dick Wald, Dave Ward, Russ Ward, George Watson, Richard Watt, Kay Way, Milt Weiss, Betty Wells, Linda Werthheimer, Betsy West, Sylvia Westerman, Wallace Westfeldt, James Whalen, Jeff Wheat, Kate White, Joe Wiedenmeyer, Richard Weisman, Bob Wolfe, Tom Wolzien, Don Woodman, Judy Woodruff, Jim Wooten, Jim Yeargin, Marvin Zindler.

For background material, I found certain books particularly helpful. Jessica Savitch's autobiography, *Anchorwoman* (G. P. Putnam's Sons), was, of course, a key source. As is the case in many autobiographies, her recollection of events differs, sometimes markedly, from that of others, and, in some instances, from the version of events that I found in my research and include here. Five other books were invaluable: *Tube of Plenty,* by Erik Barnouw (Oxford University Press, 1975); *Up the Tube,* by Sally Bedell (Viking, 1981); *The Powers That Be,* by David Halberstam (Dell, 1979); *The Evening Stars,* by Barbara Matusow (Ballantine, 1984), and *Waiting for Prime Time: The Women of Television News,* by Marlene Sanders and Marsha Rock (University of Illinois Press, 1988). Also of assistance were *The General: David Sarnoff and the Rise of the Communications Industry,* by Kenneth Bilby (Harper & Row, 1986); *The Boys on the Bus,* by Timothy Crouse (Ballantine, 1986); *Among Those Present,* by Nancy Dickerson (Random House, 1976); *"And So It Goes": Adventures in Television,* by Linda Ellerbee (G. P. Putnam's Sons, 1986); *The Newscasters,* by Ron Powers (St. Martin's Press, 1977); *The Main Source: Learning from Television News,* by John P. Robinson & Mark R. Levy (Sage Publications, 1986); *Newswatch: How TV Decides the News,* by Av Westin (Touchstone, 1983); *"This Is Judy Woodruff at the White House,"* by

Judy Woodruff with Kathleen Maxa (Addison-Wesley, 1982). Here and there, I consulted *Houston: The Once and Future City,* by George Fuermann (Doubleday, 1971); *The Ithaca College Story,* by John B. Harcourt (Ithaca College, 1983); *Women in Television,* by Anita Klever (Westminster Press, 1975); *Total Television,* by Alex McNeil (Penguin, 1984); *Amusing Ourselves to Death,* By Neil Postman (Viking, 1984); and *We're Going to Make You a Star,* by Sally Quinn (Simon and Schuster, 1975).

I used many newspaper and magazine articles, far too many to list; direct quotations are cited in the text. Here I would like to mention two particularly helpful articles: "Keepers of the Flame," an interview with David Adams, published in *Broadcasting,* June 9, 1986; and "The Communicator," a two-part profile of Sylvester Weaver by Thomas Whiteside, published in *The New Yorker,* October 16 & 23, 1954. In addition, I would like to thank Claudia Dreifus for letting me listen to an interview she conducted with Jessica Savitch in 1982.

I am grateful to the many people who helped me along the way with advice, support, and, when I was traveling, a place to stay: Drs. Dick and Dawna Armstrong, Vina Armstrong, Newell and Greta Blair, Barbara Bloom, Bonnie Fraser, Eva Gold, Dr. Eli Goldensohn, Judah and Micah Gold-Markel, Joanmarie Kalter, Elizabeth Kaye, Susan Landau, Nathaniel, Sarah, and Steve Loevy, Josh Markel, Daisy, Katherine and Steve Salant, Amanda Spake, Dr. Seymour Spivack, Bob, Emma, and Juliette Spertus, and the women in my writers' group. Avis Lang's transcriptions were also invaluable.

My agent, Gloria Loomis, and her able associate, Beth Vesel, provided valuable encouragement, help, and assistance at every step of the way. I am grateful as well to Alice Mayhew; in an age in which editors all too often never set blue pencil to manuscript, her sharp eye and detailed suggestions were priceless. Thanks, too, to her assistant, David Shipley, for patience and enthusiasm through the arduous process of rushing this book to press.

Finally, I would like to thank the folks at home, who helped me and put up with me: Ilaria, Newell, Sasha, Stephen, Bracken, Rainy, and, of course, Cam, without whom there would be no book.

With love to my husband, editor, and best friend,
    CAM,
and to the two other stars in my life,
    SASHA *and* NEWELL

Contents

1

*N*ew York

At 8:58 on the evening of Monday, October 3, 1983, a woman named Jessica Savitch appeared on an *NBC News Digest,* a sort of broadcast headline service, and proceeded to have what looked like the beginnings of a nervous breakdown. It is possible to know the details of this episode in considerable detail, almost moment by moment, because the *Digest* in question, like everything else in television, was part of the vast electronic communication system which is one of the marvels of our time, and which necessarily functions in split-second coordination across the country. The *Digest,* the first of two broadcast live every evening at 8:58 and 9:58, was sixty seconds long. The opening sequence, in this case a computer-animated globe that swam across the screen and merged with the sun, used seven seconds of that time. The *Digest* was further reduced by a ten-second commercial at the halfway point, leaving a total of forty-three seconds for the actual news content, which was delivered by Jessica Savitch. Her role—a role that had helped make her one of the most famous women in contemporary America—was to read fewer than two hundred words of prose. When she failed to perform this task properly, the result was something close to panic in the third-floor studio of NBC News.

On October 3, the first *Digest* was, in the jargon, led into by *Boone,* a short-lived dramatic series dreamed up by Earl Hamner, who had already won a place in television history by creating *The Waltons*. Set in Tennessee, *Boone* was the story of a young country-and-western singer dreaming of the big time, despite his parents' hopes that he would become either a garage mechanic or a preacher. The *Digest* was to cover four items, which had been selected and written by a man named Bill O'Connell, a bearded television veteran who received no screen credit on the broadcast. Like others on the program—although it was less than a minute in duration, the *Digest* required a producer, director, assistant director, technical director, floor director, camera operator, TelePrompTer operator, and audio engineer, as well as two graphic artists and a technician to handle the insertion of their computer drawings into the show —O'Connell had long ago been bumped from the fast track and was serving out his days until retirement and pension. One of his routine assignments was the *Digest,* which was generally regarded as a journalistic backwater.

There is considerable irony in this view, because, in truth, the two evening *Digest*s, broadcast seven nights a week, were the most widely seen news programs in NBC's daily schedule. They were shown in prime time, giving them a larger audience than the half-hour evening news and making them, arguably, the single most important source of information about current events for millions of Americans.

Few viewers tuned in specifically to see the *Digest;* rather, its audience consisted of people who had turned on their television for entertainment and kept it on when a *Digest* appeared. Nonetheless, they far outnumbered the people who watched the network's full-length news program, *NBC Nightly News.* ★ The previous Tuesday, for example, according to Nielsen Media Research, *The A-Team* delivered more than nineteen million households to Savitch and the *Digest* at two minutes before 9:00 P.M., and she undoubtedly picked up even more extra viewers who tuned in a few minutes early for *Remington*

★ *The word "network" is used in this book in its popular sense, to refer to all the broadcast operations of NBC, ABC, and CBS, although technically the NBC, ABC, and CBS networks are only one division of the companies to which they belong.*

Steele; that same week, the *Nightly News,* with Tom Brokaw, drew an average of eight and a half million households.

Savitch, a fine-featured, blue-eyed blond whose diminutive stature was disguised by the standard close-up shot used for anchors, had been a substitute anchor on the weekday *Nightly News* fewer than two dozen times during her six years at NBC; instead she anchored the far less prestigious weekend version of the broadcast, first on Sundays and then later on Saturdays. But she also anchored the prime-time *Digest* more often than anyone else; in October 1983, she was doing two of them at least three nights every week. As a result, she was easily as recognizable to viewers as Brokaw, who had recently succeeded John Chancellor and Roger Mudd to become sole anchor of the evening newscast. Her secret "Q-ratings," the network measure of viewers' responsiveness to newscasters, were said to be higher. One poll, released in January 1982, pegged Savitch and Dan Rather as the sexiest anchors in the U.S.; a second poll, conducted by *TV Guide* and released in September 1982, found that she was regarded as the fourth most trustworthy anchor on television—right behind Dan Rather, Roger Mudd, and Frank Reynolds, and ahead of Brokaw. Within the tiny *Digest,* she was the only on-air figure; there was no feed from a correspondent in San Salvador or Moscow, no avuncular commentary from a former anchor. At two minutes to nine in the evening, and again at two minutes to ten, Jessica Savitch did not simply deliver the news; in the minds of millions of Americans, Savitch *was* the news. And when she broke down, what those millions saw was not the breakdown of an individual woman, but the breakdown of the *news*—or, rather, the collapse of the elaborate, expensive, and mostly invisible machinery which maintained it, revealing at its center a frightened and lonely person twitching like a small creature snared in an incomprehensibly large net.

The *Digest* was invented in the middle 1970s as simple promotion for the news. Originally called *Update,* renamed *Capsule,* and then re-renamed *Digest* (and promptly dubbed "Di-Gel" by newsroom staffers), this live news bulletin was an unloved stepchild in the NBC news division. Because it had no staff of its own but rather used personnel from other news operations, its annual cost was less than $2 million at a time

15

when the news division budget was in the vicinity of $250 million. In other words, the *Digest* spent in a year what the rest of the department spent in less than two days. Even in a medium where the average story runs less than two minutes, the *Digest*'s brevity was considered ridiculous. Although there was always the worry, as one *Digest* producer put it, that "some little guy with a fat pencil out in Iowa would phone in and say that fact is wrong," the program was considered an elocutionary challenge, not a journalistic one, for there was barely enough time to wrap several tersely worded bulletins around a commercial.

Because this assignment meant sticking around 30 Rockefeller Center, NBC headquarters, until 10:00 P.M., just to read eighty-six seconds' worth of headlines off a TelePrompTer, it was not a great favorite. Although people in the news division were mindful of the exposure the news bulletin offered, most of them did not take it particularly seriously; they assigned real importance only to Brokaw's show.

The network executives had a somewhat different view of the *Digest*. They were attracted by a prime-time program, however short, that had a large audience and was extremely cheap to produce. As cited in *New York* magazine, in 1981, when the average *Nightly News* brought in $153,000 a night and cost $88,000, thus profiting about $3,000 per minute, the cost of what was then called the *Update* was $2,000 and the ten-second commercial within it brought in $25,000, leaving a profit of $23,000 for one minute. By 1983, the fee for the ten-second *Digest* commercial had jumped to $40,000, making that one minute at 8:58 and again at 9:58 even more profitable. Thus, Savitch's short stint on the air every night was the object of considerable attention not only from viewers but also from company brass. When things went wrong on October 3, alarm bells rang throughout NBC and, subsequently, in the larger world outside.

But nobody took the *Digest* as seriously as Jessica Savitch did. In September 1977 she had come to NBC from a local Philadelphia station, and her arrival as the anchor for Sunday nights and the *Digest* as well as Senate correspondent on *NBC Nightly News* had been covered in newspapers and magazines across the country. Within the industry, she was already a legend for her ability to sit in an empty television studio, look into the camera, and read from a TelePrompTer with a unique combination of authority and warmth that inspired a viewer response of awesome proportions. Requests for public appearances poured into her office. In 1979, *Newsweek* had called her "NBC's Golden Girl," and she had been widely described as the woman who might eventually become co-anchor or even solo anchor of the *Nightly News* when John Chancellor finally put his microphone down. No woman had ever held this exalted position, or had even been in line for it. Then again, no one at NBC had ever been faced with the situation then emerging in network news.

In terms of both news and entertainment programs, NBC had been used to being a comfortable second behind CBS. But in the mid-1970s, under programming czar Fred Silverman, ABC began pouring money and energy into its prime-time programs and attracting enormous audiences to such mindless fare as *Happy Days, The Six Million Dollar Man,* and *Charlie's Angels.* Then ABC brass had turned their attention to their lackluster news operation. Their opening move was to seduce Barbara Walters away from NBC to co-anchor *ABC News* with Harry Reasoner; although that particular combination proved unworkable, the enormous publicity generated by Walters's million-dollar salary, the first in television history, gave ABC's news operation a public recognition it had never had. The next year, Roone Arledge, whose pioneering use of new broadcast technology, including instant replays and lively electronic graphics, had put ABC's sports division on the map, became head of ABC News. He immediately began upgrading the division with such top-notch correspondents as Cassie Mackin (formerly NBC), Sander Vanocur (then at *The Washington Post*), and, from CBS, Richard Threlkeld, Barry Serafin, and Sylvia Chase. Arledge also reinstated Av Westin, a veteran ABC producer who had been fired, hired Dick Wald, outgoing president of NBC News, and began skimming off some of the best producers at the rival networks, including Mike Buddy, John Armstrong, Don Bowers, and Rick Kaplan. With *NBC Nightly News* now facing the possibility of slipping into third place, executives at 30 Rock were pushed to desperate expedients, which for some included entertaining the still-fantastic notion that a woman might ascend the peacock throne. "Hell, when you're number two and think you may be headed for number three, you'll blue-sky anything," said network vice-president Dick Fischer long after the fact.

Ever since she had arrived at NBC, Jessica Savitch had been a favorite topic of conversation. In the overworked, over-intense, highly collaborative environment that prevails in most daily media, gossip about everyone, high and low, flourishes like bacteria in a petri dish; nonetheless, few figures attracted as much speculation, the majority of it negative, as Jessica Savitch. She had come to NBC a young, beautiful, blond rising star— hardly a welcome sight in an environment where dozens of reporters and producers were already engaged in near-murder-ous competition for airtime. Worse, she did not come as simply one more working stiff, vying to get on the air; she received not only the plum assignment of Senate correspondent for the evening news, but guaranteed appearances on air as the anchor on Sunday nights and on the prime-time *Digest*. By tradition, regardless of any prior experience on local stations, future net-work anchors toiled in the network trenches and proved them-selves before they earned the top slot. Savitch, however, had never worked for any of the three national networks before becoming an anchorwoman, a post that guaranteed an extraor-dinary degree of national recognition. It did not help that it was widely rumored that Edgar Griffiths, the chairman of RCA, which owned NBC, had seen Savitch on local television in Philadelphia and had told network officials to hire her. In fact, the officials discovered her on their own, but the notion that Savitch owed her new eminence to outside intervention stuck in the craw of her new NBC colleagues.

Perhaps a saint might have turned the situation around, but Savitch's demeanor was never remotely beatific. Encoun-tering the lethal competition and relentless pressure of NBC's Washington bureau at the relatively tender age of thirty (she consistently represented herself as a year younger on all public-ity releases) would have been hard on even the most mature and well balanced of broadcasters, and Savitch was neither. Instead she was a star, and she acted like one; few at NBC ever forgave her for it. Newsroom regulars traded tales of her tem-per tantrums, her high-hat demands, her reportorial fumbles, and her alleged affairs with various news division VIPs. None-theless, even her most bitter critics had to acknowledge that she had a red-light reflex to die for; when the scarlet bulb went on over a studio camera, signaling that she was on the air, Savitch summoned up every ounce of her hundred-pound frame and projected herself straight through the television set into the viewer's living room.

Over the next six years, she moved around the schedule, serving as principal reporter for a magazine show, as a substitute anchor on *Today* and *Tomorrow,* and as a guest reporter on *Meet the Press.* Whatever the program, the camera continued to love her, and she continued to enthrall the television audience. But she did not satisfy a second, equally demanding audience: the network news executives who had hired her. They had chosen Savitch for her ability to look like she knew what she was talking about—on air, she seemed coolness itself, the essence of a great reporter—but could never reconcile themselves to the show-business implications of their action. Appalled at the thought of appearing to pander to the unthinking tastes of the masses, they decided that looks were not enough and coolness was not enough; Savitch would have to *be* an authority as well. They changed the rules; in addition to knowing how to read a TelePrompTer better than almost anyone in the business, she would have to become knowledgeable on matters political, financial, scientific, and cultural. Savitch bought into this, trying to balance the contradictions of her role by acting ever more like a star at NBC and ever more serious in every public appearance. It was an impossible balancing act, and she failed miserably. By the fall of 1983, the *Digest* was all she had left from a national career that had started to fall apart almost before it began.

In 1983, Savitch was no longer young, nor was she a rising star. She'd been through two short, unhappy marriages; the first union was over almost before it began, and the second ended when her husband of five months hung himself with the leash for Chewy, her pet Siberian husky. She had also discovered the unpleasant realities involved in achieving her lifelong dream of celebrity. A crazed Nebraska farmer had written letters threatening to kill Ronald Reagan, George Bush, and Alexander Haig if she did not return his affections, then managed to get into her office when she was alone; terrified, she shoved him out the door, locked it, then hid under her desk, shaking uncontrollably until network security arrived. From then on, a uniformed bodyguard was assigned to her whenever she

19

was at 30 Rock. The same week, she had a miscarriage. Without makeup, she looked tired and gaunt, so thin that even her detractors worried about her health. Although she was still besieged with interview requests and speaking invitations, received more fan mail than anyone else in the entire news division, and had recently written a best-selling autobiography entitled *Anchorwoman,* no one at NBC spoke of her as a golden girl any longer, or mentioned her as a candidate for the *Nightly News* anchor chair. At this point, she couldn't even get an ordinary reporting assignment from *Nightly.* The head of NBC News, Reuven Frank, wouldn't trust her to cover a fire and assigned her to do the highly visible *Digest* only because he thought she was too incompetent to handle anything more demanding and she was too popular with viewers to let her go. Savitch had gained a certain measure of respect for serving as host on *Frontline,* a new public affairs documentary program on public television, but the very fact that NBC allowed her to participate was a sign that the network did not greatly value her services. But she was still a featured favorite on the network rumor mills; among the many stories concerning Savitch, the hottest were those that depicted her as hopelessly addicted to cocaine and the lover of yet another VIP—this time, a woman. But then, on October 3, real life outstripped the rumor mill. The one thing nobody had ever expected happened. The red light went on, and Jessica Savitch couldn't respond.

Jessica Savitch was often late when she did the *Digest,* and on Monday, October 3, she was very late. The program was broadcast from the same studio, 3K, and used many of the same technical staff as a late-night news show called *Overnight.* The writers and reporters for *Overnight* reported to 3K shortly after 7:30, when the regular *NBC Nightly News* was over and its staff had cleared out. Although the studio looked like a newsroom on air, it was actually a cavernous, multipurpose space, like a movie studio, in which the illusion of a newsroom was created nightly. The solid walls seen by viewers were theatrical flats that could be moved about by stagehands and positioned to conceal lighting cables, duct tape, and sets for other television shows. Unlike most news staffers, those on *Overnight* actually worked on the set, and were sometimes annoyed by the necessity to be silent during the *Digest,* which took place just a few feet from their pounding typewriters. By 8:30 that night, the camera was positioned for the tight head shot that would be used for the entire *Digest* and the TelePrompTer had been loaded with the program's twenty-line script. The lighting had been tested on a news division staffer who was given extra pay to sit in the anchor seat every night just for this purpose, and technical director Peter Basil was routinely checking out the panel of controls with which he would switch the actual broadcast. All systems and personnel were go, except for Savitch, who had still not shown up.

In the past year, Savitch had missed a number of *Digest* appearances. When this occurred, one of the *Overnight* co-anchors, usually Linda Ellerbee but occasionally Bill Schechner, took Savitch's place. Ellerbee regularly did the program on Wednesday, the one weekday Savitch was not assigned to it. At 8:40 Savitch was still missing, so Jerry Polikoff, the *Digest* director, decided to alert a substitute. Because Ellerbee had flown to Texas for her mother's funeral, Polikoff told Schechner to prepare to go on the air. A curly-haired man with the sort of ruggedly handsome features that look good on television, Schechner walked down the hall to Makeup, read through the *Digest* script, and went back to his desk to work on *Overnight*. Having worked at the Pacifica radio network, a countercultural bastion in the 1960s and 1970s, and KQED, San Francisco's pioneering public television station, Schechner was, in network terms, a bit of a rebel. He used to imagine what would happen if one night as he was doing the *Digest* he announced that there was no news, that nothing had happened, and that he was going to spend the time telling people stories that he had made up. After all, what could anybody do? The show was live; the whole network would just have to hold its breath until he finished. That night he would see one particular version of his daydream come to life.

Savitch finally walked into the studio around 8:50. Her appearance was normal, as was the presence of the group— personal hairdresser, personal makeup artist, personal wardrobe mistress, and personal security guard—accompanying her. The security guard had been assigned by NBC, but the other three were there because her contract so specified. It was a perquisite that did not sit well with newsroom regulars, who ridiculed the whole retinue as further evidence of Savitch's nonjournalistic orientation. But to Savitch, these people, whose only job was to make her look good, were not merely perks; to this lonely, isolated woman, they were among the few people in the entire news department that she trusted. They were not trying to undermine her. They were not trying to get on air ahead of her. They were only trying to make her look good, and by so doing they made her feel good, at least for the time each day that they were working on her and talking to her and letting her know that they still thought she was important and valuable and intelligent and beautiful.

As usual, Savitch had been made up heavily, a network requirement for female anchors. Her bleached blond hair was perfectly combed and sprayed, her pale blue eyes were emphasized and accented, and the high cheekbones that made her face one of the most photogenic on television were carefully contoured and highlighted. She wore a black blazer and a rust-colored blouse. As soon as she arrived, she sat in the anchor chair and began to practice. There was time for only one run-through. To Polikoff's shock, she blew it, stumbling through the words as if she were drunk. Nonetheless, she insisted that she was ready to go on.

Affable Jerry Polikoff, who did not relish confrontation, knew that if she did that on the air, heads might roll. He asked Savitch if she was all right; tersely, she nodded yes. He had no notion of what to do. Ejecting the anchor could cost him his job; allowing a fiasco to occur might also bring a pink slip. Nor was there anyone else in the building he could ask, for all the executives had long since gone home. Polikoff had worked on every news show at NBC since the *Camel News Caravan* with John Cameron Swayze made its debut in 1949, but he had never been faced with a problem like this one. After a few words of discussion, he and O'Connell unhappily agreed that Savitch could go on air. "It was almost nine o'clock, and our hands were tied," Polikoff said later. "She said she wanted to go on, and it wasn't up to us to pull her off. She could complain, and she had weight."

In another corner of the control room, Gloria Rivera, Savitch's hairdresser, and Candy Carell, who did her makeup, were also worried about the situation. Jessica Savitch, famed for being wound tight as a coiled spring, had been lethargic and groggy while being made up for the show. As Rivera worked frantically to get Savitch's fine, thin hair ready, the anchor-woman kept dozing off. She insisted she would be fine, but Rivera and Carell didn't believe her. During the countdown to airtime, Rivera became so upset she left the control room and walked back to the makeup room. "I just couldn't stand it," she said afterward. "I got angry they allowed her to go on. Even though she said she was okay, you could see she wasn't. I don't think she was prepared to make a decision. I should have said something, but I'm not allowed to. They'd just laugh at me."

Boone ended at 8:57 and was followed by two thirty-second commercials. Savitch sat waiting at the anchor desk, which was shaped like a small bar and covered in salmon-pink plastic. Behind her was the backdrop, a large map of the world. Her head was in front of the Pacific Ocean. On the monitors, the visuals for the first story, a still photograph of Ronald Reagan and a tiny outline map of the Philippines, were projected above her right shoulder. The president had canceled a scheduled trip to Manila.

Assistant director Bern Meyer began counting loudly backward from thirty. Conversation ceased in the *Overnight* newsroom, and Savitch began her usual pre-broadcast exercise. During the opening sequence, as the globe swam across millions of television screens to the sun, she closed her eyes, waved her right hand in front of her face four times, and rotated her head on her shoulders. Then, suddenly, as Polikoff cued the cameras to roll tape and a red light appeared on the camera, she snapped to attention, eyes open wide, mouth smiling broadly. "Good evening," she said to some ten million viewers. "I'm Jessica Savitch." *

A few seconds into the first item, which was about the cancellation of Reagan's visit to the Philippines, Savitch's voice began to wobble. The briskness disappeared; words began to slur and melt into one another. During the second bulletin, on a Supreme Court ruling reaffirming U.S. citizens' right to own a handgun, she struggled frantically with the word "constitu-

---

* There is no exact figure available for how many households were watching this Digest. According to Nielsen Media Research, 8,630,000 households saw the preceding show Boone, and 17,000,000 tuned in to the Johnny Carson special that followed. A conservative estimate would be that at least 10 million households viewed Jessica Savitch at 8:58 P.M. on October 3, 1983.

tional." The carefully cultivated, orotund vowels fell from her voice. Her eyes looked strained and anxious. By the end of her twenty-second speech, she sounded like a clockwork mechanism that was abruptly running down.

Cut to a word from Sealy Posturepedic mattresses. The interruption gave O'Connell, Polikoff, and Meyer a few seconds to stare at each other in shock. Although Savitch was notoriously difficult to work with on a personal level, she was always a model of professional conduct on camera. Now something was dreadfully awry. They did not have enough time— just ten seconds of commercial—to yank Savitch off the air, even if they had possessed the authority. There was also no other subject to cut to. The only alternative was blank screen, which of course was not an alternative. During the commercial, Savitch sat like a stone, and Bern Meyer recalled that he had once been in a radio studio when the newscaster had started babbling incoherently and it had been impossible to take him off the air. After his show was over, the station manager fired the guy on the spot, and it turned out later that he was diabetic and had been going into insulin shock. Once again Meyer was in the middle of a studio disaster, and once again there was nothing to be done. The dead time crawled past with awful slowness.

Savitch reappeared to deliver the last two items, one about an Eastern Airlines strike settlement and the other regarding a walkout by Continental Airlines pilots. Now she sounded worse, like a 33-rpm recording played at 16 rpm, the words still intelligible but stretched and distorted into unfamiliar lengths and sounds. Her face looked drawn as she fought to control her mouth and tongue, to make them form the words that kept racing across the TelePrompTer in front of her.

Evidently the effort was exhausting. By the end of the *Digest,* her eyes were bleak, her face haggard. Her famous thousand-watt smile was downcast. Just as well, perhaps, the viewers did not see all of the show; for one of the few times in her career, Jessica Savitch, who always exactly filled the time allotted, was too slow in her delivery. Before she finished her sign-off, she was "upcut"—that is, cut off—by the time clock at Central Control, the master computer that automatically ends one feed and begins another, in this case a promotion for the Johnny Carson special that followed at 9:00.

In Studio 3K, the sense of disaster was palpable. In the control room, O'Connell was pale. His hands were shaking. The incident could bode no good for his career. He seemed to have no idea of what to say. Polikoff and Meyer were silent as well. "The sense was, we got through it," one observer in the control room that evening said afterward. "I had the impression nobody wanted to mess with it."

On the set, Schechner, too, was shocked. Savitch had just freaked out on national TV. Live. He couldn't imagine why Savitch had been allowed to go on, especially with another anchor available in the same room. "It was something I didn't want to see," he said. "I didn't like it. It was something I wasn't *entitled* to see—a devastating private moment, and none of my business. At home, maybe I would've had a different reaction. It would just seem incredible, something you could cackle at. But I was in the newsroom, with someone who I knew poured all of herself into that one minute. It set my teeth on edge.

"Ordinarily," he continued, "as soon as the *Digest* was over, we'd start talking and typing again. But this time it stayed really quiet. *Nobody* said a word."

Crew members silently unhooked the microphone from Savitch's blouse. She sat watching everyone avoid her eyes. No one in the control room came out to speak to her, or even called on one of the half-dozen phones connected to the anchor desk. They didn't know how to approach her. Finally Savitch resolved the social dilemma. She rose and walked out of the room without saying a word or giving any indication that something had happened. Then she went upstairs to the fourteenth floor, locked herself into her corner office, and cried.

Up in the nearly deserted main newsroom on the fifth floor, Alan Statsky, a writer, was preparing news copy. As usual, he stopped to watch the *Digest* at 8:58. Mounted on the wall in front of his desk were three monitors, next to an upside-down THINK sign stuck up by some office wit. Statsky was thirty-six and had been working at NBC ever since he graduated from college. He had started out as a page on game shows and the *Tonight Show,* and slowly worked his way into the news department. He readily admitted that news was a male preserve, a place of cigars and football pools where almost every woman, especially one who was young and pretty and seemed to be

25

headed to the top, had a rough time. But he still didn't much like Jessica Savitch, whom he thought stuck-up and demanding and not a real journalist. He didn't refer to her by the kinds of names some of the guys used—"Plastic Cunt," for example—but he could see why they detested her. Whenever she came down to the newsroom from her fourteenth-floor office, she would make people turn off the Jets game because she said sports were too distracting. Statsky and the other news writers used to joke that she paid so little attention to the copy that one day they were going to give her a resignation speech to read live, and she would do it, and management would give everybody bonuses. But it was only a joke; the truth was that to Statsky she was still a major star. No matter how unpleasant she was to people off screen, on air she always had an amazing power to communicate.

This time was different. Before Savitch was halfway through the first item, Statsky was riveted to the screen. "Holy shit, it's really happening!" he exclaimed. People liked to work on the news because it was live; crisis junkies to begin with, they were further enraptured by the atmosphere of controlled panic that inevitably accompanied the live nightly news. But the *Digest,* which wasn't real news, had never seemed as frantic —that is, until tonight. Tonight was a disaster, a live disaster, the authentic article.

By the middle of the announcement of the Supreme Court's decision on handguns, the phones had started ringing. Statsky was one of the few in the newsroom, and he answered the calls. One of the first was from J. Gordon Manning, the vice-president for special projects. A former top honcho at CBS, Manning had washed up at NBC in the late 1970s, still a honcho but a little farther down the pecking order. Plump-faced and gray-haired, Manning was known for his political and social contacts, his penchant for writing endless memos and notes—known as "Manning-grams"—to friends, and his enthusiasm for his own ideas, of which he had many. A man who never thought small, Manning had a special love for trying to arrange exclusive interviews with important world leaders; every once in a while, he succeeded. On an everyday basis, he was the kind of executive who performed most brilliantly at a front table at the Four Seasons; back at 30 Rock, he sometimes seemed merely scatterbrained and had been nicknamed "J. Gordon Missing" by subordinates. His superiors were also critical; "Gordon generates consternation," said Reuven Frank, president of NBC News at the time. "He tends to twitter." But on October 3, Gordon Manning was not twittering at Statsky. He was yelling. "What the hell's going on?" he barked. "What's the matter with Savitch?" When Statsky told him that he had no idea and hadn't seen her in person, Manning decided that his presence was needed and grabbed a cab to 30 Rock. Meanwhile, Statsky was left to field questions from the wires and the papers. He knew that the worst thing that he could do would be to answer those questions—"That kind of mistake could end your career on the spot," he said afterward—so he bounced every call straight to the press department.

When Manning arrived at 30 Rock, he encountered Art Kent, a former correspondent recently appointed vice president in charge of affiliate news services. After a brief conversation, Manning closeted himself with Savitch in her office and grilled her, while Kent went around the newsroom and the studio asking people what they'd seen. Every few minutes *Overnight* executive producer Deborah Johnson was advised that Savitch either would or would not do the second *Digest,* and that Schechner should or should not stand by. Assuming that he would fill in for Savitch, Schechner left his makeup on and tried to concentrate on finishing his *Overnight* script. But by 9:40, Manning and Kent concluded that Savitch could do her second spot, and she returned to Makeup. "She was crying and angry," Candy Carell remembered later. "She was really worried." When Gloria Rivera asked Savitch if she was all right, Savitch insisted that she was perfectly fine. "She didn't seem better to me," Rivera said. "She still seemed completely out of it."

Manning accompanied Savitch back to the studio, and she rehearsed her lines. For once, nobody had to tell the *Overnight* staff to be quiet; when Savitch sat down to do her run-through, Studio 3K was quiet enough to hear ice melting. As she read through each item, Bern Meyer said, Savitch sounded almost like her normal self—"Nervous, but you've got to understand this was a lady who *always* sounded nervous." He did the countdown, Central Control switched the feed from the Johnny Carson special to the studio at 30 Rock, and some 17 million households heard Savitch say, "Good evening, I'm Jessica Savitch." This time, she kept going. She didn't have her usual sharpness and precision, but she was no longer a woman falling apart; she was simply not quite up to snuff, like a recording played at the right speed but with a little dust on it.

At 10:00, the *Digest* was over. *Overnight* people plunged back into preparing their show. Manning and Kent went home. The crisis, of course, was not over. Messages from the press continued to pile up, and Reuven Frank had not yet been heard from. Jessica Savitch could not have imagined that nobody would say another word after she had provided millions of Americans with such unexpected drama. She returned to her office and, by using the power of her name, managed to yank a close friend, Mary Manilla, out of an exercise class at the New York Health & Racquet Club. Under her maiden name, Mary Pangalos, Manilla had been the first woman reporter at WCBS-TV, the local CBS station in New York; as such, she had been a model for Savitch, who had just graduated from college and was a lowly go-for at WCBS Radio. Disgusted by the cutthroat competitiveness that to her seemed rampant in the broadcast media, Manilla had eventually left television and become a merchandising executive at J.C. Penney and, later, Federated Department Stores.

"The men in television—and they were all men—were horrible to me," Manilla said. "But they would act the same way if you were green or orange or fat. You were just more competition, as far as they were concerned." She had remained active in professional media organizations and eventually developed a warm relationship with Savitch. The woman despised by her co-workers as impossibly demanding was known to Manilla as a shy, insecure person buffeted by an ambition she could not control. "Lots of people wanted her to help them, but I wanted to help her," Manilla said. "I used to joke about being Mother Mary—I was born with orthopedic shoes and a bowl of chicken soup in my hand—but I knew her yearnings and could identify with them."

When Manilla heard Savitch's voice on the health club phone, she knew her friend was in trouble. "She was crying and said, 'You have to come right over,' " Manilla said. "When I told her I was supposed to eat with another woman in the class, she said, 'Bring her too, I have to see you.' " They agreed to meet at Hurley's, a restaurant at the corner of Sixth Avenue and 49th Street. Half a century earlier, Rockefeller Center had been designed to fill the entire block bordered by Fifth and Sixth avenues and 49th and 50th streets, but Hurley's owner had refused to sell his land; as a result, Rockefeller Center, one of the major triumphs of modernist architecture, has embedded in one corner a small, nineteenth-century brick building. The wood-paneled restaurant had been an NBC hangout since the network's move to Rockefeller Center in 1933. Although the barroom on the ground floor was a place where network friendships were made and office alliances forged, Jessica Savitch had always been too uncomfortable to spend much time there. This evening, as usual, she preferred to wait for Manilla and her friend, Nancy Solomon, in the upstairs dining room, a large, elegantly appointed salon that was nearly empty at this late hour.

To Manilla's shock, she saw that Savitch, nervous at the best of times, was near hysteria—almost out of control. "She was absolutely frantic," Manilla said, "just flagellating herself for what had happened." Savitch said she had been told that a writer in the newsroom had told the press she was high from cocaine. The *real* reason for what had happened, she said, was that she had taken a sedative because she was still recovering from nose surgery after a sailboat boom hit her across the face; in addition, she said that she had been thrown off by errors in the *Digest* script, which she had not had time to read over properly. "Someone else flubs up on air and they don't say anything," she complained, "but when it's me, the first thing they say is that I'm on dope."

Mary Manilla blew up. Savitch's anguish made Manilla furious with the network in general and with the control room and the newsroom in particular. But she was also furious with Savitch. Once again, little Jessica was refusing to grow up; once again, she was acting like a wide-eyed, naive twelve-year-old child who just doesn't understand why everybody is so mad at her. For months Manilla had been telling her friend of the rumors in broadcast circles about her drug habits, sex life, and professional competence, but Savitch had paid no attention. She also ignored Manilla when the older woman begged Savitch not to throw fits in the studio, no matter how justified,

and warned Savitch that she was surrounded by hangers-on—
"a whole entourage of star-fuckers"—who were taking advantage of Savitch's neediness and vulnerability.

Jabbing her forefinger at Savitch's face, Manilla let the
anchorwoman have it. "Jessica," she declared, "you have to
stop pissing it all away. You have to stop with the lost-little-
girl, love-me stuff. If you don't stop, *right now,* I'll never speak
to you again." Manilla told Savitch to retain a top-notch
professional business manager and do exactly what he said.
Manilla also insisted that Savitch hire a reputable press agent
and work at building a positive image. A good reputation is
not the kind of thing that just happens, Manilla said. It has to
be consciously created. "You have to seize control," she told
Savitch. "You have to deal from strength—not this little girl
shit."

Manilla was astounded by the reaction: Savitch fell to her
knees, grabbed Manilla's hand, and started kissing it. "It was
humiliating and embarrassing," Manilla said. "But the truth
was, it wasn't really for me—it was Jessica talking to Jessica.
She knew she was this far from losing everything. She was this
far from losing it, and she finally understood it."

Whether Jessica Savitch could come back from that edge,
however, was another story. Despite the resolutions to change,
to do everything differently, to be a new person, she and Manilla knew that the crisis that had begun that evening was far
from over. Savitch was only on air for forty-three seconds, an
appearance so fleeting that many viewers may not even have
noted the disaster. But as far as the network and the news
business were concerned, it was an eternity. "Airtime is sacred
in this business," Tom Wolzien, an NBC vice-president, said
later. "It's the one thing you don't waste, not even forty-three
seconds of it."

Jessica Savitch knew this. To save her career, she would
have to explain away the debacle, first to the outside media,
then to NBC itself. She decided that what mattered was credibility, not truth; it would be an exercise in spin control. Over
the next several days, she came up with a wide variety of explanations. She told NBC president Bob Mulholland that nothing
had happened. She told the New York *Daily News* that it was
computer trouble, and added, "I hope you're not going to write
about it." She told her agent, Ed Hookstratten, and Tom Wol-

zien that it was a painkiller. She told one of her staff that it had been a glass of wine she'd had during dinner with her new friend, *New York Post* vice-president Martin Fischbein. She started to tell *The Washington Post* that it had been her grief over the death of her dear phone friend, Linda Ellerbee's mother, but the call was abruptly terminated by Tom Pettit, deputy director of the NBC news division, who knew that Ellerbee's mother had been paralyzed and unable to speak for years. In a second call to the *Post,* she pinned the blame on a faulty Tele-PrompTer. The one thing Savitch told everybody who asked her was that it was not drugs, absolutely not, no way.

Jerry Polikoff and Bill O'Connell didn't wait for explanations. The next day they went to their unit manager and asked for a budget to pretape the *Digest.* They'd been caught short once, and they were not about to let it happen twice. If they taped the run-throughs, they could cobble together a taped version in a pinch. They could also use the tapes to cover their asses. In the event that an anchor was in such bad shape that even a taped *Digest* could not be produced and a last-minute substitute had to be used, the producer and director would have taped evidence to back up their decision to do so. People in the fifth-floor newsroom didn't wait for explanations either. Shortly after the incident, a Xeroxed photograph of Jessica Savitch was taped on a corridor wall, near the third-floor elevators. Taped below her nostrils were two cutoff straws, the universal symbol of a coke head.

Tom Wolzien also didn't wait for explanations. He kept on Savitch day after day, asking her over and over what had happened and whether she was taking drugs. When he wasn't talking to her, he was grilling her staff. Every time Savitch went into a room, every time she walked down the hall or entered the studio, people stopped talking and looked at her. She felt like she was in the middle of a nightmare. People in network news are snakes, Mary Manilla had often told her, and it had never seemed more true. They are all ego, ego, ego, Manilla had said; the business is all about power and money, and the hell with the story. Terrified, Jessica Savitch began to realize, more than she ever had before, that television was something altogether different from that dream she had spent her life pursuing, and to fear that she had made a mistake to crave the attention of the camera.

2

Kennett Square

Jessica Savitch's life was so embroiled with television news, and her career so emblematic of an enormous change in its values —indeed, in the values of journalism itself—that it is startling to realize that she, like most network anchors, was born at a time and place still unlighted by the electronic glow of the cathode ray. The woman whose days exemplified the brutal, speedy, relentlessly urban culture of Big Media grew up thirty-five long miles from Philadelphia, in Kennett Square, Pennsylvania, a small town of such innocence and tranquillity that it is almost impossible to evoke today without irony. On February 1, 1947, the day Jessica Beth Savitch was born, just fifteen thousand American families had TV sets, and the modern television colossi ABC, CBS, and NBC—the last to become baby Jessica's corporate home—were mere striplings, younger siblings of radio, belittled and despised even by many of their employees. As Jessica grew up, Kennett Square remained the same, a town of horses and maple trees and old rustic houses made from stone, but television rose to become . . . well, *television,* lucrative and transcontinental, powerful as a dictator's army, filling the disturbed air with a wash of the day's events, transmitted instantly by satellite across the globe. Young Jessica was curious, insatiably curious, about what she saw on the screen, but her personal evolution ran parallel to that of the medium until she was in her twenties, and at last was able to work before the camera.

In Savitch's arch phrase, Kennett Square was the sort of place where people ate "all-American dinners of meat-loaf and canned peas and fruit cocktail." Drugs, crime, homelessness, and poverty, the familiar social evils of the modern era, were then confined to the sorts of books and articles that relatively few people in Kennett Square read. Still, despite her professed cynicism, the town remained a point of reference to Savitch all her life; when she addressed America through the video camera, she spoke to the five thousand souls of Kennett, and in some sense she never let go of being the perky little girl from Taylor Street.

It was a marvelous place to grow up. Situated amidst a jumble of gentle hills crisscrossed with low stone fences and well-trimmed hedgerows, Kennett was dotted with carefully tended fruit trees and beds of flowers. Summer and winter, children rode bicycles down the main streets, their dogs loyally trotting after. Red Clay Creek meandered through town, its banks providing fishing spots for local boys and modeling clay for local potters. Scattered throughout the vicinity were three-story homes made in colonial times of dark gray hornblende stone quarried nearby. Many of their owners had prosperous farms with big wooden barns built in a style peculiar to Kennett, with one wing of the barn cantilevered over white conical stone supports. In olden days the farms were filled with milk cows, clean and contented, but by 1950 the dairies were mostly replaced by cut flowers, fruit, and mushrooms. Indeed, when baby Jessica took her first steps in the world, she was toddling about a place that boasted of its status as the mushroom capital of America.

She belonged to a prominent local family. At that time Kennett Square had a four- or five-block central business district, depending on who did the counting, filled with tidy shops, a rough dozen of which were run by Jewish merchants who had migrated from New York or Philadelphia. One of the most prominent was Jessica's grandfather, Ben Savitch. He was born Ben Yussavitch in 1898 or 1899 in Bessarabia, an agricultural state in southwest Russia. As a teenager, he had left Russia

33

to join his two older brothers who had already emigrated to the United States, shortened his name to Savitch, and settled for a while in Oxford, Pennsylvania. Many of the other energetic, ambitious young Jewish immigrants he met became doctors or lawyers, but Ben and his brother Theodore became entrepreneurs. While still a teenager, Ben opened a department store in Coatesville, a steel town fourteen miles from Kennett; meanwhile, back in Oxford, Ted had a clothing and furniture store which during the depression became just a furniture store.

In the early 1930s, with Coatesville near economic collapse, Ben closed shop and moved to Kennett Square, where he opened a small men's clothing store called Benny's. He made monthly buying trips to Philadelphia to keep the store's stock up-to-date and cultivated customer loyalty by eagerly fulfilling special requests. Eventually he moved the business to a much larger space at the corner of State and Union, right in the heart of Kennett Square. In the original location he opened the Triangle Shop, a children's store. He then started a third store, Adele's, which catered to the "upstairs" trade—the kind of place which charged $5.00 for a skirt back when everybody else was asking $1.98.

It was a good time and place for Ben Savitch to create something. In those days, State Street was a busy spot, especially on Friday and Saturday evenings. Shoppers ran the gamut from du Ponts in worn-out jeans that smelled of horses to Puerto Rican migrant laborers and prosperous Italian-American mushroom growers; strolling from store to store, they made Ben Savitch's cash registers ring until he reluctantly pulled the shades. He was untroubled by anti-Semitism. The fifteen or so Jewish families in Kennett Square were not enough to support a local synagogue or even to huddle, voluntarily or not, in a ghetto. The Savitches mingled unselfconsciously with the larger community even as they formed part of the small, cohesive group of Jews within that community. Members of that smaller group formed car pools to cart the kids back and forth to the synagogue in nearby Coatesville, held seders together, and closed the downtown shopping district every year on Yom Kippur.

Ben and his family lived in a big stone house on the corner of Magnolia and Lafayette. Built in the early decades of this century, it had stout white columns and a wide front porch. In the yard were large yew bushes and a towering spruce, grown from one of the seedlings distributed by the local Farmer's Grange back during the centennial celebration of 1876. Ben had met Lil Dinaburg, his future wife, in Youngstown, Ohio, when she was a recent Polish immigrant and he was working briefly as a traveling salesman. They were married in 1921, when she was sixteen. By all accounts, it was a good match: Both were strong-minded and ambitious. Ben, short, elegant, and handsome, with greenish-blue eyes and high cheekbones, was bursting with energy and constantly joking in a raspy voice with a thick Yiddish accent. Never seen in public without a cigar in his mouth, he left a trail of ashes wherever he went, including, to his clerks' despair, his own stores. Fair, small-boned Lil also spoke English with a Yiddish accent, although it was less pronounced. A tough-minded woman who did not hesitate to speak her mind, she was always active in her husband's business, and served as manager of Adele's Dress Shop.

In the first five years of their marriage they had three boys and one girl, a boisterous crew who worked in the stores after school and during vacations. The oldest child, Leon, known as Sonny, and the middle boy, Emmanuel, called Manny, became attorneys, courtesy of the GI Bill; Leon eventually became a civil court judge in Los Angeles. Exhibiting their parents' drive and ambition, the three older children eventually opted for big-city life in southern California.

The baby of the family, David, known as Buddy, was different. A tall, slim man with Ben's light hair and eyes, he worked for his father in Kennett Square all his adult life. He was an affable child, enfeebled by kidney ailments, who never pushed past the limited horizons of his hometown. The one time he left Kennett Square for long was when he served in the navy as a pharmacist's mate during World War II. While in the service he was hospitalized for his kidney problems, which had become serious. There he met a small, dark-haired navy nurse named Florence Spadoni, who was from South Philadelphia.

After the war, Florence and Buddy were wed in her hometown and then went to live in Kennett Square. Ben Savitch sold the Triangle Shop and Adele's and focused his attention on the University Shop, a department store he had purchased in nearby Newark, Delaware. Meanwhile, Buddy became manager of Benny's. He and Florence lived on Taylor Street in a small red brick bungalow. Purchased with a GI Bill loan, it was trimmed with white and was more or less interchangeable with its neighbors.

While Buddy went off to State Street every day, Florence took on the full-time job of raising their three daughters, Jessica, Stephanie, and Lori. Admired by other Kennett housewives for her baking, Florence turned out pastries and yeast breads—made from scratch, of course—by the dozens. Every week she carted the kids to swimming lessons at the Y. In the autumn she took them to Resnick's Department Store on State Street to buy Cinderella costumes for Halloween, and every summer she drove them to Girl Scout camp.

And then there were all the special demands. When Stephanie was born many weeks premature, Florence had to nurse the desperately frail infant night and day. Because Jessica's February birthdate would not allow her to enter public school until she was six and a half, her parents sent her to a private school in Wilmington for first grade, a decision that required Florence to make the two-hour round-trip twice a day for an entire year. Florence wanted her children to have the same dentist she'd had as a child, which meant a two-and-a-half-hour round-trip to Philadelphia every time somebody needed a checkup. Although Florence came from an Italian family and was raised a Roman Catholic, she did so many things with the Jewish community —schlepping the kids to Hebrew classes, helping her neighbors sit shiva when someone died—that few people realized she wasn't Jewish herself.

Later Kennett became a bedroom community for employees at the chemical plants in Wilmington and Philadelphia, but in the 1950s relatively few people drove that far to work. Kennett Square was small and self-sufficient; despite the Korean War, the deep divisions of the McCarthy period, and the growing concern about the possibility of atomic war, from the corner of State and Union streets America seemed a safe and happy land. For entertainment the mothers met for canasta and bridge, fathers got together for a night of poker or a Rotary Club meeting, and children played in their backyards. In the summer, families went to Bicknell's Pond, in nearby Oxford, for a day of swimming and picnicking. Outside Jessica's front door was a great sledding hill, and nearby was a small park with a pond that the local volunteer fire department flooded for

36

ice skating in winter. Kennett Consolidated School, an imposing 1920s neoclassical edifice complete with massive Corinthian columns, was only a few blocks away. There Jessica learned of Kennett's inglorious record as a Tory stronghold during the Revolutionary War. According to local legend, while General Washington and the British commander Lord Cornwallis squared off at nearby Brandywine, Peggy Shippen, Benedict Arnold's wife, passed the afternoon sipping tea in her uncle's palatial home in downtown Kennett Square. Indeed, the overwhelming British victory at Brandywine is sometimes attributed to the assistance of James Fitzpatrick, a Kennett man who acted as guide to the king's army. After the British evacuated Philadelphia, Fitzpatrick became a bandit, celebrated for his audacious deeds; once he appeared in disguise at a meeting called to plan his capture and robbed the militia captain in charge.

From Jessica's house it was also a short walk to the Presbyterian church where the Brownies and Girl Scouts met, and it wasn't much farther to her father's store in the center of town. After school, Jessica and her sisters would sit on the steps located just inside the front door and watch the people walking by, and on Saturdays they went to movie matinees at the Firemen's Auditorium, where the local volunteer fire department showed films to raise money.

With her curly brown hair and her slim, quick body, Jessica was a pretty little girl; people often commented that she looked just like a little Shirley Temple doll. A precocious talker who said her first word at eight months, Jessica was an imaginative child who always added her own dramatic flair to any story. At night, when she was going to sleep, she would stare at the shadow made on the floor of her bedroom by the big tree outside the window and see fantastic shapes and figures. She also loved to perform, and in the summer she and her playmates declaimed lustily from the back porch to anyone who would listen. On family occasions, her mother told one interviewer, Jessica "would dance for relatives, kick and twist around"; later, in junior high school, she recited "Annabel Lee" with such emotion that her mother burst into tears.

Jessica was always Daddy's little girl. Whenever someone said she looked like him, or when he threw her up in the air and called her by her middle name, Beth, she felt she had a special connection to him. She loved it when he gave her pig-gyback rides or hunted around with her on hands and knees for four-leaf clovers; he promised her that if they found one—and sometimes they did—they would all live happily ever after. She was very proud when he bought the family a large brick ranch house on the west side of town, in the New Garden section. A Civil War buff, he told her about the numerous local battle-fields and showed her the houses in town that had served as stops on the Underground Railroad used by runaway slaves. Buddy was also keenly interested in contemporary affairs, and Jessica later recalled studying *My Weekly Reader* so that she would have something to discuss with her father at the dinner table. Unlike her friends' fathers, she said, he didn't limit his conversations with her to kid stuff; he would tell her about civil rights and Eisenhower and Jimmy Hoffa. After the Savitches got their first television set, in 1954, Jessica would sit and watch the news with Buddy, registering his interest as the small man on the box spun stories of dire events remote from their special world together. Buddy's approval meant everything; one of Jessica's earliest memories was of the time her father was using his new home movie camera and she lifted up her skirt so that her bemused father could take a picture of her new ruffled underpants.

Florence's cool, reserved nature did not mix well with the aggressive, volatile style of the Savitch family, and her relation-ships with her in-laws, particularly Buddy's sister, Sissy, were at times uneasy. Buddy also did not always get along with his family, and sometimes found working for his father uncom-fortable because of the older man's controlling hand. There were arguments between Florence and Buddy. Although it seems unlikely that, as Jessica told friends many years later, Buddy lived apart from Florence and his children at a certain point, there is no doubt that the atmosphere in the house on Taylor Street was often strained.

Such problems paled in comparison with Buddy's health. He had nephritis, an incurable inflammation of the kidneys that may have been caused by a streptococcal infection early in life. Today the chances of developing nephritis are small, for anti-biotics are routinely prescribed at the first sign of strep; more-over, modern kidney dialysis techniques or, in severe cases, kidney transplants can help those who are stricken to lead an active and productive life. But during Buddy's childhood strep was nearly impossible to check, and there was no dialysis to assist its victims.

There was little that Florence or the doctors in the area could do for Buddy's slowly worsening condition. As his kidneys became unable to eliminate wastes, his body swelled with poison; pictures of Buddy in later years show a puffy-faced man with little resemblance to the handsome young man everyone called the best looking of the Savitch boys. The poison sometimes made his breath smell, gave his skin a waxy pallor, and crystallized in his perspiration. He was often unable to move for the pain.

Jessica could not understand the illness or truly grasp that her adored father was dying in front of her eyes. But this bright, inquisitive little girl must have caught the worried glances, must have felt disoriented and disturbed when her own daddy didn't get up and go to work but lay in bed all day looking pale and bloated and weak. She knew that her father was a frail, tired man, a truly frightening fact for a child, and one that made her relationship with him seem all the more important. She sat with him as he watched TV, and it was the most precious time in the world.

A charter member of the baby boom, Jessica Savitch belonged to the last generation of American children for whom it was possible to have a truly small-town childhood—and to the first generation to grow up with television. The United States was conquered by television with startling rapidity; commerical broadcasting began, most tentatively, in 1941, but within a decade television was poised to outstrip radio in popularity. In cities with television stations, book sales slumped, movie attendance plummeted, and restaurants reported empty dining rooms, especially on big television nights. By 1954, the year Buddy installed a set in the Savitch living room, there were 32 million televisions in the United States, nearly one for every five Americans, and their owners watched the tube more than they did anything else except working and sleeping.

The Savitches were no exception. During the daytime, Jessica and her two sisters looked at Captain Kangaroo and game shows like *The Big Payoff.* Florence didn't need a watch to know it was time to start dinner; in late afternoon, Jessica would dash over to the television set and turn down the volume because she hated the voice of the announcer for *The Kate Smith Hour*. In her fascination with the world behind the small glass plate, Jessica was in the forefront of a kind of sociological revolution, as American life became centered upon the box in the living room. As Jessica watched her small, shimmering screen in Kennett Square, three hours away, in New York City, an institution of enormous size was being created; into that vessel she would pour her entire adult life.

Few would have predicted the growth of television or TV news in the new medium's first years. Postwar America was a nation of avid radio listeners who depended on their large living-room consoles for both entertainment and news. During the war, the public hunger for information about the fight had allowed Edward R. Murrow and his team of crack foreign correspondents at CBS Radio to mold the nation into a single electronic ear; now network executives wanted to continue exploring the peacetime possibilities of this still relatively new medium. Although Paley was interested in television, he did not rush to establish dominance in this new broadcast medium; because CBS was busy pursuing research into its own form of color television, in 1946 it passed up four of the station licenses to which it was entitled by FCC allocation and advised its affiliates to postpone any involvement with this newfangled medium until the kinks in color broadcasting had been ironed out.

Unable to imagine that radio could be superseded, radio broadcasters concentrated almost exclusively on such pressing issues as whether it was ethical for radio broadcasts, which were done live, to use recorded announcements, which would fraudulently imbue listeners with the belief that the studios were thronged with people who employed their deep, resonant voices only to read commercials. Television was regarded by radio professionals as a passing novelty with slight potential as a news medium because its equipment was too bulky to be dragged anywhere that something newsworthy was happening. Moreover, because the 35mm film stock used at the time was coated with highly inflammable nitrate, television news divisions had to be exiled to old movie studios with special fire doors and fireproof vaults for film storage. From October 1948 until the mid-1950s, for example, NBC news and documentaries were both located on East 106th Street near Park Avenue, a

40

$1.50 cab ride and half a city away from network headquarters down at 30 Rock.

The one person who was convinced that television would rapidly overtake radio in both news and entertainment was David Sarnoff, chairman of the Radio Corporation of America, which owned NBC. Born in Russia, raised in a section on Manhattan's West Side known as Hell's Kitchen, taught by Guglielmo Marconi, the inventor of wireless communication, Sarnoff was already the stuff of legend when he assumed the chairmanship of RCA in 1930, at the age of thirty-nine. A dandy in all respects, he began each day in his fifty-third-floor office with a shave and a haircut from his personal barber while a manicurist buffed his nails. His clothes were elegant, tending toward bright-colored vests, snappily turned fedoras, and expensive canes with gold heads. He insisted on being addressed as "General," despite the fact that his title was honorary, bestowed for a year of civilian service in the Army Communication Corps during World War II; indeed, he lobbied Washington actively for another star. The title fit his management style, which was dictatorial. During his thirty-five years at RCA, Sarnoff's word was as unquestioned as the law of gravity. According to network lore, he once told the board, "I'm glad I don't have a lot of yes-men around me!" Everyone present shouted, "Yes, General!" Under his leadership, RCA had become the leading manufacturer of radios by the 1920s; because there was nothing to listen to on the radios, Sarnoff had then founded the first radio network, NBC, in 1926.

Two decades later, Sarnoff again became bullish on a new technological breakthrough—more bullish than almost anyone else at NBC. "You are the generation that created radio," he told his station managers in 1947. "Seldom is it given to one generation to have such an opportunity rise again, but now before you is that opportunity in television—a larger, richer, broader opportunity than ever existed in radio." The General, was, as the world knows, correct, but until the day of his death in 1971 he never understood why. At bottom, Sarnoff was interested far less in news, entertainment, or even profits than in the technology involved in the development and manufacture of televisions. Once that technology was invented, however, television grew not because viewers had any particular appreciation of the engineering involved or even because television is an excellent medium for entertainment or news, though it may indeed be that, but because it is an unsurpassed medium for advertising, able to reach tens of millions of consumers at a stroke.

From the beginning, NBC—and television in general—made money, but it was not until the early 1950s, when a tall, lanky man named Sylvester ("Pat") Weaver became president of NBC, that the money started to pour in. A Phi Beta Kappa graduate of Dartmouth who had been a hard-sell advertising man from Young & Rubicam, Weaver, father of actress Sigourney Weaver, was the first of the legendary wild men to inhabit television's executive suites. During his years at NBC, his antic behavior and bizarre vocabulary drew much press coverage, including a two-part profile in *The New Yorker* in 1954. He lined the walls of his office with leather-bound volumes of endless memos that Weaver himself described as "pre-semantic" and David Adams, NBC's corporate counsel at the time, once compared to "convoluted works of art written by Picasso backwards." Weaver drove subordinates crazy during meetings by acting out passages from Greek drama to make a point and rocking back and forth on a Bongo board, a sort of one-person teeter-totter. He used a distinctive lingo in which soliciting others' opinions was called "earing the ground" and special programs became "spectaculars" intended to shake "the robotry of habit viewing," unless the spectacular had documentary content, in which case it was a "telementary" and part of "operation frontal lobes." In between memos and meetings, Weaver kept busy thinking up new ideas like the Survivor's Library (a complete record of all human history, to be printed in an edition of 20,000 and stored all over the world) as well as such strictly pragmatic inventions as an eternally flaming fireplace log and an inhaling device filled with different scents, such as a pine forest, that one sniffed or "smacked" and which was intended to replace cigarette smoking.

Distinctly out of place in the quiet, orderly world of Sarnoff, Weaver peppered the executive suites with rapid-fire bursts of ideas designed to elevate American culture through television; "I am an information optimist," he once said. He suggested to NBC News producer Reuven Frank that he beef up coverage by stationing a camera permanently in the living rooms of the one hundred greatest Americans in order to televise their reactions whenever any important event occurred. The prime minister of England has a heart attack? Let's get Linus Pauling's thoughts on the matter! When Frank pointed out that the hundred greats might not want cameras aimed at them twenty-four hours a day, an exasperated Weaver retorted that this was the kind of nattering negativism that held back the progress of television.

Undaunted by Sarnoff's ferocity, Weaver scornfully referred to his boss as "Fangs" or "Old Meg" (for megalomaniac). A year after Weaver's arrival, he was promoted to be chairman of the NBC board so that the General's son, Robert Sarnoff, already a high executive at NBC, could become NBC president. Soon afterward, at a memorable board meeting, Weaver asked Sarnoff to stop sitting at the head of the table, an action that those present watched in shocked silence. After a year and a half, Sarnoff tired of Weaver's antics (and the size of his expense account, four times higher than the General's). He let Weaver know who ran the company. Sulking, Weaver entered what staffers referred to as his "Elba period": He withdrew into a conference room and did almost nothing for several months, after which he left with a large severance package.

Despite his strange habits, Weaver managed to revolutionize the broadcast industry during his brief involvement in it. He invented early morning television with *Today,* which was first telecast from a ground-floor studio in 30 Rock with a big plate-glass window where passersby could look in and be seen when cameras panned the crowd. Because most viewers were busy getting ready for work and did not watch the entire show, it was divided into short, independent segments, an idea that was ridiculed until Dave Garroway and his chimpanzee pal, J. Fred Muggs, began drawing large and loyal audiences. Weaver also introduced late night television when he put on *Tonight,* with Steve Allen. Both shows were great advertising success stories and became permanent features on the American television landscape, as did another Weaver concept, the special program, which he launched with shows like *Peter Pan,* with Mary Martin. But his most important contribution to television was his restructuring of the commercial end of the business. Because Sarnoff thought of broadcasting as a public service, NBC had never attempted to maximize profits—a course of action difficult to imagine nowadays, when the networks chase frantically after every dime. By the early 1950s, when the number of viewers was rising, it was clear that advertising rates should follow suit, but it had taken Pat Weaver to figure out how. Rather than following the old radio arrangement with advertisers, whereby sponsors bought time in blocks of quarter, half, and full hours and produced the programs to fill it, Weaver began selling advertisers individual spot ads in programs produced by the network. Splitting up the time allowed smaller advertisers to buy space, which vastly increased the pool of potential advertising dollars. Now sponsors would have to compete for the limited amount of advertising time available, which, in accord with the laws of supply and demand, allowed the networks to jack up their prices each season.

The impact of Weaver's brainstorm was enormous. It greatly increased the number of commercials; despite the howls of the public, ads appeared for the first time in the middle of dramatic programs. More important, the already wealthy networks became staggeringly profitable. Television's rapid capture of the hearts of everyday Americans led to its equally rapid capture of the pocketbooks of the people who wanted to sell things to those average Americans. Advertisers thronged to the new medium; in one year, 1954, CBS's gross billings doubled, and three years later the total for all three networks had reached nearly a billion dollars. With profits so far beyond Sarnoff's wildest dreams, the networks could afford to become bloated and inefficient, which they soon did. They could also afford to spend money on programs that gave the illusion of public service, such as the news, which Jessica Savitch and her father watched almost every evening.

What they saw was very different from newscasts today. Although NBC and CBS began broadcasting prime-time programs in color in 1954, regular news programming was not in color until the mid-1960s. Even if the news had been broadcast in color, the Savitches would still have seen a monochrome version because, like most Americans, they did not own a color set. In 1955 there were only about 5,000 such sets in the country, and it was not until the early 1960s that color sales began to become significant. In addition, local and network news lasted only fifteen minutes each and used motion-picture film instead of videotape, which was available only in a rudimentary and unwieldy form until many years later. Film units included a silent camera, sound camera (also known as a film camera), lights and light stands, reel-to-reel tape recorder, and endless cable requiring hours to install; moreover, film had to be developed and edited, which required still more time. As a result, television film crews covered little but press conferences and other pre-scheduled events. By the mid-fifties correspondents were providing some on-the-spot stories; in 1955, John Chancellor of NBC earned a national reputation when he covered a police shootout in Chicago by lying in a gutter and cranking up a spring-powered tape recorder so that his report would include the sound of the bullets flying overhead. But viewers often did not see the action until days after it had occurred, and much of what appeared on their screens was the same sort of generic file footage—aerial shots of marching troops and the like—they watched in movie newsreels.

Even then, though, the networks fought for ratings. For many years, the race was primarily between CBS and NBC; ABC, which had been spun off from NBC in 1943 as a result of antitrust proceedings, did not begin its nightly news until several years after its two competitors, and its news operation remained marginal for some time. The networks clawed for any advantage they could find, and they decided almost immediately that viewers were more likely to watch a news program if they liked the man—and it was always a man—who delivered the stories. This man became known as the "anchor," presumably because he provided the weight and stamina that kept the program in one place.

At first, news anchors were not the living network logos they have become today. Their sole responsibility was to read the news in an engaging fashion every evening in the studio; journalists were assigned to handle any news events that might require special knowledge, such as political conventions. Accordingly, the first three network anchors, John Cameron Swayze on NBC, Douglas Edwards on CBS, and John Daly on ABC, were chosen not for their journalistic competence, but for their appeal on camera. In fact, these three and many of their local counterparts had worked for newspapers and magazines, but such expertise would have been relevant only if they had been correspondents entrusted with digging out facts; as anchors, who merely read others' stories, what counted was how they looked on screen.

One of the first newscasters to realize the potential of television news as a personal showcase was NBC's Swayze. A one-time acting student from Kansas City, he wore a fresh carnation in his lapel every night on the *Camel News Caravan* (so named because it was sponsored by Camel cigarettes) and lavished considerable attention on a dapper wardrobe of eye-catching ties and sports jackets designed to stand out on the fuzzy broadcasts of the day. Another racy touch was Swayze's habit of engaging the viewer's eye by looking directly into the camera. Nowadays everyone on television looks straight ahead, courtesy of a TelePrompTer, but before that miracle device was invented, Swayze, who could memorize each night's script on the spot, was one of the few able to do so. It was a style that attracted millions of viewers, including Buddy Savitch and his daughter Jessica. A childhood friend, Faith Thomas, later told one reporter that both she and Jessica liked to sit in the back seat of their parents' cars and recite "John Cameron Swayze" over and over, like a mantra.

Swayze's show-business flourishes were disdained by CBS's Edward R. Murrow, the longtime CBS correspondent and dean of radio news, who moved to television when its audience grew large enough to matter. Murrow regarded himself as a man of lofty standards, and he attempted to maintain them in the new medium. At once dismissing the very idea of a daily news program as too superficial, he and his producer, Fred Friendly, concentrated on *See It Now,* the TV successor to their radio news analysis show, *Hear It Now.* A thoughtful and prestigious public-affairs program, *See It Now* explored such subjects as postwar Berlin, the U.S. Supreme Court's desegregation decision, and the refusal of the American Legion in Indianapolis to rent its hall to the American Civil Liberties Union. In October 1953, and again in March 1954, when *See It Now* attacked and helped to destroy Senator Joseph McCarthy, Murrow emerged as a national hero. His program was one of the reasons Buddy Savitch bought a TV set, and Jessica set great store by sitting in her father's lap and watching Murrow dissect the American political process.

Murrow's boss, CBS president William Paley, was less enchanted. Unlike Sarnoff, whose idea of simple good fun was listening to the NBC Orchestra under the baton of Arturo Toscanini, Paley understood that entertaining the masses meant show biz. The heir to a Philadelphia cigar fortune—La Palina was the brand—Paley purchased the fledgling CBS radio network in 1928. In its early years he concentrated on news, ceding the entertainment field to NBC, which despite Sarnoff's own inclination had acquired some popular comedians. By the late forties, however, Paley had grasped the importance of the funny men better than Sarnoff. CBS enticed Amos 'n' Andy, Jack Benny, Burns and Allen, and many other big names from NBC Radio; upon being informed of this disaster, Sarnoff replied loftily, "A business built on a few comedians isn't a business worth being in." After catching up with NBC in radio, Paley used the same instinct for popular culture to make CBS the top-ranked television network until the late 1970s. It was that instinct that rankled Paley about Murrow.

To Paley, the sober analytic abilities that had made Murrow a radio great were passé. Murrow wrote well-turned essays, which he delivered in a slow, mellifluous baritone. But what was wanted now were punchy headline summaries, a rapid and excited style, and the ability to ad-lib gracefully— qualities which were altogether lacking in Murrow, who sweated whenever he had to appear before a camera without a carefully rehearsed script in hand. In part, Murrow had been the beneficiary of radio's sheer novelty; in a way difficult for Americans to imagine today, families sat spellbound in their parlors, listening with fierce concentration to the crackling messages emerging from the speaker. (The radio consoles of those years were enormous, big as Great Danes; often shaped like a cathedral arch, they formed the first American shrines to technology.) Radio had no competition, and when Murrow expatiated like Thomas Jefferson, Americans happily followed his poetic phrases—he once described the incendiaries dropped during night raids on London as "white rice being thrown on black velvet"—and his convoluted sentences and probing explorations of contemporary society.

For many radio stars, the shock of the new medium was as great as the appearance of talkies had been to silent film stars two decades earlier. Murrow disliked intensely the layers of producers and sound engineers and makeup artists and light technicians that were necessarily inserted between the correspondent and the audience, so unlike radio where the reporter simply wrote his copy and then read it into a microphone. And, indeed, viewers were less than pleased to learn that the cadences that they had thrilled to on radio belonged to a sweaty guy who smiled at the camera as if his underwear were fighting back.

Moreover, the powerful immediacy of television gave network executives pause, particularly during the cold war. Wary of touching off popular resentment or even official curbs, networks emphasized personality and fun, not controversial subjects. To all appearances, Murrow was still on top. While the evening newscast made do with a damp, dark warren of offices high above Grand Central Terminal, a skeleton staff, and a minuscule budget that forced CBS executive producer Don Hewitt to such oddball expediencies as interviewing a brewer and his billy goat during bock beer season, *See It Now* had luxurious quarters, a big crew, and the public benediction of CBS brass. Even so, when *See It Now* first took on McCarthy, CBS refused to promote the show; Murrow and Friendly paid for an ad in *The New York Times* out of their own pockets.

See It Now won Murrow more awards than any other broadcaster, but not enough people watched it to prevent its sponsor, Alcoa Aluminum, from dropping the show. Paley relegated it to an occasional special, and gave its prime-time slot to the latest television craze, a quiz program called *The $64,000 Question*. In July 1958 *See It Now* disappeared altogether. Paley was tired, he told Murrow and Friendly, of the stomachache the program had given him.

Murrow did not disappear with *See It Now*. Although he had been disdainful of network politics, he had not been ignorant of how to play the game; to retain enough clout to keep *See It Now* going even as long as he did had required that he show a certain amount of commercial savvy. He had done so with a second weekly program, *Person to Person,* which consisted entirely of interviews with celebrities and newsmakers at their homes and was a sort of precursor to *Lifestyles of the Rich and Famous.* Major scoops included dropping in on Liberace, Eddie Fisher and Debbie Reynolds, Jayne Mansfield, Lawrence Welk, Marilyn Monroe, and Humphrey Bogart and Lauren Bacall. An indication of the general tone of the show may be seen in the fact that of the ninety-three people interviewed in 1956, when Martin Luther King was leading a boycott of the Montgomery bus system and the civil rights movement was

48

convulsing America, only two guests were black. They were, of course, jazz musicians—Dizzy Gillespie and Cab Calloway.

By 1961, *Person to Person* was gone, and Murrow, who took little pains to hide his disgust that much of television journalism had become almost as superficial as he had predicted, had been reduced to an occasional appearance on a new documentary program called *CBS Reports.* Shortly after he did one of his most famous programs, a report on migrant agricultural workers entitled "Harvest of Shame," he quit TV to become head of the United States Information Agency for the incoming president, John Kennedy. Although Murrow actually spent more of his TV career doing *Person to Person* than any other show, including *See It Now,* he became an icon of quality for television journalists. Those who favored more thoughtful and weighty coverage—"Murrowites," as they came to be known—invoked his name as a watchword against the champions of advertising and entertainment that were forever encroaching upon the sacred precincts of broadcast integrity. But such was the power of Murrow's name that those very champions themselves would invoke it, paying lip service to the ideal of quality while trying to pep up the schedule in ways that would garner top ratings and, in turn, top advertising dollars.

If Murrow's mantle was taken up by anyone, it was Chet Huntley and David Brinkley. In 1955 Pat Weaver saw Huntley, then a successful local anchor at the ABC affiliate in Los Angeles, give a short speech at an industry luncheon, and was so impressed that he ordered a subordinate to hire Huntley to anchor for NBC. But when the newsroom regulars at 30 Rock got their first look at this tall, square-jawed Westerner, they were distinctly unimpressed. "The day he got there we sat in the control booth and watched him in the studio," recalled Pat Trese, a writer in the news department at the time. "He didn't have many skills. He could lean on one arm and then the other [while speaking], and he had a pipe." Then, for no particular reason, the director told Huntley to stand up. "That was it," Trese said. "Standing up *made* him, and he did it for the next few years. It broke all the clichés that he was stuck in about how an anchor was supposed to look—it freed him to be himself. When he stood up, he was really a presence. He filled the screen."

Despite his utter inexperience as a reporter, Huntley's performance on air was so impressive that he was assigned to the 1956 political conventions (at that time, the anchor on the evening news did not automatically assume the same role at conventions). As the conventions approached, however, Huntley's' lack of journalistic skills began to disturb the news executives, and they started to explore other possibilities. One day producer Reuven Frank and news executive Joe Meyers suggested pairing Huntley with someone who would make up for Huntley's apparent deficiencies: David Brinkley, a former newspaper reporter and the Washington correspondent for Swayze's nightly news show. In other words, pairing physical substance and wit, an air of reliability and irreverence, heft and deftness; it was a brainstorm, and it was to make Frank's career as well as that of Huntley and Brinkley. The two were an immediate hit both with critics and with the public. During the 1952 conventions, a previously unknown anchor named Walter Cronkite had earned top ratings for CBS; this time the audience went with the new pair on NBC. Within a few months, Swayze was out of a job, and his *Camel News Caravan* had been replaced by the *Huntley-Brinkley Report.*

A fundamental groundshift had occurred in broadcast journalism, but it was to be several years before this would become apparent to those outside the industry. Despite their quick success at the convention, initial reactions to Huntley and Brinkley as co-anchors—the one based in New York, the other in Washington, D.C.—were not all positive. The anchor of *CBS Evening News,* Douglas Edwards, who had edged out Swayze in the ratings a few years back, surged further ahead. Indeed, Huntley and Brinkley, whom CBS staff members dubbed Mutt and Jeff, could not even find a sponsor. But slowly the nation began to accustom itself to a newscast in which two anchors sat in different cities, used their first names, and signed off by bidding each other good-night. Soon they were being sung about in a parody of the Top 40 tune "Love and Marriage": "Huntley-Brinkley, Huntley-Brinkley / One is solemn and the other twinkly."

Like everything else on the show, "Chet" and "David" were touches dreamed up by the executive producer, Reuven Frank. Born in Canada, Frank attended Columbia Journalism School and started out as an editor at *The Newark (N.J.) Eve-*

ning News. "Television (then) was something you watched baseball on in bars," he once said. "I had no interest in it." In 1950 he chanced into a job as a newswriter at NBC–TV largely because radio newswriters wouldn't take a chance on the new medium. Frank was later to make his mark as the chief architect of the *Huntley-Brinkley Report.* A small man with sharp features and a sardonic, scornful manner, he sometimes went for days without talking to anyone and was notoriously hard to work with. But once he managed to get his ideas across, television news was never the same.

Most of Frank's contributions have been so incorporated into contemporary television news practices that it is hard to imagine how novel they appeared at the time. The hint of informality in the use of first names, for example, was practically revolutionary; in time it was to spawn a whole new definition of journalism, a sort of fun-time show about facts and people, that Frank himself would deplore. Similarly, before *Huntley-Brinkley,* television reporting operated almost solely on old newsreel clichés, according to which all doctors are selfless saints, all businessmen upstanding citizens, and all professional ballplayers inspirations to youth. "Unless you were a murderer, you were a nice guy," Pat Trese said. "*Huntley-Brinkley* was the first to say that Everett Dirksen wasn't always a leading statesman and that congressmen were often pretty foolish. We didn't just have a bishop giving a speech—we showed the same guy scratching his behind. *Huntley-Brinkley* really reflected Reuven's personality and judgment. It wasn't just a news show, it was a sophisticated moral show."

"Television is, above all, a visual medium," Frank told his newsroom. "It is not very good at the transmission of information, but it is matchless at the transmission of experience." Therefore, instead of writing what were essentially radio dispatches and then looking for shots to illustrate the text, Frank's writers at NBC were to look at what the camera crew had photographed and then provide transition material to fill in any blanks. Such radical steps electrified the news staff up at 106th Street. "Everybody believed what they were doing was more than a job," Pat Trese said. "We were building the machine. It was like baking a cake from scratch. You had to go find out how to shoot an interview, how to cover a convention or a space shot."

Under Frank, the result was a powerful kind of news reporting that let viewers get far closer to being at the scene of the story than ever before. But there were drawbacks; the most obvious was that certain stories, especially those dealing with business and economics, are difficult to reduce to a picture, particularly when "picture" is defined as meaning an event rather than someone sitting in a studio talking intelligently. Frank felt that having reporters on camera doing what were called "stand-uppers"—that is, adding more words—interfered with the picture, so he used them as little as possible; as a result, the anchors, in this case Huntley and Brinkley, were often the only people the viewer saw.

Huntley and Brinkley became stars. By 1960, when David Brinkley went out on the campaign trail with Hubert Humphrey, he had to retreat to the studio because he was drawing more attention than the candidate. Paradoxically, although Brinkley was one of the two most famous newsmen in the country, he could not function as a working journalist because he had lost his anonymity.

Although few completely realized it at the time, Brinkley was an exemplar of a new kind of celebrity. The stars of the past had been the unapproachable icons of the movies, remote gods and goddesses whose images filled a huge screen and who could be seen only every so often, when a new film came out; someone like Brinkley, on the other hand, seemed like a friendly neighbor, someone who quite naturally appeared in one's own home every day. He looked good on a small screen and seemed to belong in an ordinary living room, yet was linked to news of faraway people and places and events. When Jessica Savitch watched these new stars, she saw that the world was divided into two parts, the serene but dull postcard that she lived in, and the tiny but exciting and glamorous world inside the television box where handsome men spoke about great things and thousands upon thousands of people listened to the fountain of those men's voices with great approval. And slowly, as she pressed her nose against the screen, there began to grow in her a dream of how she would actually climb inside the box herself. She did not know what fulfilling that dream would mean, did not even know what the word "ambition" meant, but as she sat next to her sickly father and watched the flickering images, the dream kept quietly growing.

3

*M*argate

On the day after Mother's Day, 1959, Buddy Savitch died. He was thirty-three years old. As a matter of course, the small Jewish community in Kennett Square rallied around the survivors. The day Buddy died, friends draped Florence's mirrors with black cloth and did their best to comfort the children. Buddy was buried and mourned in proper Jewish fashion, with a funeral at a synagogue in Wilmington and interment in the synagogue cemetery. Jessica and her sisters were not taken to the funeral, but instead remained at home as the neighborhood wives filled the house with food for family members to eat while they sat shiva. For the next week, normal life stopped as family and friends came again and again to pay their respects to the new widow and her fatherless daughters.

Family friends remember talking to Jessica about her father's death; according to Doris Haber, who knew Florence well, Jessica pledged on the day of Buddy's death to become a doctor "so that no one else will ever have to die the way my daddy did." Yet in later years Savitch said that she was never explicitly told that her father had died, only that he was away. When she cried over her father's absence, she told friends, Florence rebuked her harshly and told her she wasn't allowed to cry; according to Savitch, her mother, still angry at Buddy, considered her daughter disloyal for mourning. The truth of these stories is difficult to assess, but Savitch told them to so many people that it is likely she believed them. Inexplicably abandoned, as she saw it, by her father and cruelly cold-shouldered by her mother, Jessica Savitch felt alone and desolate.

Unlike Jessica, Florence knew that they had lost not only a husband and father, but also a home and a way of life. Buddy had left little money, so she would have to find a job, no easy task after having been home for so long. Almost as worrisome as the money was the problem of being in what remained fundamentally alien territory. Florence had lived in Kennett Square for over a dozen years, but it would always be Buddy's town. She was an outsider now, and she would have to leave.

A year after Buddy's death, his family and a few close friends went to the cemetery. As Jessica and her sisters listened, a rabbi said a few prayers and then, as is the Jewish custom, lifted a black cloth to reveal Buddy's gravestone. On it was engraved his name and the dates of his birth and death. In that split second, Jessica knew, terribly and at last, that her father was truly dead, that he would never again ask her what she had learned in school that day, or sit next to her on the sofa and watch television, or tell her to smile while he took her picture.

Within a short time, all the Savitches had left Kennett Square. Grandfather Ben Savitch sold Benny's, and he and Lil moved south to Newark, Delaware. Florence moved her family to Margate, New Jersey, a modest residential community down the boardwalk from Atlantic City. A brother who lived in Atlantic City helped her to find a job as a nurse at a specialized hospital called the Children's Seashore House, and she was only a short distance away from her own parents, who had retired to the beach resort of Tuckertown.

Margate and its larger northern neighbor, Atlantic City, are two of the four independent townships on Absecon Island, one of the chain of skinny barrier islands strung along the southern New Jersey coastline. The town was strikingly different than Kennett Square, for instead of being based on the stolid traditions of farming, Atlantic City and its environs were a product of a decayed brand of American razzle-dazzle. Because of its wide, white beaches, wild berries, and abundant shellfish, Absecon Island had attracted summer visitors for centuries. In the nineteenth century, a physician named Jonathan Pitney came up with the novel idea of making Absecon Island into a summer health resort, for he was convinced that the salubrious salt air would cure all known diseases and those unknown as well. As it happened, however, Pitney's major legacy was his role in persuading the Camden and Atlantic Railroad to build a spur track to the shore. In 1854, the last spike was driven into the track, and a seemingly endless stream of tourists began to arrive in the brand-new town of Atlantic City. Soon the beach was lined with hotels and restaurants. In 1870, their complaints about visitors' tracking sand from beach to storefront led to the construction of the first of Atlantic City's famous boardwalks.

Almost from the first day it opened for business, Atlantic City was home to the best and the worst of American life. On the beach side of Atlantic Avenue was a row of stately hotels, pleasure domes reserved for a wealthy clientele; on the other side of the avenue, a shantytown housed the chambermaids, dishwashers, and other downstairs denizens, most of them black, required to keep the pleasure domes going, as well as bookmakers, prostitutes, numbers runners, and others on the periphery of the law. The other three communities of Absecon —Longport, Margate, and Ventnor—were created for the doctors, lawyers, teachers, retail merchants, and other middle- and upper-class professionals who came to live and work in the new resort industry. Public entertainment on the commercial amusement piers was lavish, spectacular, yet somehow touchingly innocent: Visitors could ride the Ferris wheel, watch Al Jolson, or sit in on a tryout of the next season's Ziegfeld Follies. And what could be more evocative of a certain charming naïveté than Atlantic City's particular contributions to American culture—the picture postcard, the Easter Parade, the Miss America Pageant, and saltwater taffy, said to have been created when a storm flooded a candy store on the boardwalk.

The combination of innocent and not-so-innocent charms proved irresistible; during the twenties, a sunny Memorial Day weekend alone could attract some quarter of a million visitors. But the glory days came to an abrupt halt in 1929, when the stock market went through the floor. The beaches were soon thronged with another sort of visitor, tourists who arrived on discount one-day return train tickets and carried their own beach chairs. They counted their pennies so closely they even brought the family's lunch in a shoebox—a frugality that earned them the nickname "Shoebies" from unhappy local merchants.

The postwar recovery did nothing for Atlantic City. The gilded age and the jazz age had been succeeded by the jet age, in which well-to-do vacationers could reach the wider, cleaner beaches of Florida or California in not much more time than it took them to drive to Atlantic City. Summer tourism slackened and winter tourism fell off to the point that, for the first time that anyone could remember, the beachfront hotels began boarding up off-season. To the casual eye, a visit there was still like a tour around the Monopoly board, the houses and hotels all lined up in neat little rows. Even strangers could recite the street names with their eyes closed: Tennessee, St. James, New York, Kentucky, North Carolina, all so wonderfully familiar. (Unfamiliar streets like Adriatic and Drexel and Congress had been excluded from Monopoly because blacks lived on them.) But the job market was shrinking, and though few outside people realized it, the Queen of the Coast was on the verge of collapse.

In Margate, Jessica felt, as she put it later, like Dorothy in *The Wizard of Oz*, swept away by a tornado to a strange land. Used to being a member of one of the more well-to-do and important families in town, here she abruptly became a lower-middle-class nobody. People nodded in recognition when she said her name in Kennett Square. Here they did nothing, or even said "Jessica Who?" Instead of having a lovely new house like the one in New Garden, she now lived in one of a long row of small brick ranch houses that were squeezed into lots so narrow that the asbestos siding from one house almost scraped that on the next. When she went to sleep at night, there was no shadow from a tree outside her window to spark her fantasies, for the tiny lawn contained only a few small shrubs and a little magnolia tree. When Jessica asked for a new party dress, she was told for the first time in her life that the family couldn't afford it. Occasionally her Savitch grandparents did send expensive presents, usually clothes, but such lavishness sometimes caused friction and resentment in the little house in Margate.

When Florence's father died, her mother came to live with

her. The household was not a particularly happy one. Florence, now the sole source of support for five people, went to work every day at the hospital, and when she returned she was often tired and worried. She had always been a level-headed, no-nonsense person, but now, one of Jessica's friends said later, Florence seemed to have less patience than ever for Jessica's vivid imagination or for the crises that arise so frequently in any adolescent's life. "Don't be so dramatic, Jessica," Florence would say, putting an odd, hard emphasis on the first syllable of her daughter's name.

Feeling anonymous, Jessica began her freshman year at Atlantic City High School, two blocks away from the board-walk. Back in Pennsylvania her grade had only one hundred students, most of them white and middle class, and she had been a class officer; in the new school, there were 925 freshmen of all races and classes. Yet it was hardly a blackboard jungle filled with teenage thugs and its hall scarred by graffiti; with Jessica at Atlantic City High was everyone from the offspring of the elite to children whose families barely survived on food stamps. The dropout rate was still low, two figures, and the height of misbehavior was to cut classes and smoke cigarettes in the little park across the street.

An enormous brick neo-Gothic citadel with a central clock tower and crenellations, the high school was the central hub of social activity not just for teenagers but for all of the island. Like Kennett Square, the communities of Absecon offered little to the young adults who did not have the good fortune to inherit a family business; in the off-season there were no jobs and few forms of public entertainment with which to pass the time. People who were able to do so moved elsewhere after they grew up, abandoning the field to high school kids who, after their own brief moment in the Atlantic City spotlight, would then hightail it out of town themselves. Although the only person connected to Atlantic City that the rest of the country ever heard about was Miss America, the annual beauty contest was strictly business to the people who lived there year-round; to them, the real stars were the local teenagers.

Their sports events were major activities for the whole town, their sororities and fraternities were key social institutions, and their plays were major dramatic presentations. No one in the area needed a watch to know when it was three o'clock, for that was the time the kids streamed out of the high school doors and began milling up and down Atlantic Avenue. Those on the academic track—the "good" kids—strolled down the avenue to the Super Sub Shop for cheese steaks and a few tunes on the jukebox, while the hoods and the girls taking steno wound up at The Great Josh's, a sandwich joint across the street from school. *American Bandstand* fans hustled home to rock out with Dick Clark, hoping that when the weather turned warm Justine and Bobby and the rest of the *Bandstand* crew would come again to the Chelsea section of the Atlantic City beach. Meanwhile, anybody interested in pizza would take a jitney bus uptown to Tony's, where they piled up the cheese on a pie and served beer to any kids who looked like they wouldn't throw up on the spot.

Jessica, always a quick study, could see right away that her old Kennett Square look, with knee socks that didn't even match her sweaters, would never do. By sophomore year she had transformed herself into a page out of *Seventeen,* right down to the pageboy, the penny loafers, and the perfectly pressed A-line skirt. For good kids like Jessica, the main goal in life was not to stick out; they did their homework, always laid out their clothes the night before to make sure there were no wrinkles, and guarded their reps with their lives. It was okay for a good girl to admit she thought James Dean and Elvis were cute, but only as long as she wore a bra that molded her breasts into perfect cones and her panty girdle was tight enough to eliminate even a hint of a jiggle as she walked; she knew with the absolute certainty of adolescence that she would be totally dead, wiped off the face of the earth, zero, if she were ever to look one iota different than the girl standing next to her in front of the mirror in the girls' bathroom.

Trying to cover up acne, Jessica wore such thick, heavily scented makeup one classmate called it "boy repellent"; in fact, however, her appearance seemed to have exactly the opposite effect. One day in the cafeteria she caught the eye of a senior named Steve Berger, who asked her out. Most fourteen-year-old girls wouldn't have thought much of his idea of a first date, to come over to WOND, the local ABC radio affiliate, where he had a part-time job, and watch him work. But Jessica was game. The next Saturday morning, Steve drove her in his family's car to a wetlands area just off the mainland. Everywhere they looked, they saw brown, dead weeds. The station itself was hardly prepossessing: a faded wood shack on stilts that was built out in the marsh because it was cheaper to build a transmitter tower there. As a result, WOND was always bathed in a miasma of rotting vegetation. Indeed, when there was a downwind from the large sewage plant that was the station's nearest neighbor, working there could be unbearable. Whenever it rained, the station was flooded, and the staff had to be rescued several times by fire department ladders.

Steve's cohorts were pleased by the pretty girl's arrival at the swamp. With some reluctance, Jessica, who was self-conscious about the "lazy tongue" that occasionally gave her a slight lisp, allowed herself to be cajoled into recording some introductions for Steve's afternoon show. Stepping into a tiny recording studio, she recited the WOND call letters over and over in as breathy and sexy a voice as she could muster while Steve turned the dials and added layer upon layer of reverberation for a classic 1960s sound. When Jessica went home, she sat down in the kitchen with her mother and listened to the show. "As soon as I heard my voice on the airwaves," she later wrote, "my destiny was fixed." Her apprehensions about how she would sound vanished, replaced by the intoxicating prospect of being able to communicate with thousands of people at once, of her very own voice coming into their kitchens and their living rooms and their bedrooms and telling them what was going on in the faraway outside world of events and meetings and important decisions. She began accompanying Steve to the station for all his shifts, and soon she had a rip-'n'-read news shift of her own, so named because it involved ripping news feeds off the wire-service machines and reading them directly on the air. At the age of fourteen, she had become the first regularly scheduled female on air in the whole region.

Despite a year-round population in the total market area that numbered under 200,000, Atlantic City had four radio stations. They flourished during the summer season, when tens of thousands of tourists tuned in. The Steel Pier, an amusement pier running out to sea from the boardwalk, was still a major stop for everyone from Jack E. Leonard to Brenda Lee and Fats Domino; live broadcasts of their concerts and, at season's end, all the festivities associated with the Miss America contest, provided plenty of ad revenue. Off-season, however, when the pier was dark and the number of tourists fell off, the stations barely eked out a living.

Howard Green, the plump, round-faced owner of WOND, had made it the leading station in the area by hiring radio personalities like Gene Packard, a local DJ whose specialty was funny characters and exotic accents. In 1962, Green decided that he needed something new and exciting to bring in the region's teenagers. He didn't have far to look; before he had made up his mind what to do, Jessica and Jeff Greenhawt, an Atlantic City High School classmate and Margate neighbor who also hung around WOND, volunteered to co-host a half-hour roundup of school news every Saturday. Soon *Teen Corner* was launched, and teenagers for miles around tuned in to find out about senior proms, scholastic awards, spring plays, club meetings, and sports, sports, sports. During the week Jessica and Jeff would talk to teachers and students from every high school in the area, write up their scheduled events, and select the records they'd play between items. On Saturday morning, Jeff's parents would drive him to Jessica's house, wait fifteen minutes while she retouched her makeup and checked for any runs in her stockings—"I always said, 'Jessica, it's only radio,' " Greenhawt said later, "but she never paid any attention"—and take the two of them to the station to go over last-minute questions with the interviewee for that day.

At the age of fourteen, Jessica was already in her element, and loving it. "If there is such a thing as a natural, she was it," Howard Green said years later. "Lots of kids come to work but lose interest after a few weeks or months, but not Jessica. She was very driven and coveted any suggestions made to improve her program, to get ahead in the broadcast world." An obvious step was to join the high school's audiovisual club. "I said, 'Girls can't work equipment,' " the club's sponsor, Robert Davies, recalled later, "but she just said, 'Yes, I can.' " The first girl in the club, she was promptly dubbed "Brenda Starr." More important, membership enabled her to borrow equipment for her show and to get pointers from Davies and others on how to conduct interviews.

Soon Howard Green hired Jessica to do a regular paid shift on Sunday afternoon as Atlantic City's first female DJ, starting at the princely rate of $1.50 an hour. Like every other successful AM rock station at the time, WOND used a highly stylized

Top 40 format, which included giving most on-air people cute aliases like "Red Car" and "Kelly Green"; Jessica, so young that she didn't have a driver's license and had to ride her bicycle to work, was given the sexy sobriquet of "Jesse James." It was the time of Motown and the British invasion, of the Temptations and Herman's Hermits, but Jessica had so many commercials to get through that she often ended up spending most of the hour pushing products like men's cologne—"Tiger, tiger," she'd whisper in her most seductive voice—and playing only a handful of songs in an hour.

She was always fiercely anxious about her performance; whenever she mispronounced a word or miscued a record, she was certain of being fired on the spot. On her first Sunday DJ shift, she was so frantic that after each tune she yanked the record off the turntable and tossed it in the corner, eventually creating such a mess that Jeff was summoned to come in an hour before his own shift to put the studio back into working order. But what came across the airwaves always sounded so good that other broadcasters began calling Green and asking who this Jesse James was, and if she was available for further shifts elsewhere. When he told them she wasn't old enough to drive, they backed off, but he knew already that her days at WOND were limited. Basking in Green's approval, Jessica Savitch had an experience of near-instant success that would be the standard against which every other achievement would be judged in years to come.

At the same time she was entering the broadcast world of "The Jukebox on the Swamp," she pledged a high school sorority called Delta Omega Beta or DOBS, acted in school plays, and became best friends with Rusty Nicholl, a redhead who sat next to her in Spanish class. Soon she was part of a crowd of a dozen or so other teenagers who got together to play records and drink soda. Social groups at Atlantic City High were as neatly stratified as geological epochs; the children of wealthy professionals, for example, all hung around together and were into drinking. Jessica's crowd, a small out-group composed largely of local storekeepers' kids, tended to meet at Rusty's house, where they would automatically head for the refrigerator and load up on cake and milk. Even if they had been out on dates, kids dropped by Rusty's for a snack afterward. In the summer they went to the beach to swim and water-ski. A major activity was devising complicated maneuvers in which up to twenty teenagers would ski in formation and climb atop each other's backs to form elaborate pyramids. Agile and light, Jessica would scramble to the apex and wave triumphantly to those on shore. It was an era long before environmental concerns outlawed fires on the beach, and every year the teens celebrated summer's end with a big bonfire where they ate and drank and played bongo drums until late at night. Much of the evening would be devoted to dancing with what was called a limbo stick, a long wooden rod. It was held parallel to and several feet over the ground, and dancers, arching their bodies backward, would try to wriggle under without touching it. Savitch, a natural gymnast who could do backbends and walk on her hands, was one of the local champions, able to squeeze under a stick only a short distance above the sand.

During the school year, the Margate kids sat in a group on the public bus to and from school, and on Friday night they'd attend sorority and fraternity meetings in the neighborhood. Some of them attended Beth Judah, the local synagogue where Florence Savitch had enrolled her daughters, but Jessica went to temple regularly only on her father's death day; the Jewish identity that had been so central in Kennett Square had become less important. She had become a teenager from Margate, a quiet little town whose most famous resident was Lucy the Elephant, a huge gray metal behemoth built on a vacant lot on Atlantic Avenue as a gimmick to promote real-estate sales in the 1940s. Now Jessica's friends were the most important people in her life, and her idea of an important holiday event was getting together with the gang at Rusty's and helping trim the Christmas tree.

As one might expect, the drive that had already landed Jessica her own radio show and was later to take her to the top of the broadcast industry showed up off the air as well. Her way of trying to get her way, Jeff Greenhawt said afterward, was "ask first, then see how it plays." Although they were close friends, he said, "she could be very pushy sometimes. When she'd innocently suggest we do something or go somewhere I had absolutely no interest in, I'd say 'You're even asking me?' When she did it to her mother, Florence would just say, 'You want to get there? Start walking, you'll be there in a week.' "

The First Family, Vaughn Meader's album parodying the Kennedys, was popular at that time, and a favorite party game among Jessica's friends was to tape each other doing their imitations of JFK and Jackie. Sometimes they used Jessica's tape recorder, a shiny, chrome top-of-the-line Wollensack which was a treasured birthday present. Jessica was always in charge of the broadcast and would make a commentary to go along with the others' voices. "She was the Edward R. Murrow of the evening," Rusty Nicholl said later. "She worked so hard on her accent we used to call her Queen Elizabeth. She was always bugging all of us to speak right, not to say At-*lan*-tic *Ci*-ty but At-lan-*tic Ci-ty*." On weekends she often spent the night at Rusty's house; dressed in shortie pajamas, they would spend hours setting their hair in bristly rollers and drying it under the big bonnet hair dryers no self-respecting teenage girl at that time would think of leaving behind for even one night.

Thin was not really in then, but Jessica was always worried about her weight, despite her evident skinniness; those who knew her then later concluded that she must have been anorectic, a term unknown to them at the time. "We used to joke that if she turned sideways, she'd disappear," Rusty said. In spare moments she would lie on the floor with her legs tucked under the sofa, doing sit-ups, and on Sunday mornings, when Steve Berger and Rusty's boyfriend, Gary Calderwood, would show up with lox and bagels, Jessica would eat unbuttered, deliberately burned toast and lemon juice because she'd heard they shrink the stomach. "I said, 'If you've got a tapeworm, that toast'll take care of it,' " Rusty said. Jessica seemed to take the teasing in stride; in "Portrait of Rusty," a poem she wrote in the spring of her junior year, she called Rusty "my bestest friend."

Jessica wore Steve Berger's fraternity pin, but after he went away to Temple University the Savitch phone rang off the hook with calls from other boys eager to ask out this fifteen-year-old who could, and occasionally did, pass for an adult. One frequent date was Steve Altman, who lived a few blocks away in Margate and was a year ahead of her in school. His father had died, too, and their common loss drew the two young people together. When Steve was still too young to drive, he and Jessica would walk out to the driftwood-strewn beach on the Bay side of the island and talk about their sense of desolation and abandonment. "She was consumed by her father's death," Altman said later. "Because she idolized him, she was always embellishing her descriptions of him."

But the relationship was not simply a matter of sharing melancholy feelings. "Jessica was this sexy little girl," Altman said. "She had a marvelous sense of humor and loved teasing me." After he got his license, he and Savitch would cut school and go swimming at a nearby lake where the clean, fresh water had a brown tint from the cedars that lined the shore. Once on the way home a bee flew in the car and Steve, who had known someone who had been paralyzed by a bee sting, brought the car to a screeching halt and leaped out in terror. After taking off her sandal and neatly crushing the bee, Jessica batted her eyelashes at Steve and said in her best Southern belle manner, "Can we keep on going now?" In the evenings, Steve would take Jessica to The Point, the southernmost tip of the island, for a favorite teenage pastime, known in the 1960s as "watching the submarine races"—that is, necking and heavy petting—and then race home to meet the stiff curfew Florence Savitch had imposed on her popular daughter. Because Jessica was underage, she and Steve had a running joke about how he could be arrested for driving her across a state line, and she signed his yearbook "Your Favorite Jailbait."

Savitch also dated a boy named Barry Swartz, another upperclassman. He was smitten the first time he met her, when she was wearing sunglasses and a trenchcoat two sizes too big and belted at the waist like Bogart's in *Casablanca*. Barry Swartz was not an obvious choice for Jessica; Rusty Nicholl told him years later that he was the only boy Jessica ever dated who couldn't help her. Barry, now a successful cosmetic surgeon in San Antonio, was not connected to WOND, and his family lived in the Inlet, a shabby section at the other end of the island. Whenever he and Jessica were with her Savitch grandparents, he said later, they made it clear that they were uptown folks and he was beneath them. What Jessica and Barry had in common, though, were a thirst for sophistication and glamour and a burning desire to escape their current impoverishment.

At fraternity parties, as everybody else was getting blitzed on beer, Jessica and Barry would slowly sip from a bottle of Asti Spumante; when the rest of the crowd went out to grab a sub, Jessica and Barry would slip over to the Flying Dutchman, a local piano bar, and order a bowl of *soupe à l'oignon,* which they knew to be very French. While their friends were spending money on movies and other teenage fare, Jessica and Barry would hoard their funds, then buy tickets to see *Camelot* in summer stock and dress up in their best clothes for a grown-up night on the town.

Jessica and Barry also shared fierce tempers. According to Gary Calderwood, Barry and Jessica fought constantly, in part because Barry was intensely jealous of the other boys Jessica was dating at the time, Steve Berger and Steve Altman. "I was surprised Barry and Jessica stayed together," Calderwood said later. "Once at his house he threw plates and broke things and screamed at her." Barry's flashes of anger were also recalled by Steve Altman. One day, he said, Barry, who already had his heart set on being a doctor, told Steve that he looked forward to the day when Steve needed surgery and Barry would have him on the operating table.

"She had two sides," Swartz said later. "One was 'I'm the best,' the hard-driving personality she presented to the world niney-nine percent of the time. In my yearbook she wrote 'From the Best to the Best.' " She made no secret of the fact that her career came first; when Swartz gave her his fraternity pin, she told him, "I'll wear it, but I just want you to realize I'll do anything I can to get ahead." But the other side, he said, was soft and vulnerable, the kind of girl who sent him a home-made brownie and a letter signed J/BS (their combined initials) every day after he went off to college to be a pre-med, who sometimes talked to him in babytalk, and who still worshipped her father's memory. On one of their first dates she asked him to go with her to her father's grave in Wilmington and told him that her favorite quotation was the first line of *The Waste Land*—"April is the cruellest month"—because that was when her father's last, fatal bout with his illness occurred. "He was a very strong presence in her life," Swartz said. "He had told her to be the best, and she never considered being anything else."

According to Swartz, having "the Best" for a sister did not bother Lori, a chubby-faced grade schooler who was nick-named "Lorchie" and who idolized her oldest sister. Jessica took a particular interest in her youngest sister and seemed to want an active role in her upbringing. But her attitude toward her middle sister, Stephanie, was considerably cooler. "Basically, she seemed to ignore her," Rusty Nicholl said. A plump dark-haired girl two years younger than Jessica, Stephanie was a better student but received neither the public attention nor the eager phone calls from boys. "Stephanie and Jessica were opposite ends of the world," Swartz said. "It was as if a lion cub had been secretly placed into a family of lambs. Stephanie was just like her mother, the kind of person who would want to sit home and knit. But Jessica was like a rocket ship, ready to fly off to Paris at any moment." Jessica had it all, but apparently even for a teenager this was not without cost; in later years, she told friends that her mother never stopped pushing her to make up to her sisters for being prettier and more popular.

For two years, Jessica and Barry were together constantly. She dedicated records to him on the air, mentioned him in her senior yearbook inscription, and accepted his fraternity pin. They secretly made love, talked often about marriage, and even picked out children's names (David Scott, after her father, for a boy and Dacey Lynn for a girl). But what their relationship meant—or indeed, if it meant anything at all—remained a mystery for Barry. "I don't know if any of that was actually real," he said years later. "She always did whatever was appropriate at any particular point. Maybe it was just 'in' to be like Rusty and her boyfriend, to act real close to someone. It was the thing to date a boy in high school, so she did. But somehow she wasn't very involved. You never really knew who she was. In my mind I was thinking rose-covered cottages and the whole bit, but she was going somewhere and we were just stops along the way."

In the summer of 1964, Atlantic City's businessmen felt an unwonted optimism. In the salt air was an upbeat conviction that Atlantic City was at long last going to beat its stretch of bad luck. This wasn't pie-in-the-sky talk; this year, Atlantic City had finally hit the jackpot: the Democratic National Convention. The boardwalk would be jammed, gleeful residents told each other. Hotels and restaurants would hire extra shifts, and conventioneer dollars would be flowing like water. Atlantic City had seen hundreds of conventions, but this one would be different. It would bring the city some badly needed attention, for all the people from newspapers, radio, and television would be there. One of them was Jessica Savitch. WOND was an affiliate of ABC Radio, and Green had managed to obtain ABC press passes for some of his staff. As Jessica headed over to Convention Hall the first morning, she was thrilled at the prospect of actually being at an event that the entire country would be watching on live television.

National political conventions had always been important for television, for the opportunity to watch these historic events as they occurred had convinced countless Americans to buy their own sets. Such gatherings were even more important for the fledgling network news divisions, for they offered one of the few opportunities for news departments to take over the air for hours at a time. As late as the mid-fifties, Reuven Frank told journalist Barbara Matusow, "News never got on the air —no bulletins, no preemptions, no late-night specials, nothing except the fifteen-minute evening news. So the conventions gave you the first real whack at the audience. If they liked you, maybe they would come back."

NBC had provided the first live television coverage of a convention in 1940, before Frank came to the network, when the Republicans' nomination of Wendell Willkie in Philadelphia was broadcast in New York City via an AT&T coaxial cable. Eight years later, both political parties chose Philadelphia to house their conventions solely because it offered the best access to television. The old coaxial cable had been expanded to provide a live feed to fourteen stations, which meant a combined audience of up to ten million viewers. It was an impressive showing for a new medium, but was still only a fraction of the audience for radio; when John Cameron Swayze and Douglas Edwards were ordered by NBC and CBS, respectively, to anchor the conventions for television, they regarded the assignments as demotions. The politicians, however, had no such reservations. Despite the seat-of-the-pants quality of the coverage, they couldn't wait to climb up to the jerry-built broadcast studios in which Swayze and Edwards held forth.

Four years later, in 1952, both the conventions and the campaigns were full-fledged television events. Radio still had a large audience, but the coaxial cable connecting television networks and affiliates now spanned the entire continent, and over one-third of the nation's families, including those demographers considered "influentials," had sets. By the time the conventions were over, two stars were born: Betty Furness, who gave live gavel-to-gavel demonstrations of Westinghouse refrigerators on NBC, and Walter Cronkite, who made his first appearance as a national anchor for CBS. A former UPI reporter, Cronkite looked and sounded exactly like what he was, a man from Missouri. Equally important, he still retained the basic wire service values: Get it fast, get it right, and keep it simple. Such an orientation was the exact opposite of that espoused by Edward R. Murrow within his wing of the CBS news division. Murrow esteemed sophistication, thoughtfulness, and complexity; as might be expected, he had no interest in the weeklong, live assignment of anchoring the convention. Cronkite jumped at the opportunity. By the end of the first day, it was obvious that his reportorial sensibilities, combined with his reassuring physical presence—like Chet Huntley, he filled the screen—played superbly on the new medium. Before the convention was over, Murrow's colleagues were poking their heads into Cronkite's broadcast booth looking for work.

But something even more fundamental to the story of television news than the debut of Walter Cronkite occurred at the conventions that year. As the candidates stood in front of an audience that by now reached into the tens of millions, it became unmistakably clear that televised conventions could make not only a news division, an audience, and a star anchor; they could also make a candidate. Senator Robert Taft of Ohio lost the spot at the top of the Republican ticket in large part because he looked remote and unfeeling on camera compared to the spectacularly telegenic Eisenhower.

Television also affected the election. Adlai Stevenson, the Democratic nominee for president, had a witty and urbane speaking style that was perfect for radio; on TV, however, he seemed cold and long-winded, especially when compared to Eisenhower, a war hero with a grin that stretched from one side of the screen to the other. According to broadcast historian Erik Barnouw, Stevenson, who abhorred television and did not own a set, refused to be packaged "like a breakfast food." To him, a televised speech was just like any other speech, to be tinkered with until the last minute; as a result, there was no time to transfer the manuscript to the TelePrompTer and Stevenson delivered it with his nose buried in his beautifully written text.

Although Eisenhower was equally unenthusiastic about the new medium, he appreciated its power. He announced his candidacy on live television, and a Republican advertising agency, Batten, Barton, Durstine & Osborn, choreographed his spontaneous-looking appearances on the screen. Whenever Eisenhower spoke, the actual text was but a single, relatively unimportant element in the mélange of triumphal entry, tumultuous applause, exchange of smiles with Mamie, and even more triumphal farewell. Perhaps the most serious threat to Ike's campaign came not from Stevenson but from his own vice-presidential candidate, Richard M. Nixon, who was accused of having pocketed campaign money raised by California supporters. The issue was resolved on nationwide television when Nixon produced a half-hour-long tear-jerker of an address. In it he recounted the origins of his family's border collie, Checkers, a tale of heartrending innocence which implied that anyone who doubted Nixon's veracity was the moral equivalent of a dognapper.

By 1956, television had completely taken over the conventions. The convention halls and the candidates' suites were knee-deep in the miles of TV cable needed for NBC's five tons of equipment and CBS's hundred cameras, and the hallways were full of correspondents staggering under their barely portable battery packs. With over five hundred television stations in the country and sets in 85 percent of the nation's homes, Stevenson finally acknowledged that the ability to come across well on the tube was crucial. He attempted to improve his video presentation, but it was too little, too late. Once again Ike came across the air better than anyone else at either convention, although a young senator from Massachusetts named John F. Kennedy emerged as a national figure because of his attractive performance as narrator of a film shown during the Democratic convention and his brief (but highly visible) attempt to challenge Senator Estes Kefauver for second place on the ticket. With the candidates a foregone conclusion, viewers focused their attention on something far more interesting: the new NBC anchor team of Huntley and Brinkley. After the convention Cronkite returned to his regular reporting duties, but Huntley and Brinkley were promoted to full-time anchors on the *Huntley-Brinkley Report*.

•

The new show would mark the beginning of the period in which television news became a major player not just during presidential elections but all year, every year. The Republican administration had already waved a beckoning finger; in 1955, when new lighting techniques made television cameras less blindingly intrusive, Eisenhower shattered precedent by inviting them to cover his regular news conferences. Print reporters, who used to control both the conference and its coverage, were permanently scooped.

The televising of the presidency would proceed under Kennedy, who used the media with an adroitness matching, if not surpassing, that of Franklin Roosevelt. He knew how to throw a party, television style; his inauguration, featuring snowy-haired Robert Frost at the podium and a dazzling lineup of Hollywood stars at the ball, left viewers spellbound. He televised his press conferences live and encouraged CBS to broadcast a tour of the White House, narrated by the First Lady. He covered up the Bay of Pigs invasion on the airwaves, then announced and finally took responsibility for its failure in the same way. When U.S. intelligence detected Russian missiles on Cuban soil, he supplemented traditional diplomatic channels by demanding on television that Khrushchev remove the weapons.

Whenever Kennedy appeared at an event, it became a television story. Sound trucks, lighting technicians, camera crews, and correspondents all converged on the spot, elbowing print and radio journalists aside, jockeying for the most advantageous spot. Once in place, they hurled questions at the president, who batted them back with an easy, telegenic smile. Despite his love for the camera, Kennedy was responsible for television's first public scolding; his FCC chairman, a lawyer from Chicago named Newton Minow, called television "a vast wasteland" and declared that station license renewals would no longer be automatic but subject to a review of their public-affairs programming. In part as a response to Minow, in 1963 the networks extended their nightly newscasts to a half hour.

Even Kennedy's assassination was a television event. Within moments of the shooting, NBC preempted all programming, a move that the other networks were forced to follow if they were not to appear unconcerned. Journalists everywhere reacted with a curious mixture of personal horror and professional excitement. To cite one small example, as soon as Jessica Savitch heard the news, she raced to a pay phone and called in a report to WOND on the reactions of Atlantic City High School students. Jessica and Jeff Greenhawt thought of trying to do a special edition of *Teen Corner,* but in the end they were overtaken by the dimensions of the event. The show was canceled, and Jessica watched the president's funeral in her living room and cried. The whole nation watched together, linked in a vast and sorrowful electronic web. At the end of the year, the Roper Organization, which conducts national polls on public perceptions of the media, reported that television had eclipsed radio and print to become the nation's basic news source.

Despite their predominance, however, television reporters were not respected in their profession. Print reporters regarded TV as a creature of great size and greater vapidity, and in many readily apparent ways the belief was absolutely correct. In part because the cumbersome equipment ruled out most on-the-spot reporting, television news relied on print to dig up its stories; moreover, even after the evening newscasts were extended to a half hour, little more than headlines got covered in the twenty-two minutes actually devoted to news. But newspaper people understood very well the *power* of the rival medium. Wallace Westfeldt, a reporter for the *Nashville Tennessean* in the 1950s, recalled years afterward what happened when Governor Frank Clement arrived at the Nashville airport after he had abandoned favorite son Estes Kefauver at the 1956 Democratic convention to vote for Senator Kennedy. Waving his white Stetson to the crowd, Clement found himself greeted by a hostile chant: "We saw you! We saw you!" The crowd wouldn't let Clement open his mouth, Westfeldt said. "Television had leapfrogged the entire institution of the press. It went straight from the event to the people."

The big story of that period was the civil rights struggle, and there, too, Westfeldt saw the power of the video camera. "Television didn't cause the civil rights movement," he said, "but it gave that story a color and attraction and emphasis that newspapers couldn't do. Even without any commentary, a shot of big white men spitting and cursing at black children did more to open up the national intellect than my stories ever could." Yet like so many print people, Westfeldt remained contemptuous of the box; when NBC called the *Nashville Tennessean* in July 1960 and asked him to work on a civil rights documentary, Westfeldt said no way. "We just didn't believe in TV," Westfeldt said. "At press conferences we would include profanities in our questions so they couldn't be used on television. We would bring in little metal beetles to interfere with the sound track, and some people even pulled out the cables." A year later, when NBC told Westfeldt that he should take it as a positive sign that the network wanted someone of his caliber, he surrendered. His television career was to span the next two decades and to include being executive producer of the *Huntley-Brinkley Report* and senior producer of *Prime Time Sunday,* a magazine show that was modeled after *60 Minutes* and featured Jessica Savitch as principal correspondent.

Westfeldt joined a network on the move. A few years before, Reuven Frank had begun his new, more pictorial concept of broadcast journalism, and it was paying off. To some extent, Frank was lucky in his timing. The revelation that *Twenty-One, The $64,000 Question,* and other leading quiz shows were rigged left NBC scurrying to salvage its reputation with more public-service and news broadcasts. In addition, CBS, which had a particularly strong entertainment side at that time, had such a firm grip on first place in ratings and revenues that the newly chosen president of NBC, Robert Kintner, decided it would be futile to make an all-out assault on Paley's empire. A stout man with Coke-bottle glasses, a gravelly voice, and a brusque demeanor, Kintner ran the company with a cigarette in one hand and a glass of vodka in the other. Having been a columnist at the New York *Herald-Tribune,* Kintner loved journalism; instead of attacking CBS directly, he chose instead to promote his own network's news department.

He'd already earned his broadcast journalism stripes as president of ABC. In 1954, he had done the unthinkable and preempted daytime programming to broadcast the Army-McCarthy hearings; an audacious move (and also an economical one as it required only one camera), it gave ABC's neophyte news operation much-needed attention and credibility. At NBC, Kintner gave his love for news full rein, providing the news division with more money, more airtime, and more promotion than ever before. As far as Kintner was concerned,

NBC News was engaged in all-out war with CBS News; accordingly, he adopted a dictum of "CBS plus thirty," which meant that all special news programs had to be thirty minutes longer than whatever the rival network presented. In one year alone, Kintner interrupted the regular schedule for a news special more than one hundred times; years later, general counsel David Adams would joke that it seemed as if every time LBJ had a bowel movement, NBC would do a report about it.

Kintner watched everything on all three networks each evening and expected his top twenty executives to do the same; early the next morning he would call all twenty into his office, where they would be closely questioned on their reactions to the other networks' shows. His unbridled competitiveness was coupled with an unusual warmth toward his staff. Every upper-level birthday merited a party complete with champagne and solid-gold cuff links. As a result, employee morale surged. So did the news standings. In 1958 NBC News pulled even with CBS, and by the end of the 1960 conventions, NBC had a whopping 51 percent share of the audience compared to CBS's 36 percent. Kintner could not resist crowing; within days, the *Huntley-Brinkley Report* had a new tagline boasting that it was the most-listened-to newscast in the country.

Kintner's methods were to keep NBC News in the top spot for years to come, but they were also to spawn an increasingly fierce emphasis on ratings above all else. Long present on the entertainment side, the fight for market share was now unleashed in network newsrooms. As time went on, fractional shifts in ratings would make and then destroy reputations and careers; the higher up the ladder one climbed, the shakier the perch. The huge stakes meant that nobody was really safe.

The competition was brutal at the 1964 Democratic convention, but Jessica saw little other than the sheer crush of the media. Although the official proceedings did not begin until late August, the crews began arriving in Atlantic City weeks beforehand. The preparations were enormous in scale, as if an army were expected. Dozens of trucks double-parked outside Convention Hall as crews constructed multileveled control booths, each outfitted like a small apartment, over the upper level of the balcony. In part because NBC was preparing for the first live color broadcast of a convention, the hall was outfitted with so much auxiliary lighting that even a bolt of lightning would have been practically invisible. The new wireless microphones and cameras meant the elimination of the miles of cable that had mired previous conventions, but much transmission line still had to be taped to the floor. Creepy-peepies, the semi-portable videocameras powered by enormous backpacks and used for live feeds, were readied for action. Even more enormous videotape recorders, used for material that would not be broadcast immediately, were installed and 16mm-film cameras, far more flexible than the old 35mm models, were cleaned and loaded for use.

All that was lacking was a real story. The 1964 convention was to be the coronation of Lyndon Johnson, and everyone knew it. The only unknown was the vice-presidential selection, and it was not a tantalizing enough mystery to hold the press corps' attention indefinitely. (The most significant development of the entire event was the Mississippi Freedom Democratic Party's protest against the all-white official delegation sent to Atlantic City by the regular Democratic Party machinery of that state. The networks did their best to follow this development; Sander Vanocur and John Chancellor, two of the NBC journalistic team known as "the Four Horsemen," even staked out the motel where Walter Reuther and Martin Luther King labored to work out a compromise seating arrangement for the convention that would include the MFDP. Such coverage was anathema to Johnson, who emphatically preferred that the cameras stay on the rostrum throughout the proceedings. Once when NBC's cameras ventured in the direction of the protestors, Johnson called up network headquarters at the convention. Expecting to reach Bob Kintner, with whom he had close ties, he instead got a startled Bob Sarnoff. Undeterred, Johnson barked out, "Get those goddamn cameras off those niggers!") *

---

* According to documents disclosed in 1975 in U.S. Senate hearings, Johnson was worried that he would be "embarrassed" by civil rights protests at the convention and requested FBI surveillance of the MFDP at Atlantic City; whether the concerns were related to security or political considerations—such as an anxiety on the part of LBJ that the MFDP was somehow linked with a Bobby Kennedy plot to wrest the nomination away from him—is a matter of debate. Johnson's trusted lieutenants, Bill Moyers and Walter Jenkins, served as liaisons to the FBI; unbeknownst to NBC reporters and producers, the FBI's infiltration of the convention was facilitated by NBC press passes secretly provided by network management. In a letter to "Bishop"

Restless, the correspondents looked around outside Convention Hall and came up with another story: the deterioration of Atlantic City. Shocked by the conditions they saw, delegates spoke of dirty, sweltering rooms and terrible service at hotels, of dreadful food and jacked-up prices at restaurants. Most of the town had been built at least forty years earlier and had no air conditioning; by the 1960s, summer visitors found this unacceptable. Modernization and, in some cases, simple maintenance had been skipped because hotel money had gone to more profitable new resort areas elsewhere; the town seemed shabby and ridiculous next to the promise of immense wealth associated with its street names through millions of games of Monopoly.

Before the entire nation, what was to have been Atlantic City's finest hour turned into a catastrophe. As the negative comments about the historic resort appeared in newspapers across the nation and on network television, the chamber of commerce protested vigorously but to little avail. Its members had fondly imagined the cameras would glamorize Atlantic City; they never dreamed that a medium strong enough to elect a president could damage a city without thinking twice about it. In a week, Jessica Savitch's future home, television, pushed her current hometown over the edge, onto a downhill slide that would continue for a dozen more years, until casino gambling was finally approved in 1976 and the tattered Queen of the Coast could begin slowly to scramble to her feet.

For Walter Cronkite, too, the convention represented a humiliating failure. As anchor of the *CBS Evening News* since 1962, he had failed to make a dent in Huntley and Brinkley's lead. At the 1964 Republican convention, held in July at San Francisco's Cow Palace, CBS had trailed miserably in the ratings. Faced with a rout, Paley yanked Cronkite, replacing him in Atlantic City with Bob Trout, a veteran correspondent, and a promising newcomer named Roger Mudd. Once again, NBC grabbed more than 80 percent of the audience.

Such an achievement would leave most NBC executives chortling with delight, but not Bob Kintner. During NBC's

(the nickname given to Moyers because of his ministerial background), dated September 10, 1964, FBI special agent Cartha "Deke" DeLoach acknowledged a letter of thanks from Moyers for a job well done and wrote, "I'm certainly glad we were able to come through with vital tidbits."

triumph in San Francisco, a disconsolate Kintner called the control room at the convention. Because Bill McAndrew, president of NBC News, and Julian Goodman, vice president, were in the men's room, Kintner reached the news division's number three, Shad Northshield, who answered the phone newsroom-style with his name, "Northshield." Speaking in his usual gruff, rasping voice, Kintner said, "NBC has eighty-six percent of the audience." Northshield started to reply, and Kintner, as was his custom, hung up before Northshield had finished. A moment later, the phone rang again. As soon as Northshield identified himself, Kintner said, "I don't think you were excited enough. Did you understand what I said?" When Northshield started to reply, Kintner again slammed down the phone. Within a minute, Kintner called once more and said, "I still don't think you understand." By now, Northshield was thoroughly exasperated. "Look, we're very busy here," he said. "What do you want, one hundred percent?" Kintner replied, "At least you've got that part right"—and then banged the receiver down.

For Jessica Savitch, the convention was the most thrilling experience of her life. It had been a year of triumphant moments: playing Titania in the senior production of *A Midsummer Night's Dream,* writing a sarcastic class skit with Jeff and then seeing it produced, getting pinned to Barry. But none of these events measured up to being able to see in person the people who had been in her living room every night for years. During convention week, Jessica accompanied WOND owner Howard Green to the parties Perle Mesta threw for Democratic party patrons; at Mesta's rented mansion, Jessica stood near Hubert Humphrey, Eugene McCarthy, and Pat Brown, as well as her famous hostess, whom Green later described as "embalmed—I couldn't figure out if she was elderly or pickled or maybe both." Hanging from a chain around Jessica's neck that week was the laminated ABC press pass she had received from Green. It was chartreuse, the lowest level, and provided access only to the arena, not the floor; to Jessica, though, it was a magic ticket that proved that she belonged to a special, privileged group. Green, Jeff Greenhawt, and Jessica came to Convention Hall early the first morning. Before anyone noticed that Jessica had taken off on her own, they heard her voice shouting down from the ABC control booth, which was some thirty feet above the floor. WOND, the local ABC affiliate, had lent the network some equipment, and WOND staffers had been invited to come and view the proceedings from the network's perch in the balcony. Grinning, Jessica stood in the place where ABC anchors Edward P. Morgan and Howard K. Smith would broadcast their coverage.

Looking down at the glaring lights and the bulky black cameras and the spaghetti mass of cables on the convention floor, Jessica saw not only that what was really going on was television, but that television was far more interesting than the ostensible business of the convention. She spent as much time as she could over the next week in the press area, walking in and out of the different control booths, overhearing hundreds of conversations, and watching everything that happened with the intensity of an adolescent in love, which is exactly what she was. She began to put together names and faces familiar to her from television with the people around her, and she noted what they did. One of the names she heard again and again that week was Nancy Dickerson, who was the only woman correspondent in the entire place. Jessica kept hoping for a glimpse of her.

Nancy Dickerson, née Hanschman, grew up in Wauwatosa, Wisconsin, and shed her Middle American background as quickly as she could. After two years at Clark College, a Catholic school in Dubuque, where she majored in piano, Dickerson switched to the University of Wisconsin, majored in foreign languages, and went to Europe until her money ran out. In 1951, she was back in the States and wangled a secretarial job with the Senate Foreign Relations Committee; from there, she quickly moved into speechwriting and dating members of Congress. Dickerson bagged three: Henry ("Scoop") Jackson of Washington, Kenneth Keating of New York, and John F. Kennedy of Massachusetts. (Jackson and Kennedy were then unmarried, and Keating was separated from his wife.) She also became friendly with Senator Lyndon B. Johnson of Texas— so friendly that she spent years denying that the two were having an affair.

With a senator or a representative on her arm, it was easy to be seen in the right places. Dickerson was smart and funny and attractive and discreet, and Washington people just naturally began to invite the woman with the distinctive heart-shaped face to parties when an extra woman was needed. Looking around, it was easy to grasp that congressional staff members were close to the bottom of a very large heap, no matter how pretty they were. And it was easy, too, to realize that the coming thing was the media, and television in particular. One of the first things she had seen in Washington was General MacArthur's farewell speech after being fired for insubordination by President Truman. "Old soldiers never die, they just fade away," the old general had said, and it had occurred to Dickerson that MacArthur was taking his case directly to the people through televison and that television, not the president or Congress or even MacArthur, would determine what the people thought of this in the end.

She found a job on CBS Radio producing two shows, *The Leading Question* and *Capitol Cloakroom,* which were imitations of NBC-TV's *Meet the Press.* "Producing," in Dickerson's case, meant convincing famous politicians that appearing on these obscure radio programs would be useful to them. She used her Washington connections and was successful. In 1954, CBS-TV created *Face the Nation* to compete with *Meet the Press,* and Dickerson became an associate producer. She worked hard and delivered her guests; all the while, she plotted a way to get on the other side of the camera.

Nobody ever asked Dickerson if she wanted to go on the air, for the idea was too crazy. CBS Washington bureau chief Ted Koop had once written an entire musical comedy premised on the sidesplitting notion that the network had inexplicably hired a bunch of girls to deliver the news. Cold-bloodedly, Dickerson decided to force the network's hand by bringing in stories nobody else could. She approached Sam Rayburn, the legendary Speaker of the House and Lyndon Johnson's political mentor, and asked—begged, rather—for an interview. Rayburn hated TV, which he thought, correctly, made him look even balder than he was; the old politician understood that the cameras emphasized style over substance. But he had a weakness for attractive, perky young women, and after she promised that he could keep his hat on, he granted her his first-ever televised interview. The next day, *CBS Evening News* producer Don Hewitt asked Dickerson if she wanted a correspondent's job. Senate majority leader Lyndon Johnson promptly threw her a celebratory party in his office.

The situation Dickerson confronted was definitely an improvement over what Pauline Frederick had faced a dozen years earlier. As recounted by broadcast veteran Marlene Sanders, Frederick, a former print reporter in Washington, first appeared on television at the 1948 conventions as a part-time correspondent to interview candidates' wives and such few female politicians as existed at the time. The only advice Frederick could obtain was not to wear black, red, or white. For makeup instruction, she had to turn to Elizabeth Arden—and a good thing she did, for when she arrived in Philadelphia she found she was expected to apply it not only to herself but to her subjects, including Helen Gahagan Douglas and Esther Stassen, wife of perennial presidential candidate Harold Stassen. In the 1950s, Frederick went to NBC, where she was assigned the backwater UN beat and thereupon became the first full-time woman correspondent on network news.

By contrast, Dickerson's assignment, the White House, was a plum. She bypassed the whole makeup question by applying her own at home (male correspondents continued to have their makeup applied at the office). A small, slim woman with beautiful skin and slender hands, she may not have been the world's greatest investigative reporter but she always got the pol in front of the camera. Although she showed up for work in a limousine and wore mink to the office, habits hardly calculated to endear her to her colleagues, she kept rising. In 1963 she went to NBC, where she was the first woman correspondent to have her own news show, *Nancy Dickerson with the News,* on for five minutes every afternoon; a year later, at the 1964 conventions, she was the first to report from the floor and to serve as a sort of co-subanchor, with correspondent Ray Scherer. She was also the first to be promoted as an attractive woman. "Pauline was handsome, but not a showstopper," NBC writer Pat Trese said. "She came off as a reporter. Nancy came off like a *dame.*"

As part of her climb up the social ladder, Dickerson married a rich widower named C. Wyatt Dickerson in 1962; when she had her two children, she worked almost to the beginning of labor. Many years later, Dickerson would complain that, unlike *Today* co-host Jane Pauley, who received much attention during her pregnancies in the 1980s, Dickerson was simply ignored when she produced children back in the 1960s. The cameras did not actually photograph her growing belly, of course; instead, Dickerson was photographed in what she jokingly called a "two-shot," with the image running from the top of the head to chest level. "All you could see," she said, "were two breasts."

By the time of the convention, Dickerson was in the catbird seat. Her friend LBJ was president, and she had direct access to the Oval Office, access that was to give her the biggest scoop of the entire week. The evening before Johnson's nomination, as most of the press sat in Convention Hall, Dickerson was at Bader Field, the private airstrip located next to the high school. She had seen Muriel Humphrey meeting with Lady Bird Johnson and had realized that the vice-presidential choice would be Hubert Humphrey. When she was tipped off that the president was coming early, she hied herself to the airport. There on the tarmac when the helicopter landed, Dickerson walked directly up to the president, a microphone in one hand and a cable as thick as a garden hose in the other. The Secret Service lights shone on her pink linen suit, her pearls, and her perfectly coiffed bouffant hairdo. Johnson walked directly over to Dickerson, and said, "Hello, Nancy, I've been watching you all day and you're doing a wonderful job." He then proceeded to confirm her speculation about Hubert Humphrey. It was a resounding triumph for NBC; back at the convention, Bob Kintner and Bob Sarnoff drank a toast and even did a little victory shuffle.

Jessica Savitch, who was watching the proceedings on television with Jeff Greenhawt, could hardly believe her eyes. Right in front of her a glamorous, sophisticated woman was getting an exclusive from the president of the United States. Every time Nancy Dickerson asked a question, millions of Americans heard her speak. The town was crawling with newsmen, but this woman was the one who finally broke the vice-presidential story. More than anything in the world, Jessica wanted to be like her, to be that one link between millions of viewers and the things that were happening all around them. "That's why I want to be a correspondent," she told Greenhawt, her eyes shining. "They all know your first name."

Back at NBC, the hard-core journalists were less than thrilled with Jessica Savitch's putative role model. People like Reuven

Frank thought that nothing good could come from their correspondent's chummy relationship with the White House. It is an unfortunate truth that reporters who are friendly with their subjects tend to treat them with excessive kindness, and Dickerson, who liked Lady Bird Johnson, soon validated Frank's fears in a pretaped convention interview with the first lady. In an embarrassing display of sentiment, Dickerson, Lady Bird, and the two Johnson daughters pored over the first family's photo albums for endless minutes. At the time, Pat Trese was in the control room with Reuven Frank; George Murray, Frank's top assistant; and a senior producer named Bill Hill. Taking his cue from satirist Dorothy Parker, who occasionally referred to herself in her *New Yorker* columns as "Constant Reader," Hill sometimes spoke of himself as "Constant Viewer."

At a certain point during the convention, Trese recalled, Murray asked when NBC was planning to run the Johnson family album tape. "Reuven said, 'Oh, come on, give me a break,' " Trese said. "But George said, 'The president of the United States wants to know.' So the tape went on. It was awful—early Barbara Walters stuff. After a few minutes, Bill Hill said, 'If this is news, Constant Viewer is going to throw up.' "

4

*I*thaca

Just a few weeks after the last of the tickertape was swept up from Atlantic Avenue, Jessica Savitch was enrolled in the communications department of Ithaca College, in Ithaca, New York, an old college town of 30,000 on the southern edge of Lake Cayuga. Founded in the 1890s as a music conservatory, Ithaca College languished for many years in the shadow of what its students referred to as "the other school," Cornell University. Dwarfed by its large and prestigious neighbor, IC, as it was known locally, occupied several old buildings in downtown Ithaca and barely managed to scrape together enough students to keep the doors open. By 1937, everything down to the knives, forks, and spoons in the cafeteria had been mortgaged, and the college was saved from going under only by an agreement among town merchants to forgive years of unpaid bills.

Although IC continued to offer a musical education and counted bandleaders Hugo Winterhalter and Les Brown among its most renowned graduates, it also began adding academic departments in areas that might have more drawing power. In this way the curriculum came to be a hodgepodge of modish specialties such as physical education, physical therapy, and "physics for engineers." The School of Fine Arts, added in 1943, would later graduate Gavin MacLeod, the reassuring captain of television's *Love Boat*. Back in 1931, a look around the educational marketplace had suggested that radio might also be a good bet; forthwith, the faculty had hired Dr. Sydney Landon, well-known performer on the Chautauqua circuit, and, before his move to IC, a professor in the Williams School of Expression and Dramatic Art. Landon's course would include program making, announcing, timing, and the use of the microphone, all for a laboratory fee of only $10 a semester. In 1946, several courses on television, possibly the first in the nation, were established, and in the 1950s seminars featured such luminaries as the director of the TV series *Superman*. By then, IC had a full-fledged department of radio and television; its chairman, Robert Earle, later gained considerable fame as the first host of *College Bowl*, and its students were broadcasting their own AM and FM radio programs as well as their own cable television shows.

The town of Ithaca was too small to support its own television station, and its geographic location, in a shallow depression, prevented viewers from receiving signals from stations in the surrounding larger cities of Syracuse, Binghamton, and Utica without large commercial antennae set up on high ground. Thus, long before "cable" became a household word, the Ceracche Cable Corporation had wired the town, and Ithaca College students were allowed to fill empty airtime with their own performances, documentaries, talk shows, and learned lectures.

By the mid-1960s, what had become the communications department had a growing reputation as one of the few places in the country where students could master the esoterica of the electronic media. They learned how to produce, direct, record, film, mix, edit, and engineer radio and television broadcasts, as well as how to anchor newscasts, run control boards, provide election night coverage, and be disc jockeys. What they didn't learn was journalism, or at least not journalism as it had been traditionally defined. Without really intending it, IC made choices in its approach that would condition its graduates' views of radio and, especially, television. When those graduates, and the graduates of other, similar schools of communication that would develop over the next two decades, went on, as they often did, to positions of importance in the media, the IC-style curriculum had a powerful, albeit indirect, influence on television itself—an influence that the Murrowites would decry for decades.

A number of the instructors at IC had been broadcasters themselves, and the department thus derived much of its program directly from the broadcast media. From the content of the curriculum, it is apparent that television and radio students at IC were being trained to work in a large commercial industry that required new technical expertise and communications skills. But unlike, say, the Graduate School of Journalism at Columbia University, which provided graduate, professional training after a broad liberal arts education at the undergraduate level, Ithaca College was an undergraduate trade school, with a program that acknowledged the liberal arts but emphasized technical proficiency. Aspiring correspondents did learn a bit about journalistic history, but the only course in actual reporting—that is, digging out facts, following up leads, putting together a complicated story, following out its implications, and interpreting its significance—was offered in the English department. Similarly, the school newspaper was a completely separate enterprise from the communications department, which regarded its mandate to be not so much the content of a news broadcast as the technical means required to put it together and the style with which it was presented.

When the graduates obtained jobs in broadcast news, they established, willy-nilly, a new standard of journalism with an accent on proficiency and style that embodied the lessons they had learned at IC. They judged newscasts not by the stories that were written but by the way they sounded and the way they looked. "Other schools developed journalists first, and then they made the transfer into broadcasting," explained Marvin Diskin, a former IC professor who went on to teach communications at Purdue University. "This seemed the right sequence to me—not what happened at Ithaca, where they developed technicians, and then maybe let them figure out how to be journalists."

To Jessica Savitch, who wanted solely to be on the air, the communications department at Ithaca College seemed made to order, but her mother had reservations. When they visited for an interview, Florence was impressed by the new campus going up on South Hill, on the edge of town, and the panoramic view of Lake Cayuga. The surrounding countryside, with the clean, sparkling Finger Lakes and rolling hills, was spectacularly beautiful, just the sort of place any parents would want to send their child. Nonetheless, Ithaca was a good eight hours away from Margate by car, and the whole idea of communications seemed to Florence a career choice that was impractical in the extreme. As her own experience had shown, even the most secure life can suddenly be turned upside down, leaving a woman with no one to depend on but herself. Florence was grateful for her own R.N., and thought her pretty, flighty daughter should get a degree of equally demonstrable utility. Indeed, Jessica later wrote, her mother was determined that she earn a teaching certificate so that she would always have something to fall back on. Jessica's grandparents, too, found her college plans unacceptable, but for different reasons. They thought Jessica should go to a school more in the center of the Ivy League, where husband material would be more promising.

After arguments, tears, and long silences, the matter was resolved. Stubborn Jessica was allowed to go to Ithaca, but she would have to pay most of the way herself. Putting together two small scholarships for veterans' children, a merit award, and the Social Security check she received each month as the minor child of a deceased parent, she was still short of the sum she needed. Jessica told friends she refused to ask her well-to-do grandparents for the cash because doing so would put her in a supplicatory position she abhorred. She said she was determined to do it on her own, and to be beholden to nobody. After her high school graduation, she found a summer job at the switchboard of the Coronet Motel on Kentucky Avenue and hoped she could earn enough to go to school. She also continued to work at WOND.

As the moment of her departure came closer, Jessica had a bout of uncertainty about her choice. The star of the senior class play and a big wheel at the top local radio station, she was well known among the young people in town; few would say "Jessica Who?" now. She had made a warm and comfortable spot for herself, and the prospect of heading off once again into the unknown was frightening. As the summer drew to a close, she told Barry Swartz she was scared stiff. "I told her the last thing she needed was to worry, and that guys in Ithaca would fall all over her," Swartz said later. "Unfortunately for our relationship, I was right."

The first thing Savitch discovered when she arrived at college was that she would be spending most of her time not in the spanking new structures on South Hill but on the old IC campus, several shabby structures on Buffalo Street in downtown Ithaca. The bulk of her classes were in dilapidated studios and classrooms in the old wooden building assigned to the communications department. She would be living next door, over the cafeteria, in a makeshift girls' dorm. She hated it.

The second was that, for the first time in her life, being young and female could be a distinct liability. Of the seventy students in her department, only a handful were female. Although the students had a surprising degree of control over the actual workings of the department, the male majority thought that the idea of a woman in a prominent on-air position was out of the question. WICB, the college's AM station, had just switched to a rock 'n' roll format, which meant that for the first time students could be actual DJs, grooving on air for hours on end. It was a wonderful opportunity for everyone in the department who didn't happen to be female.

When Savitch appeared at WICB's AM studio to arrange for a DJ shift, she was told by John von Soosten, the upperclassman who was handling the schedule, that most of the spots were earmarked for sophomores, juniors, and seniors. She would have to audition for whatever places were left over. Fresh from her triumphs in Atlantic City, Savitch was furious. Proceeding about as diplomatically as a steamroller, she declared that she had a third-class broadcast restricted radiotelephone operator's license and had worked commercially as a DJ for three years. Von Soosten's answer remained the same: Lots of students had done some on-air work, and she would have to read samples of news and commercial copy and ad-lib for one minute. Gritting her teeth, Savitch did so. She did not make the cut.

"She was above average but not outstanding," von Soosten, now head of programming for the Katz Television Group, an advertising brokerage in New York City, recalled years afterward. "The problem was that she was desperate to be a DJ and just assumed she would get a shift." To add to Savitch's dismay, a freshman named Bill Groody *did* get a DJ shift, even

86

though his credentials were no better than hers. Von Soosten told her that she could read the news or do public-service announcements.

Jessica Savitch wasn't interested in the news. She wanted the glamour spot, a DJ shift on the AM station, and she complained to Marvin Diskin, the professor who acted as station adviser. Diskin had little sympathy for the kids whose only concern seemed to be getting on air. He thought Savitch's distress in particular was unrealistic. Radio stations didn't hire women DJs, he told her. "Make sure you know shorthand and typing," he said. "That way you'll be able to get your foot in the door." (Years later, Savitch wrote that the take-home message was clear: "There's no place for broads in broadcasting.")

The college had an FM station, which was smaller and less prestigious, but Savitch was turned down there, too. She confronted Bob Eolin, John von Soosten's counterpart at that station. Eolin was stunned to be buttonholed in the hallway by this angry new student. Claiming that anyone who paid tuition should be given a shot on the air, Savitch refused to listen to Eolin's explanation that all the spots were filled. "She had a habit of sucking the sides of her face in when she got mad," he said years later. "It accented her dimples. It was an odd affectation, a sign of frustration and anger."

Disgruntled, Savitch accepted a rip-'n'-read news shift under the *nom de radio* of Jill Jackson, and was eventually given a weekly shift on FM playing classical music. She also worked on *Town Talk,* a daily AM talk show set aside for women in the communications department when other female students complained that they were excluded from the airwaves. It was on from seven to seven-thirty every evening, smack in the middle of dinner, and featured such scintillating subjects as holiday traditions. The women also tried reading poetry, including, on occasion, their own. Embarrassed by the show, Savitch did not give it her all, and managed to antagonize her co-hosts considerably in the process. They thought her aloof, cold, and a social climber, and, to a certain extent, they were right. "She came to college with the notion that she was above it all because she'd worked professionally," said one classmate, Judy Girard, now program director for WTBJ-TV in Miami, Florida. "We immediately—*immediately*—disliked her." A principal reason, Girard said, was that Savitch had no tolerance for people who weren't as serious about their work as she was. "She was so intense, she made us feel like we were dipshits if we were off having a beer on Saturday night."

That fall, Savitch plotted to get into the mainstream by wrangling interviews with musicians who played at Cornell, such as Bob Dylan and Peter, Paul, and Mary. The hope was that the interviews would be so astounding—*Peter, Paul, and Mary on WICB!*—that the station would somehow be forced into letting her be a DJ. She asked Judy Girard, one of the few classmates who ended up being friends with Savitch, to be her producer, and the two showed up at Cornell's Barton Hall several hours before each concert. When they caught all three members of Peter, Paul, and Mary, Girard was sufficiently thrilled that she chronicled the event in a paper.

Paul was a very congenial and brilliant young man. (About 30) His candid remarks were unbelievable. He said he would get Peter for us shortly. . . . Both young men congratulated Jessica on a well-organized job. They seemed highly impressed. A man came over and told us how polite we were to all concerned. (being here since 5:00). . . .

It is 8:45 and the M.C. is telling a joke to kill time. Peter Paul and Mary's road manager just asked us if we knew where they went. This could lead to trouble—like a riot . . . [We] have decided if there is a riot we're definitely going to get it on tape. . . . It is difficult to believe that represented here tonight is the top intelligence of the up coming generation. (Some of the murmurs were—"There goes Cornell's reputation down another three notches." and "By the time I graduate Cornell won't be an Ivy League School anymore") . . .

We're still in a daze about the ease and manner of both Peter and Paul. It gave us the feeling as if we were doing them a big favor interviewing them for College Radio-WICB. Incidentally, they very rarely hold any type of interview. This [getting the interview] may possibly be accounted for because we gave that "innocence of youth" appearance. The stereotype of the college kid trying to make good. Plus no attempt was made to pressure them. We were here to take it as it came and the world just bowed to our feet. I don't know why—but it certainly is worth the $3,000 tuition.

Savitch and her roommate, Dee Adamczyk, detested each other in orthodox *Odd Couple* style. In addition to sharing a tiny dorm room, they worked together on *Town Talk,* a forced association that did nothing to improve the relationship. Adamczyk was, by Ithaca College standards, a neatnik. She had a locked metal box in her desk filled with quarters for the laundromat and refused to open her books all the way because she didn't want to break the bindings. Savitch, on the other hand, slept through fire drills. She took up one and a half of the two closets and scattered her papers everywhere. She borrowed her dormmates' clothes and returned them uncleaned. It didn't help matters that guys were, as Swartz had predicted, falling all over her.

On election night in November 1964, Savitch served on the crew of the IC television station, which was covering the local contests. When she showed up in tan chinos and a rumpled man's shirt, she was promptly ejected. Tony Busch, the dark-haired, preppy-looking senior in charge of the broadcast, loftily informed her that such vile garments would not be permitted in the studio. Savitch came back in better clothing and was given the job of writing the returns on a blackboard while anchor Don Alhart, a junior, chewed on an empty pipe for a Cronkite-like effect and read the numbers. Her first experience before the TV camera was so thrilling that Savitch hardly minded when the blackboard fell down in the middle of the show and she was forced to set it up again while the cameras rolled.

Savitch and Busch began to work together, and he became the first in a long line of men to realize that Jessica Savitch had a remarkable affinity for the camera. "Most people were scared of it or somehow withdrew from it," Busch said, "but she could somehow play it where she could reach out and grab you." Although Savitch needed a lot of polish, he said, she already knew what to concentrate on: convincing those watching that what she was saying was both truthful and something they wanted to hear. On the air, she gave an immediate impression of her physical presence; she seemed to be in the viewer's own living room, a woman who was cool and collected but not cold, competent but not overbearing, intense but not alarming, powerful but not threatening. She had a marvelous smile, and the smile suggested that something surprising might happen soon, and that the people watching her would like whatever that surprise turned out to be. It was, Busch thought, a remarkable talent, and finally as inexplicable as a genius for writing operas or designing buildings or racing stock cars. The camera just liked her, and she liked it, and that was all there was to it.

Busch asked Savitch out soon after they met. Although she was still pinned to Barry Swartz, she and Busch soon were not only working together but sleeping together. (Swartz, whose college dorm room was plastered with photos of Savitch, was furious when she lost interest in him; after many telephone fights, they broke up in the spring. He later became a successful cosmetic surgeon in San Antonio.) Busch discovered that Savitch's favorite song was "I Am a Rock," a Paul Simon song about a man who builds a protective wall around himself to avoid pain. And indeed Savitch avoided overly personal relationships. When something did get through, she was thrown into a tizzy. The pain she was trying to keep at bay, Busch thought, was the death of her father, whose portrait she kept in her dorm room. When he first addressed her as "Beth," she got a stark look of horror on her face and told him that her father had called her that. When she told him about the funeral and sitting shiva, Busch realized that the experience had left a deep emotional scar.

Tony Busch graduated in the spring, and Savitch hung around the campus for the ceremony. She returned to Margate a considerably different young woman than she had been only nine months earlier. To begin with, her brown hair had become platinum blond. In addition, by summer she and Busch were pinned; once again, Savitch's sweater was adorned with Greek symbols, but this time they came from a Roman Catholic. Although Savitch still went to temple on the anniversary of her father's death, she often went to mass with Busch and she wore the St. Christopher's medal that Busch had carried since being in a bad car accident at the age of sixteen. When he came to Margate that summer, they went swimming at the swanky Deauville Hotel, where Ben and Lil Savitch were staying for a family visit. At one point, Busch recalled later, he was stretched out in a deck chair between the Savitch grandparents while Jessica—lithe, blond, the St. Christopher medal glinting between her breasts—stood on the diving board. A rotund Jewish lady leaned over to Lil and said, "What a nice grandson you have, but the *shiksa* he's going out with, oy, that's terrible!" Ben and Lil were not amused; thereafter, Busch felt a certain chilliness whenever he was in their vicinity.

Busch went home to Rochester, an old manufacturing center on the edge of Lake Ontario, and found a job in a video production group and, later, an advertising agency. (He now is a vice-president of a Rochester television production company.) He still went out with Savitch, driving the two hours to Ithaca to pick her up for a date. They became engaged in the autumn of her sophomore year, and Savitch sported a diamond that seemed the largest and most amazing thing her dormmates had ever seen. Busch took her around Rochester, introducing her to people he met in the course of his own work. She seized every opportunity he gave her, made a few more for herself, and was furiously, alarmingly busy. For the first time, her capacity for endless work was unleashed. Over the course of that year, she did on- and off-camera work in commercials for several businesses in Rochester as well as for such larger firms as Taylor Wine, Marine Midland Bank, Star Markets, and Sears (dressed as one of Santa's helpers); did filmstrips for Kodak, Bausch & Lomb, and R. T. French; interviewed professional tennis and golf players before matches; introduced dance contestants on a local rock 'n' roll dance show called by the deliberately illiterate title of *The Joe Deane Sok-Hop;* and became the official Dodge Girl for a Rochester Dodge dealership called Culver City.

For the last, she had been brought by Busch to a meeting with his boss, Bill Schwing, who was in the middle of filming a bowling show. Schwing, a tall, handsome man with bright blue eyes, took one look at Savitch and thought—Dodge Girl! —of the Culver City account, which he had been trying to land. Because the national Dodge campaign featured cute, white-hatted cowgirls, Schwing bought Savitch a white Stetson hat, and told her to wear white boots to the meeting he had arranged with the owner of the Dodge dealership. As soon as the owner saw her, Schwing had the account. Unlike the national Dodge Girl, who did impossible feats like falling out of a helicopter into a moving vehicle, Savitch, the local counterpart, was merely to be seen jumping from a horse into the driver's seat. At the shoot, Savitch clambered inexpertly on the horse. Asked if she knew how to ride, she said eagerly, "Yes, yes." The horse promptly ran away with her, causing panic on the set.

Schwing produced the commercials for a local ad agency that was owned by Ann Rogers. Well known around town, Rogers had spent years hosting Rochester-area talk shows before concluding that as a woman she would never be able to rise further in broadcasting without going elsewhere, a move she was unwilling to force on her family. In 1949, she began the first regularly scheduled TV show in Rochester; thirteen years later, when she was still doing "women's programs" about pediatricians and kids, Rogers quit to set up her own advertising agency. A spunky, hard-driving blond with a deep cigarette-smoker's voice, she was stunned by Savitch's rapport with the camera. "I looked at her and said to myself, 'Your time on camera is over,' " Rogers said later. " 'You're too old—here's the next ingenue.' " Although she thought the camera improved Savitch's looks, she was still surprised to note that the engineers editing commercials featuring Savitch often didn't recognize the star even when she was standing right next to them. Rogers, who liked the younger woman's grit and determination, advised Savitch to pare down the makeup and did her best to answer Savitch's constant questions about the broadcast industry.

As Rogers's employee, Savitch was reliable, even excessively so: Day or night, rain or snow, she made the two-hour drive from Ithaca to Rochester. Her classmates, who thought Savitch a spoiled brat, would have been astonished by the polite, quiet, gung-ho Savitch in Rochester, a diligent young woman who would do anything she was asked and never appeared to think about herself. Once she took the bus to Rochester and was followed through the terminal by a lunatic. Savitch ran through the streets until the crazy man gave up his chase. When Rogers asked why she hadn't simply called and asked to be picked up, Savitch said she hadn't wanted to bother anybody. Another time she hurt her leg, and literally crawled out of her car to get to the studio. Rogers tried to get her to relax, but Savitch refused to listen. She worked in a daze of exhaustion, balancing college, modeling assignments, and the onerous four-hour round-trip between school and work. Sometimes the stress load was so high that to Rogers's dismay Savitch would walk into the studio with bags under her eyes and a nervous rash spreading across her face. But she always relaxed before the camera, and on the screen, with makeup covering signs of wear and tear, she always looked good.

Savitch's relationship with Tony Busch suffered as well. They fought in person and they fought on the telephone, shouting into the receiver "I won't talk to you," hanging up, and then immediately calling back and starting the whole furious cycle all over again. Because the dorm phone was in the corridor, Savitch's end of the conversation was overheard by everyone on the floor; Debi Fortune Farnham, who lived down the hall, later recalled seeing Savitch become so agitated during one conversation that she scraped her knuckles across the rough wall until they bled. According to Busch, Savitch's intensity and drive made it impossible for her to have "a normal guy–girl-type relationship." Only someone extraordinary could put up with Savitch, he said. "I certainly wasn't good enough. That was it, the career was utmost."

The career was to become even more utmost at the end of Savitch's sophomore year, when she earned a DJ shift on WBBF, the leading AM station in Rochester. Jack Palvino, the program director, had been introduced to Savitch by Bill Schwing, former sports and sales director at the station. This time, being a woman—an unknown species on AM radio, as Marvin Diskin had correctly pointed out—was an unexpected asset. The competition for the rock audience in Rochester had started to heat up, and when Palvino heard that Savitch had been a high school DJ, it occurred to him that he might be able to stun his adversaries by offering listeners something novel, something amazing, something positively unheard-of. He asked Savitch for an audition tape and played it for Bob Kieve, the general manager. "Having a woman hadn't come up before because none had presented themselves," Kieve said later. "But suddenly there was a woman who sounded very good on air, and the fact she was a woman only added to her presence."

Like WOND back in New Jersey, WBBF was a Top 40 station, meaning that disc jockeys played the same forty tunes over and over and over. According to industry legend, Top 40

93

was invented in the early 1950s, when television had started to overtake radio by doing exactly what radio had always done—provide a wide variety of programming—in a visual medium. In the legend, a young man from Nebraska named Tod Storz stopped in a San Francisco bar. As he quietly sipped his beer, Storz noticed that people his age were putting their coins in the jukebox and playing the same hits from singers like Patti Paige and Tony Bennett again and again. Storz, who had been a ham radio operator as a kid and now worked in the radio industry, thought that perhaps such repetition would appeal to radio listeners as well.

Storz and his father, a brewer and real estate magnate in Omaha, then purchased a daytime radio station, KOWH (now KCRO). The young Storz discarded the standard programs and instructed his staff to play nothing but the most popular songs in town, as determined through record sales. Soon his station had taken Omaha by storm, and a new programming format was born. Old-style DJs like Cleveland's Bill Randle, the man who discovered Elvis Presley, were used to selecting their own records and offering a healthy dose of their own opinions on the side. They had to make way for the new-style radio jock who talked rapidly in a stylized patter and aired records strictly according to the play list handed out by the music directors and program directors that now began to appear on the scene. Listeners no longer had to wait for a particular show to hear their favorite songs, for now there was a whole station on which they could hear those tunes all day long.

It was exactly what America's teenagers had been waiting for, but not everybody was quite so enthusiastic. "It took the fun out of radio," said Joe Deane, who became a disc jockey at WBBF in 1955. "It took away the personality aspect—after all, how many different ways could you introduce the same record?" In the past, he said, people tuned in to a particular person, but with Top 40 they were just listening to a station. What station managers heard on Top 40, however, was the jingle of a cash register, and over the next several years hundreds of stations switched to the new format. In 1958, WBBF brought Top 40 to Rochester, and won half the audience in its very first rating period.

Deane changed with the station, but he didn't care much for his new role. Jessica Savitch, on the other hand, was part of a new generation of young disc jockeys who had grown up on Top 40. They knew the songs, they knew the jokes, they knew the pacing, and they could churn it out with ease, hour after hour. The new format may have sacrificed some of the qualities that had made radio special, but for Savitch there was a net gain: When deep-voiced personalities like Randle reigned supreme, she would never have been hired. It had taken Top 40, with all its brassy vulgarity, to crack things open sufficiently that a woman's voice was no longer anathema on radio; a few years later, it was to take a roughly parallel revolution in television news to make that all-male preserve accessible to women —and once again, one of the first in line would be Jessica Savitch.

Fashioning a nickname from its call letters, WBBF had long touted itself as the "Busy Bee" station, incorporating two buzzing insects in its logo, referring to its DJs as "Busy Bees," and using a jazzed-up rendition of Rimsky-Korsakov's "Flight of the Bumblebee" as a station theme song. Whenever there was a record hop or a gathering at a shopping mall, WBBF sent the "Beemobile," a customized trailer with a glass-enclosed portable studio for remote broadcasts. On the side of the trailer were the omnipresent oversized bees, and on the roof was a large brownish-yellow object intended to represent a beehive; to Savitch's eyes, it resembled a giant cow flop. (Such corny promotion was not unusual at the time; one IC classmate, Dave Stewart, who worked at a Binghamton station, had to dress up as a hippo.)

In 1966, when she was hired, WBBF was still the leading station in metropolitan Rochester, ruling a radio domain of some 700,000 people, more than seven times the population of Atlantic City. One of the station's special features was that every Saturday and Sunday were "Million Dollar Weekends," so called because every other record played on those two days had already sold one million copies. Savitch, who began to attract an audience as soon as she started her Saturday afternoon slot, called herself the "Honeybee." She would buzz into the station at three o'clock, put the colossal hit "Wild Thing," by the Troggs, on the turntable, and wait breathlessly for the end—or, at any rate, almost the end—of the song. As the guitar chords diminished, she leaned into the mike and motor-mouthed, "That's-appearing-from-the-charts-in

. . . *1966!* . . . That's called 'Wild Thing,' and we've got *morrre animals* on this show! We've got chickens and turkeys and seals —rrrright? Ferdinand J. has got the zoo scene, I'm calling this a *barnyard* scene—" At which point she flipped a switch to cut in a pre-recorded tape that screamed *oohhhh NNNOOO!* and then gave station identification for (hold your breath!) double-yew bee-bee eff, channel NINETY-FIVE. She even had her own logo, a quick "Jessica!" from a honeyed chorus of guys and gals. And so it went through the afternoon, a stream of Fifth Dimension and Beatles and Jefferson Airplane and commercials for Johnny Antonelli night at the local ballpark, Jack Nicklaus golfballs (three for one-ninety-five!), and Mountain Dew, here's your chance to win a free camping trailer, and don't forget the . . . Welcome Wagon. At 7:00, she thanked her engineer and signed off with the intro to "W! B! B! F! Rochester! New York! Earrrrr-witness NEWS!!!!" Savitch loved it.

As the show became more popular, Savitch was sent out in the Beemobile to sign record albums, give out fuzzy yellow bees, and have her picture taken in the company of local merchants. The female DJ attracted crowds, and WBBF capitalized on her nascent celebrity by decorating the city with billboards featuring her face blown up to the size of a Mack truck. She had it made, although her frenetic pace gave little indication that she realized it. At nineteen, her combined income from modeling, commercials, and radio work was already more than many of her teachers at IC. Back in Margate, her mother was astonished and even awed by her daughter's success, and Savitch experienced the exquisite pleasure of excelling utterly in a course on which others had predicted only failure. She also experienced the downside of celebrity: She was sometimes mobbed during her public appearances, and once needed the police to chase local toughs away from the Beemobile.

Savitch was now in the bizarre position of being a famous DJ on the biggest station in the biggest city in the region, while being unable to get an AM shift at a tiny station in a tiny college town. Because Ithaca was too far from Rochester, none of her classmates could hear her as the Honeybee. Worse, her multiple duties in the big town meant that she experienced none of the joys of campus life. While Savitch was stepping into the big time, her fellow students were staying in the small time—and having wonderful fun. Although there were those on the communications faculty who knew less than the students, and the textbooks, if they existed at all, were sadly outdated relics of the 1930s and 1940s, the kids didn't mind. They reveled in a laissez-faire atmosphere that put the teachers on the sidelines and allowed the students to learn for themselves as they went along.

The AM station at Ithaca College, WICB, didn't actually broadcast over the air but sent its signal through a wiring system connected to the dormitories. Listeners had to plug their radios in with a special jack. Nonetheless, it was the only station in town that had programs after sundown, which meant that it had a captive audience of every IC student who wanted to listen to rock 'n' roll. Because the station was supposed to provide real-life experience, students controlled their own programming, did their own engineering, and sold advertising space to local merchants, without the real-life requirement of having actually to support the station with the revenues. If something broke, nobody got mad—everybody just rolled up their sleeves and fixed it. If students didn't have something, they figured out how to obtain it. To get their hands on more catchy station identification material, for example, they drove one weekend to New York, where they taped jingles off the air from WABC; back in Ithaca, they edited out the call letters in happy ignorance of copyright law and dubbed in WICB.

Life was similar at the college television station. Although it did not broadcast a full schedule, the TV kids also spent their every waking hour in the studio, where they worked on shows, maintained the old vacuum-tube equipment, and erected and tore down sets, including a spectacularly unstable kidney-shaped anchor desk for newscasts. They rewired the place by themselves, knocking down walls, carpeting the studios from floor to ceiling, and completely rearranging the transmitting equipment. Although the college buildings were supposedly locked at night, communications students managed to enter and exit round the clock, and the more hard-core undergraduates lived at the station for days at a time. Like the radio students, they learned a lot about working with other people in close quarters, a kind of savvy that Savitch, who was hardly on campus, never quite picked up. "It was really very business-like," said Bob Kur, another IC classmate who is now a White

House correspondent for NBC. "It was extremely aggressive and cutthroat, which surprised me. It was a good introduction to this business, but it was very unreal for a college experience."

The IC crews developed a sense of camaraderie, the feeling that, like so many broadcasting musketeers, they were all in an adventure together. Jessica Savitch, by contrast, was on her own, always in transit from one place to another, almost friendless at campus and without a real base in Rochester. In both places, she appeared at the studio only when she had a role in a production; neither at school nor at work did she ever simply hang out and pitch in where needed. She had asked at IC for a spot on the air, and when she hadn't received it immediately, she had gone off and done something else—something, she told her classmates on any number of occasions, that was bigger and better than what they were doing. Even in college she was a poor winner.

The one Ithaca activity Savitch did put effort into was Alpha Epsilon Rho, a professional fraternity whose pin she had already received from Tony Busch. She was the only woman who made it through the standard hazing process, which involved standing in the cafeteria line for upper-class students, reciting lists of silly rules on demand, and making her way back to school after being dumped on a country road twenty miles away. Her doggedness did not help her standing with the other students in the department, who saw that tenacity simply as a career move to list the organization on her résumé. A few of the women did see her crying and miserable in the dorm and tried to make her feel better. "We complained about helping her and yet we all did it," Debi Fortune Farnham said. "She made you feel needed, made you feel good to help her out—it was an honor, like working for a queen bee." But most of her classmates didn't understand her apparent arrogance as compensation for insecurity; they did not know that she slept with her fingers in her mouth and was convinced that she was ugly. They saw her coldness as just that, and thought her detestable. And thus Jessica Savitch spent her almost friendless college years driving back and forth, going from commercial to sociology class to radio studio, sometimes until the wee hours of the morning.

Early in 1967, not long after Savitch had finally split up

with Tony Busch, one of her teachers, Martin Rand, a professor of psychology and campus counselor, interviewed Savitch at the student health service. He had barely noticed her in his lecture class, "The Psychology of Family Life," until another student told him that the blond in the second row needed some help. And indeed, when Rand spoke to Savitch, he found that she was almost incoherent. Alarmed, he realized that, as he put it later, "she was burning too many candles at too many ends." He arranged for her to stay briefly in the IC infirmary, whose chief, Jake Hammond, was extremely discreet. Used to the ordinary run of adolescent problems—birth control, drugs and alcohol, suicidal gestures, and the necessity of deciding when to talk to parents—Hammond was a bit startled to find a student who was burning out from professional overload. He gave Savitch a bed, listened to her desperate-sounding outpourings about future career plans, and suggested she keep talking to Martin Rand.

A big man with a pipe and an easygoing manner that encouraged students to confide in him, Rand cut quite a figure at IC in those days. He was not truly a rebel; unlike Cornell and practically every other campus in the nation at that time, Ithaca College seemed to have no radicals in either the faculty or the student body. Nonetheless, Rand was definitely a nonconformist, with an air that slyly suggested he was looking for something more interesting than could be found on campus. He invited Savitch to spend the weekend with his family, which included his wife, Jo, an energetic redhead who taught nursing students from Alfred University, and two children, at their lakeside home in Geneva, halfway between Ithaca and Rochester. The house, an overgrown cottage in a state of comfortable confusion, was a retreat for IC students, and Savitch quickly made herself at home, carving out a niche as a kind of older daughter. Being there not only eased her Ithaca-Rochester commute, but also gave her a warm, secure, unthreatening alternative to being around her unsympathetic peers at school.

"This was one of the few places she could afford to be just Jess, instead of Jess, the Budding Star," Rand said later. There was, he said, a part of her that was very hurt, crying out for help, but it was hidden from most people by the aggressiveness, the assertiveness, and the apparent self-confidence. From what Rand could see, Savitch hated herself and was convinced that she was unattractive, even though everyone she met treated her as a good-looking young woman. At night she stayed up late talking with Rand about politics and philosophy; whenever the conversation got around to religion, she would refer to God as "Sky Chief." The next morning, she would sit in the kitchen with no makeup and her hair in rollers, drinking coffee with a sleepy informality that few people in her life were allowed to see. She also babysat for the kids, occasionally taking them to the movies or to a shoot for a commercial, and once she drove them all the way to Rochester and back to see the Beach Boys. She also established the same sort of relationship in Rochester with the Schwings, staying there overnight and during the summers and sometimes babysitting for their two children. The friendships with these two families helped glue Savitch together for a while, as did, of course, having a new boyfriend.

Jeff Wheat, a cameraman, was one of Bill Schwing's assistants. He was a part-time student at the University of Rochester, and he had chiseled features and friendly brown eyes. In addition to his work behind the lens, Wheat was in several local bands; before she met him, Savitch had already played hits by two of his bands on WBBF. His parents lived on the same street as the Schwings, where Savitch sometimes stayed the night. The families had been friends for a long time. In the winter of 1966–1967, Schwing arranged for Savitch and Wheat to coproduce a weekly program for local television called *It's Happening Now*. An *American Bandstand*-type show that changed locations each week, it was shot in various spots around Rochester, including a ski lodge, an amusement park, and a bowling alley.

After working together for months, Wheat and Savitch had finally gone out on a date: a Kingston Trio concert in Rochester. Within weeks they were a steady couple, spending weekends in remote country motels, hiking by a mountain stream, climbing a rural fire-watch tower from which they could see a panorama of upstate New York. When they went to a fancy restaurant, Savitch wore her favorite outfit: a sleeveless white satin miniskirted dress with rhinestone buckles on each shoulder, worn with shimmering white stockings and white satin pumps. As a final touch, she twisted her hair up in a chignon and secured it with a rhinestone hairpin. A warm protective presence in Savitch's life, Wheat became "Jeffie Bear," a nickname which directed the choice of his Christmas gift to her, a stuffed ursine creature of vast size. Savitch gave Wheat several books of poetry, including *The Prophet,* a life-long favorite. As Wheat later recalled, the relationship was generally calm but did occasionally have "spikes"; sometimes Savitch and Wheat even had "yell-outs." He was particularly annoyed whenever she was talking to him on the telephone and she slipped into her on-air voice. "I'd say, 'Wait, I want to talk to Jessica, not the Honeybee.' "

Perhaps because her father had died young, Savitch had premonitions of an early, violent death; she told Wheat she had dreams that foretold the future, and that she did not have long to accomplish all she had to do. She wrote a poem called "Strawberrys" and asked Wheat to set it to music; in it she declared, "It has occurred to me early/that it is already too late." According to the dreams, her future would include reading the news into a microphone, but there would be some catastrophic end to everything.

Rochester's bedrock conservatism is well known in both sociological and marketing circles. Although it is the headquarters of such major corporate players as Eastman Kodak and Bausch & Lomb, the city is such a hidebound place that it has been used for decades as a test market for new products, the theory being that if something can overcome consumer resistance there it can succeed anywhere. Thus, although the summer of 1967 was the Summer of Love in the rest of the country, Savitch and Wheat, happily ensconced in Rochester, seemed blissfully unaware that their peers elsewhere were in the midst of a thoroughgoing cultural revolution; still less did the Rochester lovebirds appear to notice the deep rent in the national fabric caused by urban riots or the gathering political thunderstorms over the Vietnam War. While Jimi Hendrix was startling his listeners with a sea of feedback, the Rolling Stones were singing "Street Fighting Man," and Jefferson Airplane concert-goers were passing around cups of Electric Kool-Aid Acid, Savitch and Wheat clapped along with the Monkees. Afterward, Savitch, ever the professional, took the opportunity to interview the group for WBBF and then did a backstage promotion for Clairol.

Savitch spent most of her senior year speeding on the two-lane blacktop road between Ithaca and Rochester. The pace was impossible to maintain. "There was a frightened little girl in there who would shake in fear," Wheat said. "She could get up in the morning, put on a skintight sweater, and by the end of the day she would have lost five pounds from nerves and the sweater would be baggy." At times she called Wheat from her college dorm, crying incoherently. He would put her on hold and use the other line to call Rand, who would go over, pry her out of her room, try to induce her to eat, and sign her into the health center for a night's sleep. Years later Rand said that Savitch was undoubtedly anorectic and bulemic; in other words, she ate almost nothing, but on the rare occasions she actually consumed a meal she would force herself to vomit so as not to gain weight. One night when Rand was at home in Geneva, he was startled by a knock on his front door. It was a neighbor, saying that he had found Savitch after she had driven her tan Chevelle off the road. She was wandering in a field, unhurt but disoriented; luckily, the neighbor recognized her as one of Rand's kids, and brought her to Rand's house.

When Savitch graduated in the spring of 1968, the Rands gave her a graduation party and invited her family, Rusty Nicholl, the Schwings, and Jeff Wheat. Her grandmother Lil, a vivacious woman with elegantly coiffed dyed blond hair, expensive clothes and jewelry, and perfectly manicured nails, made a strong impression on the guests, particularly when compared to the demure, quiet Florence. But the star of the afternoon was Jessica, who basked in the circle of approval. Fueled by several glasses of champagne, she spent much of the party flirting with Wheat and waving around the sheer yellow negligee and peignoir he had given her. A few months later, they picked out an engagement ring and asked for Florence's blessing. Although she willingly bestowed it, somehow the ring never actually made it to Jessica's finger.

That summer Savitch worked at WBBF and set about getting herself to New York City, the heart of the American media. After sending off dozens of letters of application and receiving not one offer in response, she decided that she would have to hit the Manhattan pavement in person. In the fall, she moved to a gloomy residential hotel for women on East 36th Street. Supporting herself with occasional modeling work and commercials in Rochester, she registered with casting directors

102

for ad agencies and continued to search for a job in broadcasting. After several months, she finally caught the eye of the personnel director for CBS, Joan Showalter. Despite Savitch's lack of secretarial skills, Showalter, a transplanted Virginian with short dark hair and the cheery manner of a Girl Scout leader, hired her as a floating administrative assistant. Eventually she was assigned to work for Marvin Friedman, the news director of WCBS Radio, an all-news AM station. At last, Savitch's foot was in the door.

The CBS headquarters building, a black marble monolith designed by Eero Saarinen and opened in 1966, was the ultimate minimalist statement. Spare, severe, unsentimental, and totally functional, it was widely and appropriately known as Black Rock. CBS chairman William Paley's office was on the thirty-fifth floor, one down from the top. According to office lore, Paley chose his location because he was afraid the roof might leak on his extensive art collection and so put the lawyers on the top floor. The radio station's offices were on the sixteenth floor; from Savitch's desk, located in the corner of the large room used by anchors and reporters, she had a direct view into the executive washroom of the Sperry-Rand Building.

Until the year before, WCBS-AM had been a traditional station, offering a variety of programming that included the Mormon Tabernacle Choir, Arthur Godfrey, Art Linkletter, and an all-night broadcast of show music. Spurred by the success of the local Westinghouse-owned station WINS, which had gone to an all-news format in 1965, Paley decreed that his network's flagship station would do likewise, despite the heavy costs involved in such a switch. Only a few hours before the historic shift was scheduled to take place, a light plane hit the AM transmitter, located on High Island, just off City Island in the East River. The pilot was killed, and the new format's debut was shifted to WCBS-FM, a dramatic turn of events that netted wide publicity but left New York's second all-news station with few listeners until a new transmitter was constructed, some months later. By the end of 1968, when Jessica Savitch arrived in the office, the all-news station's audience had grown rapidly but was still trailing that of WINS.

Like many of the people who worked for him, WCBS news director Marvin Friedman was a news junkie. A small, slim man with glasses, Friedman had worked at UPI and then spent five years as WCBS news editor under the old format. "Radio news is the purest form of news there is," he said later. "It's instant, immediate, ongoing—whenever anything happens, you can go right on the air with it because there's nothing to interrupt." But even Friedman was blown away by the volume of history-making events during the first year of the station's all-news operation. And indeed, 1968 was an extraordinary period, marked by space shots, assassinations, riots, and the growing public disenchantment with the Vietnam War. A major story seemed to be breaking every time Friedman turned around, and he was desperate for an assistant to handle the complex job of scheduling the large staff of writers and support personnel. Years later, Friedman still remembered the day he looked up and saw Joe Dembo, vice-president and general manager of the station, and an attractive young blond woman walking down the hall toward him.

After a perfunctory interview, Friedman turned the task over to Savitch. In addition to handling the schedule, her responsibilities would include filing scripts, labeling tapes, and coordinating mobile units to be sure they were gassed, oiled, and ready to roll. She told Friedman right off the bat that she wanted to be doing news, but as far as he was concerned, all of her experience was worthless because it was not in news. He told her that if she wanted to be a reporter, she would have to go elsewhere because WCBS was not a beginner's shop. Savitch did not want to hear this. She stayed in New York. Unused to having only one job, she soon filled her schedule with graduate courses in cinematography at New York University, modeling and doing commercials for clients back in Rochester and for Bill Schwing, who now worked in Manhattan, and as much skiing as she could manage.

Savitch had been hired at CBS for what she later called an "A" position—the sort of assistant, associate, or alternate slots that women always seemed to end up in. Nonetheless, her job did have its share of excitement. Shortly after her arrival, Savitch told friends, she made her first network TV appearance, when she was assigned to post election returns on the *CBS Evening News*. "I was the blonde blur in the lower right-hand corner of your home receiver," she wrote to the Rands. And every day at the radio station had its share of crises, with reporters urgently phoning in stories and the wire service machines churning out miles of copy. In the newsroom, the writers faced at least half a dozen deadlines each shift and banged away nonstop at their typewriters; whenever one of the old manual machines broke down, which was often, they would snitch one from the next desk and keep going. "It was a very hip, smart bunch," said one man who was a staffer at the time. "We were older than the flower kids, and we were ambitious, but we were anti-establishment, into Vietnam War protests. If there was ever a pot raid half the newsroom would have been hauled off."

Pretty and impeccably dressed, Savitch caught the attention and the sympathy of several newsroom regulars, including Charles Osgood, one of the morning anchors. "She was always so cool and poised, much more than the rest of us," recalled Osgood, now a top anchor for CBS television and radio. "It looked like she was auditioning, even then." A friendly-looking man with bright blue eyes, Osgood had come to WCBS a few years earlier from ABC network radio. At ABC he had worked as a reporter alongside such future broadcast luminaries as Ted Koppel, Steve Bell, and Howard Cosell; Mort Crim, another reporter and eventual anchor at ABC Radio, was to be Jessica Savitch's co-anchor in Philadelphia a decade later. Moving to WCBS, a local station, had been a step down for Osgood, who was discouraged by seeing Koppel and other colleagues shoot past him. But with the change in format at WCBS, Osgood was given anchor duties during one of the prime-time slots, 6:00 to 8:00 A.M., known as "morning drive time" because of the commuters who tuned in, and soon Osgood, too, was shooting to the top.

When Savitch arrived each morning in the cavernous WCBS newsroom, Osgood would be sitting at his desk and turning out copy until he went back on the air at 11:00 A.M. Learning that Savitch wanted nothing more than to be doing his job, Osgood suggested that she rewrite AP newswire into broadcast copy and that he would look over her work. He had done the same sort of tutoring with other beginners in the past, but Osgood's frank criticism seemed to scare most of them from doing it more than once. Savitch appeared to have no problems with his style of teaching. "She wouldn't argue with my criticism to turn a sentence around," Osgood said. "She would just ask why."

Despite her efforts, Savitch was unable to convince Friedman or his co-news director, Ed Joyce, to promote her. Friedman insisted that the only criterion for advancement was experience, and in fact everyone else in a professional capacity in the newsroom did have stronger news credentials than Savitch. "She wasn't discriminated against," Jim Cusick, then a news writer at the station, said afterward. "Marvin treated us all like dogs, whether you were a man or a woman. Lots of people were beating on the door and they were all told to go out and get experience first." But Savitch remained convinced that she was being passed over because the station, like the business as a whole, was a bastion of white men. Her view was not entirely unreasonable. There was one woman reporter, Irene Cornell, and several female news writers and editors, but the place and the point of view were overwhelmingly male. At one point, shortly after Savitch had left, a group of several dozen women formed a sit-in outside Joe Dembo's office, demanding more sympathetic treatment of women's issues. The station's reporters were forbidden to cover the incident.

Frustrated as she was at work, Savitch did not want anyone to know she had not started at the top. When Jeff Greenhawt and Rusty Nicholl phoned her at the office, she chirruped, "Jessica Savitch's line," put the caller on hold, and then returned as herself. In letters she spoke of dictating correspondence to her secretary (she had none) and awarded herself inflated job titles. She was also unwilling to tell anyone that life as a low-level clerical employee living in a small, one-bedroom apartment in Queens was often lonely, penurious, and dull. Her letters described a glittering social life, filled with handsome men who took her to jet-set parties and showered her with gifts, fabulous job offers, proposals of marriage, and trips to exotic foreign destinations. Afterward, her escorts remembered things somewhat differently. One frequently mentioned date, Joel Davis, said he took her to Boston, not the Bahamas; another, a producer named Howard Marks, said he never owned a yacht, had never given Savitch expensive jewelry, did not offer her an apartment or a job as an executive producer, and did not send her dozens of roses every week. John Hart, at the time the *CBS Morning News* anchor, said that he was not a regular date but had simply taken Savitch to lunch at the Russian Tea Room. "She was pretty and I was interested," he said later. "I kept wanting to talk about the job and the news, but she was all technique and ambition. I thought, Oh dear, here's another person who wants to be a star, not a reporter."

Such exaggeration was nothing new to her friends from Atlantic City. "She was always a little to the left of the truth," said Rusty Nicholl. "It was just part of Jessica that you had to learn to accept." Such strong denial in the face of adversity allowed Savitch to persevere in circumstances, such as WCBS, that most other young women found overwhelmingly discouraging. At the same time, however, Savitch was learning another, less helpful lesson, how to avoid dealing with disappointment and rejection. Instead of talking about her frustration and loneliness, she refused to admit their existence and invented a fantasy version of her life. Wanting to believe she was caught up in a glamorous, fast-track life, she told people she was, and in the process she apparently persuaded herself this was the case. "We've all bent the truth now and then, but she actually believed what she told us," Nicholl said. "Maybe she really had problems we just didn't recognize."

The one subject on which Savitch apparently reported more or less accurately was her relationship with Jeff Wheat. In theory, they were still engaged, and he visited her frequently. During one period of several months when he was working as a producer for Caedmon Records, he even shared her apartment. But the relationship that had been such an important source of stability to Savitch back in Ithaca and Rochester now seemed to her simply an impediment. "Jeff is the same," she wrote to the Rands in April 1969. "Wonderfully sadening [sic]." From the time she arrived in New York in the fall of 1968, Savitch had dated other men, fitting them around Jeff's visits; now she began fitting Jeff around the other men. By early 1970 Jeff Wheat was history, and Savitch had gone on to a romance with Ed Bradley, a black journalist who is now a prinicipal correspondent on *60 Minutes*. At that time a WCBS radio reporter covering racial conflict in the Oceanhill-Brownsville neighborhood of Brooklyn, Bradley gave Savitch career advice and, according to her letters, offered to take her along when he was assigned abroad; she wrote that she reluctantly turned him down. It was a heady existence for a young woman not yet two years out of college. "Someday when I am a real important executive with this company, you could dredge out these eclectic epistles and blackmail me," she wrote in one letter. In another she asked, "Save these letters . . . I'll need them for my book."

After a year of getting nowhere at CBS, Savitch finally did prevail in one matter: She managed to convince Ed Joyce, by then the news director of the local CBS television station, to let her use his facilities to make a television audition tape. It was not a small matter, for it meant making a film with a three-person camera crew, then developing, editing, and transferring it to videotape; if done on the outside, the total tab would have run at least $5,000.

After being coached by Ed Bradley one Saturday morning in the radio station tape library, Savitch stepped in front of the camera. Dressed in a blue jacket, with a red, white, and blue scarf tucked inside the collar of her white blouse, her face covered with thick pancake makeup and her silver hair sprayed within an inch of its life, she looked almost too nervous to speak. The producer came out with the big black clap sticks and shouted, "Savitch, take one!" She swallowed visibly and began reading the script she had labored over for three weeks from the TelePrompTer. After plowing her way through the first story, on the Paris peace conference, she swallowed visibly, paused, then plunged into the latest firefight in the Vietnam War (swallow), the inauguration of Off-Track Betting in New York (swallow), Nixon's chastisement of hecklers (swallow), and the scarcity of jobs for college graduates. Although her voice was uneven, the tone was perfectly placed: energetic, buoyant, aggressive but not unpleasantly so. The heavy makeup did not prevent her from blooming in front of the lens. Her jaw, which later tightened up considerably, was just stiff enough to hint at a certain authority, while at the same time her mouth hinted at a smile and her pale blue eyes looked straight into the viewer's face.

When it was over, Savitch had two copies: enormous reels in heavy steel containers. She spent the next several weeks writing several hundred letters, one to every station director in a market big enough to have all three networks represented. She received fewer than a dozen responses, and only one offer of an interview for a reporting job materialized. It was at KHOU, a CBS affiliate in Houston, Texas. The news director, Dick John, paid for a plane ticket, and on a sweltering, ninety-degree day in May 1971, she flew into Hobby Airport.

The interview could hardly have begun less auspiciously. Savitch was dressed in her best outfit, a tan suede pants suit which was meant for considerably cooler temperatures. She was also nervous, and, as she later told Dick John, more than a little hung over from a wild party the night before. To top things off, the flight had been especially bumpy. No sooner had Savitch gotten into John's car than she had to stop at a ladies room to throw up. Gallantly supplying a linen handkerchief, John took her by the station and then out to lunch, where she announced she intended to be a network anchor by the time she was thirty. Such brashness had turned off her college class-mates, but John, who wanted somebody with gumption, was delighted. "I was going to put her on the air unless she sucked her thumb," he said later. Within a week he offered her a job at the munificent salary of $135 a week. Finally, at the age of twenty-three, Jessica Savitch was on camera.

5

*h*ouston

In June of 1971, when Jessica Savitch at last inserted herself into television news, she became a small component in an immense electronic system whose rapid expansion was driven by an extraordinarily brutal competition. KHOU, the Houston station that hired her, was one of approximately 600 television stations then broadcasting in the United States. Its programming went through the air on Channel 11, which covers the frequency range between 198,000,000 and 206,000,000 cycles per second, placing the KHOU signal, like that of most other stations, on what is known as the very-high frequency (VHF) band; the only other stations at the time were a few ultra-high frequency (UHF) broadcasters, which used Channels 14 to 85, and some cable facilities which sent signals through a wire into their subscribers' homes and offices. Houston was then the fifteenth-largest television market in the nation. Diffused by a tower located just south of Houston in the small town of Dewalt, KHOU's shows could be seen by over two million people in three quarters of a million homes. Although KHOU was in second place among the four stations in Houston, it was still immensely profitable, a circumstance that played a considerable role in Jessica Savitch's future.

KHOU was owned by the Corinthian Broadcasting Corporation, which also had stations in Indianapolis, Ft. Wayne, Tulsa, and Sacramento. Corinthian's properties, like most other VHF stations in the country, were "affiliates" of one of the three major networks, in this case CBS, in a legal and financial relationship of considerable tension and complexity. Fearful that a few powerful interests could end up controlling the electronic media, the Federal Communications Commission had mandated in 1954 that a single company could own no more than seven television stations, of which only five could be VHF (the company could also only have seven FM and seven AM radio stations).★ Accordingly, in 1972, the year Savitch came to KHOU, the networks each owned and operated five VHF stations, which were known, inevitably, as "O&Os." With these five O&Os, the networks were allowed to have a relatively free hand, although their licenses were subject to periodic FCC renewal. With the other stations, such as KHOU, the networks were strictly controlled. The networks provided programs, primarily entertainment shows, seen in the 8:00 to 11:00 P.M. slot known as prime time, but also the morning and evening news as well as documentaries and special reports, and paid the affiliates a nominal sum (compensation or "comp" money) for every show aired; in turn, the networks sold advertising to be shown during these programs and kept the revenue.

A network—and this is key to understanding the system —could not force its affiliates to broadcast its material. Nonetheless, because entertainment programs, the heart and soul of the television schedule, are expensive to produce, the local stations in fact used the bulk of what the networks had to offer. Indeed, for many years the affiliates were, despite regulation designed to ensure their independence, more or less docile creatures of the networks. This relationship began to change at the end of the 1960s, when the affiliates discovered that they could make a lot of money from local news, and the already bitter struggle among the networks became complicated by a battle between the networks and their affiliates.

The FCC required of every station that it devote a certain portion of the day to programs of verifiable worth to the gen-

★ *This has since been changed; networks can now own up to 12 television stations, and there is no restriction on what proportion are VHF.*

eral public. Most affiliates met this obligation primarily by broadcasting news, which was demonstratively of interest to the community and relatively inexpensive to produce; a single set served for years on end and history provided the plot lines. News could also be touted as a great public service, although this did not mean that either the networks or the affiliates felt obligated to present much of it. At first, local stations produced an evening news broadcast that filled the screen just before or after the network news and lasted the same length of time, fifteen minutes. In 1963, when NBC and CBS lengthened their news programs to half an hour (two years later, ABC did the same), the affiliates grudgingly extended theirs as well. There the situation remained until the mid- to late 1960s, when managers for local stations began to comprehend that local advertisers, such as banks, car dealerships, and appliance warehouses, were particularly eager for their commercials to appear on local news programs for the simple reason that, in the estimation of the advertisers, such programs provided a prestigious environment in which to showcase their products. Because most local managers had come from their stations' sales departments and spent a large part of their day selling airtime, they grasped the increasing desirability of the news faster than their counterparts in the networks. William Paley, for many years the president of CBS, might have lunch and dinner with Hollywood stars and top newscasters; Dean Borba, at that time the general manager of KHOU, ate with the marketing men of Foley's Department Store and knew what they were thinking.

Accordingly, the daily news coverage at local stations, including KHOU, increased to at least an hour and a half, and some stations jumped it to as much as three hours. As it turned out, the great unwashed on the other side of the screen actually preferred an hour or two of local news to an hour or two of old sitcoms. Ratings for the longer newscasts went up, as did advertising rates. To the amazement of many, the news departments, previously sleepy little divisions regarded as the price of doing business with the FCC, became bonanzas. The cheapest program to produce generated the highest demand for commercials and the biggest audiences; little wonder, then, that local stations couldn't get enough news. According to Chet Collier, a news director in Cleveland who was one of the first to act on the sudden spurt of interest in TV journalism, news at a station in a Top 10 market could account for up to 35 percent of annual revenues. "It was *way* out of proportion to the amount of time that news was on," Collier said. "Think about it—only an hour or two a day making a third of your profits!"

At the same time that local news was becoming a cash cow, network news was heading inexorably toward a future as an ever-larger money loser. Certain network news programs, such as NBC's *Today*, had been highly profitable for some time, but the news divisions' signature programs, the nightly newscasts, had always been in the red. By the time that the leadership of NBC, CBS, and ABC realized that a longer evening news could be a gold mine—*news*, of all things!—the affiliates did not want to give up the time; they had already filled it with their own newscasts, which in turn were filled with their own advertising. Although the networks became increasingly interested in expanding their nightly newscasts, they, too, were unwilling to give up any of their own time to do so. By now, however, when the networks leaned on the affiliates, the affiliates leaned back, and the network news divisions' flagship broadcasts remained only a half hour long. A decade later, this situation would become a disaster as expensive new technology increased the cost of preparing network news far beyond the revenue that could be realized from a thirty-minute show.

Unsurprisingly, the networks' relationship with local news became increasingly fractious, and the annual network clambakes for all their affiliates sometimes turned into angry gripe sessions on both sides. Network had always regarded local as—to use the term of art—"bush." To the people who worked at the network level, their news was the *New York Times*; local was the *Squibb Valley Herald-Gazette*. Network thought of itself as smart, sophisticated, important; local, by contrast, was amateurish, fumbling, a parade of unimportant fires and school lunch menus. To put it mildly, network did not like local's new prominence; local, for its part, enjoyed turning the tables. Relations soured further after Vice-President Spiro Agnew blasted the networks for excessive influence and liberal bias in a famous speech delivered at a Republican gathering in Des Moines in November 1969. When White House director of communications Clay T. Whitehead suggested the next year that affiliates could make their FCC renewals more secure and for a longer time period if they were more selective about the news they accepted from the networks, some local stations slapped disclaimers over network material.

In the past, the network that topped the evening news ratings and thus "owned" the news was usually able to deliver the local audience to its affiliates for their own news; now, however, local stations did not depend on network performance but instead competed directly among themselves for dominance. In Houston, for example, KPRC, an NBC affiliate, had just edged out KHOU, a CBS station, even though the *NBC Nightly News,* which succeeded the *Huntley-Brinkley Report* and was anchored by John Chancellor, was behind Walter Cronkite in the national ratings. Nonetheless, affiliates still needed the networks to provide the prime-time shows that would pull in large audiences for the 11:00 local news and the ads contained therein; likewise, the networks needed the affiliates to obtain a maximum audience and maximum advertising rate base for network shows. Neither was happy about being so dependent on the other. "They were like two scorpions in a bottle," said David Adams, the former NBC lawyer. "They were locked together. Unless they could figure out how to live together, they'd kill each other."

Smelling money, local news executives set out to increase viewership by any and all means possible. Because newscasts in the same city necessarily covered the same fires and strikes, station managers began to focus on what might differentiate one station's broadcasts from another's—that is, on how the news was delivered. If the contents of the boxes were basically the same, news directors began to reason, why not change the packaging? Thus, for example, Chet Collier, taking a cue from how much viewers seemed to like having Chet Huntley and David Brinkley acknowledge each other's existence during a broadcast, told his Cleveland crew to stop looking so serious and to *smile* at each other on the air. They were all in the same room, Collier thought, so they might as well *act* like they were in the same room. He also pointed out to them that a report on a topic covered on all the local stations could still stand out if it took a direct, personal approach. "You have to say what the relevance is to the viewer," he said. "Will I pay more or less taxes? Will there be more or less difficulties in my life? No matter what the story, you have to relate it to these concerns."

As the competition in local markets grew stiffer, many stations hired a new breed of professional: the news consultant, a media expert equipped with a package of surefire methods to increase audiences. The principal means of audience building was jazzing up the old news business with a healthy dose of show business. Following this logic, local newscasters began to crack jokes, talk in funny voices, or even, on occasion, don absurd costumes. A new ensemble-style approach emerged in which the on-air cast expanded to include such stock figures as a roué anchor, a "kid sister" female reporter, an off-the-wall weatherman, and a sportscaster of the handsome jock variety.

In the early seventies, this "happy-talk" approach was becoming the talk of the local news industry. Although many news directors, including KHOU's Dick John, resented the emphasis on what they considered show-business values, they could not ignore the fact that personalities were becoming ever more important to the profession. A native of Tulsa, John had spent his teenage years working after school at a radio station in which he served as announcer, ran the engineering board, signed the station off at night, and then swept the floor. His first full-time job was at WKY-TV in Oklahoma City. By station decree, John went on air under the name "Charlie Bishop"; his co-anchor, Frank McGee, later a top anchor at NBC, was "Mac Rogers." John's subsequent broadcast career as a radio and television reporter, writer, anchor, and news director took him around the country, including a stint at Rockefeller Center where he worked as a writer for *Today* show host Frank Blair, anchored NBC radio newscasts, rode on the elevator with Huntley and Brinkley, and drank at Hurley's bar.

Although John considered himself a Murrowite, he readily acknowledged that KHOU had finally climbed to the number one spot at the end of the 1960s only because of its distinctive on-air talent: John himself, the six o'clock anchor, an engaging redhead; Ron Stone, the solid, square-jawed ten o'clock anchor; Johnny Temple, the sportscaster who was a former major-league second baseman; and, most important, Sid Lascher, the hugely popular weatherman whose warmth and friendliness enchanted viewers. "He could have been elected governor, although he never made more than fifteen thousand a year," John said years later. "People tuned in to watch Sid and Dick and Johnny and Ron, not Cronkite or the stories. It didn't *matter* how well we covered things."

Lascher was a genial man with a mustache who smoked three packs of cigarettes a day and chewed gum incessantly, including when he was on air; John often had to interrupt the newscast to tell Lascher to take the wad out of his mouth. In between the six and ten o'clock newscasts, Lascher played jazz trumpet in his office because his wife wouldn't let him play it at home. Everyone at KHOU loved him, and so did the viewers. In the spring of 1971, he dropped dead of a heart attack in the hallway outside Dick John's office after the six o'clock news, his gum still stuck to the weatherboard. KHOU plummeted to number two almost immediately.

Soon Dick John was desperate. Before Lascher's death, he had been told to provide three times as much news with no increase in staff, budget, or equipment. Now his biggest star was dead. The competition was on the move: KPRC, the NBC affiliate, had jumped to first place and had Frank Magid, a leading news consultant, flying in to provide research and advice, and KTRK, the ABC station, had hired McHugh and Hoffman, one of the biggest consulting firms in the country. John detested news consultants; when Corinthian sent one down to take a look at KHOU, John chased him out of the building. Nonetheless, he recognized their power and was alarmed by their looming presence in his market. Then, to top things off, executives from Corinthian told John at a meeting in May 1971 that he had to hire a new woman reporter. Pressure from blacks threatening to challenge FCC license renewals had already led Corinthian to approve John's hiring a black newscaster from Cleveland named Bob Nicholas; now Corinthian was getting nervous about potential FCC and feminist pressure and wanted a female in a high-profile spot. According to John, he thought women usually did a better job than men because they thought they had to prove themselves. Ordinarily, he would have been happy to comply. At the time, however, the demand seemed simply one more nuisance. Besides, he had no qualified candidates on file.

The next day John received a big brown envelope. When

he opened it, out fell a striking black-and-white glossy of Savitch and an artfully composed résumé that suggested, but did not actually say, that she'd had broadcast news experience. John called and asked her to come for an interview. Within an hour of Jessica Savitch's arrival at the station, John said later, he knew he wanted to hire her. "She was the most ambitious, career-oriented person I ever saw," he said. "You'd have to tie her down to keep her from making it."

Savitch accepted the job offer immediately; even if KHOU had not been the station from which Dan Rather had burst onto the national scene after his heroic round-the-clock coverage of Hurricane Carla back in 1962, it was the only station that offered her employment. Despite Savitch's enthusiasm, however, her friends and family had reservations about the city to which she would have to move. When she returned to start work, she was escorted by Joan Showalter, her CBS mentor, who apparently wanted to be sure Savitch wouldn't be raped or pillaged. To John, Savitch and Showalter were astonishingly provincial. "They thought Houston was the Australian outback, a place with swamps where they say 'bid-ness,' " he said. Shortly afterward, Jessica's youngest sister, Lori, also came down to take a look around this uncivilized outpost.

The Houston that Savitch and her protectors found was hardly the cowtown they had anticipated. Houston did have swamps, known locally as bayous, and some of its inhabitants spoke of being in "the awl bid-ness," but the town also had the Houston Symphony Orchestra, the NASA manned space center, Drs. Michael DeBakey and Denton Cooley's heart transplant unit at the Texas Medical Center, and more cars per capita than any other city in the country. People wore cowboy hats and boots, but Houston, the Magnolia City, was really a southern town, right down to having members of the Ku Klux Klan in the police department and being engaged in a struggle over school integration that continued throughout Savitch's stay. As far as native Houstonians were concerned, the real West began over the horizon, at Ft. Worth. Houston did have a huge annual rodeo, but it hadn't gotten under way until the late 1930s, when it was invented as a promotional event; likewise, the trail ride that opened the rodeo each February was inaugurated in 1952 as a public relations stunt for KTRK-TV, the ABC affiliate. Every year, hundreds of cowboys would leave their desks, drive out forty miles to the town of Brenham, and ride back to Houston along the last leg of the old Salt Grass Trail. Saddle-weary but triumphant, they would surge up Memorial Parkway, right past KHOU, and finally dismount at the modern version of trail's end, the Astrodome. Riding high on the oil boom, Houston in 1971 was a city on a roll, with new apartments and office buildings going up everywhere. With a population of nearly one and a quarter million people and a metropolitan area far larger than the state of Rhode Island, Houston was already the biggest city in the South and getting bigger every day. Yet at the same time, Houston was still the kind of small town where the sidewalks were rolled up by nine in the evening, the fireplugs were always painted orange and black because some long-ago water commissioner was a Princeton grad, and people actually said hello on the streets.

Savitch's first weeks at KHOU, a modern, two-story concrete structure on the north side of town, were not promising. She despised the small-town atmosphere of Houston and the deep-fried southern cuisine. "I hate the humidity and the puppy dog open friendliness of the people," she wrote in a letter. "Maybe I am just getting old." Nor was the station itself all that comfortable for a Yankee with a pro–civil rights, pro–women's movement outlook. According to Steve Edwards, then a reporter and talk-show host at KHOU, the station was basically a mirror of the city—"half a shit-kicker, good-old-boy, redneck place, half a boomtown which was extremely progressive and had a lot of positive energy, and a touch of the counterculture thrown in on top." Although a few female reporters had already passed through, KHOU remained a resolutely male enclave; when Savitch arrived, the only other woman in the newsroom was Dick John's secretary, Roseanne Colletti.

A more immediate problem was that Savitch did not have the right background for her job. In fact, the station's newest reporter didn't know anything about what she had been hired to do. "We couldn't figure out why John hired her," said John Shaw, a cameraman who shot many of Jessica's stories. A slim man with tow-colored hair and a luxuriant mustache who is now head cameraman at KHOU, Shaw had initially sized Savitch up as a skinny young woman with bad skin and hair like straw from too much bleach; he was stunned to discover how different she appeared on camera. Shaw taught Savitch the basics, from how to write, produce, film, and edit stories to the use of "cutaways," shots in which the camera "cuts away" from the subject of an interview to the reporter. Although cutaways do serve to showcase a reporter, their basic function is to provide a transitional picture to cover spots where the film has been edited. Shaw also insisted that she stop nodding her head during interviews, which he saw as an outdated touch that was meant to indicate involvement but often looked like editorial commentary. Another important technique, used for appearing in front of the camera outside the studio (and thus away from the TelePrompTer), involved pre-taping a script, placing a tape recorder behind her back and an earphone in her ear, and repeating what she heard. This method freed her to look straight into the camera with the firm, unwavering gaze—what Dick John called Savitch's "pleasant aggressiveness"—that was to become her trademark.

Unlike much of the broadcast industry elsewhere, that in Texas, a right-to-work state, was non-union.* Although Savitch was later to participate in an unsuccessful union drive at KHOU, the open shop was to her advantage as a beginner. The downside was that salaries were low, working conditions were often crude, and job security was marginal; the upside was that a neophyte like Savitch was free—indeed, obliged—to try out anything and everything, to go behind the camera as well as in front of it and to experience directly all that went into the making of a news program. At KHOU, Shaw said later, reporters learned to do everything from writing and editing a story to shooting it because there were no support personnel. "If you wanted to get something on air, you had to do it yourself," he said. "Whenever reporters left to go somewhere else and finally got to do just reporting, it was a snap." Yet although Savitch became technically proficient, she never became an investigative journalist who broke stories because she never paid the required dues. "She never got into the nitty-gritty and found money being spent under the table, or got into

* By state law, all businesses have to remain "open shops," meaning that union membership cannot be mandatory for employment.

119

the cops," said John Shaw. "It takes reporters a year to get cops to return their calls. Jess knew that but didn't know how, so she just acted tough and covered already breaking stories."

Shaw was an exception. Most of the station's cameramen were not about to help the new blond out; as far as they were concerned, she should just pack up and head back east, the sooner the better. Whenever she ventured into the station's dingy little snack bar, they practically snarled. One old-timer, Bob Wolfe, a big man with a low, gravelly voice, later admitted that he had detested the new reporter. "Nobody liked her," he said. "We thought she was an interloper, a pain in the butt." In turn, Savitch took every remark or sideways look as a declaration of war. Instead of keeping a low profile until she'd figured out the lay of the land and the politics of KHOU, she told off anyone she thought was standing in her way. "She was a kick-ass kind of person," said another camera operator, Don Benskin. "She wasn't afraid to tell you to get screwed in a minute —she'd get right up in your face and she wouldn't let go."

The first story Wolfe and Savitch did together was about a dead body, or "floater," that had been fished out of the ship channel between Houston and Galveston, a waterway so polluted that a federal inspector had once called its waters "too thick to drink and too thin to plow." Well known in local circles for having been Rather's cameraman on the Hurricane Carla story, the pistol-packing Wolfe had the local "fuzz factory"—police headquarters—as his beat and had photographed dozens of floaters. When he and Savitch arrived at the piers, he said, he tried to keep her away from the rotting, maggot-filled corpse. But when Savitch insisted on viewing the body herself, Wolfe recalled, "I got sadistic. I took her right down close and got her downwind. She turned pale and walked away. I probably thought to myself, Goody, goody, that's what you deserve, you nosy little broad."

Benskin, a taciturn but handsome man, felt the same way. When Dick John first assigned him to work with Savitch, he came into the news director's office and complained furiously. Soon afterward, Savitch and Benskin were driving downtown to do a story when they heard on the radio that a tank car filled with oil had derailed and caught on fire several miles to the south, on Mykawa Road. From the car they could see a column of thick, black smoke and immediately turned toward it, driving down the wrong side of the freeway. Savitch leaned out of the window and screamed at other cars to get out of the way. Back at the station, anchor Ron Stone tried to tell Savitch where to go, but she was so excited by the gathering flames and the sirens and Benskin's crazy driving that she forgot to take her thumb off the button on the two-way radio. "All we could hear was her complaining about how we weren't talking back," said Stone, now an anchor at KPRC, the NBC affiliate.

As they approached the scene, Savitch later recalled in her autobiography, *Anchorwoman,* they had the following shouted exchange:

SAVITCH: I think our game plan should be—
BENSKIN: I think our game plan should be that you stay in the car.
SAVITCH: You take the sound gear. I'll shoot silent with the Bell and Howell and roll wild sound on my tape recorder. I'll hook up with you for the interviews and on-camera inserts.
BENSKIN: You're on your own, Savitch.

Savitch was ready to explode with rage, but Benskin was completely oblivious. From his point of view, it was still a time when it was assumed that a man would look after a woman and he was simply trying to warn her that he would not be able to do so. Because another KHOU photographer, Wally Athey, was already at the fire, Benskin and Savitch stopped about seventy-five yards back so that she could give a report with smoke rising dramatically in the background. Resting his silent camera between his legs, Benskin started to rig up a sound camera. Still furious, Savitch stood in front of him, her back to the fire and a microphone in her hand, waiting for him to start rolling film.

"There was a funny sound," Benskin said. "A hissing sound, like something was sucking air." It was a vacuum forming inside the tank car. A few seconds later, the car imploded with terrific violence. Benskin found himself lying in a ditch with his sound camera smashed on the ground and the grass around him afire. Savitch lay near him, her pants leg torn and her microphone thrown to one side. "The explosion knocked me smooth off my feet," Benskin said. Although Benskin was not injured, the blast was so hot that at first he thought he might be badly burned. As he picked up his silent camera and went in for some close-ups, Savitch ran down the road screaming, her hands up in the air. "What else could she do?" Benskin said. "She couldn't shoot pictures. If I'd been her, I'd have done the same thing."

Back at the studio, John and Stone were in a state of panic because they were unable to raise Benskin or Savitch on the radio. Finally they heard Savitch, panting and sobbing and barely able to get the words out. "By God, I've got the lead story tonight!" she shouted into the two-way radio. "You guys get out of the way!" When she stepped in front of the camera, she had recovered her aplomb; indeed, much of her later success would be due to the remarkable concentration that she could bring to bear in such a situation, willing herself to appear composed and collected on air no matter what was happening behind the scenes. Savitch's report on the fire appeared that night on the *CBS Evening News,* a coup that only strengthened her resolve to get herself to the network level as soon as possible. Every morning she was on the phone to CBS, keeping in touch with Joan Showalter and Ed Bradley and reminding them that her absence from New York was only temporary.

After the Mykawa Road fire, Don Benskin made Savitch part of the crew, an exalted status that meant Savitch would now be allowed to get just as wet as he did, open her own car door, and help carry the camera equipment. "I didn't give her any slack as a woman," Benskin said. "I think that was maybe the best thing that ever happened to her."

Over the months that followed, Savitch filed a wide range of stories. In the period from October 15 to November 9, 1971, for example, she reported on an oil spill and fire in the Gulf of Mexico; covered four election stories, including a Barbara Jordan rally and a meeting of Harris County commissioners; interviewed Ralph Nader and a female executive in the maritime industry; did features on shoplifting, drugs in school, and local prisons; and summed up an EPA conference. Wearing dark sunglasses and dressed in a pants suit, a scarf around her neck and her teased, silver-blond hair arranged in a perfect flip, she would go out every day and throw herself into her assignment. And every day, she expected the result to be the lead story, a view not always shared by those in charge of the evening lineup, the news director and the anchor. "If she didn't get the top story of the day, she'd be pissed," Benskin said. "She'd say, 'I could do a better job.' She'd slam doors, scream, and maybe start to cry. Then sometimes—but not always—she'd get her way."

Such behavior was nothing, however, compared to what happened whenever anyone else made a mistake when Savitch was on air. She would yell obscenities, crumple up pages and throw them on the floor, and hurl anything that happened to be sitting on her desk across the room. Once she smashed a door into a metal file cabinet so hard that the entire side of the cabinet was crushed; another time she was so angry at an engineer who had miscued a tape that Dick John had to come and pry her fingers off the engineer's throat. "I didn't know whether to fire her or promote her," he said. "After all, that drive was the reason I'd hired her." Savitch spent much of her stay in Houston in John's office, pouring out her frustrations and crying into his ever-ready handkerchief; every two months she routinely gave him a dozen new Irish linen handkerchiefs, and just as routinely she cried her way through all of them. John offered sympathy, but also something else: the accumulated wisdom of thirty years in broadcasting. Included in this store was his knack of slightly raising an eyebrow to express a comment, a touch that was to become a standard part of Savitch's on-air performance.

To the rest of the staff, it appeared that Savitch had John wrapped around her little finger. According to Roseanne Colletti, now the troubleshooter reporter at WCBS-TV in New York, once Jessica's roots were showing and she told Dick John she needed half a day off to get her hair bleached. When John said no way, she said that if he didn't let her go she'd go natural. He had a fit, said, "We hired a blond!" and gave Savitch the time off. As far as John was concerned, such concessions were simply what it cost to keep talent happy, and keeping Savitch happy was worth whatever it took. "She breathed new fire into the operation," he said. "She was made to order for us."

Three months after Savitch arrived, John announced that he was holding auditions for a Saturday night anchor. For her tryout, Savitch did her best to look as unfeminine as possible. She pulled back her hair, wore a tailored blue suit, and spoke in as deep a voice as she could muster; although she wrote afterward that she "tried to look authoritative but instead looked silly," there never was any question that the job was hers.

The audience loved her. In the space of only a few months, Jessica Savitch, the woman who couldn't get to first base in the WCBS Radio newsroom, had become the first woman television anchor in the South. The role was so novel that no term had yet been coined for it. One headline read "Jessica Savitch: South's First Anchorone," and she was featured in *TV Guide* and in newspapers across the region. The appearance several months earlier of black anchor Bob Nicholas on weekends caused little comment, but a woman—a *woman!*—telling people what had happened that day was a must-see. Letters poured in from viewers, especially women. Flowers began arriving. Suddenly, KHOU was hot again; when the next rating period was over, Channel 11 had recaptured the top spot from Channel 2. The kind of public attention Savitch had experienced in Rochester was back; soon she couldn't walk down the street without being recognized, and when she turned on the radio she heard a DJ croon, "I've never been to heaven, but I've seen Jessica on Channel Eleven."

Within the station, her reviews were mixed. Although Dick John called her "gangbusters" and most staffers were pleased that she was bringing new attention to the station, some criticized her for not being a real journalist. Others, such as Bruce Halford, weekend news producer at the time, were dismayed that the on-screen and off-screen Savitches seemed like two different women. "The other anchorpeople were all these guys who just went out and were themselves," Halford said. "Jessica went out and was somebody else." Off camera, Halford said, she had a great sense of humor and would regale staffers with stories of her former life as a Honeybee, but on air her voice would go into what he called "that upper-register, girls'-finishing-school pattern of speaking that was nothing like her real voice." To Halford's way of thinking, if only the side of Savitch that he had seen around the station were to appear on air, no one could touch her. "But when Jessica looked into a camera," he said, "the real warmth wasn't there."

Savitch spent little time resting on her laurels. During the weeks she was still a reporter, covering everything from the annual Ringling Brothers circus parade—a terrified Savitch was ordered to do a story from atop an elephant—to Sissy Faren-thold's campaign for the Democratic nomination for governor. Farenthold, a state legislator and outspoken feminist, was the first woman to run for statewide office since 1924, when im-peached former governor James E. Ferguson had arranged the election of his wife, Ma Ferguson, so that he could still run the state. Although Farenthold lost, her shoestring operation, which whistle-stopped around Texas in a 1941 DC-3 that was painted pea green and nicknamed the "Vomit Comet" for its effects on its passengers' stomachs, gave Savitch a taste for campaign coverage.

But the highlight of Savitch's week was Saturday, which she spent rigorously practicing her script, something no anchor at KHOU had ever done. She demanded that her copy be ready hours before airtime so that she could go on the dark set and read it aloud, over and over. So anxious that she would chew her fingernails until they bled, she would underline the words she wanted to emphasize and rehearse the turns she would have to make when shifting her gaze from one camera to another. To Halford, Savitch was the ex-Honeybee who desperately wanted to be considered a bona-fide journalist. "Maybe she thought that she wouldn't be taken seriously if the real Jessica went on the air," he said. "She seemed scared to death of failure and drove herself way beyond what was necessary. I used to wonder who she was trying to please."

One day in early 1972, Ron Kershaw, a reporter at KTRK, the ABC affiliate in Houston, was editing a piece he'd done on a news conference held that morning. Suddenly, in the middle of the KTRK photographer's footage, Jessica Savitch appeared. "She looked beautiful," Kershaw said afterward in the course of a long interview. "I couldn't use the competition's reporter for the shot, but she was very stunning." The next time they were on the same assignment, Kershaw, a husky man with a Beatle-style haircut and penetrating blue eyes, sized her up fur-ther. A little while later, they both covered a strike at KPFT, a local underground radio station, and Kershaw asked her if she wanted to see the popular synthesizer rock-band Yes.

During her first months in Houston, Jessica Savitch hadn't had time for a private life. On his way to Vietnam, Ed Bradley came to visit her—a mildly scandalous event in Houston at that time—and she had occasional dates with other KHOU staffers, but most of her waking hours were spent at work. Then Ron Kershaw asked her on a date, and everything changed. Almost instantly, they became a couple, and remained so for many years. As Savitch rose in national prominence, Kershaw became well known in the world of local news for his extraordinary ability to reshape a weak news operation into one that would dominate its market. Although they never married, and Jessica Savitch went on to have two other husbands, probably no one else was ever as close to her as Kershaw.

Two years earlier, Kershaw had left a job in the wire room at *The Washington Post* and come to Houston, where his estranged wife and children were living. He was hoping to salvage his marriage and to land a job as a reporter at the *Houston Post*. He was successful at neither, but along the way he had an interview for a job in a local radio station's news department. When the general manager's wife spotted him in the waiting room, she told him that he was good-looking and ought to get into television. She sent him over to KTRK, one of a handful of stations owned by Capital Cities Broadcasting. The newsroom receptionist, Chris Curle, later an anchor at CNN, also gave Kershaw a useful tip: If he wanted a job, he should go get his shoulder-length hair cut, because the guy in charge was just to the right of Hitler. When Kershaw returned, newly shorn, he was hired on the spot.

As Kershaw later told the story, he became hopelessly infatuated with TV news as soon as he got to KTRK. "I'm a good writer, but I don't have a good linear thought process," he said. "I want to sit down and go great guns, or else I get a total block. But then I walked into a television edit room and found that you could just grab all these little strips of film, all these little pieces of reality, and put them together and it all works—it just comes together as a picture. That's when I fell in love." Although he had never paid any attention to broadcast journalism, he proceeded to absorb Marshall McLuhan's theories on electronic media, to watch all the TV news he could, and to mull over ways of making his assignments come out better. At that time, reporters at KTRK didn't actually appear on screen; instead, they would find out what happened, go shoot film and do any necessary interviews, develop and edit the footage, and then write up the story for the anchor to read.

126

It was a simple, straightforward approach; it was also boring, which was part of the reason that KTRK was the distant third-place shop in town. After watching network reporters deliver their own stories, complete with closing stand-up, Kershaw realized that including similar reports in the evening newscast at KTRK would improve the program both journalistically and in terms of pacing. On weekends he practiced this new approach by choosing a story, doing the research and the interviews, shooting it, and then standing in front of the camera and delivering a final comment.

Then KTRK hired McHugh and Hoffman to help the station improve its ratings, and soon news director Walt Hawber, a former newspaperman from Albany, was telling all his reporters to step in front of the camera. "Reporter involvement," a favorite theme of most news consultants, became the new buzzword in the KTRK studio. In the classic example, reporters were told that if they were sent to cover a fire, they should not stop with the standard five W's—who, what, when, where, why—but should come up with footage of themselves holding a charred doll or a blackened photo album. Kershaw was infuriated by such advice, considering it a travesty of McLuhan's insights into the nature of television. "McLuhan meant that the medium itself is involving," Kershaw said, "but the consultants thought 'involvement' was if you were going out and doing a story, you needed [someone] telling you how it smelled, how it felt to be there." He was hardly alone; Dan Lovett, the KTRK sportscaster, regarded the consultants as parasites who were reducing newscasts to the level of fast food. After every six o'clock newscast, Lovett said, the reporters and anchors would have to meet for a critique of what they'd just done, a process which Lovett managed to get through only by sitting with a notepad and writing down the call letters of all the places he'd rather be.

Afterward, Kershaw, Lovett, and a few other newsroom buddies would go out for a drink and a gripe session. Caustic and sarcastic, Kershaw tended to form close friendships with a small number of people, usually men. Most of the time, he would simply ignore the others in the newsroom; occasionally, he would taunt them. "There was always a little devil in him," said Ed Kilgore, then a sports reporter at KTRK. According to Kilgore, one of Kershaw's favorite amusements when out in the field was to lead the assistant news director in circles over the two-way radio. Kershaw would call in and say he was headed back to the station. When the assistant news director, obviously planning to assign Kershaw to another story, would ask him his location, he would not answer but instead would ask where the other man wanted him to be. When the assistant news director eventually gave up and revealed where he wanted Kershaw to go, Kershaw would say he wasn't going that way and hang up.

Despite Kershaw's and Lovett's reluctance to admit it, McHugh and Hoffman did seem to be on to something. Viewers *were* choosing news programs on the basis of personalities, and one of the most obvious beneficiaries was Kershaw's own girlfriend, Jessica Savitch. "She was one of the first people to figure out what worked on television and to put it into practice," said Ray Miller, then news director at KPRC, the NBC affiliate that Savitch helped to knock back into second place. "She had a real knack for the personal approach, for making herself the center of the story. She understood TV news for what it is—show business. She didn't worry about what journalists with a capital 'J' worry about—she was concerned with putting on a show."

Savitch and Kershaw were first drawn to each other because of their consuming interest in everything to do with the medium in which they both worked. "We were both in love with television and with rock 'n' roll," said Kershaw, now news director at WBBM, CBS's O&O in Chicago. "But mostly and endlessly television—how you do stories." They were consumed by the business, not only at work, when they were doing it, but also away from work, when they were talking about it. Best of all were the times when they were both assigned to the same story, when they could compete directly and then compare their results.

More often than not, spending an evening together would mean sitting in front of the TV, watching every news show and hashing out not only how every story was covered but how such-and-such a reporter on another network might have covered it. Often Jessica took notes. For these two members of the first generation to grow up on television, Kershaw said, working in it felt like being backstage at the *Howdy Doody Show,* with the important difference that they were actually

The Savitch family at home in Kennett Square, Pennsylvania, in 1951. From left: David, Jessica, Stephanie, Florence. With her blond curls and blue eyes, Jessica looked "just like a little Shirley Temple doll," according to one family friend.

Jessica (right), age six, and Stephanie, age four, in December 1953. Their parents used this photograph on a holiday greeting card.

The Savitch girls head off to Sabbath services with neighborhood children, November 1956. Clockwise from upper right: Jessica, Stephanie, Kerry Haber, and Jeffrey Haber.

RUSTY NICOLL WILSON

Savitch in 1963, at age sixteen, wearing thick pancake makeup to conceal teenage acne. Three years earlier, her family had moved to the Jersey shore, where her widowed mother found a job as a nurse.

A Midsummer Night's Dream, Atlantic City High School, senior class play, 1964. Although Savitch's performance as Titania was well received, she had her heart set on a future in broadcasting and spurned any suggestions that she consider the stage.

Jessica Savitch, Atlantic City High School Yearbook, 1964. That summer an enthralled Savitch watched the national television networks at work in Atlantic City covering the Democratic National Convention.

Radio station WOND-AM. Savitch worked there after school and on weekends, riding her bicycle to this ramshackle structure built on stilts in a swampy area on the outskirts of Atlantic City.

TWO PHOTOS COURTESY OF JOHN CLEMENT

BYRON JENKINS/WOND

E ADAMCZYK EOLIN   JUDITH GIRARD

Savitch wearing a freshman beanie at Ithaca
College in the fall of 1964. A pioneering institution in the new field of "communications," Ithaca first offered courses in
television in 1946, and in the 1950s heard
guest lectures from such luminaries as the
director of the television series *Superman*.

Savitch in her college dormitory in the fall
of 1964. Her intolerance for students who
weren't as serious about their work as she
was made her an outcast during her college
years.

This photograph was used in Savitch's modeling portfolio. Between her work as a
model and as a disc jockey, Savitch earned
more during her college years than some of
her professors.

Savitch in the Ithaca College yearbook,
1968. "She was so intense, she made us feel
like we were dipshits if we were off having
a beer on Saturday nights," said one former
classmate.

ANN ROGERS

ITHACA COLLEGE

OPPOSITE: The broadcast studio of the Ithaca College television station on election night, November 3, 1964. From right: Savitch, Griffith Harrison, and Don Alhart, who chews on a pipe for Cronkite-like credibility.

Savitch, then a freshman at Ithaca, interviewing Paul Stookey of the folk-singing group Peter, Paul, and Mary, at Cornell University in the fall of 1964. Still smarting because only men were assigned on-air DJ shifts on the college's AM radio station, Savitch hoped that this exclusive interview would win her entry.

Savitch as seen in advertisements for a local Dodge dealership in Rochester, New York, in 1965. Commuting the ninety miles between Ithaca and Rochester several times a week, Savitch kept such a hectic pace that she was hospitalized for exhaustion.

BELOW: Savitch was a Top 40 disc jockey at WBBF-AM in Rochester from 1966 to 1968. Savitch, who spun platters on Saturday afternoons, was called the "Honeybee." Her shift was part of the station's "Million Dollar Weekends," during which every other record played had sold more than one million copies.

"JESSICA"

WBBF-AM, WBBF-FM 850 MIDTOWN TOWER, ROCHESTER, N.Y. 14604 TELEPHONE: HAMILTON 6-8920

JESSICA

Railroad tracks on Mykawa Road, Houston, Texas, in 1971. Savitch and KHOU camera operator Ron Cutchall stand at the scene of the disastrous fire that was Savitch's first major story for KHOU.

The broadcast studio at KHOU on a typical Sunday in 1972. From left: producer Bruce Halford, Savitch, and sportscaster Ted Groves. When Savitch became the first female anchor in a major market in the South, one newspaper called her an "anchorone."

The *Eyewitness News* team, KYW-TV, Philadelphia, early 1975. From left: Al Meltzer, sports; Mort Crim, anchor; Vince Leonard, anchor; Savitch, anchor; Bill Kuster, weather. Her rapid success at KYW-TV brought Savitch to the attention of the networks.

Savitch as seen from the KYW-TV control room in early 1975. Located in the fourth-largest broadcast market in the nation, KYW-TV was NBC's largest affiliate station.

Savitch editing news film at KYW-TV. Tied by an iron-clad five-year contract, Savitch was furious that she could not accept the offers of other, more prestigious jobs that were already coming her way.

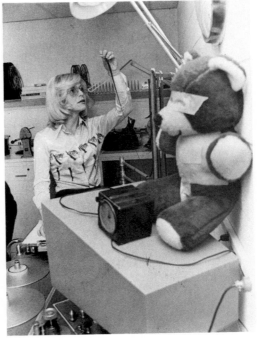

PHILADELPHIA MAGAZINE/NEIL BENSON

PHILADELPHIA MAGAZINE

Cover of *Philadelphia Magazine,* March 1975, with Crim, Savitch, and Leonard. The article on KYW-TV chronicles the stunning success and subsequent disillusionment of the *Eyewitness News* team.

Savitch and fan Ed Gebhart, who presented her with a handmade wooden box personalized with her initials. Savitch's frequent mentions in *Philadelphia Magazine* gave a big boost to her career.

The home of Martin Rand, a professor at Ithaca College, and his wife, Jo, in Geneva, New York, in 1975. The Rands' house, located midway between Ithaca and Rochester, was an important refuge for Savitch during her college years. From right: Jo Rand, Savitch, and Ron Kershaw. Savitch met Kershaw in Houston and began an affair with him that lasted nearly the rest of her life.

MARTIN RAND

TWO PHOTOS:
MARY PANGALOS MANILLA

Savitch and her first husband, advertising executive Mel Korn, at his apartment in Philadelphia in December 1979. Although they were married two weeks later, Savitch and Korn continued to maintain separate residences in separate cities.

Savitch and Mel Korn at their wedding, a lavish Jewish ceremony held at the Plaza Hotel in New York on January 6, 1980. Ten months later, Korn filed for divorce.

Savitch and her former newsroom colleagues from Philadelphia at the wedding. From left: Al Meltzer, Vince Leonard, Savitch, and Mort Crim.

MORT CRIM

NBC Senate correspondent Jessica Savitch on Capitol Hill in the late 1970s. Savitch's assignment to the Senate, one of the most visible and difficult beats in the business, proved her undoing.

The old Senate radio and television press gallery in 1978. From left: NBC news artist Betty Wells, Savitch, and Freda Reiter, ABC news artist. Because cameras were not allowed into the Senate chamber at the time, sketch artists provided the visuals for television news coverage of activity on the Senate floor.

Savitch's second husband, Dr. Donald Payne. They were married in Washington, D.C., three weeks after Savitch's divorce from Mel Korn became final. Shortly afterward, Savitch had a miscarriage, and four months later Payne hung himself with the leash of her dog.

Dick Wald, president of NBC News 1973–1977. Head of the news division when Savitch was hired, he was let go a month after her arrival. During Savitch's six years at NBC she worked under four news presidents, a rapid turnover that caused disarray within the division and left Savitch increasingly on the margin.

Les Crystal, president of NBC News 1977–1979. Executive producer of *NBC Nightly News* at the time Wald was let go, Crystal reluctantly became news president. Two years later, he was dismissed for not being tough enough.

Bill Small, president of NBC News 1979–1982. Passed over for the presidency of CBS News, Small brought to NBC the hard-driving, competitive spirit that made him a legend in the industry. Resentful of what they perceived as attempts to "CBS-ify" them, most NBC veterans disliked him from the day he arrived at 30 Rock.

Reuven Frank, twice president of NBC News (1968–1973, 1982–1984). Widely considered to be the man who invented modern television news, Frank was not a fan of Savitch. "I wouldn't have trusted her to cover a fire," he said some years later.

Fred Silverman, NBC president 1978–1981. Dubbed "the Man with the Golden Gut" because of his seemingly infallible instinct for selecting hit television shows, Silverman brought first CBS, then ABC to the number one spot. During his tenure at NBC, however, the peacock plummeted to a dismal third—and near ruin.

Savitch at the NBC anchor desk, November 20, 1978. After a year at the network, Savitch was more popular than ever with the public—but not with her network coworkers.

Members of the NBC news team at the 1980 Republican National Convention, Cobo Hall, Detroit, Michigan. From right: Tom Pettit, Garrick Utley, Tom Brokaw, and Chris Wallace, all serving as floor reporters, and podium correspondent Savitch. Despite her rigorous preparations for the event, her performance got negative reviews from many of her colleagues.

MICHAEL LUTCH/WGBH

Jessica Savitch, host, and David Fanning, executive producer of the PBS documentary series *Frontline,* shortly before the show made its premiere on January 17, 1983. Savitch hoped that *Frontline* would supply the credibility she lacked within the industry.

In 1979, Ron Kershaw came to New York to work as director of news operations at WNBC. He brought the news broadcasts at the NBC-owned station, also in 30 Rock, from third place to first place in record time.

JODY CARAVAGLIA

In 1979, eleven years after she graduated, Savitch received an honorary doctorate from Ithaca College, the same school that would not give her a regular shift as a disc jockey on AM radio. In 1980, she was appointed to the college's board of trustees.

Savitch and CBS correspondent Ed Bradley at the estate of Sam and Rita Rappaport in Gladwyne, Pennsylvania, in 1982. Savitch dated Bradley in the early 1970s, when she was an administrative assistant at WCBS Radio, and remained a close friend.

Kentucky Derby, May 1, 1982. From left: Sam Rappaport, Savitch, unidentified figure, Walter Cronkite, Kentucky Governor Martha Layne Collins. Savitch, who had been personally invited by Governor Collins, asked Rappaport, a close friend from her days in Philadelphia, to accompany her.

RITA RAPPAPORT

Savitch and model Cheryl Tiegs at Xenon, a fashionable Manhattan nightclub, during a party held on September 20, 1982, to celebrate the publication of Savitch's book, *Anchorwoman*.

Savitch and her mother, Florence, October 3, 1982, waiting for guests to arrive at a second party for *Anchorwoman* held at the Rappaports' estate in Gladwyne, Pennsylvania.

Martin Fischbein, December 1982. A successful newspaper executive, Fischbein tried for over a year to meet Savitch. Finally, in September 1983, a mutual friend introduced them. A little over a month later, Savitch and Fischbein were dead.

New Hope, Pennsylvania, October 1983. In the foreground is the canal in which Savitch and Fischbein drowned; on the left is the leaf-covered driveway that Fischbein mistook for an exit from the restaurant parking lot, which is in the rear. In the far distance is the restaurant, Chez Odette, where Fischbein and Savitch ate dinner.

TWO PHOTOS: LEIF SKOOGFORS/WOODFIN CAMP

The blue Oldsmobile station wagon in which Savitch and Fischbein died.

People magazine, November 7, 1983. According to Ron Kershaw, the man with whom Savitch was involved for most of her adult life, a cover-story obituary was exactly what she would have wanted. "I was so proud of her," he said later. "She'd made it."

being paid. Where they differed, he said, was that although they both desired to be good at their work, Savitch was far more ambitious and wanted her success to be on the largest possible scale. It was a difference that was eventually to drive a deep and painful wedge between them, separating them emotionally and geographically.

"Jessica was nothing more and nothing less than the bright, pretty little girl who just wanted to do well and wanted people to be proud of her," Kershaw said. "That's all. But then she hit some twists and turns that denied her that secondary reinforcement—'Oh, you're such a good girl'—and it really twisted her life." Over and over, he said, she told him about the death of her father, her failure to obtain an AM-radio shift at Ithaca College, her inability to land a job as Ed Joyce's desk assistant. And as she talked, he saw someone who could not suffer rejection and was forever insecure.

Kershaw, born at the time of World War II, was one of five kids raised in a poor household in Asheville, North Carolina. He had been born out of wedlock, a fact which was for many years hidden from him. Nonetheless, the silence of the adults in his life did not protect him from discerning that something was dreadfully wrong. In response, he developed a hard, protective shell to keep the world at a distance. Although he had been married and had two children, he had never really let anyone inside until he met someone else who had dealt with a childhood trauma by hiding behind a shell—Jessica Savitch.

"We were kids with each other," Kershaw said. "[Together] we had our missing childhood. We were buddies, we were lovers, we were friends. But more than anything else, [we had] the closeness of being brother and sister." Like kids, they gave each other nicknames: She was the Brat, and he was Rabbit, because of the space between his front teeth that he later had capped. Sometimes she teased him about being gruff and said he was acting like a peasant prince; other times she said he was a real Leo, always nursing a thorn in his paw. Occasionally she took him hunting for four-leaf clovers, once a favorite pastime with her father. Savitch's sharp memory of what it felt like to be a child stood her in good stead with Kershaw's own children, a boy and a girl who lived most of the time with their mother. When they visited him, the children found a strange woman in the house, an inevitably uneasy situation that Savitch cheerfully defused. As she had with the children of the Rands and the Schwings in her college days, Savitch bought them candy and told them stories. Soon, Kershaw thought, they were coming more to see her than him.

Although Savitch and Kershaw both treasured the intimacy neither had ever experienced before, they also found being so open and, in turn, so vulnerable to another human being to be profoundly threatening. "We did hateful things to each other," Kershaw said. "We repelled each other out of self-protection. You don't want somebody that close to you, really knowing you." Savitch was a manager, he said, a list maker who liked to keep her professional life, her public life, and her personal life all in separate little compartments; when she became involved with someone who was part of all three categories, her carefully developed system for keeping her life under control was thrown into terrifying chaos. There were fights, ugly screaming affairs that sometimes turned violent. "We knew where the buttons were to drive each other crazy, and it would escalate," Kershaw said. "I think the first time we had a physical fight was . . . [in order] to create such a bad situation that we could not recover from it." More than once, Dick John said, he had to help Savitch get medical treatment after a scrap, and KHOU staff members whispered to each other that the sunglasses and neck scarves Savitch favored sometimes covered up bruises.

Although he was employed by the competition, Kershaw gave Savitch pointers and sometimes spent all day Saturday at KHOU, helping her prepare for her anchor spot that evening. "It's a simple business when you break it down into the fine points of what works and what doesn't," Kershaw said. He emphasized the value of a well-paced report and the need to see each story as a microcosm of reality. Another lesson was that when Savitch sat at the anchor desk, all viewers saw was her face. Kershaw told her that all primates, from chimpanzees to Hollywood starlets, signal both vulnerability and friendship by showing their teeth, and Savitch should do the same.

Savitch valued Kershaw's advice and always considered him her most important teacher, but much of what she did was intuitive. She took the three basic rules of journalism—get the story, get the story, and get the story—and added a fourth: Put

130

yourself smack dab in the front. "She was an elbow-oriented street reporter," said Fred Hofheinz, whose first, unsuccessful campaign for mayor of Houston she covered in 1971. "Nobody ever got ahead of her for the first question." The next year, she covered another political campaign that included a whistle-stop tour around the state by train. According to Dave Glodt, who was reporting on the campaign for KTRK, Savitch's determination to be first on every story was the talk of the press car. Once when the train was just pulling into a station where a crowd awaited the candidate, Savitch, intent on being in position to pop the first question, jumped off the still-moving train, ripping her pants and rolling into several bystanders in the process. "You would consider it normally aggressive in a woman now," said Glodt, currently ABC bureau chief in Los Angeles, "but then it was still a little unusual."

She didn't always use her elbows. When she was sent to cover an exhibit of World War II bombers and fighter planes, she wore red hotpants and did her closing stand-up posing like a pinup out on the end of a wing. "After the six o'clock news the switchboard lit up like a Christmas tree," said cameraman Wally Athey. "Everybody wanted to know if that report was going to be rebroadcast at ten." On another occasion, when Savitch was over in Abilene covering the bribery conviction of Gus Mutscher, former Speaker of the Texas House, and a deputy sheriff shoved her camera operator, she hit the law official with her microphone and was promptly (albeit briefly) detained. Although KHOU ended up with only abbreviated coverage of Mutscher, the behavior of its correspondent was written up in all the local papers and a photo went out over the AP wire.

Savitch made her biggest splash the following summer, when covering a plane hijacking by two Cuban political dissidents. On Monday, July 10, 1972, they had commandeered a National Airlines jet en route from Washington to New York and demanded that it fly them, a large sum of money, and two parachutes to Cuba. After a twenty-one-hour ordeal that included several interim stops, the plane finally landed early the next morning, in the rain, at a small private airfield on the outskirts of Lake Jackson, thirty-five miles south of Houston. Soon FBI agents, the police forces of Lake Jackson and the nearby town of Freeport, and local press began to arrive by car, van, and in the case of Jessica Savitch and her photographer, helicopter.

By mid-morning, law enforcement officials had thrown up a roadblock to keep out any further reporters, even though the plane was at the far end of the tarmac, more than a quarter mile away from the press area. Shortly afterward, a battered blue Ford came blasting through the roadblock and made the turnoff toward the hangars where Savitch and the rest of the press were clustered. It was immediately surrounded and forced to stop—"curbed," in local police lingo—by a throng of state troopers and hastily deputized local citizens. KTRK photographer Greg Moore got out on the passenger side and began to protest, but Ron Kershaw sat behind the steering wheel and refused to budge. Grabbing his Bell & Howell Filmo silent camera in his hand, Kershaw kicked furiously as an army reservist tried to pull him out of the car by his feet. Moments later, Kershaw was rolling around in the mud and having a fistfight with a helmeted motorcycle policeman. The uproar was enormous as the press and the cops screamed and shook their fists at each other over the two struggling bodies. Savitch, her red-and-white plaid pants suit splattered with mud, shrieked, "Leave him alone, leave him alone!" After futilely trying to pull the cop away from Kershaw, she finally kicked her boyfriend's assailant several times, hard, with the toe of her shoe.

Savitch, Kershaw, and Moore were all arrested and then released on personal recognizance a few hours later, about the same time the hijackers finally surrendered and freed their last hostages. KHOU, left without a correspondent, had only the briefest coverage of the story. KTRK was luckier; a second photographer filmed the entire altercation, and it was shown on air that night. "There's Jessica Savitch, standing up for the freedom of the press," Kershaw said in a voice-over as Savitch gave it to his opponent in the ribs.

As might be expected, others in the local press corps resented seeing Savitch eclipse the stories she was covering. Once Savitch was late for a press conference at the Texas Medical Center and the head of the hospital refused to go ahead, even though all the other press people were sitting there, notebooks and cameras at the ready. According to Mauri Moore, then a

CBS Radio reporter and now an NBC television producer, when Savitch finally arrived, the hospital head pulled out the chair next to him and she conducted a one-on-one interview. When she was done, everything came to a halt again while she and her crew made their departure. "Only then could the rest of us go ahead and do our stories," Moore said. "The whole thing was not taken well by the crowd there."

Surprising in someone who seemed so driven and competitive, Savitch had a considerable, albeit mostly hidden, sense of humor about her work. "She didn't let many people know it, but she was one of those people who really got the joke of this whole business we're in," said Steve Edwards, host of a daytime talk show at KHOU and now the co-host of *AM Los Angeles*. "There was a part of her that could stand outside and laugh at the whole thing." When Edwards imitated Savitch— declaring through clenched teeth, "Hi! I'm Jessica Savitch and I'm taking over the world!"—the target of his jibe would dissolve in laughter. Once Savitch and Edwards went to the local VA hospital on Veteran's Day on a goodwill tour; expecting a large reception, they found only an empty lobby. "The first guy we visited was completely out of it," Edwards said. "When we walked in, he turned over and his hospital gown fell open to his waist. Jessica froze in the doorway." As they went from room to room and bed to bed, they gradually realized the vets had no idea why they were there. "They didn't have a clue who we were," Edwards said. "Our explanations kept getting longer and longer and we got giddier and giddier. We laughed all the way home."

Less than a year after she had arrived in Houston, Savitch was receiving admiring phone calls and letters from broadcast executives elsewhere. One ardent suitor was Jim Topping, the news director at KDKA, a Pittsburgh station that was part of Westinghouse's Group W chain. Topping had recently embarked on a major talent search. Carrying a suitcase-sized Sony three-quarter-inch videotape machine, he was crisscrossing the country, setting himself up in hotel and motel rooms and recording local news shows off the air. During his sweep through Houston, he taped Savitch and then called and introduced himself. When he returned to Pittsburgh, he told his boss, program manager David Salzman, of his new find, and called Savitch periodically to express his continuing interest.

In the meantime, however, Salzman was transferred to KYW, the Group W station in Philadelphia, which was the fourth-largest market in the country. One of his first tasks was to beef up the talent in his new shop, an NBC affiliate, and he called Jessica Savitch for samples of her work. "As soon as I heard, my heart sank," said Topping, who is now news director at Kershaw's old Houston station, KTRK. "I didn't have a chance because her family was nearby. More important, Philadelphia was the right access for her to New York—and that was Mecca to her."

By the time Savitch's tape arrived in Philadelphia, Salzman was frantic. KYW, long number one in its market, had fallen to a humiliating second place after the ABC affiliate, WPVI, had brought in Frank Magid's troops to spark up its news team. In addition, KYW had just moved to new offices and nothing was unpacked, there was no news director, and the entire technical staff was out on strike. Ordinarily Salzman, now a group president at Lorimar Studios, would send a tape down to master control and it would be shown on closed circuit back in his office; because of the strike, however, he had to be his own crew. Accordingly, late one Saturday night, he went down to a control booth and put the tape up on the videotape machine himself. Within ten seconds he forgot all about the pickets that were marching around outside the building. "I saw this great-looking face and these eyes that were like beams reaching out and pulling me to the set," he said. "Then I listened to her voice and heard an intelligence that really set her apart." The next Monday, Salzman called Savitch and asked her to come to Philadelphia.

When she arrived there was a charity luncheon at the Belle-vue-Stratford Hotel that featured Group W radio correspondents from all over the world. To Salzman, who took Savitch around the room and introduced her to all these industry legends, she seemed like an excited schoolkid. "I can't believe it," she kept exclaiming. "What a great network! I'd love to work here." For the other broadcast veterans in the ballroom, however, the most interesting guest was Savitch, who was dressed in an olive ultrasuede suit that complemented her hair. The room buzzed with speculation about whether Salzman would succeed in hiring her. "The negotiations were under way and the schmooze was on," said Sid Davis, then chief of the Westinghouse news bureau in Washington and later Savitch's NBC bureau chief in the nation's capital.

When Salzman and Savitch walked back to the station, he told her that he hoped to work out a long-term contract. "If we play our cards right," he said, "by the end of it you'll be much bigger than any of those guys. They're radio correspondents, but you're a television star." Salzman told her he was thinking about making her an anchor, but didn't make any promises. He didn't have to. Before she left KYW that day, Savitch had signed a five-year deal at $16,000 a year and a $1,000 annual raise.

Savitch and Kershaw had known that sooner or later one or both of them would receive an offer to go elsewhere, and they had promised each other that they would only leave together. When the first real offer, Salzman's call to Savitch, came in, Kershaw said she should turn it down flat because KYW would then come back with a second offer that was better. But Savitch was not willing to wait. "She was too insecure—she never saw that *they* were getting the deal, they weren't doing her any favors," Kershaw said. "She was so eager to get her career moving. She felt like she had no time to waste." According to Kershaw, Savitch agreed to turn KYW down but said she wanted the free trip east to visit her family. When she returned, he said, she denied that she'd signed anything. But little by little, the details started to leak out, and an enormous fight ensued. Savitch protested that she had a verbal commitment that she could leave if things didn't work out, but Kershaw pointed out that she had nothing in writing. "It started an argument that probably lasted the rest of our relationship, the fact that there was a duplicity there that was absolutely demeaning," Kershaw said. "It was almost like dealing with an alcoholic who would deny drinking and slip out and have a drink. She thought I was anti-career—*her* career. But I was very pro her career—I was just anti her demeaning herself."

Although Kershaw insisted that he didn't define success as working in a major market, others thought his furious reaction stemmed at least in part from envy that Savitch had made it big before he had. In any event, their already volatile relationship became still more explosive, even as they were undertaking an ostensibly orderly withdrawal from Houston. Kershaw began exploring the possibility of going to WPVI, the Capital Cities station in Philadelphia. He gave Savitch an engagement ring and a wedding band, although she was never to use the latter. Savitch gave notice to KHOU, and after ten days, Corinthian came up with a counteroffer of $12,000 a year. "I asked them what they had been smoking, and then put the contract in the file without even showing it to her," Dick John said. "Years later I sent it to her and said, 'You may want to frame this sucker as a memento.' " On Savitch's last day at the station, she appeared as a guest on *The Steve Edwards Show* where, à la *This Is Your Life,* the viewers saw baby pictures and high school snapshots of the young star-to-be.

Edwards, his wife, and another couple threw a going-away party for Savitch in the recreation room of an apartment house on the west side of Houston. It was a cold, rainy night, and when Savitch and Kershaw walked in it was clear they had been arguing. Kershaw, looking deeply depressed, proceeded to get drunk and then to stalk out into the night. Savitch, tears streaming down her face, ran out after him. The hosts ran after her. Eventually everyone but Kershaw returned, soaking wet and shivering. "We all thought, Good riddance, let the bum go," Bruce Halford said afterward.

A few days later, Jessica Savitch headed north in her over-loaded little yellow Opal. She wrote in *Anchorwoman* that the trip took five days, two for driving and three for turning around trying to decide whether to go or stay. In the end, she went.

6

*P*hiladelphia, Part I

When Jessica Savitch came to Philadelphia, she thought it would be like coming home. She had grown up only a short distance away and was already familiar with KYW, the NBC station she had watched in Margate. Vince Leonard, the senior anchor, and Bill Kuster, the weatherman, were figures from her childhood. For the first few months, she would be moving into an apartment on School House Lane with Judy Girard, the college friend with whom she had interviewed Peter, Paul, and Mary so many years ago. Then, after Kershaw transferred to the local ABC station, WPVI, he and Savitch would get their own place. She had a rock for her finger and was thinking about setting the day for the wedding. She told friends she was looking forward to having "a nice secure plush job" and "a nice secure husband." For once, she said, Jessica Savitch had her act together.

Savitch's dream faded quickly. Kershaw, who had left his job at KTRK, was unexpectedly turned down by WPVI, which cut off negotiations when management discovered that it would be hiring the boyfriend of a reporter at a rival station. (According to Kershaw, the news director at WPVI was overheard saying he was not about to make it easier for Savitch to stay in Philadelphia.) Kershaw then tried next to sell himself and Savitch to KYW as a package. The station rejected the offer on the grounds of nepotism. Kershaw had decided to move to Philadelphia only because Savitch was there; now he couldn't find work in Philadelphia for the same reason.

Stuck in Houston and out of work, Kershaw was angry, depressed, and broke. He had put his career on the line and was enraged that Savitch, absorbed by her own new job, devoted little time to him in return. When he visited her in Philadelphia, he did not feel comfortable staying at Girard's small apartment; instead, he and Savitch slept in hotels and fought. When he was away from her, in Houston, they fought over the phone. "It was a real *Who's Afraid of Virginia Woolf*-type relationship," said Judy Girard, who was often forced to overhear Savitch's side of the phone wars. "I think they sensed they couldn't live without each other but would kill each other if they ever really stayed together." The battles were as constant and as bitter as Savitch's quarrels with Tony Busch in college, except that Kershaw was so furious and bitter that Savitch thought he was turning into some kind of monster. "I am slowly but surely going crazy and screwing up my job," she wrote the Rands. "Arguing with him and trying to work out alternatives when we know there really isn't one takes every moment."

On top of the tumult in her personal life, her early days at work were not promising. Her first morning at KYW, she went out in a downpour and was unable to turn up a single story. Her eventual debut on the Philadelphia air was a brief feature about recycling garbage at an outlying pig farm. Although Savitch did not encounter the same open hostility toward women she had faced in Houston, her co-workers dismissed her as "the new girl from Houston," a country cousin who had stumbled into the fourth-largest market in the nation with an on-air style developed in the fifteenth largest. The slight twang she had picked up in the Lone Star State rang unpleasantly in ears at Channel 3. Worse, she arrived with cowboy boots and a bouffant Barbie-like hairstyle that was, in Philadelphia terms, the essence of Totally Wrong. As a reporter and weekend anchor, she was rattled, nervous, and, by big-city standards, unprofessional. "It just wasn't the Philadelphia look or the Philadelphia sound," said Robin Mackintosh, another

138

recent recruit to KYW. "We all looked at each other and shrugged our shoulders and said, '*This* is the new anchor?' "

Fortunately, help was nearby, in the unlikely form of an assignment editor named Dave Neal. A plain-spoken man with a thick Philadelphia accent, Neal had a remarkable knack for tapping into areas of public concern just before the public sensed its concern. Although he was KYW's resident idea man, he preferred to refer to himself by the self-deprecating sobriquet of "Mr. Schtick." Neal was born with the name Dave Gomberg and grew up to be a shoe salesman and sign painter. In the early 1960s, when he was thirty-five, he broke into radio at a station owned by the city of Camden when he purchased an hour of airtime and played Jewish comedy records under the stage name Neal. Five years later he became a freelance reporter for KYW Radio and he moved to television as an assignment editor shortly after Savitch arrived. There Neal's ingenuity knew no bounds. When one-dollar movie theaters were big in town, he developed a special review feature called "Dollar Groovies." Neal's proposal that the station do a story on street food led to a long-running feature called "The Sidewalk Gourmet"; likewise, his concern for coverage of the energy crisis led to the Energy Warden, who wore a special helmet and provided regular tips on how to reduce the consumption of electricity and heat. Neal even found a city sewer worker, known as Manhole Manville, whose rabid and unerring instincts as a sports fan made him the perfect choice to pick football teams every week on the sports segment, where he gave his choices in rhyme and managed to rack up a 90 percent success rate.

But Neal's biggest schtick was Jessica Savitch. One Sunday night not long after she came to KYW, Savitch had shown up at Neal's desk and said that she'd heard he was a nice guy who would help her. He took one look and decided that Savitch had enormous potential to relate to the people of his city. He arranged for makeup instruction, found a cosmetic dentist to fix a chipped front tooth, and booked an appointment with the top hairstylist in town, Barry Leonard. Only a sliding glass door separated Neal's office from that of Jim Topping, who had come to KYW as news director shortly before Savitch arrived. When Neal heard Savitch shouting at Topping that her salary wasn't enough to support her in Philadelphia, Neal gave her some pointed advice. By the time taxes are taken out, he explained, a fifty or hundred dollar raise is nothing. "And they'll get you," he said. "They'll remember, they'll put you on lousy shifts." A better strategy, he said, was to seem to be on management's side. Rather than pressing for an out-and-out raise, she should point out that voice lessons would help her do a better job on air and then ask that management pay for them. Wagging his finger, he admonished, "Stop thinking like a shiksa—think Jewish."

On Neal's recommendation, Savitch went to Lilyan Wilder, a voice coach in New York City who had already worked with Larry Kane, then the top-rated anchor in Philadelphia. Wilder, who taught at New York's Actors Studio and maintained a private studio on the East Side, counseled clients not just on how they sounded but also on how they looked in front of the camera. In her view, the ideal television persona should appear to be not only a competent and credible authority, but also sympathetic; accordingly, she set about to make the young blond broadcaster into someone viewers would feel they had direct contact with, someone they could rely on and like. She worked with Savitch on her writing, her appearance, and her speech, particularly the faint lisp that still surfaced occasionally when Savitch hit a particularly sibilant phrase. Wilder emphasized that a broadcaster must read even the briefest news story with a sense of concern for its subjects. Every day Savitch performed a series of exercises that included such expected drills as reading aloud as well as lying on her back and attempting to bounce a telephone book by flexing her diaphragm muscles. With Wilder's help, she developed the polish she needed for major-market success; in return, Wilder gained a national reputation as the coach who "made" Jessica Savitch, an accomplishment which eventually brought her a star-studded client list, including George Bush.

A few months later, Robin Mackintosh turned on the weekend news with Jessica Savitch and found himself riveted to the screen. In front of him was a woman with the crispness and authority a good anchor had to have—someone he actually wanted to watch. "When Jessica first arrived in Philadelphia," he said, "her hair and her voice were really just noise, bothersome and distracting. The best anchors have no noise. Once

Jessica got rid of all that, she could build on the core that was left, work on her image and believability."

The work settled into routine. On weekdays, Savitch wrote to the Rands in early 1973, she did reports that were " 'in depth' (as in depth as superficiality can be)" and appeared on the 11:00 news, sitting at a desk marked "New Jersey Bureau" and reading wire copy stories about the Garden State. On the weekends, she simply came in, got made up, assumed the anchor chair at 6:00 and 11:00 P.M., and plowed through what other people had written for her. Indeed, Savitch was startled to realize that once her initial problems had been overcome, the actual work she did at KYW seemed far less demanding than what she had done in Houston. Whereas the non-union operation in Houston had allowed and often required her to produce, shoot, write, report, and edit, the union shop in Philadelphia asked her only to stand up in front of the camera. It was, she thought, mostly Hollywood—and low-grade Hollywood at that, for the stories she was sent to cover were of the most routine sort. Writing to friends in the characteristically elliptical style that often made her letters look like speeches, complete with pauses for added emphasis, she said:

> It has taken me three months to realize that the reason they hired me was not because I am a good journalist (which I believe I am) but because I can "cosmeticize" up the news. The fact that I can walk and chew gum at the same time is an added plus . . . but if I couldn't . . . it wouldn't have mattered. So you see . . . I haven't really come such a long way since I stood on the top of dodge [sic] chargers and spun records at bargain basement openings. . . . The words are different, but it's really the same old song.

Several months after Savitch's entry into Philadelphia, Kershaw found a job a hundred miles away, at WBAL, an NBC affiliate in Baltimore that was owned by the Hearst Corporation. Within a year he was news director at an operation that was, to use the term of art, "in the toilet." Working off camera was something of a lark at first. "I was given the opportunity either to stay a reporter that's always going to be bitching about the management and how stupid they were, or to do the format

141

myself, to be the asshole in charge," he said later. "I did it almost to prove a point, that if you let the inmates take over, they'd do all right."

But as Kershaw quickly learned, the keeper of an asylum has to be on call twenty-four hours a day. "For the first time I was faced with failure," he said. "I'd never run a shop, and boy, suddenly it dawned on me—we're number three, and all these people are depending on me, and I don't know what the fuck I'm doing." The job was maddening, exhausting, never-ending. Savitch would drive down to Baltimore on Friday evening, speeding on the dark roads, and left early Sunday to be back in time for her 6:00 P.M. broadcast. It was a heavy burden on an already hectic life—and now it was Kershaw's turn to have no time. "You can't visit into that kind of environment," Kershaw said. "It's almost like if you're riding a carousel, you can't jump on and off [to greet anyone.]" Preoccupied with the task in front of him, he was barely aware of her presence and unable to relate to her disappointment with KYW. Much of her visit would be spent in the newsroom, impatiently waiting for Kershaw to be finished, an arrangement that did not sit well with either of them; often staffers would hear screaming fights between Savitch and Kershaw in the latter's office.

Although Kershaw and Savitch still considered themselves engaged, her trips to Baltimore seemed to produce only disappointment, frustration, explosive arguments, and, sometimes, physical violence. When Savitch returned to Philadelphia, she was despondent. Sometimes co-workers saw black-and-blue marks on her body, and they suspected that the sunglasses she wore at such times covered facial bruises. After one particularly horrific fight, Carol Bell, the wife of KYW station manager Alan Bell and a close friend of Savitch, came over to Savitch's apartment and removed all the letters and photos and gifts she could find that were connected with Kershaw. She told Savitch she could have everything back whenever she asked, but that at the moment it was better for Savitch to have some time off from being around anything to do with Kershaw.

The tears, arguments, fights, and bruises went on and on. When Savitch discovered she was pregnant, she went to New York for an abortion, and Kershaw did not accompany her. She was upset for some time afterward. One morning she told Jim Topping she had to speak with him privately. The rest of the day they sat huddled in a small alcove in a remote corner of the building and Savitch told him of her feelings of distress and sadness about what had seemed the only possible decision.

As in Houston, Savitch soon became noticed within the local broadcast community for her drive and competitiveness. "I would see her out of the corner of my eye [when we were both] on a story, and I had to admire the steel in her," said Kati Marton, at the time an investigative reporter for WCAU, the CBS-owned station in Philadelphia. "I didn't have the blinders on that she had. I could see if a cameraman had a headache or a soundman didn't feel like scaling a rock to get a particular sound. All kinds of stuff got in my way, but I knew nothing would get in her way." Marton and Savitch lived in the same apartment building, and whenever Marton ran into Savitch on the weekend, a time Marton relished, she had the impression that Savitch couldn't wait for Monday to come so she could get back to work.

Although Savitch displayed increasing mastery of the form at KYW, she became ever more sardonic about the work itself. "I'm really getting in the ole newsbusiness-showbusiness gro[o]ve," she wrote in an ironic note to the Rands. "Today I covered a tripple [sic] shooting where a guy shot his wife, her sister and himself. The husband and wife died . . . I got nice close-ups of the blood, the entrance and exit wounds and the screaming kids . . . and then went to the hospital where they took the sister and did 2 standups in front . . . one saying she was in critical . . . the other saying she was dead, in case she died before the six o'clock news. I guess that makes me a dynamite reporter."

Indeed, KYW management did think that Savitch was dynamite, and decided to give her additional exposure by having her concentrate on longer stories that would be divided into segments and featured on the news every night for a week. It was a signal honor, but Savitch didn't see it that way at first. Determined to make her mark by covering hard news, Savitch was horrified when Jim Topping informed her that she would be filming a five-part series on natural childbirth. To Savitch, the story smacked of "women's news"—the fluff beat—which she'd always tried to avoid. Waving her arms in agitation, she did her best to talk Topping out of an assignment she considered degrading. "I'm not even married!" she protested. But Topping, who was taking Lamaze classes with his wife, was adamant. "The subject was flamboyant, it was provocative, and it hadn't been done," he said afterward. "I was struck by the class as an incredible slice of Americana. There were high school dropouts and gas station attendants—it was perfect for television."

A reluctant Savitch and her crew, camera operator Joe Vandergast, sound recordist Paul Dowie, and film editor Allen Kohler, began working on the story of the preparations by typical American couple John and Ellen Condello for the birth of their second child. The first material Savitch came back with looked great, Topping recalled, but there was one problem: Savitch herself was not part of the story. "I suggested to her it was clinically exact, but there was no emotion, no sense of Jessica as the viewer's surrogate." Sent out a second time, the crew came back with film Topping found more engaging. Soon, however, there was a second, more urgent problem. For the first time, KYW had launched a full-scale promotional campaign for one story by one reporter—for weeks Savitch's picture had smiled out from the local edition of *TV Guide*—but the Condello baby was late. In *Anchorwoman,* Savitch recalled that an alarmed Topping suggested that labor be induced, but was dissuaded by Savitch's admonition that the series was about *natural* childbirth. Instead, Savitch wrote, she and crew members compiled a list of every woman in the area expected to deliver within the next forty-eight hours so that a substitute childbirth could be filmed if necessary.

On the evening of November 16, 1973, four days before airtime, Savitch and crew were eating dinner in a Chinese restaurant when a phone call warned them to get to the delivery room fast. Stuffing their food into little take-out cartons, the KYW team raced to Pennsylvania Hospital and threw on their gray-green scrub suits. While the crew filmed the event, Savitch helped John Condello to hold Ellen's hand, swab her forehead, and give her encouraging words. After Sarah Margaret Condello finally entered this world and gave a loud scream by way of greeting, Savitch did a closing stand-up in front of the delivery room in which she looked and sounded as proud—and as exhausted—as if she were a member of the family. "Watching the birth of the Condello baby," she concluded with a

144

triumphant smile, "is one of the most emotionally moving things I've ever experienced."

Three days later, on a Monday, the series was launched on air. The fourth segment was shown on Thursday, which was Thanksgiving. Sarah's birth, now accompanied by the old English folk tune "Greensleeves," was seen across Philadelphia. Because childbirth was then regarded as a medical procedure that required masses of complex equipment, watching it seemed as strange as observing open-heart surgery. Few had ever seen even the most discreet images of someone else giving birth; when KYW brought the scene into the audience's living rooms on a warm holiday evening, it made for powerful television. All three papers gave the series and Jessica Savitch rave reviews. She had been an effective stand-in for the viewer, involved yet collected, alert yet relaxed. "You've made your career," Topping told her.

The next five-part series, entitled "Rape . . . the Ultimate Violation" and made in early 1974, clinched it. This time the subject was as challenging, timely, and little known, but much racier. As with the first series, Savitch's initial reaction to the idea had been a flat *no*. "She was always insecure, always saying, 'I can't do it, this won't work,' " Topping said. "But I just viewed that as Jessica's warming-up exercises." As usual, she threw herself into the project when it began. Although most of the segments consisted of interviews with law enforcement officials, social workers, and anonymous rape victims, the public's attention was caught by the sequences in which Savitch and her crew portrayed the dreadful vulnerability of rape victims. In one segment, Vandergast's camera wandered with agonizing slowness through the scene of a rape, an empty laundry room late at night. As a dryer spun in the background, a voice-over by Savitch described the victim's desperation as she was cornered and attacked in the basement room. Taking the victim's point of view, the camera looked futilely through a half window at the feet of heedless passersby, then scurried around the room looking for a place to hide. The episode that captured the most notice, however, was one in which Savitch, wearing a white trenchcoat, walked down a desolate street in the warehouse district late at night and spoke about her feelings of apprehension. It had been Mr. Schtick's idea: "This wasn't a documentary on public TV," he said. "It was commercial TV, and you only had two or three minutes to create an impression and get people to tune in the next night."

Getting those few minutes on film was, technically, one of the more ambitious projects in KYW's history. Filming at night required renting a Javelin Nightscope lens, an expensive piece of custom military equipment. With it, a camera could be used in pitch darkness—"You could go inside a closet and get a picture," said Joe Vandergast. Police were posted unobtrusively along the route, and the crew set up in a van pulled next to an old building. As Savitch walked down barren, trash-strewn South Street, she carried a concealed, cordless microphone. She could be a relatively free agent, limited only by the need to stay within view, and the camera could create the impression of actually eavesdropping on a lone woman as she crept fearfully through the urban nightmare. "It was like we were stealing an honest moment of her real life," Vandergast said.

The series was successful beyond Topping's wildest hopes. The critics gushed, and more important, people watched. Acceding to requests for rebroadcast, the station showed the series again and then again. It was screened in community groups and state legislatures in Pennsylvania, New Jersey, and Delaware, and was credited with helping to push local and state governments to open rape crisis centers and pass new legislation. And, as in Rochester and Houston, Savitch once more found herself the darling of a city, her name dropped regularly by DJs and gossip columnists. She received the prestigious 1974 Clarion Award from Women in Communications, Inc. Requests to give speeches arrived, and Ida McGuinness, head of the Philadelphia Speaker's Bureau, began booking engagements for her. The first, at a local luncheon, paid a fee of $125, but soon Savitch was the hit of the Philly lecture circuit and was pulling in several times that amount. She was also asked to participate in such civic events as the ribbon cutting at a new branch of Blum's Department Store. When Savitch discovered she had split a seam in her dress, Rita Rappaport, wife of the store owner, offered Savitch the pink ultrasuede Halston suit off her back. The two women became fast friends, and afterward Rita and her husband, Sam, a major commercial real estate owner in Philadelphia, arranged to supply Savitch with fresh outfits every day for her broadcasts.

146

The balloon of Savitch's fame expanded as she became the frequent subject of panegyrics by local print reporters. In an article entitled "Queen of the News Jungle," *Philadelphia* magazine's television critic, Maury Levy, declared that Savitch was "the sex symbol of the '70s." Indeed, Levy concluded after one particularly effusive description of her body parts, "the way it all falls together is enough to knock you over." Her bra size, he breathlessly informed his readers, was 34-A.

Until Savitch's arrival, the first lady of KYW had been Marciarose Shestak. During the sixties and early seventies, Shestak, a slim woman with perfectly coiffed brown hair and a prominent place in the city's Social Register, had served as a gracious hostess on the station's daytime talk shows. Crisp but not overly aggressive, intelligent but not too assertive, she had interviewed book authors, introduced new fashions and furs from exclusive shops, and done special reports on such timeless subjects as an archaeological dig, where she might be seen gingerly holding a just-excavated ancient bowl. She was, Topping said afterward, traditional television: a larger-than-life personality, witty and attractive, who traveled in the best circles and was appropriately attired, appropriately married, and appropriately distant. "Then, suddenly, enter Jessica—tough, earthy, sleeves rolled up," Topping said. "She was equally classy, but she was driven, with the word 'journalist' on her hat." Although in theory there was plenty of room for both women at the station, in fact there was an edgy sense of competition when they were together. "There was elbowing at a subconscious level," Topping said. "It was like two women who arrive at a social event wearing the same dress—it should be all right, but it really isn't."

Shestak's stature diminished visibly under the onslaught of Savitch's sudden popularity. Word began to leak that people turned the sound off so they could watch Savitch without the distraction of the news, and KYW realized it had something more special than it had ever had with Shestak. When viewers formed a Jessica Savitch Fan Club and started sending her embroidered panties in the mail, KYW began to relieve Shestak of her duties. Although no poll ever showed that she had lost any ratings or credibility, her star fell as Savitch's rose. She lost her most popular show. Eventually she left the station, and then television altogether.

By the time Savitch had been at KYW for eighteen months, the station was turning out one series after another. Mort Crim went to Canada and interviewed Vietnam War draft resisters. Reporter Matt Quinn posed as a doctor and showed that a white coat and a phone listing were all it took to dispense narcotic prescriptions. From other correspondents, viewers learned about depression, crib death, and breast cancer. But the series that invariably received the most attention were those done by Savitch, many of which focused on some aspect of contemporary life-styles. In one she looked at the world of singles, sipping a drink at a singles' bar, attending meetings of singles' clubs and a self-awareness seminar, coming home to a lonely studio apartment with a single bed, and concluding the final segment with a wry smile and the observation (borrowed for the occasion from songwriter Kris Kristofferson) that "freedom's just another word for nothin' left to lose." In subsequent series, she covered the marriage mills of Las Vegas, the impact of divorce on American society, and (with Vince Leonard) the complex issue of when life begins and ends. Other reports were more lighthearted. She went to Hollywood to interview Joey Bishop, Peter Boyle, Eddie Fisher, and other Philadelphians who had made it big in show biz. For one series she went skiing at a lodge in Pennsylvania's Pocono Mountains, testing the powder with photographer Vandergast strapped to her skis and shooting up into her face. She had indeed drifted far from hard news, but being famous eased any misgivings.

Over the months, Savitch the reporter, Vandergast the camera operator, Dowie the sound editor, and Kohler the film editor became a team. Because Savitch had learned to work a camera and splice film in Houston, the technical people respected her more than they did most reporters in Philadelphia, who were forbidden by union regulations to touch the equipment and were inclined to be supremely uninterested in it and its servants. When Savitch showed Vandergast a photograph of herself shooting a story with a heavy Auricon Pro 600 camera, he was thrilled by the idea of working with a reporter who could relate to what he was doing and went the extra mile, pulling out additional lights and reflectors and umbrellas just to get the perfect shot. He photographed Savitch with a No. 2 Fog Filter that produced a slight, almost subliminal aura around her blond hair. "The effect was like looking through a shower door that was just slightly steamy," he said. "It was what you would do with Doris Day." During interviews, the filter couldn't be used, because it made a haze around everyone else, too. On those occasions he lighted Savitch from the front, shooting straight into her face as if she were a fashion model, to ensure that the acne scars on her skin threw no shadows and hence could not be seen. In turn, Dowie and Kohler, the other half of the close-knit group, made sure people never heard the lisp. Unlike the daily news, where reporters get only one or two fast cracks at a location shot, Savitch and her crew did scenes over and over; when shooting a staged wedding for a story on divorce, for example, they filmed from a dozen different angles.

Typically, a series began when Topping, Neal, or Savitch came up with an idea for a piece—runaway wives, say. They bounced the notion around, discussing time, budget, and the target audience with Bob Sutton, who in the fall of 1973 replaced David Salzman as program director. The most important decision was how Jessica would play the story. If women were abandoning their responsibilities, should Jessica be angry? If Jessica was sympathetic, would that mean losing the men? Or was it better for her to stand to one side, giving the Sincere Observer Look, hoping that Wiser Counsel Would Prevail? What was the spin? Spin settled upon, Savitch and the producers would research the story, make phone calls, scout locations, line up interviews, maybe crack a couple of books. Filming began. Savitch produced scripts, did interviews, watched Kohler cut them on the board, rewrote the scripts. Slowly, over several weeks, the sequences came together.

They had a good time, the three men watching out for the fragile, talented, nervous woman who stood in front of the camera. She worried them a bit. Ordinary things like balancing a checkbook or fixing a door seemed beyond her; she frequently called up the station and asked for somebody to come over and deal with such matters. Dave Neal had to arrange for the purchase of a new car, a yellow Jensen-Healy, and he usually ended up taking care of it as well. She acted as if moving to an apartment on the fifteenth floor of Hopkinson House, a new high-rise only a few blocks away from the station, were a life-threatening situation. Although she seemed to have little stamina, was frequently sick, and was often doubled over in pain during her monthly periods, she appeared to go out of her way to set up a punishing schedule. She smoked a fair amount of marijuana, but then so did many twenty-six-year-olds in the mid-1970s. There was that boyfriend in Baltimore who hit her, or seemed to—she wouldn't talk about it. On overnight trips, Vandergast and Dowie and Kohler saw her in nighttime Dr. Denton's, skinny as a rail because she never ate, and they would make her drink milkshakes with an egg in them. Coming back from a shoot in a station car, Dowie always drove and Savitch invariably fell asleep with her head on his thigh. "Jessica's pacing herself," the men said fondly. Just as invariably, she woke up with a start only a few blocks from the station. The men were always amazed at her timing.

They kept doing series, and Jessica Savitch kept becoming more popular. Eventually she was too popular, too big, to be limited to periodic reports and weekend news. The station management wanted her on every day, in a prime anchor role. In August 1974 she began co-anchoring the 5:30 news with Mort Crim, and the ratings exploded. After four years of being a reporter and a subsidiary anchor—a member of the chorus, as it were—she had now fully ascended into another realm of stardom in a major, Top 10 market. She loved it.

KYW is part of a chain of five television and eleven radio stations known as Group W, which in turn form part of the Westinghouse Electric Corporation. Group W, which has television stations in Philadelphia, Boston, Baltimore, Pittsburgh, and San Francisco, broadcasts into more than 10 percent of American households, and its radio stations, scattered through seven states, serve more than ten million listeners each week. Because Group W is not a network, it is, in the jargon of the industry, "local"—but it is big, rich, powerful local. Despite its enormous revenues, it has remained, like the smallest of local stations, more supple and in touch with its constituent populations than the networks; similarly, being local, its news divisions have become both increasingly important and ever less committed to the system of beliefs held by the Murrowites at the networks. Indeed, those who ran Group W's flagship station, KYW, during Jessica Savitch's tenure there were, if anything, scornful of that system of beliefs—to them, the M in Murrow stood for My Eyes Glaze Over.

In television terms, Group W has a long and distinguished history. Its Pittsburgh station, KDKA, was the nation's first commercially licensed radio station; its premiere broadcast, made on November 2, 1920, from a tiny, makeshift studio that bore a startling resemblance to an outhouse as it sat on the roof of a Westinghouse factory, was an announcement of Warren Harding's presidential victory. Westinghouse began television operations in 1948 in Boston with WBZ, New England's first television station. The chain grew quickly in both size and assertiveness. For years Westinghouse took it upon itself to advocate the claims of local before the networks and the FCC, even though many local stations opposed the Westinghouse point of view.

KYW occupies a prominent and not always happy place in the history of network-affiliate wars. Granted the country's second commercial television license in 1941 under the call letters WPTZ and purchased by Westinghouse a dozen years later, it was the home of comedian Ernie Kovacs and other early video stars. Later on, *The Mike Douglas Show* was shot at the station and shipped in fat film canisters to hundreds of other stations around the nation. In 1956, WPTZ became the object of an unseemly tug-of-war between NBC and Westinghouse. Hostilities broke out when NBC, which already had O&Os in the nation's top three markets, New York, Chicago, and Los Angeles, decided to acquire a station in the fourth market. Because the three VHF channels allocated by the FCC to Philadelphia were already taken, NBC could only acquire an outlet by inducing someone else to give up a station—which, of course, was tantamount to asking that someone hand over a gold mine. Accordingly, the network informed Westinghouse that unless it agreed to swap WPTZ, its biggest station, for the station then bearing the call letters KYW, a smaller, less profitable NBC-owned station in Cleveland, the network would cut off WPTZ and WBZ, the Group W station in Boston. Loss of affiliate status would force two out of Westinghouse's five stations to become independents, which, in the time before TV had built up a huge bank of reruns, meant condemning them to commercial purgatory, for they would have nothing to broadcast. Westinghouse had no choice but to obey. The nakedness of the deal ruffled sensibilities at the Justice Department's Anti-Trust Division and the FCC, and both waged long and bitter battle against NBC. The fight eventually went to the Supreme Court, which ruled against the network, forcing it to return the Philadelphia station, whose call letters NBC had changed to KYW, to Westinghouse. In 1965, NBC slunk back to its former Cleveland property, and Don McGannon, the president of Westinghouse Broadcasting, was handed the keys to KYW. This success, with its aura of David and Goliath, delighted McGannon, and he resolved to remain ever vigilant against the network giants' attempts to muscle in on local outfits.

Even in an industry with a surprising tolerance for eccentricity, McGannon was an anomaly. A devout Catholic who went to mass every morning and fathered thirteen children, he was, in television terms, a rebel, an idealist, and a visionary. After graduating from Fordham Law School and establishing a private practice in Connecticut, he made a mid-career switch to being an executive at the DuMont Television Network, headquartered in Pittsburgh. In 1955 DuMont folded and McGannon moved to Westinghouse, where he became president and chairman. Like many of his peers in broadcasting, McGannon was brutally competitive, regarding his subordinates as chess pieces to be shifted around from station to station in a ceaseless search for a combination that could generate an extra tenth of a point in ratings. Unlike his peers, however, he was a fanatic about maintaining stringent ethical standards, no matter what the effect on the balance sheet. During his tenure, Westinghouse refused to cram extra commercial moments into popular programs and films; turned down ads for products of dubious value, such as feminine hygiene sprays; and regulated children's advertising long before the FCC came up with official guidelines.

In the late 1960s, when the broadcast industry discovered that reformers actually might be able to induce Congress to ban cigarette advertising, most local station owners were appalled at the prospective loss in revenue. At Westinghouse, however, McGannon seized the high ground and cut all cigarette commercials in 1970, a year before the congressional prohibition went into effect. "He thought the ads should go," said Win Baker, a longtime Westinghouse broadcasting executive. "But he also saw the chance to grab some ink." McGannon emerged as that television rarity, the man of principle, but his stations took a beating, losing up to 15 percent of their annual advertising income a year earlier than was necessary.

A tall, portly man with red Irish cheeks and an angelic face, McGannon was active in the Urban League and in liberal Democratic party circles. At one point, he even considered (but eventually rejected) a run for public office in Connecticut. In 1963, he was one of the prominent businessmen appointed by President John F. Kennedy to monitor elections in South Vietnam; upon his return, he held a staff meeting and spoke of his deep disappointment with the caliber of U.S. press coverage of the event. "Journalists are men and women who haven't really grown up," he declared. "There's a war going on, and they've got to get serious about covering it."

For his entire thirty-year career in broadcasting, McGannon, who died in 1984, was in constant revolt, struggling to pry local broadcasting from what he saw as the strangling and unscrupulous grasp of the networks. He was a singularly canny opponent, and often won. Perhaps his most important victory occurred in 1970, when, to the dismay of less ambitious station owners, he pushed the FCC to rule that during the prime-time period between 7:00 and 11:00 P.M., only three hours can be filled with network programming (with additional time allowed for network-produced news, documentaries, children's shows, and certain sports events). The idealist in McGannon believed that the fourth hour should be filled with worthy programming of local origin in which the many voices of the local community, heretofore denied expression by the malevolent media powers in New York, would at last be represented on the airwaves. And indeed, Group W proceeded, flags waving and trumpet fanfare blowing, to provide such programming. Unfortunately, Group W was, despite its size and power, local. When it suddenly tried to produce hours of extra programming each week, fifty-two weeks a year, the results were woefully executed and miserably received. Within two years, even Group W had to resort to filling the time with syndicated game shows and reruns. Certain high-quality programs for what is called the prime-time access slot or PTA have been developed on both local and network levels; the most well known is CBS's *60 Minutes,* a network news program that found room on the schedule on the most heavily watched night of the week, Sunday, solely because of the new rule and went

153

on to become one of the highest-rated prime-time series on the air. In the great majority of cases, however, programs such as *Wheel of Fortune* with Vanna White, independently produced and then sold by syndicators to local stations for broadcast during the PTA slot, have been the ultimate beneficiaries of McGannon's long-ago hopes for the betterment of local airwaves.

Because of McGannon's interest in locally produced programs, local news became important at the five Group W stations early on. In the early 1960s they were among the first to extend their newscasts to half an hour, and they continued to be a place where innovative techniques made their debut. "Westinghouse understood that if you took news seriously you had a different status than other stations in the market," said Win Baker, who started as KYW program director the day the station returned to Group W hands. "If a station had a consistent emphasis on local news, if it was the place people looked to for information and help, it had a huge advantage." Like the incoming news director at KYW, Al Primo, Baker had ambitious hopes for local news. Because many of what subsequently came to be labeled as the ideas of Baker and Primo were bubbling through the large but diffuse Westinghouse bureaucracy, there is considerable dispute over exactly what they invented and what they took from Westinghouse colleagues, such as Chet Collier, the man who told his newsroom people to smile at each other. Baker and Primo both now claim priority in the invention of the television packaging now known as *Eyewitness News;* what is indisputable, however, is that it first appeared in its full-fledged form at KYW in 1965, and that the changes of which it was a harbinger dominated, indirectly but powerfully, Jessica Savitch's career.

Until 1965, KYW's newcasts at 6:00 P.M. and again at 11:00 P.M. had been anchored by Vince Leonard, a sober, somewhat detached, middle-aged broadcaster of the Walter Cronkite mold. Although the programs included filmed stories from the station's few reporters as well as reports from a weatherman and a sportscaster, they consisted almost entirely of Vince Leonard reading story after story in a calm, steady voice. For most of his tenure, KYW had been number one in the news, but there was close competition from WCAU, a CBS O&O. WCAU's news used an identical format, with the sole difference that its Walter Cronkite, a man named John Facenda, was a warmer, more inviting presence. "They were using the same system, but it worked because Facenda had a personality," Al Primo said later. "Vince Leonard had no personality. He was very straight and businesslike—an off-the-rack newsman." It seemed to Primo that personality would inevitably beat out straight and businesslike, so he resolved to change the situation.

Tall, dark, intense, Primo arrived in Philadelphia with a fast-talking style and a well-tailored wardrobe that intimidated the KYW newsroom. People listened to Primo, but privately thought of him as a sharpie, a slick operator in a five-hundred-dollar suit and pointy shoes. Concluding that "there was no person in America who could out-personality John Facenda if you went personality to personality," Primo instead decided to field a whole lineup of personalities, an approach that Baker had already tried out as news director of WJZ, the Westinghouse station in Baltimore. Rather than focusing on a single figure, the home audience would watch (and root for) a team of reporters, a group of guys and a gal or two who could cover stories and show their warm human hearts, too. They were to serve as surrogates for the viewers, or "eyewitnesses," and their status was to be almost equal to that of the anchor. They would supplement their filmed reports by appearing live in the studio during the broadcast and talking, in a carefully developed off-the-cuff style, to the anchor about the stories they had covered that day.

The first step was to beef up the reporting staff. Primo noted that the union contracts of all newsroom employees, regardless of job title, allowed them to cover stories with no extra compensation. On the spot, he appointed as many as possible to report the news, assigning them as much as possible according to their own experience and interests—that is, setting up a rudimentary beat system. In addition, he hired new reporters, including a promising young fellow from Los Angeles named Tom Snyder who later went on to national stature as host of the *Tomorrow* show at NBC.

Everything worked beautifully. By 1966, less than a year after the introduction of *Eyewitness News,* KYW was securely on top. Soon the *Eyewitness News* format was in place at all five Westinghouse stations. (In 1968, Al Primo went to WABC, ABC's flagship O&O station in New York, and produced what might be called *Eyewitness News, Part II.* In this version, the personalities—anchor Roger Grimsby, weatherman Tex Antoine, and a whole mini-UN of reporters, including Anna Bond, Geraldo Rivera, and Roseanne Scamardella—all but eclipsed the news. But ratings went up, and the *Eyewitness News* format and name became virtually a trademark of ABC affiliates coast to coast.)

But leads in television are evanescent; only a few years after KYW had shaken off the challenge from John Facenda at WCAU, the third station in town, WFIL, Channel 6 on the dial, rose to challenge *Eyewitness News* with an even more radically restructured news format. Owned at the time by Walter Annenberg's Triangle Broadcasting Corporation, WFIL was later to be sold to Capital Cities and to change its call letters to WPVI, its current designation. The home of *American Bandstand,* Channel 6 had a strong identity in Philadelphia, but it had never been more than a distant third in the Philadelphia news game until Triangle's general manager, George Koehler, put the company's local radio station in first place by switching to a Top 40 format that squeezed the news previously covered in ten minutes into three. The rat-a-tat-tat delivery captivated the radio audience, and so Koehler, WFIL general manager Mel Kampmann, and news director Pat Polillo proceeded to devise something similar for television.

They increased the number of stories in each newscast from the usual eight or so to as many as twenty-five. Given that eight of the newscast's thirty minutes were used by commercials and another two or three were required for the opening and close, more than a score of stories had to be covered in nineteen minutes. To accomplish this, Channel 6 created a tight, shotgun format that the station called "Action News." It was strikingly different from the rival *Eyewitness News. Action News,* Channel 6 boasted, was everywhere, and *Action News* was fast. Each show began by mentioning the lead story and the two second leads, and the rest of the newscast was rigorously paced for maximum viewer appeal. Unlike *Eyewitness News,* the anchor, a deep-voiced man named Larry Kane, was never on screen for more than a minute at a time; instead, as many of the stories as possible were film packages, with the name and location of the reporter highlighted to enhance the image of *Action News* as roaming far and wide across the entire Delaware Valley. "The idea was to create the subliminal feeling that these people were giving you *all the news there was*," Koehler said.

To produce that many stories meant fielding far more camera crews than had ever been used before, which was possible only because at non-union Channel 6 employees could be pressed into service in any number of roles. At the end of the program, in a manner reminiscent of the legendary Walter Winchell "racing the red hand around the clock" at the end of his radio news broadcast by reading as many headlines as he could in one minute, the *Action News* anchor devoted the remaining seconds to news items from outlying communities— "the more obscure the better," Koehler said, "so it would seem like we really did cover *everything*." The specially composed *Action News* theme music began, softly at first, as the anchor signed off with a "kicker," a quick humorous story which finished precisely as the music ended, and then—presto!—on into a final commercial.

Koehler and the management at Channel 6 hired the ubiquitous Frank Magid as a consultant. Although they ignored his advice on the name ("Don't use 'Action News' ") and anchor ("Don't use Larry Kane"), they embraced many of Magid's other suggestions with gusto. Magid said, for example, that the scattershot program would hold together only if the anchor always seemed authoritative and in control; he might kid briefly with others on air, but they were never to upstage him. To acquire this patina of competence, the anchor was encouraged to hold in prominent view such staples of the journalistic trade as a pen and sheets of paper. Likewise, directors were given strict instructions to guard against any talent being on air with a hair out of place or a tie even slightly askew. Promotion, too, became more aggressive, stressing the title of the program, the number of stories, and the amount of film shown. In one spot, a truck driver delivered an enormous load of film to Channel 6 and the stockroom clerk complained that it was still not enough for *Action News;* in another, there was so much film for one newscast that Larry Kane was forced to throw away all but one page of his script. In a third spot, Kane and sportscaster Joe Pellegrino were riding in an elevator with an elderly woman whose excitement at the encounter was so unbounded that she was unable to refrain from striking them both with her pocketbook and umbrella.

Action News was a milestone in local news. In April 1971, exactly one year after it went on the air, Channel 6, now operating under the call letters WPVI, surged past KYW. Such success did not pass unnoticed. *Action News* clones began to pop up around the nation, joining the *Eyewitness News* clones already in place. Soon a new standard local market profile emerged: *Action News* and *Eyewitness News* slugging it out in the top two spots, with the market's other stations trailing at a distance, vainly scrambling to come up with a name and a format that could compete with the two giants. Because of the imperatives of speed, *Action News* downplayed the personalities a bit; there was no time for banter. However, despite the endless canisters of film, the stories were of necessity little more than headlines. Skimpy as the actual coverage (not to mention analysis) was in *Eyewitness News,* it was skimpier yet in *Action News.*

Attracted by skillfully produced news presentations, more people than ever watched, and the Roper Organization described television news as outdistancing radio and newspapers as the nation's primary source of information by an ever larger margin. Subsequent research, however, began to challenge this finding and to suggest that TV news viewers were actually learning—and retaining—considerably less than had been assumed. According to *The Main Source,* a study by University of Maryland sociologists John P. Robinson and Mark R. Levy, television news was becoming increasingly irrelevant as a basic source of information; by the mid-1980s, Robinson and Levy reported, the style of presentation was so compressed and frenetic that nightly news viewers understood only a third of what they saw. They were attracted by chatter and whiz-bang editing, and chatter and whiz-bang editing were what they got.

But few people at the time had the luxury of the long view. KYW was stunned by the rise of *Action News.* In 1971, less than six years after Channel 3 had reasserted its ownership of the local airwaves, it was in what Westinghouse viewed as an intolerable position: second. The next year, Group W executives began to plot a comeback. The first step was to bring in a new management team, starting with a twenty-eight-year-old, self-

described "news junkie" named David Salzman who was program manager at KDKA, Group W's station in Pittsburgh. He
had been offered a job at WABC in New York that would
mean more money and a larger market, but he chose Group W
because of McGannon's reputation as a progressive, experi-
mental broadcaster. Even more compelling, at Group W the
news reported to the program director; it was a setup that
Salzman, who had entered the news business at the age of eight
as the one-boy staff of his own neighborhood newspaper, could
not resist.

Within several months, Salzman was joined by a new general manager, Alan Bell, who had wanted to run a station ever
since his parents took him as a small boy to a live broadcast by
his favorite radio star, Gene Autry. "I remember the little door
with a huge knob for the sound effect," he said later. "The
sound man slapped his tummy for the horses' hooves. I ended
up at KYW because of that night. I didn't want to be Gene
Autry, I wanted to be the person who conceived of the whole
thing, the architect of it all." On June 9, 1948, Bell, then a
teenager and fairly dancing with impatience, spent an entire
evening outside a furniture store window in Boston waiting to
see WBZ-TV sign on the air for the first time. After Harvard,
where he worked on the student radio station, and a long apprenticeship at WNEW, a radio station in New York, Bell
finally moved into television, eventually becoming general
manager of WJZ, the Group W station in Baltimore.

Once in place at KYW, Salzman, Bell, and Jim Topping,
who was transferred to KYW in the fall of 1977, had their work
cut out for them. They were keenly aware of the journalistic
and financial potential of an expanded local news. The problem
was finding the time for it. At 6:00, the station had its half-
hour *Eyewitness News,* followed by the network news. After
that, the prime-time access hour from seven to eight was firmly
locked up with crowd-pleasing syndicated fare, including the
hugely popular *What's My Line.* Crossing his fingers, Salzman
scrapped the 5:30 P.M. rerun of *I Dream of Jeannie,* a show about
an astronaut who has a beautiful but madcap genie in a bottle,
thus opening up a "daypart"—that is, a part of the daily schedule—for a half-hour news program. Nobody had ever put
news on so early, for it had always been assumed that the
hausfraus watching only wanted soaps and reruns. Because the

159

new broadcast was to have a separate identity, it was given a new name ("Newswatch 5:30"), a new set (a complicated arrangement of stepped platforms that was instantly dubbed "Starship 5:30"), and a new informal, relaxed pace. Although *Newswatch 5:30* would provide viewers with the traditional fodder of news reports and late-breaking headlines, it would really be about longer feature pieces and live, in-studio interviews by the anchor, Mort Crim, whom KYW imported from Louisville.

Crim had been a top ABC radio correspondent and anchor, working with such later network news heavies as Ted Koppel, Howard Cosell, and Charles Osgood, the man who was to be Jessica Savitch's tutor at WCBS radio. In 1969, Crim decided to make the big switch to television. Huskily built, with light brown hair and blue eyes, Crim was successful from the moment he sat down in front of the camera. Not only did he have the smooth, orotund voice of a preacher's son—his father had been a minister in the Church of God—but he also had a warm, friendly demeanor, qualities that rapidly put *Newswatch 5:30* on the map. (The same qualities made a considerable fortune for Crim when he began privately syndicating *One Moment Please,* a series of ninety-second inspirational messages that were used at hundreds of radio and television stations across the country.) The *hausfraus,* it seemed, wanted something new; they liked watching this comforting version of the real world even more than watching a genie in a bottle.

Pleased, Salzman, Bell, and Topping turned to their next problem: persuading senior anchor Vince Leonard not to quit. Up to this point, Leonard had always rolled with broadcasting's punches; he was a survivor. He had survived his given name of Homer Vesci by changing it to Vince Leonard. He had survived an unpromising start in a minor-league market, Indianapolis, where he was one-third of a news team whose other two parts were a curvaceous "weathergirl" and an announcer who wore a Shell Oil uniform and did commercials. An anchor at KYW since 1958, he had survived two changes of ownership, seven general managers, nine program directors, and ten news directors. He had even survived the Tom Snyder years, when the man many considered the liveliest person on television seemed destined to end up in the top anchor seat at KYW. Electric and unpredictable, Snyder had kept the place hopping.

160

He rode his bicycle around the studio, poured scotch in the office water cooler, and dumped a plate of hot spaghetti on a producer's head; appropriately, the staff dubbed him "Snidely Whiplash," after a character on a children's cartoon show. Once he set reporter Malcolm Poindexter's script on fire when Poindexter was on camera; on another occasion when Poindexter was on air, Snyder, who had just come in from a tennis game, passed his sneaker under Poindexter's nose. But eventually competent, careful, stick-in-the-mud Leonard managed to amend his contract to include what came to be known as "the Tom Snyder clause," a provision guaranteeing that no matter how high Snyder rose, Leonard would rise higher. The implacable strictures of the Snyder clause ultimately sent Snyder packing off to more promising pastures in Los Angeles in 1970.

By 1972, however, Leonard thought he'd met his match. Compared to the machine-gun tempo of Larry Kane, Leonard, with his traditional, Chet Huntley-style, just-the-facts-ma'am delivery, looked like he was standing still, and he was sure he would be given the pink slip. Dreading the idea of being supplanted by some new, young hotshot, he decided to exit on his own and submitted a letter of resignation. As it happened, he could not have been more wrong about what Salzman, Bell, and Topping had in mind for him. In Philadelphia, Leonard was Mr. News; firing him, KYW management thought, would strike viewers as akin to defacing Mt. Rushmore. Across town, executives at WCAU, which was also reeling from the *Action News* onslaught, had canned Leonard's old nemesis, John Facenda, with a singular lack of grace. The audience was outraged at the treatment meted out to an old, familiar face, and WCAU had fallen from a competitive third to that proverbial television purgatory, the toilet. Bell et al. would not repeat that mistake. Eventually they managed to convince Leonard that he was still their first choice. They even gave him a raise, and he stuck his letter in a bottom drawer. The next year, he did end up sharing the 6:00 anchor chair with Mort Crim, a post Snyder had never attained; by then, however, he and Crim had become friends and co-owners of a small airplane. He did not feel threatened by Crim's cordial, conversational style. The combination, with its obvious echo of the *Huntley-Brinkley Report* back in the 1960s, was an immediate success. "Pairing Mort and Vince was like adding one and one and getting more than two," Topping said. "Mort gave Vince permission to come out more, to be more relaxed and smile once in a while."

Step number three involved utilizing Jessica Savitch, the weekend anchor and reporter from Houston who had been spotted by Topping and then snapped up by Salzman. They had wanted to hire some fresh faces to back up Leonard and give the program depth and sparkle, and thought Savitch's tapes were full of potential. When Bell arrived, he, too, became a Savitch fan. "I took one look at Jessica and thought here's my future," Bell said afterward. "It was like going into a dusty warehouse and saying, 'Hey, here's something I can really work with.' She was an enormous opportunity for me—I knew it would never happen again." As it happened, however, the three men, who would play such a role in shaping Savitch's future at KYW, were only recent arrivals themselves. Faced with so many immediate crises—the imminent loss of their main anchor, the murderous competition from WPVI, sagging morale throughout the newsroom—they had little time to work with Savitch. It would remain for Dave Neal to help her learn the ropes.

A similar process took place in Baltimore, where Ron Kershaw underwent what he ever after regarded as a trial by fire. For the first year and a half, he was flailing around, trying to keep the news operation afloat as he got his bearings and the ratings sank like lead. "Even if you're number three or four," he explained later, "there were some people watching you and liking what you were doing. When you change, you rid yourself of those people momentarily, before you attract a new audience." Worried that his program was a disaster, harassed by corporate heads at Hearst who were pressing for results, Kershaw was profoundly out of equilibrium, which contributed to this passionate man's explosive bursts of anger at Savitch. "At the time I always blamed Jessica for my life having changed," he said. "Every time I'd get into management problems, it was always back to *her* original sin." It was, he said, "as if you're driving down the road and someone says, 'Oh, can we stop and take a look at that overpass?' And you do, and then three miles down the road you have a flat tire and you blame it on the person who asked you to stop. Anything that happens in your life

162

comes back to that—if *that* hadn't happened, none of the rest of this would have gone wrong."

Kershaw's first move was to start firing staffers; at the end of the year, there was almost a complete turnover of employees in the newsroom, and considerable bitterness at the heavy-handed manner in which this had been accomplished. His budget was so small he could only afford to hire rookies as replacements, but he had a good eye for raw talent and an even better eye for people who would be loyal to him. Next he brought in a news format to match the broadcast's name, *Action News*. His goal, he said, was to create "a pace so compelling, so fast, that you wouldn't have time to get up and change the channel." The emphasis was on a high story count and perfect pacing, although Kershaw later insisted that this concern with entertainment values did not preclude actual journalism, particularly of the photographic variety, and that stories occasionally did run longer than a minute or two. "The reporters learned how to tell stories with pictures," he said. "It's a cliché that short pieces have to be simplistic. Five seconds of natural sound at the beginning [of a story] can give a lot of texture." As a training exercise, he also devised a magazine show called *People in Action,* a sort of forerunner of *20/20* that featured stories up to seven or eight minutes long. "We didn't treat cameras as simply technical positions but as artistic positions," he said. "This had already been done in print, but not at local television news."

As a boss, Kershaw was a steamroller; he worked relentlessly, and his staff was soon working round the clock with him. Like a charismatic drill sergeant committed to turning the raw recruits under his care into a cadre of professional soldiers, Kershaw was constantly in the trenches with his troops, hectoring, cajoling, praising, storming, and then turning around and doing it all over again the next day. Those he considered to be with him he treated like combat buddies; those he considered not to be with him he sacked on the spot. The breakneck pace and atmosphere of constant crisis encouraged a camaraderie that was heightened by partying and drinking together and, among certain staffers, by gathering in the bathroom over lines of cocaine. It was the 1970s, and few people knew the down side of coke; at that time, the drug seemed like fun stuff, a quick way to put a fine, sharp point on ordinary existence. With Kershaw at the helm, the WBAL news staff gained a reputation among their peers as a fast, loose crowd, working hard and playing even harder afterward, barreling ahead in the contest for market dominance. "We didn't compete with the other stations," Kershaw said. "We competed with each other, internally, which was a little something I'd picked up at *The Washington Post,* [where people] didn't compete with the other paper, they competed for space in their own paper."

As shaped by Kershaw, the WBAL news did not fit any of the image profiles associated with top stations. It was definitely not *Eyewitness News.* Despite the name, it was also unlike the standard version of *Action News* because of its photojournalism, for which it won several awards, and its occasional long reports. It was, Kershaw said proudly, something else—something better. "We didn't have the loyalty, we didn't have the lovble people," Kershaw said. "We won one question, 'If a plane crashed at five-forty-five, which newscast would you watch at six?' That's all you need to win it." In 1975, viewers proved him right; WBAL finally knocked off WJZ, the Group W station that had dominated the market for years, and became number one. Later the veterans of that newsroom went on to major roles, including weatherman Spencer Christian, now at *Good Morning America;* anchor Sue Simmons and reporter Lloyd Kramer, at WNBC in New York, and Josh Howell, at WABC. (According to Kershaw, just as his station was about to start moving up in the ratings, his boss heard that the CBS affiliate in Baltimore was set to hire news consultant Frank Magid and hired him instead. In Kershaw's recollection, Magid did little tinkering with the actual program but was naturally pleased by the audience response, and WBAL, to Kershaw's chagrin, became known in the industry as another Magid success story.)

As Kershaw's efforts finally began to pay off, in late 1974 and 1975, and Savitch was becoming increasingly successful in Philadelphia, there were occasional visits without arguments or fights. When Savitch visited him at the farm he had rented outside Baltimore, they went to the track at Pimlico and to see the trotters in Delaware; in a gesture toward her own past, Savitch liked to bet on horses with Russian names. She took Kershaw to her father's grave and to Kennett Square and to Margate, and she introduced him to her mother and her sisters and her grandparents. On another trip she took him to upstate

New York to meet the Rands. In the winter Savitch and Kershaw went skiing in Colorado with his kids and Dan Lovett, his old co-worker from Houston, as well as Lovett's wife, Livvy. Savitch, a crack downhiller who had learned to ski on weekends in Vermont back when she had worked at WCBS in New York, tried to outdo the men on the slopes and often succeeded. Afterward they would show slides of the trip, complete with a parody voice-over. In the summer Savitch and Kershaw went with the Lovetts to the Poconos 500, an all-day stock car race on a two-mile track, and had a picture of themselves laminated onto buttons which they pinned on their shirts. Kershaw didn't get along with Savitch's cat, Svelte, but both Kershaw and Savitch doted on his enormous male husky, Chewbacca, who was named for the *Star Wars* character but earned his nickname of Chewy by gnawing on whatever he could get into his mouth. Kershaw was a fast-food nut whose favorite treat was Moon Pies, and every time Chewy heard the crinkling of plastic wrappings he would come bounding over for a bite. Occasionally Savitch cooked a real soup-to-nuts dinner which she would top off with Ron's favorite dessert, earthquake cake—a big yellow spongecake, covered with chocolate frosting as soon as it came out of the oven so the center would cave in.

Within his first few weeks at Channel 3, in the fall of 1972, general manager Alan Bell came to several conclusions about his new home: First, Philadelphia was tired of being overshadowed by New York and desperate for its own celebrities; second, because the weather was bad so much of the year, Philadelphians stayed home instead of going out, and hence the easiest way to establish those celebrities was on the screen in people's own living rooms; and third, the currents of cultural change in Philadelphia were flowing in a most propitious direction for KYW in general and Jessica Savitch in particular. A predominantly blue-collar town with a relatively stable population, Philadelphia had long been a sleepy, insular place where residents' first loyalty was to Fishtown or Strawberry Mansion or Chestnut Hill or any one of the dozens of other neighborhoods that crowded together to form the City of Brotherly Love. But at the beginning of the 1970s Philadelphia was finally ready to claim its rightful place as a Big City. Plans for the bicentennial anniversary of the nation's founding were under way, with much of the celebration to take place on Independence Mall, directly across the street from KYW. Historic areas like Society Hill, adjacent to KYW, were being scrubbed and sanded and polished for the upscale baby boomers—that is, nascent yuppies—just beginning to appear on the streets. A handful of adventurous new restaurants opened to serve them, ushering in a culinary renaissance that made Philadelphia a trendsetter for the first time in many decades. Philadelphians, a group that had traditionally resisted change, began to look for it, and Alan Bell was ready to oblige.

As Bell acknowledged, one change that was long overdue had to do with the presence—more accurately, the absence—of women on television. In the early 1970s, the National Organization for Women's Media Project had revived a tactic first used by civil rights groups: challenging FCC license renewals on the grounds of discriminatory coverage, hiring practices, and salaries. By 1973, Philadelphia NOW, an unusually active chapter, was monitoring the local news and meeting with station managers to complain about what they saw—or rather, what they didn't see. "It was just mind-boggling how little women and women's issues were on the air," said Lillian Ciarrochi, an accountant at the Scott Paper Company who served as the project's co-chair. "Women were so unimportant that they barely got mentioned, and when they did it was only as somebody's wife."

KYW adopted NOW's media guidelines for nonsexist language and promoted several women to producers, but Ciarrochi wasn't satisfied. "I told Alan Bell I couldn't relate to watching four men with big shoulders at six and eleven every night," Ciarrochi said afterward. "It was like a locker room. The news would just seem much more real to me if a woman were there." After Savitch was hired, Ciarrochi waged a personal crusade to get her a weekday anchor role. "I just related to the news when she was giving it," Ciarrochi said. Although one of the standard reasons given for not making women—particularly attractive women—anchors was that female viewers would be jealous, Ciarrochi and the other members of NOW did not see Savitch as a threatening siren figure. "Women liked her," Ciarrochi said. "She was really a symbol that women were moving forward." Whenever Savitch covered a NOW story, Ciarrochi, the group's spokeswoman, would tell her she should be an anchor. "Keep saying it," Savitch replied. "Keep saying it."

In 1973, the year Ciarrochi and her sisters began toting up how many seconds the face of a woman occupied the screen and whether reporters described females over the age of eighteen as "girls," Win Baker, newly appointed as president of Group W Television, hired the news consultant firm McHugh and Hoffman. Baker was used to studying the market. Eight years earlier, when he was program manager at KYW, a study of the Philadephia market had pointed out that it was one-third black while the station's on-air staff was white as the driven snow. Baker put black reporter Claude Lewis on camera and hired two more black TV correspondents, including the city's first black woman, Trudy Haynes. But in 1973 Baker did not know what a news consultant was. "I heard everyone talking about them and I figured I'd better find out," he said later. "I wanted to have the same ammunition everyone else had. We were completely unsophisticated and didn't understand why things were changing."

At KYW, McHugh and Hoffman began by cajoling five hundred viewers, selected to represent the market, to answer open-ended questions for up to two hours in their own homes. The numbers were analyzed by a group of social scientists at the University of Chicago who specialized in figuring out why people buy particular brands of cars. Soon afterward, John Bowen, the McHugh and Hoffman vice-president who handled the KYW account, stood before station management and top talent and drew on a blackboard a diagram of society as McHugh and Hoffman saw it. The sketch, based on a standard social-class typology originally devised by Dr. W. Lloyd Warner of the University of Chicago, consisted of a diamond divided by horizontal lines into five sections that were labeled, from top to bottom, UC, UMC, LMC, ULC, and LC. Bowen suggested that KYW should immediately write off the top and bottom—the upper and lower classes—because the rich (2 percent of the audience) paid no attention to TV and the poor (15 percent) didn't have enough cash to be of interest to advertisers. Nor should the station spend much time wooing the upper middle class, professionals who account for 13 percent of the viewers, because they were not steady watchers. Instead, the station should aim for what was known as "the middle majority": the lower middle class (small proprietors and white-collar employees) and upper lower class (assembly-line workers, clerks) which together constituted 70 percent of the audience.

Bowen also reported that viewers thought Jessica Savitch was as knowledgeable and authoritative as Mort Crim and Vince Leonard, and communicated just as strong a sense of interest and concern in viewers' lives. "The conventional wisdom was that only males could be anchors," Bowen said. "One of the most-asked questions we got from general managers back then was whether the public would accept female or black anchors. The study showed that it was no real issue." On the contrary, the numbers showed that Savitch scored as high with men, who saw her as a sex object, as with women, who saw her as a role model. In part as a result of the women's movement, the image of women was changing on the screen as well as off; the traditional notion that a woman was either a desexed paragon of virtue (whether virgin, mother, or, in recent versions, career-oriented professional) or a sultry whore/sexpot was giving way to a newer notion that one and the same woman could be a role model, a sexy object, and a career gal to boot. And according to the research, in Philadelphia, that woman's name was Jessica Savitch. Management, in McHugh and Hoffman's opinion, had almost no choice: Savitch had been at KYW almost a year, and it was time to start thinking not about whether she would become a weekday anchor—as far as the consultants were concerned, that was settled—but when and how.

Although Savitch was already anchoring on weekends, Bell and his staff decided that further grooming and, more important, exposure were necessary before putting her on Monday through Friday. Management was not going to place an unknown quantity (a woman) in such an important spot without carefully preparing the city for such radical change. Things had to move slowly. In addition to her regular reporting responsibilities, Savitch was made a co-anchor of the noon news. The big step in the molding of her career, however, was the childbirth series and the multipart stories that followed, because they lent themselves to much more aggressive promotion than the news. Because nobody can know in advance when, say, the chemical plant will explode, news shows as a rule can only be pushed through what is called "image" advertising, in which the faces and voices of the reporters and anchors are featured—the idea is that viewers should tune in to watch particular people. By contrast, a series can be promoted in a hard-hitting, specific way, almost as if it were an entertainment program: Next Week at 6:00, Jessica Savitch Walks the Streets to Expose Rape. This promotional potential made the series ideal not only to showcase talent but also to maximize audiences for the official standings, which at the time were compiled four times each year by the Arbitron Ratings Company. Accordingly, series were always scheduled for the month the ratings were compiled, with the hardest-hitting productions —that on childbirth, for example—slotted for the most important rating period of the year, November.

In the past, KYW had promoted its occasional special reports with advertisements cobbled together from footage used in the series itself; it seemed foolish to spend money hustling something that was only going to be on the air for a few days or weeks. But here, too, old practices were no longer enough. In Chicago and New York, local TV stations had tried aggressive, expensive ad campaigns for special reports, and had seen the ratings skyrocket. Following suit, KYW promotion director Paul Bissonette hired a production company, complete with director, camera crew, and professional actors, to produce original, thirty-second commercials. Like everything else produced at KYW, the actual series were filmed in 16mm, a small, cheap film stock that produces dull, grainy images; the commercials, however, were done like an ad for Pepsi or Chevrolet, using larger, more expensive 35mm film, the stock used by Hollywood, to enhance the sense of atmosphere and depth. Whereas a series on crib death, say, consisted of long interviews with experts saying that the cause of the problem is unknown, Bissonette's commercials showed a crib in a studio, starkly lighted and ominously empty, which the camera approached with the slow glide familiar from horror movies. "We got a couple calls from people saying, 'You scared the pants off us,' " Bissonette, now the promotion director at WPIX-TV in New York, recalled. "But most stuff goes in one eye and out the other. You have to consider it successful if you get them to stop and concentrate."

If the crib death series had been done by Savitch, Bissonette's spots would never have centered on an empty cradle. Indeed, when she was the correspondent, the promotion often mentioned the subject in passing, the pitch centering instead on the blond, blue-eyed presence of Jessica Savitch. "She was more likely than any other reporter to figure into the promo because she handled herself so well in front of the camera," Bissonette said. "We considered her as much an asset as the subject matter. In some cases the reporter is neutral and the subject the hook, but in a Savitch story we always tried to feature the idea it was *her* report."

In August 1974, after a year of series and accelerating promotion, Jessica Savitch was appointed to co-anchor the 5:30 news. Lillian Ciarrochi spent the day walking on air. Mort Crim was considerably less elated. Solo anchor of the top-rated broadcast, Crim had no interest in sharing the spotlight with anybody, including Savitch. When Alan Bell told him that Savitch would be joining him, Crim did his best to change Bell's mind. When Bell announced the move at a general staff meeting, the general reaction was hardly more enthusiastic. "Everybody walked out muttering and mumbling, 'It'll never work, it's the end of us,' " Dave Neal said. Despite Savitch's demonstrated appeal to viewers, the newsroom still viewed a female co-anchor on a weekday evening as something like an albatross on a ship—an invitation to disaster.

The next day, however, Crim took Savitch to dinner at an exclusive little restaurant in Society Hill and made his peace. "I said I wanted to tell her up front that I wasn't thrilled about her coming on the show," he recalled some years later. "I told her she wasn't needed and the show was doing well without her. But since management had made the decision, I would do everything I could to help. I wouldn't sabotage her, and we'd make it the best five-thirty newscast we could." The following Monday, they went on together, and the show went over like gangbusters.

Within a short time, the new lineup was settled: Savitch and Crim at 5:30; Crim, Leonard, weatherman Bill Kuster, and sports commentator Al Meltzer at 6:00; and the same 6:00 group, minus Crim, at 11:00. Youth, good looks, and warmth combined with reliability, credibility, and competence; emotional power added to unassailable authority—the team was the stuff of news consultants' dreams. "They seemed so compatible

170

and balanced," McHugh and Hoffman consultant John Bowen said. "There was a family feeling, like three siblings with Vince as the oldest one." As Bowen saw it, Leonard represented "the core of authority" and appealed to the 15 percent of the audience that belonged to the upper middle class or was over fifty. Savitch and Crim, on the other hand, attracted the middle majority, the 70 percent of the audience that was from the lower middle and upper lower classes, and those under fifty.

No matter what the subject, Jim Topping made sure any report zeroed in on the local angle from the first sound bite, and, in orthodox *Eyewitness News* fashion, tried always to endear the correspondent to the home folks. If a federal tax increase was in the air, Channel 3 spoke of how big a chunk it would take from the average Philadelphian's weekly paycheck. Gasoline shortages translated into how many minutes people waited in line at a Texaco station on Market Street. Whatever else was going on, a Vietnam debacle or war in the Mideast, a snowstorm would always be the automatic lead item. Country boy Bill Kuster gave the winter weather outlook in terms of how many blankets to put on your bed that night; in the spring he planted a small garden in front of the station and gave regular bulletins on the progress of his cucumbers and tomatoes. Sports commentator "Big Al" Meltzer punctuated the sports report with loud groans when a home team lost. A reporter named Lou Wagner called himself Captain Lou and gave fishing reports wearing a boating hat. Robin Mackintosh donned a Superman suit when he covered efforts to combat inflation. As the pretty but serious-minded younger sister, someone who smiled at others' jokes but never cracked any herself, Savitch was a thoroughly modern young woman who still knew her place. "I'm the co-anchor," she told *Philadelphia* magazine's Maury Levy. "Mort and Vince take the lead. The world isn't ready for anything else. As enlightened as the viewers might be, they're really not ready for a dominant female anchor."

The show also indulged in the occasional madcap antic. One night Mort Crim ended the newscast by snipping off Al Meltzer's wide yellow tie; another evening, when Bill Kuster was snowed in, a "Mystery Weatherman"—Mort Crim wearing a clown mask—popped up on the set and proceeded to fumble his way through a parody forecast. When an orangutan escaped during a *Mike Douglas Show* taping session and wreaked havoc in the newsroom, the *Eyewitness* team pulled together a report which combined film of the orangutan leaping from desk to desk, orangutan jokes ("Is it true the monkey just wanted Jessica Savitch and a fifteen-minute head start?"), and a song called "Apeman."

When Bowen said that viewers responded to WPVI's *Action News* because they wanted to know a little bit about everything—to be able to make an informed response when a topical reference came up—KYW's producers and directors began to change the look of *Eyewitness News*. Rather than increase the number of stories, which would copy *Action News* too closely and cost too much, KYW concentrated on speeding up the pace of the program through faster editing. Reports featured multiple short scenes instead of fewer and longer takes. Instead of coming back to the anchor between each story, producers and directors cut directly from one report to another. The camera shifted back and forth between anchors more frequently. Everything popped a little more quickly, a little more sharply, but the focus was still on the viewers' surrogates: Mort, warm and chatty; Vince, steady and reliable; and Jessica, businesslike but beautiful.

Bissonette, for his part, lost no time coming up with a string of new image spots. Although some local stations were going wild on such promotion—in Chicago, WLS showed a caricatured nurse giving its anchors "compatibility tests" during which they hit each other with pillows—KYW sought to display its team as Just Plain Folks. Ordinary people, they were shown performing such down-home activities as picking out vegetables in the Italian market, rowing leisurely on a lake, and reassuring a little girl who had strayed away from a tour of the news set. Savitch, initially portrayed as a tough reporter because management was concerned about her credibility as a female, had been softened. Promotional advertisements showed her smiling and walking down a crowded street, the only figure in focus. Done with a telephoto lens, such shots provided the soft look the PR business calls "sexy."

Throughout the publicity, as in the broadcasts themselves, the images were tailored to the makeup of the viewers. Such close attention to the class structure of those who were watching him made Vince Leonard unhappy. "I never thought of the audience as separate from me back in Indianapolis," he said. "I

172

just thought about what they would be interested in and what they should hear, not whether different segments could relate to what I was saying." Now, however, the copy Leonard wrote was deliberately rewritten to a lower level. When he felt the changes went too far, he refused to read them. Although Leonard had no objection to research on viewer reaction to the news, he disapproved of what he saw as "wholesale ordering about" by news consultants. "I think the consultants have done more harm than any other single factor in this business," he said recently. "There is something wrong if you need to have . . . [someone] come in not knowing your community and say this worked in Baltimore and Denver, so let's try it here."

Jessica Savitch differed. Constantly trying to improve her performance, she had personally taped and then reviewed her own newscasts long before it was common practice. Whenever a new study of the audience was done, she combed it for useful information about trends, and she probed Bowen for his interpretation and advice. "In the mid-seventies, consultants were considered the boogeymen of the business," Bowen said. "We made most talent very nervous and weren't allowed to talk to them. But Jessica was different. She wanted to understand the viewers, to know everything she could about them and to reach them at their level."

Station manager Bell also considered it a priority to learn all he could about the viewers. "McHugh and Hoffman helped me to see what the audience was responding to," he said. "Then I could play those keys and push those buttons." Every piece of research further corroborated Bell's initial hunch that Savitch was one of the most important buttons he had to push. "When you hear that women viewers are excited to see a woman doing a man's job, you don't have to be a genius to say let's do a series that plays against type, that involves danger and a man's sense of adventure and daring," he recalled. "I said we've got to destroy her and get her dirty—otherwise she'll look like a mandarin princess."

To Bell, the great challenge of television was being able to communicate to a non–print-oriented audience. "I was perverted and ruined by print culture, which has a certain sense of logic, of who, what, where, and when," he said. "TV isn't that. It's not linear. Print culture is sequential, but television is everything all at once." He thought his role at KYW was to eliminate whatever remained of what he called the "elitism" of traditional journalism and to join "the long tradition of simplifiers and popularizers. If I'm *Reader's Digest* rather than Proust, so be it." In Bell's view, television wasn't talking to people for whom wordsmithing was a sport, who went to the right schools. "Ordinary people are not trained for abstraction, and when you talk to them it helps to have color and flash and style," he said, "to have someone like Jessica. She had an intuitive feel for how to focus an audience's attention—she was just naturally good at it."

It was populist news, and the populace ate it up. In November 1974, three months after Jessica Savitch became a weekday anchor, KYW pulled ahead of WPVI. Immediately Bissonette and his assistant, Vince Manzi, filmed a thank-you spot which showed the anchor team going through a gigantic phone book and calling viewers to express KYW's appreciation for making Channel 3 number one. When the voiceover explanation finished, the spot closed with Jessica Savitch's voice saying, "Hello, Mr. Kane." WPVI and *Action News* anchor Larry Kane sputtered, but the press and the public roared with laughter.

Early one Saturday morning that same fall, the *Eyewitness News* team headed off to Baltimore to shoot several commercials. Although the filming was done out of town in order to use a non-union production company, the rest of the arrangements were handled with a generosity unusual for Westinghouse. There were plush limousines, lavish suites at the Cross Keys Inn, and bottles of imported champagne. "We partied in Vince's room because it was the biggest," Bill Kuster said. "Everybody let down their hair." After Savitch retired, Crim, Kuster, and Leonard called her up and sang "Tell Me Why." Later they phoned each other's rooms and gave "the crow call," a loud caw which Kuster had learned as a farmboy and which the team gave each other as they left the station after the late news on Friday nights. Spouses, who had been urged to come, were given orchid corsages and envelopes containing $100 in spending money. Even Ron Kershaw appeared. "It was the first chance we got to see him close up," said Bill Kuster. "He was attentive to Jess, but he was moody. We kept getting inklings she wasn't the master of the relationship, but she seemed happy he was there."

174

Jessica Savitch was riding high. TV critic Maury Levy kept churning out puff pieces about her, and Ida McGuinness was besieged with requests for Savitch to give speeches. When the furnishings department of the local Bloomingdale's decorated rooms to suit the personalities of the city's celebrities, it included a Jessica Savitch room. A Philadelphia band cut a record with a rapturous chorus:

> *The evening lady of the air*
> *Welcomes me in my easy chair,*
> *Sweet eyes that glow and yellow blond hair,*
> *Making the bad news sound good.*
> *I wish you'd come and cover me.*
> *Jessica, I love you so,*
> *I want you, don't you know.*

In the spring of 1975, Savitch received the kind of vindication and recognition most people only dream of. "In a full circle swing of the whole of life," she wrote to the Rands, "Ithaca College, for the tenth time, has asked me to participate in college activities. This time, [communications department chairman] Dr. Keshishoglou has asked me to become a 'visiting professor.' Like Rod Serling, I would give a one week course." Seven years after her graduation, the school that would not let her be a DJ on its own AM radio station was pleading for her to come back in triumph. After a delicious period of deliberation, she accepted and taught a course there that fall and again in 1976 and 1978.

7

*P*hiladelphia, Part II

It has often been observed that Camelot has become one of the great American stories, and Americans indeed seem to call every brief, shining moment when a group of people is newly assembled and triumphant by that name. Thus, inevitably, the ascendance of KYW's *Eyewitness News* is today recalled as "Camelot." And, like its mythical predecessor, Camelot in Philadelphia was not everything it seemed.

Every evening at 5:30, the Knights of the Television Screen gathered around Ye Olde Broadcast Studio and held court before hundreds of thousands of viewers. Although the *Eyewitness* team's actual lead over *Action News* was brief—within less than a year, WPVI was again number one—KYW's gloating promotion always gave the impression that the station was solidly in first place. And even to those who knew the real numbers, Channel 3 remained the class act, the place with newscasters who were honest and reliable and trustworthy.

Most important, KYW had the beauteous young Queen of the Ratings, Jessica Savitch, whose star ascended at dazzling speed. Her name kept popping up in *Philadelphia* magazine, and her photo kept appearing in gossip columns. Clairol reportedly asked if she would be interested in being associated with its products. She turned that offer down, but did agree to play herself—Jessica Savitch, anchor/reporter—in *Nasty Habits,* a farce about nuns starring Glenda Jackson. Awards poured in: a NOW Award for Excellence, a Sales and Marketing Executives of Philadelphia Special Award for Outstanding Achievement, a Philadelphia Press Association Award for Best News Feature.

By now, her series were special events, lavishly produced and plugged relentlessly. One five-part report followed the rock music scene in Philadelphia from the days of Frankie Avalon, Fabian, and *American Bandstand,* in the early 1960s, to "The New Philadelphia Sound," the Philly-style production techniques that were then attracting B. B. King, David Bowie, Dusty Springfield, and other major stars to recording studios in the area. Savitch interviewed fans outside a David Bowie concert, watched Barry Manilow sing his jingles for McDonald's at the Philadelphia Academy of Music, and talked to a salesman in the rock 'n' roll section at Sam Goody's who pointed out that the average record buyer now was no longer a fifteen-year-old nerd, but a thirty-five-year-old with kids and a mortgage.

In another series Savitch informed viewers of ways that rape could be prevented; once again the critics applauded and the public asked for the show to be repeated. A third series, "Lady Law," took on the sticky question of whether women could be effective police officers. After seeing Savitch interview female cops in several cities, viewers watched the blond anchor go through training at the Philadelphia Police Academy. Dressed in blue T-shirt and sweatpants, her hair pulled back by a red kerchief, Savitch shot a pistol, jumped over oil cans, squeezed under a barrier, hopped through a series of tires, and scrambled over a six-foot-tall wooden barrier. For weeks afterward, Savitch complained of sore muscles and a wrenched back, but "Lady Law" eventually brought her the Broadcast Media Conference Award as well as a second award from Women in Communications.

Like all the other Group W stations, KYW created many of its own programs. In addition to the multipart series done for the news, the programming staff produced public-affairs shows and special live coverage. Once the mayor and the leaders of a teachers' strike negotiated live in the studio; on another occasion, KYW engineered an agreement on air for the federal government to make enough natural gas available to reopen schools which had been closed to save fuel. New sets were constantly thrown up, and the art department kept busy painting new backdrops. "It was a very intense, no-nonsense period of time," assistant program manager David Beddow said later. "But you felt like you accomplished something every day. It was sort of the good old days of television."

"Anytime you had a decent program idea, you could waltz into Alan Bell's office," said Jack Fentress, an executive producer who later became program manager. "If he approved, you'd zip up to New York on the Metroliner, and if the powers that be liked it, you'd have a program on the air. I couldn't wait to get up in the morning and go to work, it was so exciting." One Fentress proposal that got the green light was *Meetinghouse,* a one-hour, prime-time live studio show. Every Thursday night at 8:00, co-hosts Jessica Savitch and Matt Quinn, a veteran political reporter, would lead a discussion with a panel of experts on an issue such as gun control or school busing. Savitch and Quinn complemented each other perfectly in orthodox good-cop, bad-cop fashion. "Matt was a cleaned-up Mike Wallace," said Fentress, "and Jessica would come in and grab you by the throat with reasonableness." The program's goal was to get the studio audience involved, and almost every week it succeeded; by the end of the question-and-answer session, audiences often were yelling and shaking their fists.

Savitch inspired in young women at all three stations in Philadelphia the dizzying thought that they, too, might someday rise above their lowly entry positions. For her part, she readily acknowledged the help of Joan Showalter and the NOW chapter in Philadelphia, and she was generous with supportive words and concrete advice for other women as well as birthday presents, get-well calls, and wedding gifts. When fledgling producer Shelley Laurence found herself temporarily without a home, Savitch let her sleep on the couch in her apartment; when Sue Percival, a public-affairs producer, was discouraged and talked about quitting the business altogether, Savitch took her out to lunch and convinced her to hang in there another six months. Although Savitch was also helpful to men who were just getting started at the station, writing them notes for a job well done and encouraging them at tense moments, she went out of her way again and again for the women she saw following in her footsteps.

As is invariably the case in Camelot, however, the court was never as harmonious within as it appeared from without. Although the Knights and their Queen did have a Round Table of sorts—the front room at the nearby Lafayette House, a glorified sandwich shop they called "the French place" and went to for a bite between the 6:00 and 11:00 shows—relationships within the kingdom were in perpetual disarray. "Behind the scenes, it wasn't so golden," said Dave Neal. "My job was to be at the front door every night about five o'clock and stop anyone who was thinking of leaving." The team genuinely liked one another, but the pressures of intimacy were sometimes too much to bear. "They were just like a family," Jim Topping said. "They were fond of each other, but they fought like cats and dogs." Being there, he said, "was a rich experience in sum, but day to day, get me a bottle of aspirin."

The problem, as Topping saw it, was that the local renown had swelled everybody's head. With the exception of Vince Leonard and Bill Kuster, who were content to stay right there, the team members were constantly packing their bags for greener pastures. "As soon as you're successful, people start counting their chips," Topping said. "They liked it and it was working and they didn't want to leave, but they also thought they should use this as a bridge to something more." Mort Crim, who thought he had taken a certain demotion when he left ABC Radio for local television, was champing at the bit to get back to the network level. "Big Al" Meltzer wanted to do play-by-play coverage of football games for KABC, the ABC O&O in Los Angeles. Most eager of all to take her leave was Jessica Savitch. "She was on a fast track," Topping said, "but it still wasn't fast enough. The minute Jessica got made nightly anchor, she was looking for when she could get to New York. Everything was a stepping stone." With Savitch, he said, nothing was ever enough. "There was always a next goal. I liked her, but it was a pain in the ass."

From the talent's point of view, the problem was Westinghouse personnel policies. Although Group W was willing to try out new ideas, its salaries were low and its benefits were even lower. Westinghouse head Don McGannon liked to play musical chairs with his employees, transferring executives from one Group W station to another in an endless search for the perfect combination of talents. Sometimes it worked, but often the switches broke up winning teams and paired incompatibles, and they always created insecurity. "It was a good place to have once worked," said one former Group W employee. "It was great to have on your résumé, but you didn't want to stay there too long." Others felt more negative: "Frankly, Westinghouse would screw up a free lunch," said Bill Kuster, whose anger at the company lasted for years. "They dealt away chip after chip, like a bad poker hand. They screwed up all their TV stations by running them from New York." Group W stations, he said, were run by "a bunch of bookkeepers" who didn't know how to do anything but take orders from Westinghouse headquarters in Manhattan. "I saw little leaks in the great ship from the time Westinghouse showed up in 1965," he said.

In January 1975, while *Eyewitness News* was still in its primacy, Jim Topping left Group W and was replaced by a young man named Joe C. Harris. A wunderkind of twenty-six who had worked for Al Primo at WABC in New York, Harris arrived with a big fanfare in the press. He installed a huge rubber plant in his office, which was squeezed into the corner of the overcrowded first-floor newsroom, and immediately began to bruise egos. Coming upon the heels of the beloved and respected Topping, Harris had a hard job, and he made it harder. His first mistake was to tell a news team that had come in number one in the latest rating book that he wasn't sure if they had gotten there through talent or luck. His second mistake was not, strictly speaking, his fault: Harris gave an official contract to a sports reporter, Rod Luck, who had already started working at the station. When Luck did a feature on belly dancing in which he appeared wearing a turban, pantaloons, and a jewel in his navel, the *Eyewitness* squad went into shock. Then Harris unveiled a plan for a series called "A Day in the Life," in which Mort Crim was to spend a day as a garbage collector, Vince Leonard as a fireman, and Jessica Savitch as a waitress. The team flatly refused the assignment. Soon the rumor swept the station that a person or persons unknown had peed in Harris's rubber plant. On the March cover of *Philadelphia* magazine, Savitch, Crim, and Leonard stared out under the grim headline, "Is This Goodnight for Eyewitness News?"

One of the policies most odious to talent was Group W's insistence on holding its employees to their contracts, a practice that Jessica Savitch found particularly galling. At KYW, as at KHOU, Savitch had continued to pursue CBS. At the end of 1973, when she had just begun doing the multipart series, her tenacity had begun to pay off. "She had been sending us tapes for two years," said Sandy Socolow, a CBS News vice-president at the time. "I knew her from the days she was a secretary —she would send me a Christmas card every year." When Savitch mailed him footage from Philadelphia, he was impressed; the series clinched his interest. CBS interviewed her several times, and Socolow offered her a job as reporter. Savitch happily accepted. Although her written contract bound her to Philadelphia for nearly four more years, she believed that KYW program manager David Salzman had given his verbal agreement to a "network out"—that is, she could leave for a job with a network. But Salzman had left the station in the interim, and when Savitch gave KYW two weeks' notice, she received an injunction and a back-to-work order. Alan Bell, the general manager, told her that he knew nothing about any verbal agreement, and that he was damned if he was going to let Savitch fly the coop after the company had invested so much time and money in her.

At CBS, Socolow was appalled by Westinghouse's reaction. "Her bosses hit the roof," he said. "They sent us a ferocious lawyer's letter accusing us of messing with the contract. *Jesus,* it was a tough letter. [CBS president] Dick Salant was a lawyer, and he paid attention to lawyers' letters. I spent weeks alibi-ing my way out of that one. It was very traumatic."

Savitch was not the only one to have her hopes quashed; Al Meltzer also received court papers enjoining him from going to work elsewhere. But Savitch refused to knuckle under. Early in 1974, she contacted KYW alumnus Al Primo, who had just been made vice-president of news at ABC, and asked for an appointment. Shortly afterward, she was sitting in his large office at ABC headquarters, at 54th Street and Sixth Avenue, and telling him of her ambitions to come to New York. "Her attitude was 'Tell me to start next Tuesday and I'll be here,' " Primo said. Impressed by Savitch's conviction that she was destined for network stardom, he asked about her contract. "She said she could get out of it, but I knew it was a useless conversation from that point on," he said. "I had worked with Westinghouse, and I knew it was not a company to mess around with."

Enraged by Westinghouse's obduracy, Savitch decided to retaliate by staging a one-woman strike. Day after day, she stayed home and called in sick. Her timing was perfect. Bissonette was in the middle of shooting a series of whimsical promotional spots which played with the question, "Will success spoil the *Eyewitness News* team?" The whole group was to be photographed as they frolicked out on Independence Mall. After three days of Savitch no-shows, management cried uncle and gave her a new contract with a hefty raise but the same lengthy term of employment. Savitch returned, but her attitude toward the station had permanently soured.

"Plenty of days she'd be crying, red-eyed, bitching," Dave Neal said. "By then, I was the people guy. I was told to make sure she was on air and looking like a million dollars. What she needed was a pat on the back." Every day, Neal gave it to her. "I'd go pick her up at her apartment at about three. It meant she'd get there on time, and also by the time she arrived, most of the bitching would be over."

Most, but not all. Savitch's once-pleasant relations with a number of producers and directors headed downhill and never went back up. Always a perfectionist on the set, she became a humorless prima donna, frequently lashing out at the hapless crew. Because she perspired heavily under the 25,000-watt studio lights, she insisted on cranking up the air conditioning to such a frigid level that the crew had to huddle in overcoats around their cameras and sound equipment, resentfully warming their hands by the oversize bulbs. ("We used to joke about installing an air conditioner right between her legs," said stage director Wayne Boyer.) After a special thermometer was placed in the studio, Savitch checked it religiously; whenever the temperature crawled above Arctic levels she was on the phone, furiously informing the news director of the crew's incompetence. Even if the room were sufficiently icy, she was likely to complain that the lights weren't right or that the TelePrompTer was passing the copy by at the wrong speed. "She was becoming a major pain in the ass," said Neil Bobrick, then a news producer and director. "The little people like me knew she was trying to get back at management, but she was also getting us. People just didn't want to deal with her."

Another KYW reporter recalled, "I had a reservoir of goodwill for Jessica. When I arrived, 'thank you' was still part of her vocabulary." Once the newscast became successful, however, "Savitch, like everybody else on the news team, started to think her shit didn't stink." Part of the reason, of course, was that, along with Mort Crim, she was flooded with requests to speak at luncheons, dinners, openings, celebrations, and conventions. For delivering a twenty- or thirty-minute speech (one of the three or four she had worked up, prefaced by topical anecdotes) and perhaps answering questions afterward, she received as much as $1,000, plus limousine transportation to and from the event.

Alienated and frustrated, Savitch withdrew from station life and hid from her public. Even though she only lived a few blocks from the station, she traveled back and forth only by car, either with Dave Neal or driving her own little yellow Jensen-Healy. In between visits to Kershaw, she spent weekends with Sam and Rita Rappaport and their two children out on the Main Line, in Haverford. As with the Rands and the Schwings, back at Ithaca College, Savitch had found another surrogate family in which she could feel warm and secure. In Sam Rappaport, a successful real estate speculator who was regularly scolded by *Philadelphia* magazine for having allegedly shady connections, Savitch found a warm, supportive father figure; and Rita, his diminutive, Vienna-born wife, became a sort of older sister/mother. This time, Savitch did not have to babysit to repay her hosts, who seemed more than happy to bask quietly in the reflected glory of having a celebrity for a close friend. They gave Savitch a whole suite of rooms on an upper floor of their 48-room estate, Bally Heather, built around the turn of the century for the daughter of Joseph Newton Pew, founder of the Sun Oil Company, and purchased by the Rappaports in the mid-1970s. The affection the Rappaports felt for Savitch was unconditional; she could come and go as she wished, do as she pleased, and they would still be happy to have her there. Rita was Savitch's same tiny size, and Savitch routinely showed up with no luggage, knowing that she could find whatever she needed in Rita's bountiful closet. Sometimes when Savitch visited she shut herself up in her suite and didn't show up downstairs even for meals, but to the Rappaports such behavior simply meant that she felt at home. Their hospitality extended to Chewy as well, who had the run of the fenced-in portion of the estate during his stays there.

In mid-1975, Joe C. Harris was transferred to Westinghouse headquarters in New York. His replacement as news director at KYW was Ken Tiven, a former reporter at the *Washington Post*. Fascinated by the technical aspects of broadcasting, Tiven had followed the rapid development of newsgathering technology with an eager glee. New vistas were everywhere. When Tiven had entered broadcast journalism, in the late 1960s, videotape was used exclusively for recording in-house programs and almost all news coverage was done on film. Most foreign stories, such as the Vietnam War, could not be covered live because there was no way to get electronic imagery out directly; instead the stories were filmed, sent to the closest major processing center (Tokyo, in the case of Vietnam), developed, and "up-linked"—sent by satellite—to network headquarters in New York. Domestic reports could include live segments, but they were severely circumscribed by the crew's need to be plugged into a powerful source of electric current. Thus, for example, at the 1968 Democratic National Convention in Chicago, the live chunks consisted mainly of goings-on inside the convention hall and other places where cables could be set up beforehand. Viewers saw Mayor Richard Daley give the finger to Senator Abraham Ribicoff on live TV, but footage of demonstrators and police slugging it out in the streets had to be filmed or taped, processed, and edited before each broadcast.

Four years later, when both the Democrats and the Republicans met in Miami Beach, Tiven was assistant news director at WPLG, the local ABC affiliate. For the conventions, as for any major national event, one network provides what is commonly called pool coverage, the basic video and audio, which is designed to reduce the clutter of cameras and needless duplication of effort. Each network is still free to provide its own individual angles or views of an event and to add its own reporting and narration. Thus, for example, in coverage of a presidential news conference, each network broadcasts the same basic podium and cutaway shots from the pool cameras, supplemented by the network's own exclusive angles. In

Miami in 1972, the pool crew had the same creepy-peepies that had been around since the early 1960s; in addition, however, the crew had a helicopter-mounted camera which used a micro-wave to beam footage back to the pool control room and which could provide coverage of any street encounters between the demonstrators in Flamingo Park and the cops in Miami Beach. Meanwhile, Tiven had rented an apartment on the eighth floor of a building just outside the convention center and installed huge picture windows and studio cameras linked by microwave to the WPLG studio. When protestors and police ran along Collins Avenue, WPLG had live overhead shots from both the pool cameras and the station's own crew, and Tiven was elated. "The revolution was under way," he said later. "You could see what was just over the horizon. Now all we needed was better equipment."

In 1974, Tiven got it. By then the news director at WSB, the leading station in Atlanta, he learned that a television engi-neer in Nashville named Ralph Huckaby had come up with the zany idea of bolting a four-foot-wide microwave dish onto a tripod on the roof of a van. Huckaby then wired this ensemble to a brand-new Japanese videocamera, the Ikegami "Handy-Looky," subsequently known as the "Ike" (pronounced "Icky") or by its model number, HL-33. Unlike the creepy-peepie, a videocamera which weighed about 65 pounds and used a battery pack heavy enough to require a small hand-truck, the HL-33, the first camera to use miniaturized circuits, was no bigger than a loaf of bread and used a battery pack the size of an ordinary knapsack. With Huckaby's setup, one could point the HL-33 and beam the resulting footage directly from the dish back to a local station. Live broadcasts could occur anywhere within fifty miles of the station, a radius imposed by the limited power of the microwave transmitters then in use. Instead of cutting off news coverage at three in the afternoon so as to have enough time to get the film back to the station and processed, stories could be reported from the field as the show went on the air. Tiven immediately started lobbying his station manager for $250,000 to buy the new equipment, which he insisted was necessary for the station to retain its lead. As a compelling argument, he pointed out that videotape, which could be used immediately, cost eight dollars for twenty min-utes' worth of reusable tape, whereas film stock, which could be used only once, ran at least $125 for twenty minutes, including the cost of processing.

In mid-1975, soon after the new equipment had arrived in Atlanta, Tiven was off to a new job as news director at KYW. There he found a newsroom demoralized by the Harris fiasco and depressed by the fact that KYW had slipped behind WPVI in the latest ratings. The celebrated anchor team was ready to fly the coop at a moment's notice. When Savitch was introduced to Tiven, the first thing she told him was precisely how much time, down to the minute, was left in her contract, and that she would be leaving immediately afterward.

The KYW newsroom at the time required the political finesse and diplomatic skill of a Cardinal Richelieu; unfortunately, Tiven was a techie with a short fuse. He did what he could to keep Savitch, his flashiest talent, happy; although she made him so uncomfortable he couldn't eat, he took her out to lunch, lent a sympathetic ear to her complaints, and boosted her compensation to $100,000, a sum whose six figures had great symbolic value to Savitch and her agent Don Hamburg. But on the whole, Tiven preferred arranging live feeds to massaging egos. Such a choice did not go over well with many in the newsroom, who remembered with fondness Topping's ability to calm troubled nerves and resolve conflicts. "I always suspect news directors who know model numbers," said Matt Quinn. "Engineers need them, not news directors. What Tiven knew about machinery cost him in terms of what he knew about people." Fits of temper and freak-outs, never rare in a business beset by stress and constant deadlines, became ever more frequent. At one point a sign appeared on the wall that read "There will be no laughing."

"Tiven set the model and others emulated him," said Anne Amico, a stage director and audio engineer. "A few times people even threw typewriters at the wall—I remember the holes they made." As might be expected, Tiven saw the situation differently and placed much of the blame for the discontent within the newsroom on the fact that two-thirds of the major talent were too busy to do their jobs. Every evening, Tiven sat in Alan Bell's office watching Crim and Savitch talk on the set before the show. Over the studio mike, which the anchors did not know was live, Tiven and Bell could hear endless muttered imprecations against KYW and Westinghouse. Savitch and

186

Crim also told each other of their latest job offers, never realizing that one reason for the company's uncanny awareness of their every move was that management knew exactly whom they were talking to.

"They were all very nice people, decent sorts," Tiven said. "They wanted to win and had all the right motivations." But when the chips were down, he said, Crim and Savitch were off giving well-paid speeches. "One day Mort said he'd love to cover a story, but when he looked in his book he was scheduled up for weeks in advance. Finally he found a spare Tuesday and said he'd put me down for a story, as if something would be sure to happen that day."

Morale among the *Eyewitness* teammates sank even lower in mid-1976 when Tiven unveiled a radical new concept: the tri-anchor. Not one, not two, but three people—Savitch, Crim, and Leonard—would anchor the 11:00 news each night. Data from McHugh and Hoffman suggested that the late news needed a younger audience; adding Savitch to the existing Crim-Leonard broadcast was the logical way to do so. Logical, but not terribly sensible. Because each half-hour broadcast contained eight minutes of commercials, eight minutes of weather and sports, and three minutes of opening and closing credits, the anchor was on for only about eleven minutes. Dividing that time among three people, all of whom believed themselves capable of doing the entire newscast alone, was next to impossible. "It was a great idea, but it didn't take into account three crazy people," Tiven said later. "They all had pretty big egos —Mort's was as large as Delaware at least, and Jessica knew that what counted was being on the air, not what you said." And as for Leonard, Tiven said, "He'd been there a long time, and he *liked* doing the late news." Every night, Tiven said, each anchor complained that the other two got more to do; according to one producer, at times the three of them sat down and tallied up each other's pages. Shortly after the great tri-anchor experiment began, it ended. As Crim and Leonard had feared, there was a loser, and they were it. Henceforth, there would only be two anchors on the late news, but these two slots would be filled by all three broadcasters on an alternating basis, an arrangement that gave both Crim and Leonard one-third less air time at 11:00 P.M.

Tiven's priority was the machines. As soon as he had arrived, he launched the same lobbying drive for new equipment he had already staged in Atlanta; this time, however, he could actually take Alan Bell to Atlanta for a look at a properly equipped newsroom. Soon after visiting WSB, Tiven installed new equipment in Philadelphia. Its debut was hardly auspicious. As the anchor led into a live report on a recycling plant, engineer Anne Amico was on the phone, frantically trying to figure out how to bring in Matt Quinn, who was standing in front of the plant and wondering whether anyone back at KYW could see him or hear his words. There was a collective sigh of relief when the dark-haired Quinn popped up on the monitors, but little confidence the same feat could be duplicated the next day. "You were never sure if something would work or not," said producer Milt Weiss. "For the first year we always had our fingers crossed and made sure we had an escape plan. Maybe one out of every twenty-five times, something went wrong— enough to make you very, very nervous."

Frustratingly, the technology never seemed to catch up to Tiven's dreams. In July 1976 Savitch and a crew covered the Democratic National Convention in New York City, but the distance was too far for live feeds via microwave and satellites were not yet readily available for local uplinks. As Savitch interviewed delegates on the floor of Madison Square Garden, Group W technicians ran downstairs to Penn Station, which is located just beneath the arena, and dumped canisters of film and videotape on the Metroliner to Philadelphia. That footage was inevitably overwhelmed by the pace of events, and to Tiven's chagrin, his team was reduced to covering that ever-popular subject, how the insane pace of life in the great metropolis means that everyone at home is really better off staying there. KYW's coverage of the Republican convention, held in Kansas City a month later, was even more disappointing; forced to send film back by plane, the crew provided scintillating coverage of tourist highlights in Missouri and profiles of Pennsylvania delegates.

But it was the last time Tiven would have to resort to such expedients. A new technological era had been launched, and it would change broadcast journalism across the nation. Once the other stations in town got their own new electronic gadgetry, the race was on to see which station could flash the word "Live" on the screen most often, and trucks were dispatched to cover even minor traffic jams or fires. Although the quality of television film varied, at its best its sound and image quality surpassed that of videotape, a fact which distressed many of the technicians. "They took me into tape kicking and screaming," said cameraman Joe Vandergast, who eventually went back to film and left television news altogether. "All you could get was this harsh, cold picture. I couldn't bring my special effects to it. A summer intern could get the same shot I could." The new equipment also occasioned bitter union jurisdiction disputes at KYW and hundreds of other stations, and, in some cases, including WBZ, the Group W television station in Boston, a long strike ensued.

But for Jessica Savitch, the introduction of what came to be known as electronic newsgathering, or ENG, was a boon. Part of what she loved about news anchoring, what gave the antiseptic-looking task of sitting alone in an icy studio and talking into a camera an edge of excitement and danger, was that it was live, right now, a direct communication from her to the viewer. With ENG, even more of the broadcast could have that edge. Instead of simply introducing a film package done by a reporter in the field, the reporter and Savitch could talk on air and she would thus become part of the story. In addition, anchoring was no longer the only way she could work live; now she could have the same charge outside the studio. She could be right in the middle of a breaking story on air—an electronic Brenda Starr, out working on a story while simultaneously appearing in the living rooms of millions of viewers.

Another strain on Savitch at the time was the interminable disintegration of her affair with Ron Kershaw, which dragged violently on for years. Tormented by his inability to live with her and ambivalent about her success, Kershaw oscillated between extremes of love and anger, and the relationship became so tumultuous that the people around Savitch were appalled and could not imagine why she continued to see him. While filming the series on Philadelphians who had found Hollywood success, Joe Vandergast, who was staying in the adjacent hotel room, heard Savitch screaming so loudly that he was sure she was being raped. But when Vandergast burst into her room, he found she was only shrieking at Kershaw over the phone. At the station, Kershaw had a habit of calling Savitch up just before she went on the news. "She would get so upset she could barely work and would freak out at the least little thing," said one friend. Another co-worker recalled hearing Savitch speaking to Kershaw shortly before airtime—"she'd be sobbing like a little girl"—and being amazed that Kershaw was insensitive enough to phone then, and that Savitch was foolish enough to take the calls.

A major bone of contention between them was Savitch's five-year contract with Group W. Although Kershaw believed that she had been promised a network out, he thought she had been stupid for believing that such a promise would ever be honored. "It made her absolutely crazy," he said, "because these people that she had trusted had lied to her, and I was crazy [with anger] at her, because *of course* they had lied to her. They're in the fucking business of lies." According to Kershaw, Savitch "wanted to be naive. One of our huge, huge problems and the reason she tried to keep distancing herself from me was that she wanted it to be a fairy world. She wanted to be the princess. She didn't want to hear the shit that I was always talking, this negative shit." In Kershaw's view, "She wanted to be lied to. And when she was lied to, she didn't want anyone pointing it out."

Still irate at being uprooted from Houston and, as he saw it, forced into the horrible job of trying to put WBAL on the map, Kershaw was further enraged at seeing Savitch's transformation from a working journalist into a star. "She got a little detached from reality, as anybody in an anchor chair does, because you're only gonna run into people who are kissing your ass," he said. "She went into this cocoon where she and Mort and Vince were all 'colleagues,' and they would go to dinners and be honored by all of Philadelphia. And she fit too easily into the mode of star." Although Kershaw's work at WBAL was finally successful, he remained hostile to a life of reading *Variety* every week and being immersed in the industry. "Partly as a reaction to Jessica being burned up with career," he said, "I was always anti-career, reluctant to give myself credit for anything I'd done. It was always 'I don't want this fucking career. If we hadn't stopped [on the highway] at that overlook, I wouldn't have to be here.' "

Yet furious and brutal as their arguments were, Savitch continued to go back for more. The little girl who had been abandoned by her father could not accept being left ever again; instead of driving her away, Kershaw's fury and rejection seemed to bind her ever closer. Kershaw was so powerfully affected by her, her presence pulled out feelings so deep, and the emotions she aroused were so strong and uncontrollable, that it seemed foolish to imagine that they could ever be apart. Faced with the central and overwhelming fact of her presence in his life, he felt that they were helpless—trapped by an inexorable fate. "We couldn't get away from each other," Kershaw said. "If I left, I would be abandoning her. If we stayed, we fought. It was a vicious circle we couldn't break."

On the morning of Sunday, June 1, 1975, a man named Mel Korn had lain in bed and leafed through the *Philadelphia Inquirer*. A prominently featured interview in the magazine section caught his eye. By the time he was finished, he had decided he wanted to meet the subject, Jessica Savitch. Chasing after glamorous celebrities was not the kind of thing that Korn, a small, dapper man of forty-five with brown hair and brown eyes, had ever even thought of before that day. For eighteen years, Korn, the father of four children, had lived in a large house in Wynnewood, on the Main Line, with his second wife, Patti. President of J. M. Korn & Sons, an ad agency started by his father, Korn had spent every waking hour of his adult life building up the business. In 1975, after nearly twenty years of unrelenting effort, this self-described "two-fisted entrepreneur" had $15 million in billings from plugging Mrs. Smith's Pies and Pepsi. But now everything had changed for Mel Korn. He had separated from Patti and a divorce was under way. He had moved to a plush apartment on the Benjamin Franklin Parkway in downtown Philadelphia. He had a penthouse office, a large income, a closetful of expensive suits, and a chauffeur-driven limousine. His new life lacked just one crucial ingredient: a female companion.

That Sunday, he thought he might have found her. In the interview, which was titled "Pretty People Are Suspect," Savitch told reporter Maralyn Lois Polak that she was very different from her polished on-screen image:

[I have] a very square jaw . . . [and] awful skin—I figure I'll go through menopause with acne. Then my nose was broken when I was a kid and I never had it fixed. How'd it happen? A little boy in the neighborhood beat up my sister, then I went looking for him and beat him up and then he smashed me in the face with a baseball bat. My hair never stays, either. . . .

Ordinarily I'm very shy, except on camera. But I'm probably more real, more at ease, better adjusted in my work than in any part of my life. Maybe it has something to do with success. I'm happier, more comfortable, better able to cope while working. I even move better. My weaknesses and frailties? Privately I'm very emotional, insecure, unsure, overly sensitive to criticism, very high strung, nervous. But these things don't affect my job performance. . . .

Remember how in school all the little girls always said they wanted to be nurses or teachers or mommies when the teacher asked them? Well, my mother was a nurse so that's what I said. But what I really wanted to be was a *princess*. Except you didn't say that in school. It wasn't democratic. I wanted to be one of the princesses out of *Grimm's Fairy Tales*—really long hair and a pointed hat with a little veil hanging down.

On Monday, June 2, Korn spoke to Harold Pannepacker, an ad salesman at KYW who had been a business acquaintance of Korn's father, and asked him to bring Savitch over for a talk with Korn's staff. Always willing to oblige a potential client, Pannepacker delivered Savitch over to Korn's office. That evening, Korn took her to dinner at an expensive French restaurant not far from KYW. As far as Pannepacker was concerned, Korn was "a very smart businessman, but not my type of person. He was all business. Everything he did was business—he was not a fun kind of guy." But to Jessica Savitch, a woman completely focused on her own career, Korn's similar single-mindedness was immensely appealing.

Even more appealing, the field in which Korn had labored so diligently was marketing. He was an expert in pushing products, and Savitch had a product she wanted to push: herself. "We started talking about how you apply marketing to what she was doing, and if she was a product how do you package it and how do you promote it well," Korn said. Savitch was delighted; Korn was intrigued. For the first time in his life, Korn had met someone with more drive than himself, someone who made him seem low-key and calm, and he was attracted immediately.

"I could always relate to talent," he said. "I could understand where they were coming from and the sensitivities that they had and the commercial world that they had to deal with." With talent, he said, "there's always a certain amount of insecurity they have, we all have. The stronger the talent, many times, the stronger the insecurities, as crazy as that sounds. And yet if you help soothe that insecurity, that strength and talent really comes out. They just need confidence."

For the next five years, Mel Korn would make it his job to provide that confidence. "I felt that besides being a good journalist, you had to be packaged properly," he said. "It's a total thing that people buy." Every night he watched Savitch's broadcasts and took notes on her presentation. On the weekends he went shopping with her to find clothes that fit the smart (but not too smart), tailored (but not too tailored) look that he thought best for reaching the audience. He encouraged her to take an escort to any business-related function so as to forestall any jealousy from the wives. "The bridge between us was my interest in her career," he said. "I wasn't doing it to be the gent. I truly enjoyed it."

And Savitch obviously enjoyed Korn. "He was older, but older-hip," said Helene Swertlow, a producer on *The Mike Douglas Show* who dated Korn during a period when he and Savitch had temporarily stopped seeing each other. "He was very with it—on his office wall he had a sign that said 'I.G.,' for 'instant gratification.' He was very different from the average Philadelphia guy—more like a New York man." Despite his apparent sophistication, however, Korn was in awe of Savitch. "He looked up to her," Swertlow said. "She was a star."

As the months went by, Savitch spent an increasing amount of time with the middle-aged marketing executive. Worried about her extreme thinness, he sent her to an endocrinologist; when she was diagnosed as hypoglycemic, Korn hired a cook to provide proper meals. He routinely lent her his car and driver. Whenever Savitch admired something, he bought it for her; once when she and Korn were in a restaurant with

Carol Bell, Savitch made a complimentary remark about the china pattern, and Korn presented both women with a place setting. For her part, Savitch sent Korn a steady stream of little cards and messages in which she shared with him her thoughts. At one point, she had a passage from *Me and Other Advertising Geniuses,* a memoir by Batten, Barton, Durstine & Osborn president Charles Brower, blown up and framed. It read:

> He was one of those men who struggled for success long after they have it, who are all making touchdowns when the stadium's empty, the other team's long gone and the shadows lengthening toward them. Like most of us, he was seeking happiness and was baffled. Success itself is sort of a failure. You reach the end of the rainbow and there is no pot of gold. You get your castle in Spain and there is no plumbing.

Although it was intended as a gift for Korn, it was a description of Savitch as well.

With Korn, Savitch could be not only the ambitious journalist, but also the child who still longed for her daddy. One evening when Korn was, as usual, waiting outside the station in his limousine to take her home, Savitch offered a ride to Diane Allen, then the noon anchor. "I was amazed at what a little girl she was around him," Allen said later. "Usually she was the consummate professional." Unlike Ron Kershaw, Korn let Savitch relax and bask in the warmth of an unconditional love that she had not known since childhood. "If you love somebody, you're there for whatever happens," Korn said later. "Isn't that what it's all about? The rest is conversation."

Korn was not angry at her for uprooting his life or surging ahead of him on the career ladder; on the contrary, he was delighted to be able to stand in the margin of Savitch's life and give her whatever assistance he could. He had spent his life in what he called "unsung hero work, where you're the quiet, invisible thinker—you don't take the direct bows, you just have the ear of the king or the queen directly," and he was comfortable in that role. He did not expect Savitch to place her career to one side. He did not demand that she live with him. He did not complain about her absences or her strange working hours or her fits of rage. He did not insist that she stop seeing

Kershaw and did not interfere with the marijuana she smoked or the coke she snorted or the prescription drugs she renewed more often than she should have. He did not even expect her to become acquainted with his children. Indeed, she only met them once in their first four years together. Just before going to see them that day, Savitch told Korn, "Remember, *I* am your baby." She was.

Korn's counsel was particularly important to Savitch as she assessed the expressions of interest that continued to pour in from other stations and the networks. In November 1975, CBS, which had to withdraw its first offer to her two years earlier, got back in the act. Bill Small, then a vice-president at CBS and later to become president of NBC News and Savitch's boss, was attending a journalism convention in Philadelphia and invited Savitch to visit him and his wife in their hotel suite. When Small asked her if she would be interested in CBS, the network she had spent the last seven years pursuing, she was forced to tell him that she was not free to consider any offers.

A few months later, in early 1976, Savitch and Dave Neal went up to New York for a get-acquainted lunch with Ron Tindiglia, news director at WABC, and Al Ittleson, the vice-president of news for the network's O&Os. Tindiglia, who had been news director at WPVI, the ABC affiliate in Philadelphia, was already familiar with Savitch's work; while still at WPVI he had called a promising young woman broadcaster in Indianapolis named Jane Pauley and tried to hire her, sight unseen, in order to give Savitch and KYW some competition. But Pauley had gone to WMAQ, the NBC O&O in Chicago, and Tindiglia, who had moved on to WABC, was now interested in exploring the possibility that Savitch might want to jump to his new station. Savitch said that she wanted to go network, and Ittleson arranged for her to meet Bill Sheehan, president of ABC News.

Savitch's timing could not have been better. After a quarter century of being an also-ran, ABC was ready to make network news a three-way race. Aware of the beneficial results when local stations had added a woman co-anchor to their newscasts, Bill Sheehan decided to do the same at the network level. The first step would be to give a woman a slot as co-anchor, alongside Ted Koppel, on the Saturday evening news. Although Marlene Sanders and Lisa Howard had anchored five-minute afternoon newscasts on ABC and Sanders had appeared on the weekday evening news as a substitute, this would be the first time at ABC that a woman had been given the evening newscast as a regular assignment.* Sheehan was at the point of choosing among Jessica Savitch, Connie Chung, and Pat Harper when his boss, ABC-TV president Fred Pierce, reported that he had heard from his tennis partner, super-agent Lou Weiss, whose company, the William Morris Agency, represented Barbara Walters, that Walters might be available. Sheehan then decided to skip hiring a woman for the weekend, and to go right for Walters on weeknights. In September 1976, Barbara Walters became the first woman to co-anchor a network evening news program. Her salary was $1 million. Savitch was devastated. Although it is unlikely in the extreme that she could have bested Walters for the job even if she had already been at the network level, she was irrationally convinced that this was an opportunity that could have gone to her if it had not been for the Westinghouse contract she had been foolish enough to sign four years earlier. (Lost in the uproar about Walters's salary was the fact that the Walters-Reasoner newscast was to be expanded to one hour; because of affiliate protest, the broadcast ultimately remained only thirty minutes, too little time to showcase two major stars and a key factor in the breakdown of relations between Walters and Reasoner and the program's subsequent failure.)

In the fall of 1976, Savitch auditioned to be a regular contributor on *Who's Who,* a new prime-time, *People*-magazine-like show on CBS featuring interviews with celebrities, near-celebrities, and ordinary folk in temporary possession of such status. With Dan Rather as chief reporter and Don Hewitt, the creator of *60 Minutes,* as executive producer, *Who's Who* was the big leagues. Barbara Howar, Phyllis George, and Christine Okrent were also up for the job, but Savitch was sure it would be hers. "She showed up in a blazer that was made of some

---

* *In December 1964, Marlene Sanders had substituted for Ron Cochran at ABC; the next day, in an article entitled "A Precedent Is Set," The New York Times's critic Jack Gould called Sanders "A courageous young woman with a Vassar smile." Sanders subbed on the weekend news several times in 1965 and once more in 1971, but institutional memories were short and the latter occasion was again celebrated as the first time a woman had anchored a network newscast.*

kind of red lizard," recalled Grace Diekhaus, senior producer on *Who's Who*. "It sounds weird, but it looked fabulous. She really made an impact—I thought she was quite good." Again, however, she was dropped cold as soon as she mentioned her contract. Seething, Savitch stayed in Philadelphia, and *Who's Who* went on the air with Barbara Howar in the female contributor role (Charles Kuralt was her male counterpart). The show was pulled after six months.

At the same time, Savitch was being wooed by the CBS O&Os. Bob Hosking, the general manager of WCAU, the CBS-owned station in Philadelphia, would have hired her in a flash, as he made clear to Don Hamburg, the New York lawyer and agent she had retained on the recommendation of Hamburg client Mort Crim. When Eric Ober became news director at WCAU in the spring of 1976, one of the first things he did was press Dave Neal for an introduction to this Philadelphia legend. Such attention was gratifying, but the suitor who provided Savitch with the most emotional satisfaction was Ed Joyce. As an executive at WCBS Radio and then as news director at WCBS-TV, Joyce had refused to hire her as a desk assistant back before she went to Houston. Now he was looking for a co-anchor at WCBS-TV, the top job he could possibly have offered. His first move was to ask Don Fitzpatrick, a television news consultant hired by the five CBS O&Os, to make an exploratory call to Savitch. At the time, Fitzpatrick's firm, Entertainment Response Analysts, was working on the CBS People Project, an annual compilation of data about on-air talent which Fitzpatrick called the world's most expensive bathroom reading because it was seen by only a dozen executives. The People Project rated television figures by their popularity, and Joyce told Fitzpatrick that he had noted with much interest that in the Philadelphia market Savitch was second only to Larry Kane of *Action News,* and that her appeal cut across all segments of the audience.

This conclusion had been reached by the then-revolutionary sociological method of convening a small number of people —"a focus group"—to talk about TV for an entire weekend. Participants were paid $20 a day to answer questions like "Who do you think is the best anchor in the city?" and "Why is he/ she the best?" According to Fitzpatrick, Savitch's many fans tended to pick her as the most trustworthy dispenser of journalistic truth for reasons ranging from "I'd like to invite her over for coffee" to "I'd like her to be my friend." To back up these conclusions, focus group members had little wires attached lie-detector style to the palms of their hands. The idea was to measure whether their palms perspired at the mention of Savitch's name. They did. Of coffee cups and sweaty palms were reputations made and broken; little wonder that the business operated in an ulcerous sea of unease.

Fitzpatrick, who rarely made actual contact with the people he evaluated, was nervous about phoning someone of Savitch's stature. Nonetheless, the call went well. She was warm, friendly, and direct: Although still under contract to KYW, Savitch said she was talking to other broadcasters. In the spring of 1977, Ed Joyce, Jim Cusick, assistant news director at WCBS, and Tom Leahy, the station's general manager, took Savitch out to lunch in New York. The executives were on their best behavior; they had chosen the sort of refined, Upper East Side expense-account restaurant whose business is less satisfying appetites than making an elegant impression. By the time the dessert cart pulled up to the table, Joyce was ready with an offer of a $175,000 job as co-anchor opposite Jim Jensen. It was a handsome bid, but Savitch cut him off. Smilingly recalling that she couldn't get to first base with him only six years earlier, Savitch said that WCBS, the flagship station for America's biggest network, was certainly the only local station she would be interested in—but, she sighed, she wasn't interested in local stations anymore.

Mel Korn encouraged her quest to move away from Philadelphia, although he was, he said later, ever careful to remain an adviser, not a director. A regular reader of *Variety,* he enjoyed the peculiar atmosphere of intrigue and rumor that flourishes in show biz, and he had encouraged the negotiations that Savitch found so frustrating. He had strong opinions about where she should go (network, not local) and with whom (ABC, not NBC or CBS). "I really hoped she would go with ABC," he said. "ABC was becoming a full network at about that time. I had known [ABC president] Fred Pierce as an agency guy. I was even going to give him a ring, but I stayed out of that stuff. It was her shot."

In 1977, Savitch decided that the shot she wanted was NBC. She wanted it because it was classy, the home of Huntley and Brinkley. She wanted it because it was said to be stable, a place where people treated each other decently. She wanted it, of course, because it was network, not local. But most of all, she wanted it because it was NBC that offered her, in the summer of 1977, the chance to become a national anchor-woman.

Nineteen-seventy-seven was not a propitious year to come to NBC News. Since 1964, when Jessica Savitch had watched NBC's proudest moment, its domination of the Democratic National Convention in Atlantic City, the proud peacock had fallen on hard times, and would fall on harder. Its decline began in 1965, when Robert Kintner, the man who had thrown the network's full resources behind the news and embodied the zeal that had put Huntley and Brinkley on top for year after year, was fired for drinking too much.

Bullying yet sentimental, hard-driving yet loyal, Kintner had spent the late 1950s and early 1960s ensuring that NBC was *the* network to watch when anything happened. CBS might have the crowd-pleasing Westerns and, starting in 1962, the phenomenally successful *Beverly Hillbillies;* Kintner made sure that NBC was how people learned about the world. It was Kintner who had broken the rules and pre-empted America's soap operas for the Army-McCarthy hearings back in 1954, when he was still at ABC. It was Kintner who decided that NBC would yank all programming—and, amazingly, all commercials—for twenty-four hours after President Kennedy was shot. His competitors at CBS and ABC followed suit, but NBC garnered the credit for public-spiritedness. Kintner's fierce competitiveness spawned the brutal, childish scramble for ratings that has ever since dominated broadcast journalism.

Televisions blaring in his office morning, noon, and night, he seemed to his staff to have no need of sleep and to be utterly without a personal life. Once Kintner gathered a score of feuding agents, lawyers, advertisers, and producers to hammer out a huge contract for six Bob Hope specials and a film anthology to be hosted by Hope. He rammed through the document in a single hour-long session that left heads spinning and egos vibrating on all sides. "We marched through it," recalled Herb Schlosser, then one of Kintner's negotiators. "He kind of just *decided* those issues, and everybody went along." It was easy for Kintner to make the choices; the company was everything to him, and nothing else mattered.

But Robert Kintner had a problem: He liked vodka. Sometimes he would get drunk and tell people funny stories. Sometimes he would get drunk and be quiet. But sometimes he would get drunk and harangue people and break things. In his print days, he had become a newspaper alcoholic, able to operate full speed while half-drunk, and he became a TV alcoholic, running the show with a rapidly emptying bottle in his desk drawer. Every so often he quit drinking; then the tension of the job would get to him, and the bottle appeared again. Sometimes people would find out only when he called them in the middle of the night to deliver long, angry, self-pitying diatribes about imagined faults. It was a shameful performance, his associates thought, for a man so gifted.

In 1965, after NBC's huge triumph at the Democratic convention—more than 80 percent of the audience! Walter Cronkite yanked from the convention coverage!—Robert Kintner was promoted to the post of chief executive officer of NBC. (The title had been held previously by the General's son, Robert Sarnoff, who had succeeded his father as president of RCA, the company that owned NBC.) Kintner did not respond well to his new eminence. He had always fought with Bob Sarnoff, but these disputes had served as a necessary brake for this contentious man. "Kintner couldn't take not having an adversary," said Reuven Frank, executive producer of the *Huntley-Brinkley Report* at the time. "When he was made chairman, that was the end." Soon after Kintner's appointment to CEO, he insisted on flying a week early to a fall meeting of affiliates, scheduled for Acapulco. He had been dry all summer, and his closest associates knew the tacked-on week in Mexico meant trouble.

"He left on a morning plane," said one of his friends. "Kintner showed up with his wife and his chauffeur holding him up. His feet weren't touching the floor." In Mexico, the friend said, "we tried to hide the liquor, but he would drink Sterno." To make things worse, a plane crashed on the way to the convention, killing some of those who were to attend the meeting. The conference was a disaster; Kintner did not show up for everything he was supposed to attend, and was rambling

200

and belligerent when he did appear. When it was over, he did not return to his office. A month later, Robert Sarnoff summoned him to his office, where the pink slip was formally dispensed in a meeting that an embittered Kintner claimed lasted six minutes. He had been at the network for eight years. (Kintner then worked in the Johnson White House and eventually retired to Haiti, where he died in 1980.)

Although ads for NBC boasted that it was "the world's largest and most comprehensive broadcast news organization," the man who had been at the top for nearly a decade was not a good administrator. He inspired the people around him, but the lower levels of the network were a bureaucratic mess—the sort of network one might imagine was run by a drunk. There was no backup; nobody had a means for ensuring that good new people and ideas came flowing up the ladder. Even in the small things the network was the shakiest of giants: The files were a tangle, the logbooks a jumble, the film libraries nonexistent. The print library in the most important bureau, Washington, consisted of little more than *Time, Newsweek,* and *The New York Times,* which, because they were checked out and returned on the honor system, were missing more often than not. Nobody cared as long as the numbers were good. During Kintner's tenure, they were. And so nobody paid attention.

Kintner was replaced by two men: Julian Goodman, the second-in-command of the news division; and Walter Scott, a fellow from sales. Scott was affable and well liked, but did little. Goodman, whom people thought of as a bright young man, was left to run things. He had the wit to leave the good parts of Kintner's empire alone, but he lacked the energy, the electricity, the sheer conviction that Kintner had supplied, notwithstanding the disorganization and drinking. Things were left to run as they always had, and things did what comes naturally in such situations—they went downhill.

By the late 1960s, America's love affair with Huntley and Brinkley had come to a close. Walter Cronkite, who had been the anchor of *CBS Evening News* since 1962, took the lead. If Kintner had been at the helm, the loss would have been a source of anguish and fury. But Goodman and Scott almost didn't react—it was as if they were comfortable with the other guys taking the heat. In 1970 Huntley retired, and, after a brief and unsuccessful experiment with a three-man team composed of David Brinkley, Frank McGee, and John Chancellor, the network made Chancellor solo anchor.

Chancellor, a former reporter for the *Chicago Sun-Times,* had been with NBC since 1950, and his coverage of such key events as the school integration crisis in Little Rock and the 1964 Republican National Convention in San Francisco—Goldwater security forces kicked him out of the hall on air—had earned him a reputation as a reliable, responsible newsman. As a journalist, he could be ironically unflappable; as he was being hauled off in San Francisco, he told viewers, "I'm being taken off the arena now by police. I'll check in later. This is John Chancellor, reporting from somewhere in custody." But as anchor, he lost his capacity to be droll, and seemed to take himself and the news he reported with excessive seriousness. He was courtly in his stiff way, dependable but dull, the kind of man who is always a solid second but never in the pole position. He was a working newshound who made the phone calls and read the dull government papers and wrote his own copy, but he was not an exciting presence on the screen, or even much of a presence at all. "Chancellor had all the credentials to be anchor, but he was not a heavyweight," said NBC news writer Pat Trese. "He couldn't really fill the screen and he was also too academic. He worked well as a correspondent because he could make things clear and he wrote well to pictures. I think he could play second to Huntley or Cronkite with great effectiveness. But neither Chancellor nor Brinkley could carry the show alone." The viewers trusted Chancellor, research showed, but they had no desire to watch him.

In today's environment, where careers are broken by a few tenths of a rating point, NBC's complacence about its long, dignified slide is difficult to comprehend. It acquired a reputation as a gentlemen's club—dusty, genteel, bound by convention; people worked there without shouting at each other. They did middling well, and nobody got ulcers, and nobody rode anybody else, and everybody happily milked the cash cow that was broadcasting. In March 1975, correspondent John Hart went to NBC from CBS, and was flabbergasted by what he saw. "Things I took for granted at CBS—act fast, react quickly, do whatever it takes to do better—were missing there." Although the lack of pressure made NBC a more pleasant place to be, to Hart it seemed as though his new network had "a loser's contempt for CBS. CBS had a raw, competitive elitism. The elitism at NBC was a condescending one—we're too good to compete. Anything that sparkled was suspect."

The lackadaisical attitude came straight from the top, where RCA management happily raked in the money that seemed to come in without excessive sweat or bother. Three-quarters of RCA's profits came from the network; indeed, the men at the top in Rockefeller Center thought they were doing better by not doing too well. "The Sarnoffs did not want to be number one," said Dick Wald, who became head of NBC News in 1973. "They felt that in order to be number one, you had to maintain this enormous expenditure for news shows, for development projects, for special events, and that they could make more money by being number two. They may have been right—in the short run."

In the long run, the network suffered. In the early 1970s, CBS had begun a run of top-rated contemporary comedies (*All in the Family,* about a lovable bigot; *The Mary Tyler Moore Show,* about a long-suffering single woman and her wacky co-workers) programmed by a man named Fred Silverman, who manipulated the schedule according to the dictates of his "golden gut." These shows and their spin-offs combined with the new preeminence of Walter Cronkite on the news to give CBS a greater lead than ever before. Then, in the mid-1970s, ABC, the perennial third-place network in entertainment as well as news, started shouldering aside second place NBC with saccharine-but-peppy shows (*Six Million Dollar Man,* about an astronaut who is part robot; *Happy Days,* about a corps of unthreatening adolescents in the 1950s) for the "family viewing hour" that had been created when the FCC decreed that no violence was to be shown on television before 9:00 P.M. In 1975, ABC also managed to lure away from CBS Fred Silverman, whose gastric juices enabled him to boost his new network's ratings amazingly. Although Silverman's greatest innovation was having a crew of braless women run about in a police show called *Charlie's Angels,* which made its debut in 1976, his greatest success was the blockbuster miniseries *Roots,* a chronicle of one black family which was broadcast in January 1977 and was watched by more viewers than any other show in television history before or after.

NBC executives who had tolerated second place for so long began to worry that the network might slip into third. Third place was more than a blow to corporate pride. Third place meant that the affiliates might revolt. If affiliates dump the network, the network's ratings perforce drop—nobody can watch the shows. If ratings drop, more affiliates back out, creating a downward spiral that is the nightmare of every television executive.

In April 1974, Bob Sarnoff, chairman of RCA, had put Herb Schlosser, already president of the television network, in charge of the entire company. A graduate of Princeton and Yale Law School and a former corporate lawyer, Schlosser had a reputation as a smart, able executive and a deft negotiator: He had signed Huntley and Brinkley to their ten-year contracts, and Johnny Carson to his first contract in the early 1960s. Worried about a possible exodus by affiliates, Sarnoff had tapped Schlosser to head it off. He did. The first year of Schlosser's presidency, his emphasis on program development brought the network from a weak second place to being a strong contender for the top spot. He also put *Saturday Night Live* on the air in 1975 and followed up the next year with *Sportsworld* and *Weekend*. But because Schlosser's major experience was in the entertainment side of the industry, some of those below, especially in news, were uneasy about his appointment. Compared to his predecessor, Julian Goodman, whose orderly, genial, laid-back management style had been good for office morale if not the company fortunes, Schlosser, with his aggressive, hands-on attitude, seemed anxious and over-eager. Under enormous pressure to make things better overnight, Schlosser could be both indecisive—"Sometimes it seemed like the only thing that got decided at meetings in Herb's office was when to hold the next meeting," one former NBC executive said—and impatient. He often bypassed the official chain of command and reached down into the organization directly, an approach that brought quick results but earned him a reputation for interfering in others' business.

Matters were not helped by an embarrassing incident that occurred midway through Schlosser's tenure. With great fanfare, NBC announced plans for updating the company's image by modernizing its logo. Lippincott & Margolies, a top design firm that had already created a new logo for RCA, was retained for a handsome fee. After fourteen months and costs estimated up to $750,000, NBC unveiled an attractive stylized N and began a changeover budgeted at several million dollars. Soon afterward the network learned that for the past six months, a tiny public television station in Nebraska had been using precisely the same logo, which had been designed by Nebraska Educational Television's own art director and cost less than $100. The red-faced network then made a financial settlement and bought the rights to the logo which was already emblazoned on NBC's advertising, stationery, equipment, and employee uniforms.

A more fundamental problem was the working relationship among Schlosser, President and Chief Operating Officer; Julian Goodman, Chairman and Chief Executive Officer; and Dick Wald, president of NBC News. On paper, all company divisions, including news, reported to Schlosser, the number two, who ran the day-to-day operations and reported to Goodman, the number one. But in fact the company news veterans tended to adhere more to Goodman, who had been at 30 Rock for decades, than to Schlosser, who had spent much of his NBC career out on the West Coast. In particular, Dick Wald looked less to Schlosser, who was his immediate superior but came from the programming side of the industry, than to Goodman, who, as a former news executive, spoke the same language as Wald and knew the same people. Although Wald and Schlosser got along reasonably well at the beginning, the relationship suffered as ABC's fortunes improved and those of NBC declined, a state known within the industry as "heading south." As president of NBC, Schlosser was charged with making the network number one; not surprisingly, he paid considerable attention to program ratings, an orientation that Wald and others in the news division considered unpleasantly close to the kind of thinking news consultants had brought to local television. "There was always a rivalry between the NBC News priesthood and the grubby programming money-makers," David Adams said. "The news people liked to seem above the fray, as if they didn't give a damn about profits, but they did." Though Schlosser had the power to fire Wald, Schlosser did not have the power to tell Wald what to do. An unpleasant stasis was the almost inevitable result.

Wald was a refugee from print. Educated at Columbia

University and Clare College, Cambridge, he had made his name as a reporter at the *New York Herald Tribune;* in the early 1960s, he became its managing editor, and ever afterward took credit for enlivening the *Trib*'s dull gray columns. Despite his ministrations the paper folded in 1966, and Wald wound up as a vice-president of NBC. A man of sharp intelligence, Wald was a classic wise-guy, sometimes described by the phrase "too smart for his own good." He told friends that he had been too shy to speak as a child; they saw little of that timidity as an adult. One afternoon Wald spoke with David Adams as they waited outside Schlosser's office. Inside, Robert Stone, the president of Hertz, an RCA subsidiary, was loudly complaining to Schlosser about the treatment of rental-car agencies in a special report done by WMAQ, the NBC-owned station in Chicago. Stone came out fuming, and, according to Adams, Wald greeted him with the cheery question, "By the way, did I ever tell you I always rent Hertz cars if I can't find anything else?"

In 1976, the unthinkable happened: NBC's prime-time entertainment shows fell into third place. The network's news division was still in second place, but ABC, which had finally built its program division into a formidable powerhouse, was now turning its attention to developing an impressive news division. It was then that ABC lured Barbara Walters from NBC; it followed up by seducing talented producers, directors, editors, and camera operators from both of the other networks. Although NBC's earnings jumped 12 percent in 1976, CBS had an increase of 22 percent and ABC had an increase of 186 percent. To counteract the impression that NBC was falling apart, something would have to be done.

One of the most obvious targets for change was the news, and a first step was to borrow (but not credit) ideas from the news consultants; Wald, who remained dismissive of McHugh and Hoffman, et al., called the new, local-style innovations "making the program more acceptable to a wider audience." In the mid-1970s *NBC Nightly News* began to include a new section, titled "Segment Three," which contained longer feature stories on subjects ranging from sexuality and poverty to chemical warfare. Despite network protestations ("It was a distinct turn in a different direction than *Eyewitness News,*" asserted Joe Bartelme, a news vice-president), reports on Segment Three (later renamed "Special Segment") looked quite like some of the better series done by local stations such as KYW. And, despite network declarations against hype, the special segments were promoted heavily, much as local stations had done with their series.

Certain executives had in mind a much more fundamental change in the news, namely, getting rid of John Chancellor. It was not the first time he had been under fire; as soon as correspondent John Hart had arrived at NBC, in 1975, a vice-president had taken him to lunch and said that his faction wanted to get rid of Chancellor. The bespectacled anchor might be an emblem of journalistic integrity to correspondents, but to others at NBC he was the college professor whose obsession with boring foreign stories had induced him in November 1975 to lead the news five days running with the fact that Generalissimo Francisco Franco was on his deathbed. To make matters worse, Chancellor's leads became the subject of a running joke on the network's late-night comedy series, *Saturday Night Live.* Every time that comedian Chevy Chase began his parody of the news with the words, "Once again, Generalissimo Francisco Franco is still dead," NBC executives cringed.

In 1976 Chancellor was paired with David Brinkley in the hope that the Huntley-Brinkley magic would happen again. But the sum was less than the two parts, and rumors began to circulate that Chancellor would be replaced by Tom Snyder, the madcap anchor who had lost out to Vince Leonard at KYW. After a highly regarded stint at KNBC, the NBC O&O in Los Angeles and the place where Tom Brokaw had made his mark, Snyder had come to WNBC, the network's flagship O&O in New York City. There his abrasive hipness and electric presence had driven the station's news broadcasts, long in the doldrums, to the top of the local heap. Snyder had been sick of working local, and had only accepted the WNBC job on what he understood as a commitment from network brass, including both Dick Wald and Herb Schlosser, to give him a real future in the news division if all worked out well (unlike the other networks, NBC News administered its O&O news operations directly). To sweeten the WNBC job, Snyder was also given several network news plums—anchor of the Sunday evening newscast, prime-time newsbreaks, and a late night talk show called *Tomorrow*—and a salary of $600,000, making him the

207

highest-paid male anchor in local television. When Snyder was hugely successful, he awaited the anointment as Chancellor's successor. It didn't come. But it didn't *not* come, either.

The details of subsequent events are shrouded in conflicting accounts of the growing hostility between Herb Schlosser and Dick Wald. What to do about Chancellor was not the only issue between them. Wald had already made himself unpopular by stalling when Walters's *Today* contract came up for renewal and thus giving ABC an opportunity to offer her a job as co-anchor on its nightly newscast. Because NBC was unwilling to come up with a similar role for her, the network lost one of its biggest news stars. Another sore point was the fat contracts NBC had given former Secretary of State Henry Kissinger and former President Gerald Ford to act as network consultants. Herb Schlosser, Dick Wald, and Julian Goodman all participated in discussions of such deals at various points, but the few programs that resulted were disappointing, and Wald complained afterward that he had not been involved in the final arrangements. In addition, there was still a sharp conflict over Snyder's potential rise, which caused splintered factions, mutual recrimination, and, of course, indiscretions to the press. Schlosser was interested in Snyder, but had not made up his mind about replacing Chancellor; Wald thought that Snyder was smart and a good television writer but projected the wrong image. Cronkite, now *there* was an image. Tweedy, rough-hewn, avuncular, Cronkite would never be caught dead looking anything but steady as a rock.

Snyder was Ten Thousand Volts, so wired he had to take a drink sometimes to calm himself enough to go on the air. The anti-Chancellor, with great big eyebrows that waggled ferociously, he looked as though he might say something terrifically funny, and often he did. The potential for surprise made him a consultant's kind of anchor, but to Wald it meant that Snyder was too dangerous for viewers ever to award him their entire trust, no matter whether they were amused or not. (Wald was not alone in his rejection of Snyder; citing Chancellor's credibility, Julian Goodman came down firmly for retaining him. "Julian was afraid Tom would say 'shit' on the air," Ed Hookstratten, Snyder's agent, later told journalist Barbara Matusow.) From Schlosser's point of view, Snyder's charged personality made him appealing, and there were others in the news division who felt the same way. But Wald and Schlosser's disagreement over Snyder was symptomatic of their own deteriorating relationship. "We didn't get along," Schlosser said later. "It's as simple as that."

Chancellor, for his part, was cleverer than everyone else around him. He let the word get out that he was thinking about leaving at the same time that CBS was looking for someone to replace the retiring Eric Sevareid, the commentator on *CBS Evening News* and one of the last survivors of the Murrow days. Faced with the distressing prospect of losing the network's top anchor to a rival network, Schlosser made his decision. "I don't think Mr. Wald wanted to keep John Chancellor," he said later. "That negotiation was not going well." According to Schlosser, it was only because of his intervention and that of Julian Goodman that Chancellor got a long-term renewal as well as a hefty raise. In 1977, when Chancellor signed his new contract, Schlosser and Wald were back to Square One.

One of the reasons Square One was so uncomfortable was that for the first time in nearly half a century, there was no Sarnoff at the head of RCA. Although relations between NBC and the General (and, after his retirement, between the network and the General's son, Bob Sarnoff) were not always smooth, there was a sense of continuity, of someone on top with a strong personal connection to the network. This had come to an abrupt halt in 1975, when Bob Sarnoff was fired. Lackluster earnings had been cited as the official reason, but, according to David Adams, by then company chairman, Sarnoff's substantial personal expense account was also a factor.

Sarnoff's replacement, Andy Conrad, ruled just ten months before it was discovered that although his income taxes had been withheld, he had the unfortunate habit of not filing returns. When he refused to explain why, he was summarily sacked. His replacement was Edgar Griffiths, an RCA executive who had been in charge of several subsidiaries, including Hertz, and whose blind regard for the balance sheet led to the nickname "Bottom Line Ed." Indeed, Griffiths was so utterly devoted to the bottom line that staffers joked that he'd tripped over it when he broke his leg. According to Dick Wald, Griffiths had first made a name for himself at RCA by removing the spare tires from Hertz rental cars after calculating that it actually would be cheaper to write off the price of the rental when somebody had a blowout.

Utterly uninterested in broadcasting, Griffiths's response to his network's difficulty was the classic hard-nosed approach: He demanded that Schlosser cut costs. Schlosser was under unremitting pressure from Griffiths, and felt himself placed in an impossible bind. CBS was flexing its muscles, ABC was catching up fast, and Schlosser's boss was only looking for people to fire. Whenever Griffiths was told of plans to upgrade the news, Wald recalled, "he would say, 'Don't tell me why you need this program, just tell me how much it will cost.' " By cutting costs deeply, the news division finally began to make a little money, but *NBC Nightly News* was still going nowhere in the ratings. The House that Kintner Built was crumbling, and Wald and Schlosser had to do something about the news.

On Thursday, September 23, 1976, President Gerald Ford and former governor Jimmy Carter met at the Walnut Street Theatre in Philadelphia for the first of three nationally televised, ninety-minute debates arranged by the League of Women Voters. The pool crew was from ABC, but each network provided its own anchor, who broadcast from studios set up in the back of the theater. Nine minutes before the debate was scheduled to end, the line amplifier in the audio system blew. The microphones were dead inside the theater, and there was no audio feed from the podium to the sound trucks outside. For the next twenty-seven minutes, the candidates stood silently in front of their lecterns, and viewers around the country watched John Chancellor, Harry Reasoner, and Walter Cronkite scramble to fill the silence with trenchant remarks.

Those who tuned to KYW in Philadelphia, however, saw not the network feed but Channel 3's own coverage. Seeing NBC "sitting around with a finger up its ass," KYW news director Ken Tiven switched to the *Eyewitness* team. With Mort Crim serving as anchor back at the station, KYW provided on-the-spot, live reports on the situation. Outside the theater, Matt Quinn buttonholed debate officials. Across the street, Don Fair kept watch on protestors from a group called "Get the Rich Off Our Backs." Staking out a neighborhood bar in South Philly, Jim Hickey chatted with the man who had installed the telephone company hookup for the debate; the installer insisted that whatever had happened, it wasn't the phone company's fault. Most of the reporting, however, was provided by the correspondent inside the theater, Jessica Savitch. Dashing up and down the aisles, she quizzed ABC executives, party officials, innocent bystanders. "I remember thinking, What do I do now?" said Cliff Abromats, producer of the KYW newscast. But he soon discovered that with three live remotes and three fairly glib reporters, there was no problem, particularly when one of the three was Savitch. "She was very good on her feet," Abromats said. "She could think fast and ask the right questions, and she had the ability so many lack, to actually listen to the answer. Jessica would never miss it when someone said something unexpected."

When the sound went out, one of the more unhappy members of the audience was Bob Mulholland, the executive vice-president of NBC News who had come down to Philadelphia to oversee the event. In order for the NBC crews at the debate to see on their monitors exactly what was being broadcast from 30 Rock, he would have had to rent return phone lines back to New York, but as an economy measure he had opted not to do so; instead, he reasoned, the crews could keep track of what the network was doing by watching the broadcast on the local affiliate, KYW. Mulholland saved about $1,000, but when the audio went dead he was stuck watching KYW's local coverage. He was not thrilled at first to see any more of Jessica Savitch; watching KYW, he had missed most of the network's introduction to the debate because the local station's own promotion for the event, delivered by Savitch, had run late. Mulholland had squawked, and Savitch, who pinned blame on the KYW computers, was mortified. After a few minutes of watching her cover the case of the missing audio, however, Mulholland began to perk up. The evening was a technical disaster, a real programming screwup—Carson would be late, affiliates would be screaming—but perhaps there was a silver lining to the evening's cloud.

"It was the first time I can recall ever really seeing Jessica," Mulholland said. "It was one of the rare occasions when you have a chance to see the story yourself because you're there witnessing it with your own eyes [and] I was also able to see her reporting, on the air, of the story that I was seeing. That's a fast way to make a judgment about a reporter." That night, Mulholland gave Savitch high marks. "I thought she really had something and was doing a very, very good job. She was doing it all herself—really, really hustling."

The next morning, Mulholland called Ken Tiven to chew him out for not staying with the network. "You son of a bitch!" he yelled. "But I have to tell you, that Savitch was great." Shortly afterward, Mulholland sent for tapes of Savitch and began to talk up the idea of hiring her at NBC. "Here's someone who can anchor, [and] here's someone I've also seen work in the field," Mulholland told associates. "That's a pretty interesting combination." Actively pursuing Savitch, however, was a delicate mission. The network would be trying to lure someone from an affiliate at a time when relations between the network and local stations were dicey. Worse, KYW had more listeners than any other NBC affiliate, and it was owned by Westinghouse, an organization with which NBC had no desire to tangle ever again. "Don McGannon and the Westinghouse people could whisper in the ear of NBC," Ken Tiven said. "They could say, 'We can make your life miserable in Philly and Boston, which add up to four percent of the U.S. audience.' " Going through the proper channels, Mulholland contacted KYW first, then Savitch. The airtight contract ruled out any actual move for another year, but Mulholland did continue to keep in touch with her by phone.

Mulholland was not the only person from NBC who was becoming aware of Savitch. Since 1975, Bill Slatter, a former executive producer at WMAQ, the NBC O&O in Chicago, had been visiting every market in the nation searching for new talent for the network. Sitting in motel rooms from Peoria to San Diego, Slatter flipped back and forth among channels. Whenever a face seemed to pop out at him in the right way, Slatter told his boss, Joe Bartelme, the network vice-president in charge of O&Os. Bartelme in turn decided whether to recommend Slatter's find to his own boss, Dick Wald, or to a station manager with an opening. Sometimes Bartelme agreed with Slatter's judgment, and sometimes he didn't. Bartelme had snapped up Slatter's recommendation for Jane Pauley in a trice, for instance, but decided to pass on Oprah Winfrey. A news writer at WMAQ mentioned Savitch to Slatter, and he took a look the next time he passed through Philadelphia. Then he called Bartelme and told him to take a look. Bartelme liked what he saw. He looked up KYW's ratings and liked those, too. KYW had a steady, responsible program that didn't jump around like *Action News,* pulled in the viewers, and had a woman as a major anchor.

"There had been an advancement on the local level of women and blacks as anchors," Bartelme said. "Suddenly you looked at the networks and you saw there weren't any. There wasn't a single network then that had a woman in an anchor role." Ordinarily, Savitch probably would not have been considered at NBC for such a job. Unlike local stations, which made a practice of snapping up beautiful women as anchors, the network had hired only a small number of women, none of whom was allowed to begin as an anchor. "The network wanted women to be smart, to have a good education, and be good reporters," Slatter said. "We all had a good, gray image of a network reporter—a little vanilla." In Slatter's view, NBC executives "didn't want [the reporter] to dominate the news. They wanted men or women in their upper twenties or thirties who were attractive but not knockouts, because that would get in the way of a story."

But the times weren't ordinary. To network executives' amazement, the women on staff—still a tiny minority—were going nuts. In 1971, the entire network news division had sixty-odd on-air correspondents, of whom just five were females; Barbara Walters, Pauline Frederick, Liz Trotta, Cassie Mackin, and Aline Saarinen. Over the next few years, the network hired a handful of other women, including Betty Rollin, Carol Simpson, and Betty Furness, but the people who appeared on screen were almost all male. Nor was the situation any different on the other side of the camera. In 1971, NBC and its O&Os had scores of people in the studio and in the field producing news and documentaries, of whom three were women. At *NBC Nightly News,* no off-air woman had a job above the level of secretary, researcher, or production assistant. No men were employed in such dead-end posts; they generally began as desk assistants, and the way was open to move up the ladder.

"I was from Indiana and thrilled to be working at NBC,"

said Marilyn Schultz, at the time a production assistant for Wallace Westfeldt, executive producer of the evening news. "But something inside of me said there's something not fair about being a production assistant for the rest of my life. There was no place to go—no place." One morning in 1971, Schultz walked into her office, took one look at the men sitting there waiting for her to bring them coffee, and said no. Soon afterward, she and others in the news division held a companywide meeting and found that women elsewhere in NBC were even angrier. On the next National Secretaries' Day, the company sent its annual rose to all female employees (including reporters); in what was later dubbed "The Day of Roses," hundreds of women put their blossoms in interdepartmental envelopes—Schultz and several dozen other ringleaders stamped their envelopes "BULLSHIT" in two-inch-high letters—and sent them back to the personnel office. After a steering committee representing women employees met with NBC executives to complain that women were not promoted, hundreds of women at NBC suddenly found their jobs classified as managerial, but with no change in salary or job responsibility. According to Marlene Sanders, when the committee charged that women's concerns were ignored on air, the company replied that there was plenty of mention of adultery, abortion, and similar topics on soap operas. As time went on, the gap between the executives and the women seemed only to grow wider, as illustrated by a purloined memo from one vice-president to another. "Some of the women just are not taking us seriously," he wrote. "In answer to a question [in a survey] on what position they'd like to have with the company, many answered 'President of NBC.' Now come on!"

For the next three years, the women met several times a week. They gathered statistics, raised money, listened to encouraging words from the few women in leadership positions, including Barbara Walters and Cassie Mackin, and began a long legal battle against NBC. Armed with rulings issued by the FCC and the Department of Labor banning sex discrimination in broadcasting, sixteen NBC women filed a lawsuit in 1975 charging the network with sexual bias. The plaintiffs included Marilyn Schultz and Mary Hornickel, Barbara Walters's secretary. On February 13, 1977, the suit was settled for $2 million, which included back pay for more than one thousand women and a fund to implement affirmative-action guidelines to put women in a number of jobs where they had been absent or grossly underrepresented.

The suit and its successful outcome were a mortifying black eye for the network. Executives suddenly found themselves on the wrong side in public. Unhappy at looking dismayingly like male chauvinist pigs, network executives scrambled to find what they deemed to be appropriate additions to the cast of white males on the news. Wald and Schlosser claimed ever after that the suit had little effect on their hiring policies, but it is the case that more women (and more blacks) were hired after the judgment. The search, Bartelme said, was on. Accordingly, when he called Savitch early in 1977, it was with some eagerness. After they spoke, he phoned several dozen people and talked to them about her, trying to find out whether it was Savitch or Crim who was responsible for the success of KYW's news. Then he took Savitch to lunch at Raga, an elegant Indian restaurant a block from 30 Rock, and tried to assess her news skills in person. Afterward Bartelme said he was still uncertain who had sparked KYW's revival, but in the end he recommended Savitch to his boss, Dick Wald.

Although NBC was, as Wald later put it, "looking to who would be a successor to Chancellor in the great scheme of things," one solution that apparently never occurred to anyone was that his eventual successor could be a woman. Even a woman co-anchor was far too wild an idea for most NBC executives to contemplate; the only woman with enough status even to be a candidate, Barbara Walters, had to go to ABC to have a chance at it. Nonetheless, Wald said later, he was personally interested in increasing the number of prominent women who were working for NBC. When Mulholland and Bartelme brought in tapes of Savitch and their own glowing recommendations, Wald agreed to meet her. In addition, on July 13, 1977, Savitch did an audition as an anchor at 30 Rock. After it was over, she and Korn, who had brought her up to the city in his limousine, went to a celebratory dinner at the Four Seasons. Halfway through their meal, the lights went out for what turned out to be the second New York City blackout. They finished eating by candlelight and then drove through the Lincoln Tunnel toward Philly. When they looked back at the strangely dark skyline, Korn told Savitch she should do a story, and she called in a live report on the car phone to the 11:00 news back at KYW.

Wald was impressed with the audition, but wondered whether Savitch would be the ultimate star who would put NBC ahead. Despite the great hopes Mulholland and Bartelme expressed, Wald said later that he was "not willing to give away the farm." Savitch seemed to him to have plenty of potential, but he was still skeptical about whether she could bring it to bear on the kind of broadcasts that were done at NBC News. Finally, he decided to try to hire her. At Herb Schlosser's next weekly meeting with the news division, Wald showed him a tape of Savitch's work and told him that NBC News was going after her.

Meanwhile, Wald and his staff tried to come up with a schedule that would take maximum advantage of Savitch's talents. She could start off as an anchor on Sunday nights, and she could also be assigned several weekday prime-time news updates, a job that seemed to Wald to be made to order for Savitch. "People didn't particularly want to do the news briefs, because it meant being tied to a studio in the middle of the evening," Wald said. "But she was interested in showing off, in exhibiting how good she could be." However, she also needed a regular weekday reporting assignment. "If she was going to have any future with us, she had to prove that she was a competent reporter," Wald said. "Local anchors, especially in 1977, were not notorious for the wonders of their reporting." To round out her schedule, Wald decided, Savitch would be assigned to the Senate. "It was not a pivotal job," Wald said. "If she didn't do it right, we didn't suffer. Too much pressure on her would not be good."

The plan seemed sensible to Wald. But he was not a man to shed doubts easily, so he asked Don Meaney, NBC's Washington bureau chief, to meet with Savitch. The former executive producer of *Today*, Meaney had helped Barbara Walters become a major presence on television. "Meaney had great antennae," Wald said. "He would know if Savitch was not a bright person." In Wald's view, Meaney "is very sympathetic, and he really forms a bond with people. He doesn't do that if you're not a nice person. If Don didn't like her, that would be a real problem."

Meaney called Savitch and rode the Metroliner up to Philadelphia's 30th Street Station to meet her. Savitch was standing at the head of the escalator when he came up from the train platform, and they hit it off immediately. Soon afterward, she came down to Washington and they met in Union Station. There was a third meeting, again at the 30th Street Station; afterward, Savitch referred to Meaney as "that man who picked me up in a train station." Unlike Wald, Meaney saw the Senate post as a major spot; but, again unlike Wald, he had no doubts about taking Savitch. "I thought she was compelling on air as an anchor," he said, "the kind of broadcaster who made you listen."

The contract negotiations were long and complicated. Up until this point, someone with Jessica Savitch's background could expect to receive a contract that required her to stay for three full years and gave the network the option of firing her every thirteen weeks. Typically, the salary would be about $75,000; although for many, including Savitch, this would mean a pay cut, most local broadcasters jumped at the opportunity of going network. But Savitch had a rather different idea about how things should go. "She thought she had a lot of leverage going in because she was being hired not just as a reporter but also as an anchor," said Ken Tiven. "She was one of the first to come in the door as a great communicator, not just a journalist." As a result, Tiven said, "she saw herself along with Barbara Walters, in a very select group of half a dozen women."

Determined to strike a deal befitting a member of such rarefied company, Savitch sequestered herself with Korn for an entire weekend in Lancaster County, in the heart of Pennsylvania Dutch country, and went over all the elements to be included. Korn, who knew show biz, believed that a person's worth was measured by the little services they received along the way as well as how much they were paid. Together they prepared a list of demands for Savitch, who was thrilled by this visible manifestation of her increasing value. The actual negotiations were in the hands of her agent, Don Hamburg. Using what he called a "laundry list approach," Hamburg pursued not only money (under the final contract, Savitch's salary was set at $115,000 for the first year, $125,000 the second, and $140,000 the third and final year) but a set of perks more reminiscent of rock stars than humble journalists. The list included hairdressers, clothes, researchers, limousines, first-class travel allowances, and luxury hotels. Such benefits were not new at NBC—Barbara Walters had all these and more—but they were unheard-of for a new reporter. No one else along Correspondents' Row, the lengthy corridor that runs along the first floor of NBC's Washington bureau, had someone detailed to comb their hair or to wait outside in a limo, a circumstance that might have caused Savitch to pause had she grasped its significance.

Day after day, Hamburg haggled with NBC's chief contract negotiator, John Ghilain. After each session, Hamburg filled in Savitch, who conferred with Meaney. In turn, Meaney talked to Schlosser, who insisted on being kept informed although the matter was not his direct responsibility. In the interim, Savitch and Korn would have their own long sessions, talking on the phone between her chores at KYW. Savitch was departing in triumph, and she was increasingly impatient with those she was leaving behind in Philadelphia. Years of rancor spilled out, and every concession she won from NBC was another privilege denied her by miserly Westinghouse. Finally Schlosser called Meaney and asked what remained unresolved. When Meaney told him what Savitch would need to sign, Schlosser replied, "You've got it."

On August 19, 1977, Jessica Savitch did her final newscast at KYW. Although the rest of the nation was still in shock over the death of Elvis Presley three days earlier, the biggest story at KYW was Savitch's departure for NBC's Washington bureau. Viewers saw pictures from her Atlantic City High School yearbook, an interview with the principal, clips from KHOU and KYW, and farewell messages from the rest of the *Eyewitness* team. As Joe Cocker sang "You Know You're Going to Be a Star Someday," Savitch, wearing the gold four-leaf-clover pin given to her by Joe Vandergast, Paul Dowie, and Allen Kohler, swallowed hard, gave her trademark smile, and said good-bye. There was also a round of farewell gifts and parties, including a lavish banquet hosted by Mel Korn at LaTruffe, an exclusive French restaurant located on the newly renovated waterfront. On Labor Day weekend, Korn drove Savitch, her cat, and all her earthly possessions to an apartment the network had leased for her at the Watergate Hotel. "She said her teary good-byes and then I drove off," Korn said. "As soon as I got on the road, she called me up on the car phone. She was like a little girl you'd left at camp—she was missing her old home already."

As her time at KYW was coming to a close, Savitch had fallen into the habit of arriving later and later, often showing up at 5:15 to anchor at 5:30. Management had tried to accommodate her. Indeed, one afternoon when Savitch called to announce that a negotiating sesssion with NBC in New York had run too late for her to get back to Philadelphia by train in time for *Newswatch 5:30*, Tiven hired a helicopter. "The sense we had was that she was trying to get fired," said John Terrenzio, a KYW producer. "But management was so petrified of her leaving that they let her get away with murder." Savitch had little but contempt for local now. Gone were the days of laboring over the wording of a report and practicing camera turns. Gone were the days of even reading the script through before going on camera. She simply raced in the front door, slapped on some makeup, and dashed downstairs to the news set, a complicated, state-of-the-art platform dubbed the Starship Westinghouse because of its different levels and angles. Plopping herself in her anchor chair seconds before the newscast began, she watched for the red light to go on, smiled, and started talking.

She carried it off until the day the script pages were out of order on the TelePrompTer. Unable to improvise because she had not read the script beforehand, a few minutes into the program Savitch became hopelessly out of synch with the control room. When she should have been reading the transition into a commercial, the TelePrompTer was showing the beginning of a live, in-studio consumer report by a KYW correspondent. Because of the way the set was designed, with the contributing reporters seated behind and above the anchors, Savitch could not see the correspondent while she was introducing her. Thus she was shocked when she pivoted around to discover that nobody was sitting behind her. As soon as the broadcast went into the commercial, a humiliated Savitch threw her arms into the air and shrieked with rage. Even by the standards of TV egos, what then transpired was a major "fly act"—the KYW term for a temper tantrum. Red-faced, Savitch swore at the crew for the entire two-minute break. Or, rather, almost the entire two minutes. On this broadcast, as was always the case on *Newswatch 5:30*, the commercials were inter-

219

rupted for fifteen seconds while the camera panned the slightly darkened studio and the winning lottery numbers flashed on the screen. As the red light came on for this brief hiatus, Savitch's mouth snapped shut and she stared intently at her script. When the commercials resumed, she picked up her tirade in mid-scream, keeping it going until the director started counting back into the newscast. "Ten, nine, eight . . . " Every eye in the control room was on her, terrified that she would not stop calling the crew names. As the director continued counting down—"five, four, three,"—Savitch took a deep breath, emptied her face of fury, smiled an apparently genuine smile, and said in the crisp, competent voice Philadelphia knew and loved, "And *now* a word from our consumer reporter."

It had been quite a performance. As soon as it was over, engineer Gary Merkin decided that Savitch's fly act belonged in the station's collection of bloopers and screwups. He quickly copied it from the tape of the newscast intended for the station's library. Because this in-house version was provided by the studio camera, it did not show the commercials, which were electronically inserted into the actual broadcast that went out over the airwaves; it thus showed Savitch's tantrum in toto, including the weird moment when she had abruptly suspended screaming to concentrate on her script. However, because the air-feed microphones were turned off during breaks, the section that included Savitch's temper tantrum showed only a picture. Struck by her antic behavior, Merkin decided to add a sound track of his own, Aram Khatchaturian's "Sabre Dance," a charging Russian ballet piece that had acquired a kitschy second life as background music for comic chase scenes. It was a choice inspired by a malicious deity, for Savitch's arms flailed and her head bobbed with uncanny precision to the accompanying music. Cymbals crashed as she banged her desk top; violins raced to each flick of her blond hair. It was a stitch, Merkin thought. The edited tape quickly made the rounds of the station, where it was enjoyed by Savitch's many detractors, and was then tossed into a drawer with many dusty and long-forgotten blooper predecessors.

There it remained until an NBC crew was sent up to shoot a story in Philadelphia. As often happened, the crew came over to use the facilities at the local NBC affiliate, KYW. When the network people heard about the fly act by Jessica Savitch,

NBC's newest anchor, they asked to see the tape. It provoked much hilarity. "The next thing I knew, they were over in the next editing booth dubbing away," Merkin said. Soon copies of the tape were crisscrossing the country and Savitch's musically enhanced fly act had become a featured new addition to the subculture of outtakes that circulate throughout the country's broadcast news community. Insisting that they could read Savitch's lips, viewers traded versions of what she was saying during her tantrum; one of the most popular variations had Savitch yelling, "Who do I have to fuck to get out of here?" Back in Philadelphia, the tape was a nasty but ultimately harmless dig. Put into national circulation, however, it was harmful in the extreme to Savitch's standing, for it added to the bad first impression already created by the contract and spread a reputation for star behavior that she was never able to shake.

8

Washington, Part I

The Washington bureau of NBC, where Jessica Savitch worked, is housed, along with WRC, a network O&O, in an unattractive building of gray and turquoise brick that resembles a suburban elementary school of 1950s vintage. It is hidden from the road by other buildings; visitors see only a flagstone marker, adorned by the stylized silhouette of a peacock, and a long, winding drive. Near the road there is a naval security station bristling with antennae; in 1957, when the network moved to this spot, the navy facility was topped by barbed wire and guarded by marines wearing pistols. There was a rumor that the first-floor windows of WRC were deliberately placed too high for the journalists to look outside because the navy feared that they might manage to view some top-secret activity. By the fall of 1977, when Savitch came to town, the station had acquired two more floors and a new wing, but it was still the same crowded place in the Washington sticks—on Nebraska Avenue, near Ward Circle—that staffers had been complaining about for twenty years. Unlike the Washington bureaus of the other two networks, located just blocks from the White House, WRC was stuck in the boonies, down the street from sleepy American University. Considering the network's sagging fortunes, its Washington bureau's place on the margin had a certain gloomy appropriateness.

Before moving to Nebraska Avenue, WRC had been based in a Washington hotel, and its broadcasting facilities had been so weak that David Brinkley, who was then a WRC anchor, had sometimes received calls from viewers who wanted to congratulate him on being visible in the suburbs that night. A quarter century later, in 1977, WRC had expanded to take up most of the Nebraska Avenue building, but it shared the newsroom on the first floor with the network. For the most part, local and network worked with a certain measure of camaraderie. But whenever a big story came up, network reminded local of its place, snatching up equipment and crew and leaving WRC scrambling to pull together its local newscast from what was left over. No matter how successful reporters were at WRC, they were forever trying to leave their lowly local status behind and to take up quarters in the cramped splendor of the NBC Correspondents' Row on the first floor. This corridor of small, cheerless offices was one of the most prestigious in the network, for it was from there that the House, Senate, and president were covered. The most important national correspondents had worked there—each cubicle on both sides of the hallway fairly reeked of history—and network people who couldn't wangle an office there felt acute envy.

Most local broadcasters who switched to network would have gratefully accepted a broom closet on the inner, windowless side; Jessica Savitch, however, insisted on a highly prized window office. Although she was more than likely unaware when she moved in that others who had been waiting their turn for this coveted space would now have to wait longer, her new mates on Correspondents' Row took note of the special treatment she received. The office was only one of many perks suggested by Mel Korn and negotiated by Don Hamburg. They had imagined that they understood such contracts, for Korn had done business with Hollywood and Hamburg had worked with KYW. Unfortunately, they did not understand the differences between show business and the network news business, or that a show of glamour on Nebraska Avenue would be like waving a red flag in front of the newshounds there.

Savitch moved into a big, expensive, glacially private

high-rise on Massachusetts Avenue, just down the street from the station. It was one of the first apartment houses many of her colleagues had ever seen with a security guard who announced guests on an intercom, and its forbidding and reserved nature seemed to them somewhat like Savitch herself. Her elegant, spotless apartment had French doors and white rugs and big black-and-white plaid sofas and a huge terrace. The effect was expensive, hotel-style bland. The one exception was a large model of Nipper, the black-and-white mutt that was the RCA corporate symbol, which Savitch told visitors had been given to her by Edgar Griffiths. (It had. A lifelong Philadelphian who commuted to 30 Rock in midtown Manhattan everyday from his Main Line home by limousine, Griffiths had been a regular viewer of KYW and a fan of its young, blond anchor.) But Savitch had no need to stamp her apartment with her personality; even then, her real life was her life on air. Like the famous high-wire aerialist Karl Wallenda, who once declared, "Life is the high-wire, and everything else is in between," Savitch was her truest self in front of a camera; off camera, she was always scrambling to come up with what she considered an appropriate self-presentation. "Most people create a character to be on television, but [that's when] the real Jessica shone through," Ron Kershaw said later. "The rest of it was like creating this persona and putting on different masks for different situations."

The money, the limo, the chichi digs—all these things alarmed Savitch's co-workers and told them that the network thought she was someone special. In truth, NBC did have big expectations of her, but nobody in New York had ever quite decided what they were. Dick Wald, who had hired her, might have been able to give Savitch an idea of what, exactly, she was supposed to accomplish, but he was fired by Herb Schlosser in October 1977, a month after Savitch's arrival. Schlosser was in turn sacked in January 1978, a casualty of Edgar Griffiths's determination to close the $50 million gap between the profits of his network and those of CBS.★ The network hired Fred

---

★ *Griffiths proceeded to put Schlosser in charge of the development of programming for the video disc, a major RCA project that ultimately (through no fault of Schlosser) was a failure. Schlosser also became head of RCA's Entertainment Group, which*

Silverman to replace Schlosser, but the man with the golden gut was still bound to his contract with ABC for another five and a half months, and could not take the reins. Unable to work at either network, he jetted around the country, dogged by a phalanx of journalists who eagerly remarked every word and gesture in the hope of discovering Silverman in the act of illicitly contacting NBC. According to television journalist Sally Bedell, industry insiders joked that NBC and Silverman were trading secret messages in hollowed-out pineapples, and a character in Gary Trudeau's *Doonesbury* speculated on what sorts of programs Silverman would create at NBC.

Because Silverman had no management experience, Jane Cahill Pfeiffer, a former IBM executive who had served as a go-between in negotiations between Silverman and NBC, was made chairman of the company. Silverman, the president, theoretically reported to her, but in reality the reverse was true. When the president was able finally to assume office in June, he stunned everyone by declaring his intention to present only quality programs and canceled several of the network's more inane new shows, a move that netted him approving headlines but left NBC stranded with few potential hits. By Thanksgiving, the entire entertainment schedule of shows had been pulled and Silverman was putting together yet another lineup; its centerpiece was *Supertrain,* a loosely constructed adventure series that would take place on an extravagant resort hotel on wheels that cost $12 million to build. The program bombed. Silverman, the Wild Man of CBS and then of ABC, became the Wild Man of NBC, holding endless meetings, demanding to read scripts, insisting on approving everything. His impetuousness was famous; he signed two Japanese performers to a thirteen-week series before he learned they couldn't speak English. His temper tantrums were infamous. According to David Adams, when Silverman had to wait for an elevator he would kick the doors. By the end of the 1978 season, NBC's profits had fallen 20 percent, from $152 million in 1977 to $122 million. The network had a secure lock on third place for the next four years.

included RCA Records and RCA's participation in RCA/Columbia Pictures Home Video and the Arts and Entertainment Network. Currently he is a senior advisor at Wertheim Schroder & Co., an investment house in New York City.

Office politicking would convulse 30 Rock for years to come, and executives would be too preoccupied with the orgy of back-stabbing and hide-saving to devote much time to thinking about the welfare of their highly touted new reporter in Washington, D.C.

As the entertainment division floundered, first while waiting for Silverman and then, even more drastically, after he arrived, the news division, too, faltered. When Wald was fired, a month after Jessica Savitch had arrived in Washington, a man named Les Crystal had reluctantly taken up the reins as president of NBC News. He had been senior producer of *Nightly News* and was widely thought an extremely nice fellow. But network news is even more widely thought a place that must be run by a not-nice fellow. This is held to be especially true if the network news in question is in trouble. Not only was the *Nightly News* audience diminishing, but NBC's morning show, *Today,* the most lucrative program in the news division, was under siege from ABC's *Good Morning America.* One symptom of the malaise was allowing Savitch, before she had even arrived in Washington, to pose in front of the Capitol for an *US* article entitled "Barbara Walters, Move Over!" Another had been to promise her time as an anchor on the weekend and on what was then called *NBC News Update,* while demanding that she show her worthiness for the task by working weekdays as the chief Senate correspondent—and then, before she had a chance even to begin to learn the ropes, to tour her around the affiliate circuit as the newest, brightest star in the NBC News firmament. As a result, both her role and her image became permanently confused; she was, in Pat Trese's phrase, hired to be a sex object, but a *newsy* sex object. And nobody, least of all Savitch, knew what that was.

Every weekend she flew up to New York, checked into the suite NBC maintained at the Plaza Hotel, and spent Sunday over at 30 Rock in the fifth-floor newsroom preparing for the evening broadcast. Because the show used what was called an "open" set—that is, the anchor was visible from head to toe—Savitch anguished before her first newscast, on November 6, about inadvertently crossing her legs in a revealing position. "To protect myself," she wrote in *Anchorwoman,* "I took a piece of thick masking tape—the kind reporters say mends everything but broken hearts—and taped my ankles together."

It worked so well that after the show was over, Savitch stood up to shake hands with the crew and fell flat on her face.

Over the months that followed, Savitch's Sunday night performance received high marks. She drew particular praise in November 1979 when she went on the air with no script and narrated a videotape of the murder of Congressman Leo Ryan and his party in Jonestown. Because the tape had been fed to New York by satellite only moments before airtime, Savitch had not yet viewed the horrifying footage, which showed men with machine guns firing at the Congressional party and NBC correspondent Don Harris, and ended abruptly when NBC cameraman Bob Brown was killed. Calm and collected as ever, Savitch broke out of form only once, when she exclaimed, "Unbelievable!" Staffers later printed the word in large letters and framed it in chrome for Savitch's office. "She was flying by the seat of her pants that night," Sid Davis, director of news at the NBC Washington bureau, told one reporter. "She did a superb job of ad-libbing."

By now her anchor style was polished to a high gloss: tough, sharp, precise, seemingly invincible. She had done the impossible. She had welded together a beautiful, photogenic, perfectly put-together feminine appearance with an air of authority and credibility associated only with male anchors, and broadcasters everywhere were taking a close look. Not all liked what they saw; some found her studied presentation brittle, stiff, shellacked into place. But no one doubted that Savitch represented something new and powerful, something that could, for better or for worse, have a large and lasting impact on television news.

The first bit of history-making came on November 20, 1977, when she'd been at the network only two months. That evening, she co-anchored a special one-hour version of the Sunday night newscast that featured Savitch in New York, Brinkley in Washington, and Chancellor in Jerusalem. Waiting to go on the air, she later wrote, she looked at the studio monitors and saw "John coolly standing in Jerusalem and David coolly smoking a cigarette and shuffling through his papers in Washington and me in New York attempting to look cool. I was overcome. These men were the giants of the industry. Even if I had only read, 'Good evening, heavy rainstorms deluged the West Coast, good night,' I would have been happy." Having shown her mettle that evening, she was periodically assigned to substitute for Chancellor and Brinkley on the weekday *Nightly News*. Although other women had anchored the less prestigious weekend news, Savitch was the first in the history of NBC to occupy the peacock throne on a weeknight.

Savitch was by no means the first woman at NBC's Washington bureau. Indeed, she was stepping into some very large shoes. In 1971, a strong-minded ex-newspaper reporter from Baltimore named Cassie Mackin had barged through the door. Unlike Savitch, who was constantly being called away to give speeches or grant interviews, Mackin was allowed to learn her job and covered the Senate so well that the next year she was a network floor reporter at the national political conventions. In the last week in September of 1972, Mackin filed a story detailing Nixon's distortions of McGovern's positions that was so bluntly phrased and minutely detailed that the White House was on the phone to NBC before the end of the broadcast. Bob Mulholland, then executive producer of the *Nightly News,* was sitting in his office when the report came on the air. According to Wallace Westfeldt, Mulholland went running across the hall to see Wald, who called Mackin in the next week and told her she was being sent to California to learn about film. "It was a kind of exile," Westfeldt said. Angered, Mackin eventually left NBC and was House correspondent for ABC when Jessica Savitch came to Washington in 1977.

Covering the House for NBC when Savitch arrived was a former AP correspondent named Linda Ellerbee, who had been Savitch's replacement back at KHOU. After a stint covering crime at WCBS in New York, Ellerbee had come to NBC in 1975 as a general assignment reporter, a job otherwise known as the bottom of the heap. An irreverent broadcaster whose idea of dressing up for work was putting on a clean pair of jeans, Ellerbee was a dogged reporter and a fast, witty writer. According to Don Meaney, her elegant on-air skewering of Representative Wayne Hays for using public funds to pay a secretary, Elizabeth Ray, who did not even know how to type earned Ellerbee a regular beat as House correspondent.

Other women were covering other important beats for NBC. Hilary Brown, who had reported from Asia, the Middle East, and Europe for CBS and ABC, was now in Israel for NBC. Judy Woodruff, who had worked for the ABC and CBS affiliates in Atlanta before going to the NBC bureau there, was assigned by the network to the White House because of her expertise on fellow Georgian Jimmy Carter. Like Savitch, she had been a reporter and anchor at the local level; unlike Savitch, she was willing to start again from the bottom as a third-string White House correspondent. Once in Washington, Woodruff waited outside the Oval Office with a tenacity that earned her the sobriquet "Stake-out Queen" as well as the respect of her colleagues. Woodruff paid her dues, she didn't make a fuss, and she hung in for the endless dull waits, hugging driveways on the off-chance that a news subject might pass in front of the camera. (Later she went to the *Today* show as a reporter and then to a job as correspondent on PBS's prestigious *MacNeil-Lehrer Report*.)

Savitch did things differently. She reasoned that she had put in plenty of time as a street reporter, and that she did not need to clock any more hours chasing fires. She was already launched as a weekend anchor, and the idea of beginning anywhere except as high up as she could position herself was out of the question. Nonetheless, the network insisted that a prerequisite for going any further at NBC, either as a top correspondent or as an anchor, was a credible performance as a reporter. Regarding the Senate assignment as a temporary chore, she put up with the work, only to become aware quickly that the job was over her head.

In the grand tradition of television journalism, being a correspondent at NBC was as much of a sink-or-swim proposition as it had been at KHOU. Unfortunately, it had been some time since Savitch had to do anything more strenuous than float on her back and bask in the warm bath of stardom. With the exception of the Carter-Ford debate, it had been years since she had gone after a breaking story, and many months since she had done anything beyond the minimum exertion necessary to read the news to Philadelphia viewers at 5:30 and 11:00. Worse, she had come to the network's largest bureau, where there were dozens of other ambitious and energetic reporters, all vying to have their stories included within the few precious minutes allotted every evening to Washington.

Unlike the daily pieces Savitch had done in Houston and Philadelphia, the Senate is not a story that could be reported, filed, and forgotten. Senate reporters have to track legislation as it wends its way through committees and amendments and reconciliations and tablings and hearings. They have to follow half a dozen stories simultaneously until they can be reported on, and work the luncheons on days when there is no chance of getting a piece on the evening news. The cast of characters is huge: In addition to the one hundred senators, there are thousands of lobbyists, staff members, press agents, lawyers, and government bureaucrats. All have to be identified as players before they can be coddled and cajoled and sometimes threatened into giving up the goods. Reporters at the Senate spend their days building contacts, angling for tips, waiting for leaks. No dead bodies are fished out of the river, and no juries file into courtrooms to read the verdict. The story in the Senate is the slow, never-ending job of governing the nation.

One of the most important points for a Senate reporter to grasp, according to Linda Werthheimer, congressional correspondent for National Public Radio in the late 1970s, is that what's happening at any given moment in the Senate probably isn't happening for the first time. Without that knowledge, Werthheimer said, one is constantly—and inappropriately—amazed. "It's hard for someone without any background to understand the rituals, the relationships between farm states and urban areas, the fact that the U.S. always tries to demobilize after wars as quickly as possible and that we hate our standing armies," she said. "If you don't know this, you can be very puzzled." Congress, she said, "is very hard to cover because no matter what you do it comes down mostly to white men talking to each other. It never catches fire, it never explodes, and it isn't pretty."

Although reporters assigned to other Washington beats have been known to do little more than wait for handouts and show up for press conferences, the Senate requires steady legwork. "You cover it by moving around the Capitol, talking to staffers, being on the telephone," said Don Farmer, who was covering the Senate for ABC in 1977. The senators, Farmer said, "are spread thin and facing their own blizzard of information. They rely on their staff for detailed knowledge. Talking to the senators lets you cover the touchdowns, but you miss the grunt work."

Every time the reporters come to work at the Senate, they are confronted by a museum of Americana in the form of the

Capitol's Senate wing, an astonishingly ornate structure constructed during the Civil War in part as a symbol that the Union would endure. Overhead are elaborately carved arches and spandrels, and the walls are covered with murals depicting scenes of historical and allegorical import. On the floors are equally elaborate floral and geometric patterns made from red-, blue-, and cream-colored glazed tiles manufactured by England's Minton works in the 1850s. There seems no end to the lore about the place. As soon as Savitch learned one tidbit, like the tradition of senators' carving their names in the lids of their old-fashioned wooden desks, or the fact that the sixth desk from the left in the back row held candy for members to nibble on, there would be a dozen more such footnotes to be absorbed.

Then, of course, there is the business at hand to be comprehended and described and analyzed—a job that requires not simply recognizing faces but being able to figure out the intricate legislative ballet. Unlike the tidy process delineated in the neat little diagram in high school civics books entitled "How a Bill Becomes a Law," real lawmaking is a complex, often untidy affair, for which there is no adequate flow chart. Even Robert's Rules of Order, the bible of the chamber, provides only partial guidance to the parliamentary machinations and political considerations involved in many maneuvers. Savitch would have to note not only who had the floor and when, but who was caucusing with whom during the breaks, and who didn't speak or didn't join in caucuses. Meanwhile, she would be listening to a speech filled with legal terminology often phrased with a precision that obscured its true significance.

There was neither time nor space for quiet reflection on these weighty matters. The old plans for the Senate wing of the Capitol, of course, did not take into account the introduction and growth of electronic media. Accordingly, the print reporters were located in crammed but convenient quarters on the third floor, just off the Senate visitors' galleries, whereas the latecomers, the radio, TV, and wire correspondents, were mashed into the impossibly small Senate radio and television gallery on the other side of the building. In 1939, the thirty-nine radio correspondents at the Senate could fit into the forty-foot-square room; by the late 1970s, over seven hundred radio and television reporters wre assigned there. Most never attempted to use their official quarters, but the gallery was still wall-to-wall people all day, every day. Squeezed into one corner was a fifteen-foot-square studio with a backdrop of red leather-bound volumes of the Congressional Record—for variety, a blue curtain could be drawn in front of the books—in which legislators could hold press conferences or be interviewed. Along one wall and in much of the open floor space were telephones, tables, and manual typewriters for which several score hardy souls competed furiously every day. The Associated Press, United Press International, Mutual Radio Network, and the three television networks were the royalty of the place and were assigned to the broadcast booths set up along the east wall. Although luxurious compared to the bedlam in the rest of the room, the booths were cramped; inside NBC's six-foot by twelve-foot space were Jessica Savitch, NBC radio correspondent Russ Ward, a wire-service machine, and an even smaller recording studio. Adding to the claustrophobia, a loft area had been constructed over the booths as office space for the gallery staff.

Working in such a manic, high-pressure environment was horribly stressful for everyone. What made the assignment worse for Savitch was that her particular skills were nearly the opposite of what the job required. Her gift for moving into a new situation, sizing it up quickly, and delivering a succinct summary—the very ability that brought her to Mulholland's attention during the presidential debates in 1976—could not begin to get her through a protracted debate over a multibillion-dollar weapons system. Her skill at interviewing ordinary people on everyday subjects, such as being single or listening to rock 'n' roll, was of little help when she had to get a senator to talk about a nuance of a certain foreign policy initiative or to quiz staff members concerning parliamentary end-runs being played out on the chamber floor.

"In Jessica's day, we did really simple pieces," said John Holland, a desk producer in the Washington bureau at the time. "It was all run-and-gun. You'd have a long voice-over, a wide shot of a hearing room [or a sketch of the chamber], a sound bite from an official, and a closing stand-up. Sometimes the reporter just stood up and talked into the camera and there would be no interviews." What counted in such reports was not how Savitch looked and smiled, but her ability to penetrate the layers of legal language, political maneuvering, and regional and personal self-interest and come up with an accurate summary that nailed everything down in two minutes or less. "Washington is a one-story town where you have to take the politicians seriously," said Pat Trese. "In those days, if you wanted to do a picture story and do it right, you'd do it in New York. But if you were interested in talking heads, you'd go to D.C. It was journalism, but not human-interest material. The stories were about issues, not people."

Unfortunately for Savitch, issues were the competition's strong suit. In Houston and in Philadelphia she had come up against others covering the same story, but her aggressive manner and attractive style usually gave her the edge. In the Senate her rivals were seasoned network veterans, and the contest was of an entirely different order. Phil Jones, the CBS correspondent, had covered Vietnam and had spent the last decade reporting on regional and national politics; Don Farmer, there for ABC, had done a tour of duty in Europe and the Middle East for that network as well as two years covering the House. In Philadelphia, their laconic delivery and sober manner would have got them sent to charisma coaches if not actually yanked off the air. In D.C., however, they were the very model of everything a political correspondent should be. They were heavy hitters, men who knew the Senate cold and spent all day every day getting to know it better.

Savitch, too, spent every day she was in Washington getting to know the Senate better. In her case, however, this did not amount to a lot of time. NBC had hired a star, and it was eager to show her off whenever possible. Accordingly, management encouraged her to accept the many requests for newspaper and magazine profiles, even when this meant she would not be able to cover the Senate for a day or two. In addition, the network continually sent her to speak and be seen at conferences and regional gatherings and affiliate events. When Brown University asked alumnus Bob Kasmire, an NBC vice-president in charge of corporate information and public relations, to get Savitch to speak at a seminar, he happily obliged. Speaking invitations poured in to Ida McGuinness, and Savitch was booked months in advance on the paid lecture circuit. Although she was not an unwilling pupil at the Senate, she was often an absentee one. According to Russ Ward, her roommate in the

NBC broadcast booth, she was sometimes missing even during important Senate floor debates.

It also didn't help that she was replacing Bob McCormick, another serious-looking male who had worked with David Brinkley at WRC thirty years earlier. "McCormick was like a crony, a member of the old-boy network," said John Travieso, a news producer in the Washington bureau. "He kept in touch with certain sources. Everybody liked him—and there's always the feeling that people already there are better than newcomers." Savitch represented Change with a capital C, the arrival of a star where there had been none before, and her co-workers were less than happy about it.

In this job Jessica Savitch could not simply elbow her way around her rivals and concentrate on how she looked. The stakes were different. What counted was satisfying her invisible bosses in New York City, for without them she would not get on the air. Unlike local, network had a surplus of correspondents. In Houston and Philadelphia, the stations did not have the money to send people out to cover a lot of things that might not get broadcast. The stations were like newspapers, desperate to fill space, and the only argument was whether a story was played big or small. By contrast, the networks had money to burn, and they burned it. Vast amounts of tape were shot for every minute that appeared on the screen, and whole bureaus didn't get airtime for days on end. Being at the Senate meant that Savitch's chances were better than most, but her appearance was by no means guaranteed, a situation that she found unpalatable.

Not surprisingly in view of how little help she received and how many other obligations she was expected to fulfill, Savitch's performance at the Senate continued to disappoint network executives. "She never really had a chance," said Gerry Solomon, then a *Nightly News* producer in Washington. "She was doomed from the start." Yet at the same time, news division brass remained reluctant to do anything about the problem. "There was so much money and hype invested in her by then," said one knowledgeable source. "We didn't know what to do, so we just sat there and waited for lightning to strike."

The stories she was covering began in Washington but were finished in New York City. For the first time in Savitch's

234

life, she was not in direct contact with the people she had to please. The workday began with a discussion of story ideas with Chris Michon, head producer for the small task force within the bureau that worked directly with *NBC Nightly News.* By noon a field producer had been assigned to any story thought to have a chance of getting past the guardians of airtime in 30 Rock. A crew was dispatched to shoot videotape, unless the location was inside the Senate chamber; because cameras were not allowed within the chamber at that time, the network had to rely on sketch artists for such stories. Savitch wrote a script and put it into a Rapifax machine in the NBC booth. Moments later, an identical machine at the Nebraska Avenue office emitted a copy for Michon to go over.

A second Rapifax copy went to Gil Millstein, the news editor at 30 Rock. Pugnacious and skeptical, Millstein had spent thirteen years in the news business at the *New York Times,* where, the joke has it, the editors are trained to bark out "How do you know?" if a subordinate is rash enough to predict that the sun will rise the next morning. Like the *Times* itself, Millstein was a stickler for grammar and he looked with an unsympathetic eye at anything flashy. He had worked for years with David Brinkley, and it took him next to no time to decide that Jessica Savitch was an illiterate piece of local fluff. "When one of her scripts came over my desk, I used to scream," Millstein said. "No matter what she covered, it was badly done and needed to be corrected." Although he did not consider Savitch the worst reporter he'd ever worked with, "she was down toward the bottom of the list—so close to the bottom it doesn't make any difference." Savitch never knew what to do about Millstein. His hostility became yet another one of the crosses she had to bear, and she often lost her temper defensively.

Holding his nose, Millstein would go through Savitch's copy and then bring it to Bill Wheatley, the New York producer responsible for Washington stories. If there were further questions, the story went to the executive producer, Paul Greenberg, and, in some cases, to the anchor, John Chancellor. Changes, corrections, expansions, and reductions were discussed up and down the line. The several hundred words were massaged and re-massaged, phone calls going back and forth to Savitch all the while. Even getting this far did not guarantee that the story would be used; it might still be killed, changed into a voice-over to be delivered by the anchor, or shelved for Savitch to use for the Sunday edition of *Nightly News,* which was not considered on par with the weekday news. "Everybody had opinions," said John Holland. "You had to wait for them to be formed and conveyed. You would sit by the phone and wait for instructions." Once a final version was available, Savitch would step into the tiny studio inside the NBC booth and make a recording, which was fed by phone to Nebraska Avenue. There a tape editor, working with the field producer, would fit the sound track to the picture.

The story might open in any number of ways, but the closing seconds were almost invariably done from "Elmsite," a large elm tree on the lawn outside the House wing of the Capitol where the networks had installed a power supply and permanent phone lines back to the bureaus. Elmsite was a tradition Savitch detested: "Even when the driving snow plasters your hair to your face, you brave it in the outdoors," she wrote in *Anchorwoman.* "I have often wondered how viewers could believe anything said by a woman too stupid to come in from a blizzard, but producers are apparently convinced that a view of the elm . . . or the Capitol dome gives the story depth."

In order to include the latest developments, Savitch wrote her closing remarks at the end of the day. These, too, had to get past Millstein and up the chain of command. If they received the seal of approval, she recorded her words on a cassette and dashed out to Elmsite. As the camera crew set up to tape her standing in front of the Capitol in the fading daylight, Savitch stuck an earphone in place. She carried the tape recorder beneath her coat or attached to the back of her belt, an arrangement that allowed her to hear and repeat the recorded version with an appearance of spontaneity. Lights came on, Savitch brushed her hair back, smiled, and began speaking. The camera rolled for the ten- or fifteen-second ending. The story was done. The next morning, she would begin another.

Two days after she had begun working the Senate, Savitch did her first story at the network, a quick report on presidential candidate Ronald Reagan's opposition to the newly negotiated Panama Canal Treaty. Over the next two months, she did fifteen more stories for the weekday *Nightly News* on subjects that included a Senate vote to increase the minimum wage, an account on the status of a pending maritime cargo preference bill, and the return to the Capitol of Senator Hubert Humphrey, mortally ill with cancer. In mid-November, two months into the job, Savitch and a crew went to Panama with the Senate Foreign Relations Committee, which was discussing the canal treaty with the country's ruler, General Omar Torrijos. While Savitch was out with the senators on a helicopter and boat tour of Panama, producer Jim Lee went to the room of the tape editor, Nelson Martinez, to look at some footage. The door burst open, and Panamanian police swept in, began a frantic search, and produced a shoe filled with marijuana. Savitch came back to find a guard blocking the door to Martinez's room, Lee and Martinez sitting in the slammer, and Martinez protesting that the dope had been planted by customs agents. Savitch initiated a flurry of international phone calls and finally managed to get someone at NBC to pull strings in the State Department, which pulled strings in Panama City. Within a few hours, a shaken Lee and Martinez were setting up for a satellite feed to the *Nightly News*. To demonstrate her presence in conflicted territory, Savitch did the report in a khaki fatigue jacket. The trip produced four stories, and the arrest was almost reduced in memory to a hilarious scrape.

As she coped with her first stories, Savitch experienced the ordinary embarrassments of beginning a new job. She couldn't find the Senate gallery; she didn't recognize key senators; she battled with Millstein over her grammar. A more serious problem was the lack of any single producer for the Senate beat, which meant that she did not have anyone to orient her on a regular basis. She received some pointers from Senate staff members, but they had hundreds of other correspondents to attend to and could give her only limited assistance. She also spent a day at the White House learning the ropes from NBC correspondent Bob Jamieson, but in that amount of time she could not begin to learn all she needed. Savitch worked hard, perhaps too hard, making lists on long yellow legal pads, sweating over any copy she had to file, and going over and over her *Update* spots. Unlike Hill correspondents Linda Ellerbee and Cassie Mackin or general assignment reporter Carol Simpson, Savitch was never one of the gang in the bureau. "She seemed pleasant and energetic," Bob Jamieson said, "but she seemed to reveal very little of herself—and this is a business where people become fast friends and quick enemies." There was always a certain distance between Savitch and her co-workers, in part because of their initial mistrust of the glamorous intruder but also in part because of her fear of not being able to hold up her end of the political gossip that is the food and drink of the Washington bureau. "She knew she didn't know," said one reporter who was at the Washington bureau at the time. "At first she didn't know that, but then she learned, and it ate at her."

Paradoxically, Savitch was at the same time providing to women journalists around the country a powerful new image of what a network newswoman should look like. "She was so carefully put together," said National Public Radio's Linda Werthheimer. "The look wasn't really elegant but it hit a middle-brow spot—silk blouses and polyester suits. It was as if she dressed for the fifty-year-old gents who ran the network, as if not to be noticed for her clothing. Such attention to detail was really noticeable. Nobody invented themselves quite like she did for this role." In Werthheimer's view, "She didn't dress to be beautiful or striking or interesting. What she wore wasn't even *becoming*. She wasn't dressing for herself but for the screen, and she really had it figured out."

In January 1978, when Savitch had been at the Senate four months, NBC sent Savitch on Vice-President Fritz Mondale's fence-mending tour of the West and Northwest. Unlike the other networks, NBC did not send a camera crew for the four-day, twelve-state trip; the notion was to give Savitch some general background by letting her watch the national press corps at work and listen to Mondale. The trip was not terribly useful for her current assignment, the Senate, for which the best schooling would have been to stay right in Washington, D.C., nor did it seem to offer much help in other areas; afterward, Savitch seemed neither better informed about national politics nor more tuned into the Washington press scene. Russ Ward, the NBC radio man who shared the network booth with Savitch, noticed she was lonely and guarded—inordinately pleased if he asked her out for a sandwich. "She was always whispering on the telephone to someone in Philly," he said. "In those crammed quarters, there was nothing personal. Everybody knew everybody else's business. Except nobody knew Jessica's business, because she was so private."

As the Mondale junket was en route back to Washington,

D.C., Senator Hubert Humphrey, who had been Mondale's mentor, died. There was some thought of diverting Savitch to Minneapolis, Humphrey's home, but higher forces in New York decided to bring the Senate correspondent, who was presumably chockablock with details about Humphrey, back for the funeral in Washington. Then, at the last minute, 30 Rock chose to broadcast live the arrival of Humphrey's body at the Capitol. The decision caused havoc at NBC's Washington bureau on the cold, rainy Saturday morning of January 14, 1978. Rousted from bed by executives in the Big Apple, the D.C. bureau had to come up with hours of thoughtful, incisive, yet respectful remarks while the camera focused almost the entire time on a motionless casket. The sole activity would be the transfer of Humphrey's body from Andrews Air Force Base to the Capitol, followed by an endless parade of people filing by a flagdraped casket. Making the broadcast even more difficult was the fact that the anchor and correspondents would be off camera nearly the entire time and thus could not add to the coverage by their own physical presence; they would be simply disembodied voices, narrating a static picture.

Exhausted from the Mondale trip, Savitch had gone to bed at 1:00 A.M. Shortly after sunrise, a producer was on the phone telling her to get ready for her first live network special. Her assignment was to provide coverage inside the Rotunda, where the Happy Warrior was lying in state, an honor so rarely accorded that it was in itself enough to trigger massive coverage. Bob Jamieson was about to start cooking a big birthday dinner for his best friend's fortieth birthday party when he got the word to drop everything and get over to the bureau to serve as anchor. "It was an extremely rocky day because of the confusion in the control room over when to go on air and how long to stay there," he said later. "It took an endless amount of time for events to take place. It was a hard story for television because although history was in the making, not much was actually happening."

Speaking in the hushed tones befitting this mournful scene, Jamieson tried to fill out the airtime by noting and re-noting the highlights of Humphrey's career. Because most of the camera shots were from some distance, Jamieson, who was viewing the scene on the newsroom monitor at Nebraska Avenue, was unable to identify many of the participants. "It was tremendously frustrating," he said. "Jessica was actually at the Capitol, and she was supposed to carry half the load. But she just wasn't confident about the people and the place." Savitch found the whole occasion a nightmare. Unsure who was who in the parade of dark suits, unprepared to supply tidbits of inside info on those she did know, and unable to use her commanding appearance to paper over the gaps in her coverage, she repeated mechanically the few facts she knew: There were no rules for who could lay in state in the Rotunda, Humphrey was the fifth senator to do so, and the last person to lay atop the high black catafalque, built for Abraham Lincoln, had been a former president, Lyndon Johnson, in January 1973. During the long pauses between her remarks, the microphones picked up the footsteps that echoed from the dome overhead.

As with any live special event, network news executives were watching intently and evaluating work with particular care and rigor. It was an opportunity to shine, but Savitch did not do so, a lapse that did not pass unnoticed at Nebraska Avenue or 30 Rock. Listening to her flounder through the Humphrey funeral, her new co-workers heard what they had expected to hear: a reporter out of her depth in the Big Time. "Everyone at NBC realized the problem pretty quickly," said veteran reporter Douglas Kiker. "She was a very hot news presence but she was very unqualified as far as her news potential went. She was never mean or bitchy. Her ego was no smaller than the rest of us, but next to this intense, driven woman was a scared, shy little girl. You wanted to give her a hug and say everything is going to be all right."

In Philadelphia, Savitch would have marched into the office of Alan Bell or Jim Topping or Ken Tiven and insisted that things be done her way and, after some shouting and yelling, there would probably have been some modification if not a complete overhaul. Back in Houston, she might have cried into one of Dick John's linen handkerchiefs and extracted consoling concessions. Their official counterpart in Washington, bureau chief Don Meaney, always listened to Savitch sympathetically —too sympathetically, in the eyes of many at the bureau—but he did not have enough clout to give his new protégée much help. "He was not operating out of headquarters in New York," said Richard Valeriani, the NBC State Department correspondent at the time. "He could schmooze with the executive producer of one of the shows, but he couldn't do much more if the perception had been created that Jessica Savitch was not a good reporter."

On March 16, 1978, Savitch was again scheduled to take part in a special live report from Washington, on the Senate vote on the Panama Canal Treaty. For that night, Savitch became a sort of subanchor on the *Nightly News,* stationed at a desk in the Capitol. Unfortunately, the only place producer Bob Asman could get permission for the elaborate setup this required was Statuary Hall, a huge, circular chamber on the House side of Capitol Hill. Savitch was unhappy about the location, and she was even more unhappy that there was no place for her to sit outside of public view. To her mortification, she was ringed by gawking tourists as a makeup artist and hairstylist prepared her for the broadcast. At one point, hypoglycemia drove her into what Asman later described as "a kind of physical fit" and she said that she had to have sugar immediately. Asman sent someone to get a candy bar, and Savitch wolfed it down just before the broadcast. But it did not improve her mood.

Outside, in a heavy rainstorm, NBC's national correspondent Tom Pettit, waited, microphone in hand, to interview key senators after the vote was taken. As described in Linda Ellerbee's autobiography, *And So It Goes,* Pettit and Senator Charles Mathias, a liberal Republican from Maryland, huddled under Pettit's umbrella while waiting for NBC to cut to the interview. Shivering in the frigid downpour, they listened to a voice in their earpieces. It was NBC's on-site anchor, Jessica Savitch.

What they heard was a woman complaining that her hair didn't look right and this was network television and if the network didn't hire a hairdresser who knew what he was doing, well, they should hire another one right after they fired this one.

The rain didn't let up and neither did the noise from the Rotunda. After a while, Tom felt his nose begin to run, but with both hands occupied, there was precious little he could do about it, except stand there in the rain and listen to beauty-parlor talk coming into his ear from inside the warm, dry Rotunda. Tom's nose ran on. Finally, the Senator, saying nothing, reached into his pocket, took out his handkerchief and, with it, gently wiped the nose of a twenty-five-year veteran political reporter. Neither man mentioned the scene inside. They were professionals.

During 1978, an election year, Savitch periodically hit the Senate campaign trail. One day that summer, she rode on the press bus covering John Warner's run against Andrew Pickens Miller for the Senate seat being vacated by Harry F. Byrd, Jr. Also on the bus was Sam Donaldson, ABC's longtime Senate correspondent who had gone to the White House in 1976. "Jessica Savitch was a hot topic of conversation in the news business back then," Donaldson said later. "I have to say I felt sorry for her. She was nice enough, but she was lost. We all tried to help her, to say they'll be going here next, but she was just lost." On such jaunts, he said, reporters "are always asking each other questions, but the kind of questions you ask because you got on the bus late. She was asking really fundamental questions, which showed she didn't know what was happening."

Adding to her difficulties, Savitch was frequently sick and had minor surgery for the gynecological problems that plagued her all her adult life. A week before the election, she trudged around Maine, following the race between the Republican candidate, William Cohen, and the Democratic incumbent, Senator William Hathaway. During the shooting, she frequently had to lie down and rest, and she looked so ill and so thin that cameraman Dean Gaskill was alarmed. "She was tired all the time," he said. "Every time we went out for two hours, she'd be just wiped out."

For election night, Savitch was assigned to provide live coverage of the Senate races, and she was terrified. She made conscientious preparations for the big night, making even longer lists than usual of things to be done each day, interviewing every incumbent and opponent, and filling a file box with every scrap of information she could find. "She was teeth-rattling scared," one NBC correspondent who was not always complimentary about Savitch told a reporter. "It's the Big Time, and you aren't reading most of the time—you are talking. She made a good mix." But things did not go altogether smoothly: Early in the program, another observer recalled, she referred to David Brinkley as "Dave," a nickname he detests.

242

"That was cut-your-own-throat time. Brinkley spent much of the evening pressing her with direct questions and showing she knew very little." Afterward renowned journalist David Halberstam dismissed her as "a handsome young woman who is being brought along too quickly for her own good."

In its December 18, 1978, issue, *New York* magazine declared confidently that "the very professional Jessica Savitch" would be the female half of whatever anchor team replaced John Chancellor. As the New Year began, *Washington Post* fashion editor Nina Hyde included her on the nation's most prestigious list of What's In, and on January 15, *Newsweek* anointed her as "NBC's Golden Girl" and declared her "clearly NBC's reporter most likely to succeed." Several weeks later, Tom Pettit was named NBC Senate correspondent and Savitch was made a general assignment reporter. The shift, clearly a demotion, was made "to broaden her experience," Don Meaney noted diplomatically. Sid Davis, who succeeded Meaney as bureau chief later in 1979, was more direct: "Coming to the Senate for her was like being sent to new territory without knowing all the terrain," he said, "although like any professional she got a road map and tried to learn." Nonetheless, Savitch's public speaking, Sunday night anchoring, and expert stroking of interviewers continued to create the impression she was the hottest talent at NBC. A month after she was yanked off the Senate beat, a *TV Guide* profile called her "meteoric success at NBC News" the "Cinderella story of the year."

Network executives did their best to help maintain the image, cheerfully providing upbeat quotes about Savitch's work and discouraging any more skeptical remarks. When producer Gerry Solomon told *Ms.* writer Judith Adler Hennessee that Savitch's writing "needs work" and "doesn't sparkle," he quickly learned that he had made a strategic error. "I took flak," he said later. "Some executives implied I shouldn't have said it."

Phil Jones, covering the Senate for CBS, was dismayed by what he saw happening to Savitch. Later he recalled that during the Watergate investigation, CBS Washington bureau chief Bill Small ran Lesley Stahl and Connie Chung, rookies at the time, ragged with pre-dawn stakeouts at the home of John Dean, chief Nixon accuser, and midnight duty outside the home of White House aide John Ehrlichman. The two women didn't get on air much, and much of what they did went into Daniel Schorr's pieces, Jones said. "But Small said he wasn't going to make the same mistake CBS did with Nancy Dickerson, where the only thing that got developed was her ego. And that's *exactly* what NBC did with Jessica. It really did her a great disservice. I'd been around a little bit and I really felt for her. It was brutal to be thrown into this with no background. You want to beat your competition, but if you have any compassion you look at someone like that and you say oh, my God. Every piece she did was wrong. Everybody would sit back and say, 'She's got it wrong.' She would have a fact wrong, or the approach wrong, or just the whole story wrong." In Jones's view, "it was not a sex issue, it was a stripes issue—she hadn't earned any."

Over the spring, Savitch continued to file stories, and after much arguing back and forth on the phone, *Nightly News* continued to use a certain number of them. But her co-workers were ever more scornful of the star persona into which she increasingly retreated, and ever more likely to retail gossip about Jessica Savitch, Nose in Air. They talked about her showing up at stories in a limousine. They talked about having to pry her out of hotel rooms to do stories. They talked about her doing stand-ups in a mink coat and refusing to do them at all if her hair got mussed. (The crews thought she was talent, and *all* the talent was crazy, so what was a mink coat and a fancy hairdo?) Producer Susan LaSalla brought back a tale of flying out on a story with Savitch. At first, LaSalla told friends, she was baffled by Savitch's behavior—she was just standing there, doing nothing, while everybody else was hustling to get going. Then the answer dawned on LaSalla: Savitch was waiting for someone to carry her luggage.

But the best story was Jessica Savitch Goes to Canada. This happened during the elections of May 1979. It was an important contest, because Pierre Trudeau, the long-time prime minister, was expected to lose. NBC was the only network with a regular correspondent covering Canada, although Lee McCarthy, the reporter in question, was based in Boston. (McCarthy said later that he had been forced to browbeat the network into admitting that Canada was important.) By 1979, Canada was McCarthy's beat—he knew it backwards and forwards. About a week before the election, McCarthy got a call from NBC to the effect that he would only cover the story for *Today* and the weekend news. Jessica Savitch would do it for the weekday *Nightly News,* which was, of course, the high-profile show. McCarthy hit the roof. He never minded, he said, when the network replaced him on a story with someone who knew more about the subject, but on Canada, McCarthy was the expert. When he called to complain, *Nightly News* executive producer Paul Greenberg told him it had been a policy decision to give Savitch exposure, and he shouldn't take it personally.

McCarthy and his videotape editor drove up to their hotel in Toronto with a rented Mustang so small that their briefcases wouldn't fit into the trunk. "Up pulls a big Lincoln driven by a cameraman I recognize as being from the Washington bureau," McCarthy said. "Then Jessica Savitch steps out with Susan LaSalla." Gritting his teeth, McCarthy decided to be nice. After dinner, he got a call from LaSalla, asking him to come up to Savitch's room. In McCarthy's recollection, LaSalla broke out a bottle of Courvoisier and said, "Tell us all you know—we don't know a thing." She picked his brain for a couple of hours as Savitch sat quietly and took notes. The next day, McCarthy was editing tape at a local station when Savitch marched up to him and proceeded to deliver a lecture on nineteenth-century Canadian history. McCarthy was impressed; she had tried to prepare. Unfortunately, she still knew nothing about the election, which was taking place that day. "On election night," McCarthy said, "Jessica did a spot on the *Nightly News.* I didn't see it, but I knew it must have been *awful*—the first thing I heard was when Susan came up to me and said her own career was going down in flames."

Savitch and LaSalla flew back to Washington to edit the post-election wrap-up for the next evening news. Trudeau had lost, and a virtually unknown Conservative named Joe Clark was in the prime minister's office. In Washington, Savitch put together a presentation on the end of the Trudeau era. According to one newsroom veteran, Savitch showed the tape to executive producer Paul Greenberg. The veteran said, "Greenberg, a man of strong opinions who criticizes in the most direct manner, ripped the piece to shreds." It did not go on the air.

Humiliated and irate, Savitch flew to New York City, where she had breakfast with Les Crystal, the president of NBC News. She spent the time complaining about the treatment of the Canada story. "It took about fifteen minutes for that story to get out," the veteran said. "I would date her decline from that point." The only time Savitch would ever appear on the *Nightly News* again was over a year and a half later, on January 21, 1981, for a special report on the American hostages the day after their release by Teheran. She continued to report stories for *Today,* and, after a six-month hiatus, for *The Weekend News,* to anchor during the weekends, and to do news digests, but she was not permitted to do the one task that was supposed to establish her journalistic credentials—report stories from Washington, D.C., for *NBC Nightly News.*

For a long time Savitch continued to see Kershaw, despite her continuing involvement with Mel Korn and the fact that she and Kershaw seemed trapped in an endless cycle of arguments and violence. "I thought if that's what a relationship is, forget it," Korn said later. Several months before Savitch went to NBC, on Memorial Day weekend of 1977, Korn had brought Savitch back from a weekend in the Hamptons just in time to get ready for the KYW news. After he had left her apartment, Kershaw had showed up. According to Korn, Kershaw hit Savitch and then threatened to jump off the balcony. "Jess and I were just making the crossover from friends to lovers at that point," Korn said, "and whenever Kershaw would show up it was a real three-ring circus."

During Savitch's first months in Washington, Kershaw was a frequent visitor. After WBAL became the top news station in Baltimore, Kershaw left the station and took off in a van with his dog, Chewy, to travel around the Southeast, where he had grown up. ("I'd read *Travels with Charley* a long time ago," he said.) Every now and then he and Savitch arranged a rendezvous when she was out on the road, and eventually, when the weather got cold and he ran out of money, he and Chewy stayed with her and began looking for another job. As usual, their time together was rocky, full of loud voices and slammed-down phones and fights. In February 1978, Kershaw moved to New York, leaving Chewy behind with Savitch, and began working as senior producer of the weekend edition of *ABC News.* For the first time since Houston, he and Savitch were direct competitors, but in Kershaw's recollection this was one of the few things that they did not argue over. "She was undeniably the best anchor on weekends, but we were doing the best shows," he said. "She was hoping that NBC might catch on and make hers a little better." He kept a picture of her in his office.

Kershaw was outraged by what he saw as the brutal treatment Savitch was receiving at NBC. "They treated her as if she was just another blond-headed Barbie doll foisted on the pinstriped gray suits of NBC News," he said over the course of a long conversation. "Washington was the worst possible thing that could have happened to her. She was brought in to be a star and put into one of the stodgiest, most backward, stiffest fucking no-news places in the world. And they punished her, they really punished her, poisoning New York people against her by saying things like, 'Jessica's really a problem to manage. She's not doing this, she's not doing that.' " To Kershaw, Washington, with its dry, issue-oriented stories, was an impossible assignment for someone who had made a reputation by being involved in the stories she covered. "We considered ourselves new-generation people [at a time when] network television news was out of touch. This having the middle-aged white man standing up there in his gray suit with all hell breaking loose behind him was theater of the absurd. *Of course* the reporter should be a part of the environment and should look, feel, act human." Compounding her problems, Kershaw thought, was NBC itself—"the boringest network." Kershaw looked at NBC and saw a network trying to be CBS, but without the talent to do so. "CBS was serious," he said, "but CBS had the talent to go with being serious. NBC was just serious."

Yet when Savitch complained about her work, Kershaw offered little sympathy. "I had no patience to hear this shit," he said, "because I'd already *told* her [what was going to happen] and she didn't believe me." He had told Savitch to leave the Senate; she had dug in her heels and refused to budge. "She'd say, 'No, if I do that, then these people are going to play it as an admission that I can't do it. I'm going to prove them wrong. I'm going to prove I can.' It was always the same thing—reject Jessica, tell her no, and you would have her at your door, trying to beat the door in every fucking day, even if it bloodied her head to a pulp. And that's what Washington did to her."

Every time Savitch had another fight with Kershaw, she

turned back to Mel Korn and his unqualified support. "I didn't care what she did," Korn said later. "I would have been supportive of whatever she was doing." Whenever she had a problem at NBC, he was always available to sit down, talk about it, and then let her decide what to do. When she finished a newscast, she called him and he was prepared with a solid, positive response. As she sat in the cramped booth in the Senate day after day and anticipated the disdain she would encounter over whatever story she was doing, she called Korn for encouragement and moral support, and he provided it. Finally, on April Fool's Day, 1979, when Savitch and Korn were in California for her grandparents' fiftieth wedding anniversary, she asked him to marry her. Korn was ready and willing to do so, unlike Kershaw, who had given her a ring but could never get any closer to going through with a ceremony.

When Savitch finally told Kershaw that she planned to marry Korn, Kershaw went down to Washington to see her. When he walked into her apartment, Muzak-type background music was gushing from the stereo. "She said, 'It makes me comfortable,' " Kershaw recalled. "I said, 'It makes you brain-dead. That's Thorazine for the ears.' She had reached a point where she had retreated from music, and she had *loved* rock and roll." It was a dreadful moment for Kershaw. Rock music, Elton John and the Rolling Stones and Stephen Stills, had been the stuff of his relationship with Savitch, the thing they could share no matter how rotten every other part of their life together was, and now it was gone. Listening to the syrup from the speakers in Savitch's no-decor living room, Kershaw realized that she had changed irrevocably, that the Jessica he had assumed would be his forever was slipping away. "I cried, it was like I'd lost someone, that she had spiritually died. She'd been in such great trouble and I had not realized it, I hadn't been there, and now the person that I loved was no more."

Dismayed, Kershaw returned to New York. Korn later told friends that Kershaw was so distraught that his friends put him in a private hospital in Maryland. One evening Korn drove Savitch out to see Kershaw. "You can't do more than that," Korn said later. "You really can't."

In the spring of 1979, less than a year after Fred Silverman assumed the presidency of NBC and began his wholesale revamping of the prime-time entertainment schedule, he and his main ally, NBC chairman Jane Cahill Pfeiffer, decided something had to be done to rev up NBC News. Pfeiffer asked her Connecticut neighbor, Dick Salant, the longtime head of CBS News who had just reached mandatory retirement age, to come over to NBC. On May 1, 1979, three weeks before Jessica Savitch had gone to cover the Canadian elections, Salant reported to work as vice-chairman of NBC. The first problem he saw was that RCA, which owned NBC, was not devoted to broadcasting and saw NBC as a cash cow. He was appalled the first time he attended the regular monthly meeting between NBC and RCA. "[RCA chairman Edgar] Griffiths was yelling that they had to let all these people go," Salant said. "He was absolutely tyrannical. Afterward he asked me how I liked it and I said I was taking early retirement."

A second problem was that NBC News was located in the same building with network management. At CBS News, which is on the far west side of Manhattan, Salant had been across town from CBS network headquarters. "Whenever we got a summons from Black Rock, we'd say it was raining and there were no cabs," he said, and noted that many of the problems faced by NBC News might have been alleviated simply by moving. But the most urgent problem, in his view, was the president of NBC News, Les Crystal. Although he considered Crystal a good journalist and a superb producer, he thought him a failure as an administrator. "Unfortunately," Salant said, "he did not have the leadership dynamic to wake up a moribund news organization that was fat and lazy and self-centered." To Salant's mind, there was only one thing to do: Bring in someone from CBS.

That someone turned out to be Bill Small, who replaced Crystal as president of NBC News in the fall of 1979. Regarded as outstandingly aggressive and relentless in a business full of aggressive, relentless people, Small was a legendary figure in the world of television news. He had been the youngest head of the CBS Washington bureau and, after that, a CBS News executive in New York. Expecting to succeed Salant at CBS News, Small was still smarting from being passed over. William Paley had gone with another CBS executive, Bill Leonard, instead. At CBS, Small had expected his crews to cover everything and have it all first, an attitude that inspired both respect and fear in his subordinates; his assistant New York bureau chief, Cindy Samuels, who revered him, hated to face him when she missed a story. Once upon a time, in the days of Robert Kintner, such a competitive attitude had rallied NBC News; when Small came in 1979, however, it caused only apprehension and alarm. To the news division at 30 Rock, Bill Small was the embodiment of CBS, the place where, as Richard Valeriani, who covered the State Department for NBC, put it, correspondents would walk over their own grandmothers to get a story. "At NBC, we'd get the story, but we'd walk around the grandmothers," he said.

Indeed, one of Small's first moves was to pull Valeriani from his beat and send in Marvin Kalb, whom he had lured from CBS with a spectacular contract that gave Kalb a guaranteed minimum number of appearances on *Nightly News* each week. Even those NBC News staffers who might have welcomed Small as a new broom were appalled by Kalb's plush contract, and soon the news division was in a state of all-but-open warfare. At NBC, Bill Small represented not the man who could get NBC News going again, but The Enemy, the man who was going to replace them all with murderous troglodytes from CBS. In the NBC newsroom, it was circle-the-wagons time, a strategy that may have been useful in the Old West but was hardly conducive to a smoothly functioning news division. Savitch was affected by the duck-and-cover attitude. Having turned down CBS jobs in the past, she was in mortal fear that Small and Salant would gang up on her.

During the first six months that Richard Salant was at NBC, Jessica Savitch planned her wedding, delivered a commencement speech at Ithaca College and received an honorary doctorate degree, provided news updates several evenings a week, appeared as a guest panelist on *Meet the Press,* gave lectures all over the country, and anchored the weekend news on both Saturday and Sunday. The only reporting she did during the week was nine interviews for the *Today* show. Her suspension from doing reports for weekend *Nightly News* ended on November 24, 1979, precisely six months after the Canada fiasco, when she did a two-minute, eleven-second report on the origins of the Shi'ite sect, the dominant Islamic branch in Iran. It was in the headlines because of the anti-Shah demonstrations in Teheran by supporters of Ayatollah Khomeini, who was then based in Paris.

By that time, Savitch had already made her debut as a contributing correspondent on *Prime Time Sunday,* the latest entrant in NBC's never-ending quest for a successful prime-time magazine show. The search had in recent years been spurred on by the popularity of CBS's *60 Minutes,* which had almost half the total audience on Sunday nights at 7:00 P.M. *Prime Time* was anchored by Tom Snyder, Savitch's predecessor at KYW and a recent contender for anchor of *NBC Nightly News.* Between October 1979 and June 1980, Savitch did twenty-one stories for *Prime Time,* ranging from the threatened demise of a one-room schoolhouse in Nebraska and the exhaustive search for someone to play the title role in the musical *Annie* to profiles of Mormon dissident Sonia Johnson and of Jane Fonda and Tom Hayden on a political tour of the Midwest.

Prime Time had a brief, unhappy history on air. In theory, in order to distinguish the show from *60 Minutes,* each broadcast was to emphasize breaking news and to have as much live coverage as possible; in practice, this tended to mean conversations—"cross talk" in TV news lingo—between Snyder and story subjects, as well as interviews with correspondents after their taped reports had been shown, a gimmick lifted straight from the *Eyewitness News* approach so detested at the network level. *Primetime* had started out in February 1979 as a Fred Silverman project, and Les Crystal had selected Savitch to participate. By the time the show reached the air in the fall, however, it was being overseen by Crystal's replacement, Bill Small, and Richard Salant, who had strong reservations about the emphasis on live broadcasts. "I didn't think Tom Snyder had the patience to do live interviews, and it seemed a ridiculous waste to keep correspondents sitting out in the field, long after the story was done, just so they could answer a question the night of the broadcasts," Salant said.

Salant also had reservations about Jessica Savitch. "She asked me to lunch once when I first came there in April 1979," he said. "Perhaps she thought I would have more to say about her career than I did. A few days later I read [in the papers] that I had asked her to lunch to discuss her becoming anchor of

Nightly News. I was pretty mad when I found out the item had been planted through her."

Savitch's involvement with the *Prime Time* segments varied. When she went to Germany for a piece on the impact of the 1936 Olympics, she stayed up most of one night with producer Sid Feders writing her material. Feders had come up with the idea for the show the previous Friday, when President Carter pulled the United States out of the 1980 Moscow Olympics to protest the Russian invasion of Afghanistan. "There was some question about whether Jessica would do it because it was so demanding," Feders said, "but she was full of enthusiasm." On Sunday Feders was sitting on the Concorde, madly scribbling notes. Savitch, who had gone straight from her Sunday night anchoring to the airport, arrived in Berlin the next afternoon, and they talked the story through at dinner. "When we came into the hotel dining room, everyone's head turned," Feders said. "I thought everyone must think I have money— why else would that gorgeous creature be with that short, fat man?" Early the next morning they began interviews and reporting. They wrote that night, and the next morning, Wednesday, she did stand-ups at the stadium and then went to the airport.

Once again, however, Savitch had to fit her main reporting assignment, *Prime Time,* around a schedule already crammed with other obligations. As soon as she finished the Olympics segment, she flew to Chicago for another story, on to Miami for a speech on Friday at noon, and then to New York for another speech at 5:00 P.M. the same day. As might be expected, her contribution to many of the magazine stories was little more than asking questions prepared by field producers and reading their scripts for stand-ups. She was there not to be an investigative reporter but to look like one, and she did the job well: On camera, she looked so authoritative it would never occur to viewers to question her sources.

She was a star, and she demanded to be treated accordingly. For a *Prime Time* segment entitled "Legal and Ethical Questions Surrounding the Medical Definition of Death," Savitch flew to Miami to do what might be called a "sit-down"— sitting in a window with the moonlit ocean behind her and reading less than a minute's worth of script off the Tele-PrompTer. "My first headache comes at midafternoon," said

Alan Statsky, field producer for the story. "I'm beeped by the desk that Jessica's contract calls for a female chauffeur only." After he had obtained a woman driver for Savitch, Statsky received headache number two: Savitch announced that she needed air reservations to Greensboro, North Carolina. Again, by contract, the flight had to be first class. When Statsky discovered that there were no flights from Miami to Greensboro with first-class accommodations, Savitch demanded that he charter a plane. "Other correspondents would say, 'Okay, give me the best you can,' but no, not Jessica," Statsky said. "That was her forte, quibbling about things." She made the two-hour flight to Greensboro the next morning on a six-seat Lear jet that cost more than $4,000.

Although Wallace Westfeldt, senior producer on the show, thought Savitch's stand-ups and sit-downs were fine, she appeared to him a person who never really fit in. "She didn't seem to associate with the rough-and-tumble of journalism," he said. "She was so frenetic she was almost spastic. She never walked out of a place—she exploded out." Like Tom Snyder, the anchor of the show, Savitch never initiated anything and would much rather work in the studio than go out and actually do stories—a preference, Westfeldt said, that in reality was permissible for men in TV but not women.

There were other problems. One of the biggest was *Prime Time*'s place on the schedule, 10:00 P.M. on Sunday nights; the news magazine audience had already been satisfied three hours earlier by *60 Minutes,* and the Sunday night time slot was frequently preempted by sports events. After a few months, Silverman moved it to 10:00 P.M. on Saturday nights and changed its name to *Prime Time Saturday.* The program immediately sank even further into obscurity.

The one thing that seemed to be going well for Savitch was her wedding plans. "She was very excited about her marriage," Westfeldt recalled. "She seemed to think it would be the greatest thing in the world." Savitch wanted a real wedding, with a floor-length white dress and a long train, bridesmaids in aquamarine, flowers everywhere, and hours of dancing afterward. Although Mel Korn would have been happy going to a judge's chambers, he agreed to pick up the tab. "Every woman is entitled to that kind of pleasure if that's what she wants to do," he said later. Korn and his secretary spent the fall working on the details. Invitations went out to several hundred people, the Plaza Hotel was engaged for the wedding and reception, and a premarital agreement was hammered out that restricted each spouse's access to the other's money in case of divorce. Despite Savitch's frantic schedule, she and Korn put together the whole affair smoothly, engaging a florist to create a chapel-like effect in an elegant Plaza ballroom, quietly arranging security in case unwanted guests— including, for Korn, Ron Kershaw—showed up, and weathering an eleventh-hour summons by Korn's ex-wife, Patti, for $21,000 in back child support and other obligations.

About one hundred seventy-five people came to the Plaza on Sunday, January 6, 1980. It was as if Savitch had her whole life in one room, all the feuds forgotten and everyone in their best finery. The whole Savitch clan came, including a delighted grandfather and grandmother Savitch. At long last, their granddaughter was marrying a nice Jewish boy. The Rands drove down from Geneva, Tony Busch was in from Rochester, and the Schwings made it up from Princeton. Vince Leonard, Mort Crim, Bill Kuster, and the rest of the KYW *Eyewitness* team, now dispersed across the map, were reunited for the day. Ida McGuinness, Shelley Laurence, and Rita and Sam Rappaport came from Philadelphia. Rusty Nicholl flew in from Milwaukee with her husband. Faith Thomas, Savitch's childhood friend, and Don Meaney, her first D.C. bureau chief, came from Washington. Tom Snyder and his old noontime co-anchor from KYW, Marciarose Shestak, were there, along with Les Crystal, Bill Small, and NBC vice-presidents Ed Planer, Gordon Manning, and Joe Bartelme. Mary Manilla, the former WCBS-TV reporter who had become a close friend of Savitch, appeared with a little heart which contained a coin and was laced in blue silk; it represented something old, something new, something borrowed, and something blue, and Savitch was supposed to tuck it into her garter.

The requisite wedding near-disaster occurred when the judge was an hour late. Martin Rand, who had once become a minister for the Universal Life Church, a mail-order denomination ("Our Creed: We Believe in What's Right"), was drafted to unite the happy couple. But at the last moment the judge appeared (laughter, cheers) and the wedding began. Smiling on the arm of her mother, Savitch came down the aisle, her dress accentuating her alarming thinness. Her sister Stephanie's children, two small boys, followed behind with the rings. Gravely the judge read the passage from Kahlil Gibran's *The Prophet* that Savitch had selected for the occasion. Bride and groom kissed, and everyone retired to the dance floor, where Mel Korn sat in on the drums for a short session with the band.

The honeymoon was short. After a few days in Jamaica, Korn went back to Philadelphia to find that a second emergency support summons from his ex-wife had been described in embarrassing detail by the *Philadelphia Daily News*. Savitch went back to 30 Rock, where, after a brief period of anchoring both weekend newscasts, she had been cut back to doing only one night, Sunday. Most of the time Savitch had been at network she had worked just one of the two weekend anchor shifts, and the other had always been handed to a man. Now the assignment and the credibility attached to it were going to another woman, Jane Pauley, co-host with Tom Brokaw on *Today*. Pauley had come to NBC in 1976, a year before Savitch, when she had been chosen over Linda Ellerbee, Cassie Mackin, and Betty Rollin to replace Barbara Walters as the co-host of *Today*. Only twenty-five years old at the time, Pauley, like Savitch, had faced an uphill struggle to be taken as anything more than a pretty young woman. When Pauley had been an anchor at WMAQ, the NBC O&O in Chicago, one critic had said she had the intelligence of a cantaloupe, and at *Today*, Tom Brokaw, the former White House correspondent, had been cast as Mr. Journalist while she had been firmly positioned as a talk-show hostess.

Savitch had always steered away from any suggestion that she try to snag *Today* for herself, for she thought it would brand her as a featherbrain instead of a journalistic heavyhitter. If she did take on *Today*, she told friends, she wanted Brokaw's job, not Pauley's. When Henry Kissinger goes on *Today*, Savitch said, where's Pauley? She's talking to the consumer-affairs reporter! Kissinger's telling Brokaw about global diplomacy, and Pauley's out there asking if sugar causes cancer—forget it, no woman's job for Jessica Savitch. But now it appeared that Jane Pauley was moving out of the *Today* ghetto, and loud alarm bells went off for Savitch. To her way of thinking, it looked as if Jane Pauley, the only other woman then on air at NBC who had achieved real star status, was being groomed for greater things. By unfortunate coincidence, Pauley started her new assignment by substituting for Savitch on the day of Savitch's wedding; when one NBC executive came through the receiving line at the Plaza, Savitch greeted him by asking in an agitated tone, "How'd Jane do?"

The sole unresolved item in Korn's and Savitch's meticulous planning for their marriage had been their future together. Although there was vague mention of finding a place to live somewhere between Philadelphia and New York, bride and groom continued to live in their separate digs. Just as before their wedding, Korn would go down to Washington on Friday evening and then accompany Savitch to New York for her anchor stint. On Sunday, he would wait in her Plaza suite until the broadcast was over, take her out to dinner, grab a quick breakfast with her on Monday morning, and then head back to Philly. It was a makeshift arrangement, and it did not withstand the severe pressures that began to assail it almost immediately.

To begin with, Savitch continued to see Kershaw before and after her wedding. Their relationship was no better, but when they visited a couples' therapist for help in breaking up, they concluded that they could not do so. In addition, Korn lost two of his biggest accounts within a month of the wedding, and his business went into a tailspin. Savitch responded by telling him that she felt cheated and hoodwinked. Korn told one friend that Savitch said to him, "This is not the package that I bought." When Korn asked her to help him out by accompanying him at a few key business functions, she refused point-blank and complained that he had the temerity even to ask. "Now that we're married," she told him, "we can't be friends any longer."

In the early years of their relationship, Savitch had shown Korn her girlish side. She had been a warm, charming, fun-loving adolescent, a grown woman who still had a let's-have-a-slumber-party innocence, an unstudied sweetness and generosity of spirit that Korn had found irresistible. But now he was seeing the other side, a frantic woman seemingly obsessed by ambition who insisted that the world bow to her needs and who shut out everyone else, including her own husband, with a ruthlessness and savagery that left Korn shocked and dumbfounded. Once when Savitch and producer Susan LaSalla returned to Washington from doing a story out of town, Korn, who had told Savitch he would pick her up at the airport, was not there when the plane landed. After no more than five minutes, Korn arrived in a limousine with a dozen roses and chilled champagne. In the past, Savitch would have been delighted; now she was all icy fury. "Where have you been!" she yelled at him, and threw herself into the back seat.

Savitch felt under such pressure that she had to reserve every bit of psychic capital for herself; there was nothing left over for Korn. In addition to anchoring the Sunday night broadcast, she was busy with weekend news reports, news digests, *Prime Time Saturday,* speaking engagements, and constant public appearances, often to pick up the awards that continued to shower down on her. She had to do just as much flying in, just as much setup time, just as much fighting over copy, but nothing she did was noticeable or important, and none of it added up to a coherent body of work.

Putting the shine back on her journalistic credentials was particularly important during the negotiations on her contract, which was due to expire at the end of summer. Convinced that she needed more firepower to get the best deal, Savitch decided to supplement Don Hamburg and hired Richard Leibner, a well-known agent for television newscasters whose client list included Dan Rather, Diane Sawyer, Andrea Mitchell, and Ed Bradley. Items began appearing in the gossip columns to the effect that Savitch was busy talking with CBS and ABC. "The peacock's tail could get to look quite bedraggled unless NBC blocks some of that disgruntled and unhappy talent from taking flight," Liz Smith wrote in the *New York Daily News* on May 29, 1980.

Savitch also arranged to talk to RCA chairman Edgar Griffiths about her new contract. Beforehand, she and Korn spent a weekend figuring out an agenda for the meeting and hammering out a wish list. "We wanted a very direct discussion about the problems she was having and how she could enhance the news if given broader opportunities," Korn said. "They had her running around on the magazine show, which was a ridiculous scene." According to Bill Small, Griffiths never contacted him about Savitch's contract, but the fact that she had tried to go over the heads of the news division caused her stock with Dick Salant to sink even lower. Doing so, Salant said, was "a no-no," something that was "generally regarded as unforgivable" and "would have gone over very, very badly." In the end, Savitch did not get any sort of commitment to anchor *Nightly News,* but she did get a significant raise, to $265,000 for the first year of the new contract, $285,000 the second year, and $300,000 the third and final year.

In 1980, NBC decided that it needed a woman in a visible position during the Republican and Democratic National Conventions, scheduled for Detroit and New York, respectively. Bill Small took a calculated risk and put Savitch on the podium, the position that offered the most visibility but required the least reporting. It was a position to which Small felt a personal connection. He claimed to have been the first to see it as a television position, back when he was CBS Washington bureau chief and had told those planning the network's coverage to put a correspondent with a mike up on the platform. Because Washington politicians tend to dominate the podium, it made sense to use the D.C. bureau chief as producer for the podium correspondent; Small himself had served in that capacity for Harry Reasoner in 1968 and for Daniel Schorr in 1972. Now, in 1980, it seemed to him only fitting to tap the new head of NBC's Washington bureau, Sid Davis, to produce Savitch. "I picked her because she was an aggressive, go-getter reporter," Small said, adding that "some eyes did roll"—including, apparently, those of Sid Davis, whom Small described as "reluctant" to accept the assignment.

It was a make-or-break proposition, and Savitch was scared stiff. There was ample reason. Since the early days of television, the conventions were thought to set the agenda and the relative positions of ABC, NBC, and CBS for the next four years. Although the conventions had steadily diminished in political importance, the networks continued to put huge effort and expense into them. In 1980, NBC hired Henry Mancini, one of Hollywood's priciest composers, to compose theme music for the network's coverage. Everyone from the network went, able-bodied or not, equipped with fat little loose-leaf notebooks whose covers had special caricatures by *The New York Times*'s Al Hirschfeld of the anchors and correspondents —Savitch looked like a giraffe-necked Lauren Bacall wearing a necktie—and were packed with capsule descriptions of noteworthy delegates and the phone numbers of their hotels. (The notebooks were not of sterling accuracy; the title page listed the wrong dates for the Republican convention.) NBC customarily spent so much on this and other convention paraphernalia that the news operation usually took three years to get back in the black, or near it. As a result, extra-heavy pressure was on the reporters, who had to shine at the conventions if they were going to get anywhere. Savitch felt the burden. "Jessica was to be the equal of Chancellor and Brinkley," Wallace Westfeldt said. "They're the jazz boys—they had done it so often they could do it in their sleep. But Jessica didn't know what to say and hadn't been told what to do."

The assignment was again mismatched to her talents. True, she would be seen on the screen every time the camera panned the podium, but the podium was the place that required the most academic-style knowledge of partisan politicking and parliamentary maneuvering. "You can't do much enterprise reporting if you're on the podium," said Wally Pfister, a veteran producer who had worked at all three networks. "You have to be more of a producer of thumbsuckers. It's the best seat in the house, but in fact you're in splendid isolation." Worse, the podium correspondents were surrounded by monitors and worked in such close quarters that they were acutely aware of each and every time they were scooped by one another. Savitch would be under merciless scrutiny.

Political conventions are angels-dancing-on-the-head-of-a-pin affairs, nightmares of detail with delegations from the fifty states and the District of Columbia and Puerto Rico and the Virgin Islands and Guam and God knows where else, all selected and governed by different rules, in a maze of floor fights and platform planks and caucuses and dark horses and favorite sons, and Savitch was literally sick with worry. Once again she interviewed everyone she could, took the parliamentarians of both parties out to lunch, reviewed tapes and scripts from past conventions, and filled her file box with three-by-five cards. To build up her strength she wore small weights around her ankles and went jogging with Chewy. According to Westfeldt, the late producer Stuart Schulberg told him that at one pre-convention rehearsal, Savitch rushed off during a break. "Stuart heard racking sobs from inside the ladies' room," Westfeldt said. "He stopped outside the door and asked if he could help. When he discovered it was Jessica, he took her to his office and sat her down. She told him how scared she was, and he arranged for NBC political consultants to brief her."

As Savitch plowed through her cram course in the political system, Korn had trouble accepting that the only time she might be able to see him was during the weekend, when they visited the huge houses Korn's friend John Sculley, at the time president of Pepsi-Cola, maintained in Connecticut and Maine. Korn was also dismayed by Savitch's accelerating use of cocaine, which she claimed to need for sex, and the way she kept calling to renew prescriptions for painkillers. Matters came to a head one summer weekend at the Sculley place in Maine, when Korn raged at Savitch for constantly ducking into the bedroom or the bathroom to snort cocaine. He told her he was deathly afraid that the Sculleys would find out. He told her she would destroy her career. He told her she should know about drugs from covering the wrecked lives of athletes who used them. She ignored him. The coke, he told one friend, was like a third person in the room with them, and the third person was the biggest of all. It was the last weekend Korn and Savitch spent together.

Just before the Republican convention, NBC announced that Roger Mudd had jumped to the peacock network. Long Walter Cronkite's heir apparent, Mudd had been humiliated when CBS had chosen Dan Rather to succeed Cronkite in February 1980. By joining a rival network and a news division run by his old Washington bureau chief, Bill Small, Mudd was immediately touted as John Chancellor's new heir apparent. Even though *Time* said Savitch might be paired with Mudd on the *Nightly News* when Chancellor left, Savitch knew Small wanted Mudd alone, and the latter's arrival seemed to her to close off all hope of further advancement. The day after the announcement, she told Korn to call a lawyer about a divorce. In Korn's recollection to a friend, she said, "I don't have time for this. I've got to focus on my work. I've got another three tough years rather than the thing coming about the way I thought."

Outsiders saw only that portion of her distress that she could not contain completely. To most people, she walled off the disappointment in the same place she walled off her disintegrating marriage, telling producer Sid Davis how chipper she felt as they flew up to the convention a few days after her declaration to Korn. Gilding the lily, she blithely remarked to Davis how much she enjoyed doing Mel Korn's laundry.

"It's kind of nice being married," she said.

At 11:00 A.M. on Monday, July 14, 1980, the Republican National Convention opened in the Joe Louis Arena of Cobo Hall. Unhappy about the city's image as a riot-torn slum full of unemployed auto workers, the Detroit establishment wanted to keep the network cameras focused on the refurbished downtown, and, especially, the Renaissance Center, a complex of hotels and stores and restaurants that hugs the polluted shore of the Detroit River. But it was hard to hold all eyes trained in the desired direction. With four thousand delegates and alternate delegates, six thousand to eight thousand journalists, and perhaps ten thousand additional assorted politicians, staffers, and Republican hangers-on, the convention bureau was overwhelmed, and conventioneers as well as members of the press ended up stashing themselves across Michigan, Ohio, and southern Canada. (On the *Nightly News* the Saturday before the convention began, Savitch interviewed a delegate, Michael Retzer, who claimed that the faraway beds were actually a boon because they let one escape the impossible snarl of traffic in Detroit.)

Inside the convention was media madness, a barrage of floodlights, snapping camera shutters, and shrieked journalistic inquiries. On the raised podium, Savitch and the other reporters assigned to the rostrum were kept from thrusting their noses everywhere by a picket-style fence that was three feet high. Despite being penned in, Savitch aggressively buttonholed every important Republican that passed within arms' reach, and was constantly shouting "Come to me!" at the control booth. "She had done her homework," Davis recalled. "She knew all the parliamentary rules and never slipped up explaining them in simple English." Nonetheless, her performance did not draw raves. "Jessica Savitch, the podium reporter for NBC, should slow down when she talks," wrote Kay Gardella in the *New York Daily News* on the third day of the convention. "She's good but her high-handed manner can be offensive. There's a cutting edge that needs blunting." Jim Wooten, a former *New York Times* reporter who had joined ABC in 1976 and was that network's podium correspondent, was even less impressed. "I was up, the new kid on the block, and Bruce [Morton, the CBS podium correspondent,] was kind of bored because he'd done it so many times before," Wooten said. "But Jessica was two or three beats behind, saying the obvious, adding almost nothing to NBC's reporting of the events."

During the convention, all three networks hosted press receptions. That sponsored by NBC was a brunch, and was held late one morning. When Nancy Collins, then a *Washington Post* reporter, arrived, she saw Savitch sitting all alone and went over to say hello. "I went up because she seemed so lonely," Collins said. "She seemed thrilled to be talking to somebody." As Collins moved around the room speaking to acquaintances, she noticed that Savitch was still by herself, and invited the podium correspondent to accompany her. "It was very poignant," Collins, now a *Today* correspondent, recalled. "Here I was, not even in television at the time, taking one of the stars of the show around with me as I worked the room."

Covering the convention was difficult not only because the sheer mass of press meant that reporters were crawling everywhere, but because there was in addition very little for these droves of reporters to find out. Ronald Reagan had the nomination sewed up, and the only suspense was over his choice of running mate. The hot rumor was that Reagan's people had lured Gerald Ford out of retirement to become a very powerful vice-president in a sort of co-presidency. On the evening of Wednesday, July 16, after a day of speculation had convinced many in Cobo Hall that the co-presidency was a certainty, Sid Davis found Senator Paul Laxalt, one of Reagan's closest confidants and the original proponent of the idea, in a small meeting room beneath the podium. He asked Laxalt for an interview, and moments later, at 9:38 P.M., the senator was speaking into Jessica Savitch's microphone. When Laxalt said, "There's no firm deal yet," it was the first indication from an informed person that Ford's participation was anything but nailed down. An elated Savitch saw her colleagues looking at her scoop with envy.

Her triumph was short-lived. Within moments, NBC floor correspondent Chris Wallace was on the air with the news that Reagan's choice for vice-president was George Bush. Soon afterward, Reagan himself came to the convention to squelch the Ford rumors. This was a break with tradition, for in order to preserve suspense, the nominee is usually not seen before the moment of nomination. But Reagan wanted to turn attention away from Ford and onto Reagan, and so with a canny sense of timing he injected drama into the proceedings by showing up a day early. He told the assembled multitudes that his choice for vice-president was George Bush, his most bitter rival on the hustings. As Reagan spoke on the rostrum, Jim Wooten crept behind the security guards and stationed himself in front of the nearest exit. Quietly alerting one of the ABC camera crews in the rafters, he whispered, "Can you see me? I'm going to get him!"

Reagan swept out of the hall, accompanied by his wife and platoons of Republican strategists, and found an arm pulling him toward a microphone. Wooten quickly asked the candidate about the insults he and Bush had previously heaped on each other, and received the usual demurrals. Eventually Nancy Reagan pulled her husband away, and Wooten was left with the satisfaction of knowing he had broken the rules and gotten his own scoop.

With Reagan's announcement, the convention was over for the day. Wooten was joined in the podium's official press area by NBC correspondent Tom Pettit, who was working as a floor reporter. "He puts his big fist on my arm," Wooten recalled, "and says, 'If you ever do that again, I'll break your arm.' He was really serious, even though he broke into a grin." When Pettit, still standing on the podium, went on air to wrap the evening up, Wooten said, Jessica Savitch, NBC's official podium reporter, "was left back at the front of the stage, just staring, just standing there while Pettit muscled her aside. That's how it went all week."

Determined not to let herself be big-footed again, Savitch planted herself the next night at the edge of the picket fence. There is a tradition of sorts at the last night of party conventions that somehow San Donaldson always manages to get around the picket fence. When the candidate waves his arms to accept the huzzahs of the crowd, Donaldson is always there, arching his thick eyebrows and asking impertinent questions. In 1980, the Republicans had hired Wally Pfister to keep Donaldson off the podium altogether. "On nomination night, everything was set," Pfister said later. "I had assured the [Republican National] Committee that Sam Donaldson wouldn't get exposure." But when Reagan spoke, Donaldson was there. "He got in with a Secret Service button," Pfister said. "There were three reporters ready to kill me!"

Seeing Donaldson at the candidate's side, Wooten, Morton, and Savitch all rushed the fence, Morton and Wooten leaping the barrier in orthodox superhero fashion. Savitch, however, was required to dress like a lady, in a rust-colored suit and spike heels. She was also shorter than anyone else. Hiking the skirt up, she tried to clamber over the fence, spike heels scrabbling for purchase as the skirt slid up to her thighs. It was a sight that many people on the podium did not forget.

One of those watching the scene was Ron Kershaw, who was now working at WNBC, the NBC O&O on the seventh floor at 30 Rock. In December 1978, he had been ordered to fire people at ABC because of a sudden budget cut mandated by the network's number two in the news division, who was none other than Dick Wald, formerly of NBC. Kershaw was furious at having to toss out his staff in the week before Christmas. He did not get along with Wald, and soon found himself working for WNBC, the network's flagship O&O, in 30 Rock. There he became news director of the station's news operation, in which the main emphasis was on the newscast from 5:00 to 7:00 P.M., then a distant third in the ratings. Although the newscast had been extended to two hours, no increase in the WNBC budget was given, and Kershaw was forced to resort to desperate measures. To compete, he said, "I had somehow —to use the military phrasing—to put an overwhelming force at my point of attack, which was the six o'clock news, which meant that I had to kiss off one of the hours. And that turned into *Live at Five*."

The name itself was a joke, because the show had no live trucks, no satellite vans, no reporters bringing stories directly into viewers' homes. Instead, Kershaw gave free rein to a producer named Fred Ferrar who had the zany idea of abandoning any pretense of being an ordinary news show and instead going the celebrity route, sprinkling the show with a few headlines but concentrating on interviews with big-name guests. Anyone in Manhattan who seemed interesting might go on the show; sometimes veteran announcer Don Pardoe even played the piano. Kershaw called it "The Show Without Shame." To avoid alerting NBC that something was going on, he originally called the whole two-hour segment *News Center Four,* with the first hour being *Live at Five.* Over the months, the *News Center Four* got smaller and the *Live at Five* got larger, until the ratings books listed it as a separate program. To Kershaw's astonishment, it was hugely successful.

He spent his budget on the *real* half of *News Center Four,* the 6:00 news, trying, he said, to find a way to combine the values of flash and substance. "There had to be some room between the trivial, with-it style of [a WABC-type] *Eyewitness News* and the gray eminence that stood on Mt. Olympus," he said, "[between the one side] that had no relevance to American life, and the other side that pandered to it." Once again he started out by wholesale firings—one of the first to get canned was reporter Mary Alice Williams, who went on to become a major anchor and vice-president at Cable News Network—and surrounded himself with a tight circle of trusted associates, known as the Baltimore Mafia because several were from WBAL. He and his band of loyalists worked hard and played hard; after hours, they gathered at Hurley's or joined other WBAL veterans at Chip's, a bar on Columbus Avenue. Across the street was Kershaw's apartment, where they often repaired for a night of poker and drinking; around the station, it was widely believed that those get-togethers also included cocaine. At work, the investigative unit that had garnered shelves full of Emmies for its long, in-depth reports but little audience response was disbanded, and the newscast began to feature the short, punchy reports and tightly controlled pacing Kershaw had developed in Baltimore. Kershaw detested staff meetings and refused to hold any for the first fifteen months he was news director. He also refused to wear a coat or a tie, kept erratic hours, was sometimes rude and abusive, and intimidated staffers by announcing frequently, "I'm kicking ass and taking names." But as at WBAL, those who got along with the man his staff called "Mr. TV Eyes" flourished, and his instinct for how to put together a news operation viewers would watch brought the station's news operation from number three to number one in record time.

Working at 30 Rock, Kershaw saw Savitch in the corridors, and the romance that had never quite ended again resumed. After the Republican convention was over, Savitch and Kershaw flew to the eastern shore of Maryland for a few days.

A frantic Mel Korn didn't know where she was until he received a phone call at about four o'clock in the morning. But even this did not make him draw the line. She had told him she desired to get out of the marriage and wanted nothing further to do with him. She switched her standing weekend hotel reservation in New York from the Plaza, where the staff all knew Korn, to the Pierre, where he was a stranger. She refused to accept his calls. Yet Korn hung on, trying to phone her, trying to meet her, trying to be in her life, and thus setting the stage for a new round of anger and callous behavior.

Savitch's lost weekend with Kershaw was cut off by the need to prepare for the Democratic convention, which began exactly four weeks after its counterpart in Detroit. On Monday, August 11, the same cast of characters appeared at Madison Square Garden in New York; on this occasion, complaints about the host city focused on prostitution, crowding, and dirt. Once again, Jessica Savitch, Jim Wooten, Bruce Morton, and hundreds upon hundreds of Gray Suits flooded a political wingding. This time, however, the town image was of less crucial import to City Hall; there was too much else going on in New York for its city fathers and mothers to obsess over the comfort of the delegates.

Savitch again stood on the platform, watching the sea of balloons and banners and placards below. Here the basic story was the question of whether Ted Kennedy and Jimmy Carter would make up after a bruising primary fight. Carter had the nomination locked up, but his popularity had begun to nosedive. Kennedy's last hope was to cajole delegates into switching loyalties. To do this required changing the rules, for most delegates are sworn to vote on the first ballot for the candidate selected in the state primary. On Tuesday, Kennedy's troops set up a test vote on the rule, hoping to throw the convention into a tumult sufficient to give the impression that Carter had lost control, which in turn might open some space for a Kennedy comeback—precisely the sort of complicated maneuver that the podium correspondent was there to explain to viewers. "There was no chance the Kennedy people would actually carry the vote," Wooten said. "But Jessica presented it as a real contest." Wooten was proud of his ability to ferret out little snippets of data, the details of the deals between the Kennedy forces and those behind Carter. "It was insider baseball, filling in the

266

cracks with information which was not vital but useful," he said. "It was the kind of information Jessica didn't have. I began to have great compassion for her. It took some of the pleasure out of beating her because it was so easy."

The convention was scheduled to wind up two nights later with a final address by President Carter. It was the networks' last chance for glory for another four years, and all three opted for maximum coverage by the simple expedient of filling both of their podium slots with the most high-visibility reporters available. CBS took out producer Ed Fouhy and anchor Bruce Morton and sent in Lesley Stahl and Ed Bradley. ABC producer Bob Murphy was benched and Sam Donaldson was put in next to Wooten. NBC took off Sid Davis and put Tom Pettit next to Savitch. Faced with this flouting of the one reporter–one producer regulation, the Rules Committee promptly retaliated with a decree that each network could have only one active reporter on the podium. As Savitch watched Wooten and Bradley take off their headsets, she received the distressing news that she was to remove her headset as well, and that Tom Pettit was now the NBC podium correspondent. "One does not argue in tight, competitive field situations," she later wrote. "Pettit was, after all, the senior correspondent. Logic like that didn't help. I was devastated."

After Carter finished his speech, Martin Luther King, Sr., gave a benediction and the convention sang "We Shall Overcome." Meanwhile, Savitch replaced her headset. Taking a tip from Wooten, she headed for the exit while the rest of the correspondents surged toward the rostrum. Once again there was a picket fence in the way. As Savitch recounted the incident in her book, she pleaded with a guard she knew to let her past the barrier. " 'Now, you know I can't let you through, Jessica,' he said and paused. 'But I can't help it if I don't see you sneak past me, can I?' " Savitch charged ahead and was the only correspondent who got to Carter. It was, as she put it, "not exactly an earthshaking interview," but that didn't matter; it was the only interview, and that's what counted. "Everybody saw it," she wrote, "but by the time the other reporters rushed over, we were already being knocked to the floor by the Secret Service." Afterward, she wrote, Tom Pettit told her, "Next time, Savitch, *you* block and *I'll* carry the ball."

Savitch received mixed reviews on her work at the conventions, but in the end the one vote that counted most was that of Bill Small, and he said later that she had done just what she was supposed to do. But she did not have a chance to rest on her laurels; her life was beginning to spin out of control, and she was being Ping-Ponged among a set of mutually incompatible forces.

At the end of the summer, during what was to be one of their last encounters, Korn handed Savitch a letter. He had written it several weeks earlier, but had hung on to it until Savitch was flying to Atlantic City at her mother's insistence to explain what was happening to the marriage. At the airport, Korn gave her the letter. It said simply that they had to have a marriage, not a master-servant setup. That their relationship could not be a one-way street. That until Savitch could look beyond television she would never be a full human being. That Korn continued to love her, but he could not do all the work himself.

Savitch responded in her own way. First she sent back the letter with a few marginal notes and the remark that it contained nothing new. Then she telephoned Korn at four in the morning to announce that she had taken out a million-dollar insurance policy because she was about to have a minor operation. The sole beneficiaries, she told Korn, would be her mother, her two sisters, and Ron Kershaw's two children.

Dismayed by her cruelty and frightened by her increasing drug use, Korn called Savitch's family and friends. Then he told Savitch they might as well split up, because they never saw each other. Early in September, Savitch's lawyer and former agent, Don Hamburg, spoke to Korn. Presumably realizing that a messy divorce could do Savitch's career no good, Hamburg asked Korn what conditions he would set to keep the marriage together. First, Korn said, she had to get off drugs. Second, she had to get a handle on herself. Third, she had to decide whom she loved. Fourth, she had to learn to share. Fifth, they had to go into marriage therapy. Sixth, they had to live together.

When Hamburg reported Korn's words, Savitch exploded. She couldn't believe Korn was telling anyone this stuff. She told Korn she didn't have time for this nonsense. The elections were coming up, and she had to prepare to cover them. You don't understand, she told everyone who asked. *This is important. It's the elections.*

In November of 1980, Mel Korn sued for divorce. He had been married to Jessica Savitch for ten months.

9

Washington, Part II, and New York

When things go sour at a big corporation, the executives spend their days in a kind of frenzy, running from past disasters and hiding from those that may still be looming. NBC was a very big corporation, and when it went sour in 1980 and 1981, 30 Rock was convulsed by fear, anger, and the special manic exhilaration felt in the presence of catastrophe. Fred Silverman had not worked out. His programs had flopped, and he had become one of the favored targets of NBC's own satiric *Saturday Night Live*. In 1977, Herb Schlosser's last full year at the helm, NBC corporate profits were $152 million, In 1981, after four years of Fred Silverman, they had fallen to $48 million while double-digit inflation had pushed profits at ABC and CBS up to nearly $300 million apiece. Because cable television and the independent stations were not yet an important factor, corporate vice-president for public affairs Bud Rukeyser later recalled, it was still possible for even a network running around like a chicken with its head cut off to make a *little* money. "Of course," he said, "it did make everybody crazy." Rukeyser, a twenty-year veteran of NBC, temporarily quit the fold in 1979 and sought refuge at *Newsweek,* where he waited for Silverman to get fired.

Those Rukeyser left behind did go crazy. Despite the failures, Silverman kept all the power in his own hands and granted and took away authority by whim. (As cited in *Rolling Stone*, his chief of programming, Brandon Tartikoff, was once asked if anyone at NBC could make a decision without speaking to Silverman, and Tartikoff said, without a trace of irony, "Could I get back to you on that?") Desperate for something, anything, to break right, Silverman was convinced that he could solve the network's problems simply by hiring the right people, which of course meant firing the wrong people. He kept reshuffling positions and responsibilities as if they were slots on a television schedule, and nothing ever came right, and he kept trying over again. "NBC stands for Nothing But Chaos," *Today* critic Gene Shalit told *New York* magazine in July 1981. To the battered denizens of 30 Rock, it seemed that every two weeks a vice-president left and a new vice-president showed up. Warren Littlefield, who survived to become executive vice-president of prime-time programs, told a reporter that the staff spent Friday nights waiting to find out which people were going out on their ears. "We would walk whoever it was to their car, tell them how much we would miss them, and then go back and steal their office furniture," he said.

Affiliates left in droves, and Silverman was unable to lure them back. One of the first stations to go was KSTP, in Minneapolis–St. Paul, which had been one of the network's first affiliates. David Adams told Silverman that there was a small chance that Silverman, the head of the company, could convince the station manager, a man named Stan E. Hubbard, not to quit just because of a bad year or two. In Adams's recollection, Silverman allowed himself to be dragged onto a plane to the Twin Cities. To amuse himself during the plane ride, Silverman had a program board, and spent the hours shuffling shows around the week. A few minutes before landing, Adams tried to talk to Silverman about the meeting and what they were doing in Minneapolis, but the man with the golden gut was too interested in shuffling the slots to pay any attention. In the meeting, Silverman remained silent while Hubbard uttered a few pleasantries, Adams made his little pitch about loyalty to the network, and Mrs. Silverman sat there knitting. Finally, Adams said that Silverman would describe what he was going to do with NBC. Silverman explained glibly that there was no

271

problem. ABC, his old network, was going to collapse without him. He knew everybody at ABC, and he would bring them all over to NBC, and they would make wonderful shows, and that would be that. Adams sat there watching Hubbard recoil from this grandiosity as Silverman, more and more excited, eulogized himself. He projected that he would turn the network around in three months, and Adams realized the station was lost, and maybe the network as well.*

Silverman and his team were constantly looking for the magic bullet. One day Adams was called into the office of Jane Pfeiffer, who was chairman of the company and both Silverman's superior (when he wore his programming chief hat) and his subordinate (when he wore his chief executive officer hat). Pfeiffer had spent six months in a convent, and her imperious manner and outspoken intolerance of the network's locker-room atmosphere had given her the nickname "Attila the Nun." According to Adams, she was always trying to teach fat, stubby, rumpled Fred Silverman good table manners. At the meeting that morning, Adams said, Pfeiffer told him, "I have a brilliant idea! I think we should put ten percent of our money in good programming, and urge our affiliates to do the same." To the idealistic Pfeiffer, good programming meant evenings at the symphony and meaningful stage drama and all the other high-minded shows the network had lost money on for years. Adams demurred, for the idea was tantamount to a public admission that everything the network was doing was junk, but she told him to "staff it out" with Bob Mulholland and a lot of other people. Grumbling, Adams went out of the meeting, only to encounter Pfeiffer's assistant. "She said, 'Forget it,' " Adams said. "She told me that in three months Pfeiffer would have forgotten all about it." In the meantime, Adams said, Pfeiffer had secret luncheons with five of the seven members of the affiliate board, an advisory council elected by the affiliated stations. "They pissed all over the idea," Adams said, "and so Jane did forget about it, thank God."

---

* In 1984, Hubbard's son, Stanley S., went even further. Dissatisfied with the networks' practice of holding back the best news footage for their own use, he founded CONUS, a cooperative of dozens of local stations that share video material among themselves—one more step toward making local television news operations independent of the network news divisions.

Although Pfeiffer and Silverman had begun work at NBC as allies, their relationship deteriorated as it became clear that her idealism and his commercialism were irreconcilable. They fell out in 1980, and by the summer of that year Pfeiffer had accepted a generous severance package and become a footnote to corporate history. In the spring of 1981, RCA chairman Edgar Griffiths retired and, according to Adams, the board of directors paid one of their number $250,000 to act as a search committee of one to find a replacement. "He found the new chairman—[former Atlantic-Richfield chairman] Thornton Bradshaw—snoozing next to him at board meetings because he had to commute from California," Adams said. "So he got the two hundred fifty thousand, and also got appointed as a consultant for another two hundred thousand." Hearing of the new man on top, Silverman demanded a public vote of confidence. Bradshaw declined to give it to him, and Silverman quit, more or less gracefully. In June, Grant Tinker, the creator of the hugely successful *Mary Tyler Moore Show,* became NBC chairman and chief executive officer. He and Bob Mulholland, who replaced Silverman as president of NBC, promptly went on the road, visiting all the O&Os, soothing hurt feelings, calming jangled nerves, projecting the notion of concerned but dignified management at the top. And handsome management at that—"It didn't hurt that they were both good-looking," producer Gerry Solomon pointed out. Back at 30 Rock, Tinker set about doing the necessary repair work, which mainly consisted of staying out of everybody's way and letting them do what they were hired to do. Nonetheless, it was to be some time before Silverman's legacy played itself out. On January 16, 1982, NBC drew the lowest ratings in television history, pulling less than 7 percent of the audience.

"It's not like you've just been rejected by your wife, or your boss, or your friends," Tartikoff was later to say to a reporter about that awful time. "You've been rejected by an *entire country.*"

In the general malaise, the divisions at NBC News continued to grow apace, with Bob Mulholland gathering the old NBC staffers to his breast, and Bill Small, president of the news division, doing much the same with the new people from CBS. Had everything else been more or less equal, it might have been an even match, Mulholland's flashing Irish temper against

Small's soft voice and iron determination, but everything else was far from equal. Because Small had fewer loyalists, he was constantly on the defensive, unable to carry out his own plans, yet stuck with the rap for a third-place news organization. He couldn't even secure a desk for correspondent Betsy Aaron when she came over from CBS, much less put his own choice, Roger Mudd, in the anchor seat.

It was an impossible situation, and Small tended to act impossibly. "I'm one of the few people who likes Bill Small and thinks he has a lot of integrity," Bud Rukeyser said later. "But he had a problem dealing with people." In Rukeyser's view, the head of the news is like a general in command of any army; in both cases, it takes a certain kind of leadership to make the troops move. "You have to be perceived as standing for something," Rukeyser said, "to get all those disparate creative egos pushing in one direction." Unfortunately, despite Small's protests, he was perceived as standing for CBS—and that was the one banner NBC News would never rally round.

"Small was probably right about the fact that a lot of things were not done well," said one senior staff member who preferred to remain anonymous, "but he insulted people rather than getting them to work harder. When Small came in, everybody freaked out and froze and couldn't deal with him." To make matters worse, Small had long had less than cordial relations with Paul Greenberg, the executive producer of *Nightly News,* a former CBS man who had preceded Small to NBC. Every morning Greenberg would come back from his daily meeting with Small in a foul mood. "No matter how cheerful you were when you arrived," said the senior staffer, "you got depressed. The room was full of cigar smoke and the smoke from Chancellor's pipe. Everyone looked grim."

As a further irritant, the Chancellor succession was still unresolved, a situation that left a number of newscasters, including Tom Brokaw, on hold. Like Savitch, Brokaw had been a highly successful local reporter and anchor (in Los Angeles) who had been picked up by NBC in 1973 and put in a highly visible position (White House correspondent) to gain some national credibility. Again like Savitch, he had been initially dismissed because of his good looks and ability to communicate on camera. Unlike Savitch, however, Brokaw was able to convince the network heavies that he was not just another pretty face, and his coverage of Watergate and the Ford administration was widely respected. In 1976 he had become host of *Today,* and had again received high marks for his work. By 1981, Brokaw was an obvious candidate to be a nightly news anchor. With Mudd already in line behind Chancellor, NBC did not appear a likely possibility, and so Brokaw began talking to someone who was already a personal friend, ABC News president Roone Arledge. Just as Brokaw was about to walk uptown to ABC, however, another of Brokaw's friends, Thornton Bradshaw, became chairman of RCA. One of Bradshaw's first acts was to instruct Bill Small to keep Brokaw, no matter what it took to do so. Thus galvanized, Small got Chancellor to agree to a definite departure of April 1982 and then got Mudd to agree to accept Brokaw as a co-anchor.

The network then proceeded to give Brokaw a contract as co-anchor of *Nightly News* with an awe-inspiring salary of $1.5 million a year and even more awe-inspiring prerogatives in the running of the news division, including consultation rights and, in many cases, approval rights as well over almost everything but the number of feathers in the NBC peacock's tail. With the stroke of a pen, Brokaw's biggest job became perhaps not so much the news as the task of presenting himself as a bona-fide newsman while being paid a show-business salary and being given show-biz-style power. Yet even as that delicate balancing act (already going on at CBS where Dan Rather was being paid a package that amounted to $2.5 million a year) was being inaugurated at NBC, the question of who was going to follow John Chancellor remained open. Roger Mudd was still a co-anchor, and still the first choice of Bill Small. Although Mudd detractors claimed he was sometimes difficult to work for, he looked to many in the news division, including those who were scarcely partisans of Small, like the best bet for anchor. "Roger's a good reader and fills the chair," said the senior staffer. "If he'd been made anchor, we'd have gone to number one a lot sooner. Brokaw didn't yet have the persona or the style. He was all over the map—he stumbled and couldn't read well." The only one who didn't seem to to be in the running was Jessica Savitch. It was not that Savitch was not good enough, Small later told a reporter, but "you make these decisions based on who you think is best."

In the office warfare, few people had much extra time to

devote to an increasingly erratic anchorwoman. Savitch did have a number of duties: She continued to appear on the news updates, which she now did up to five nights a week, and to do the weekend anchoring, now switched to Saturday night; she also appeared occasionally on *Meet the Press* and substituted on the *Nightly News* and *Today*. But somehow the whole of these assignments was less than the parts. They did not add up to a plan, a program, a rational approach to her future. "The guys at the top would always say, 'Baby Doll, Sweetie Pie, we love you, we've got something special in mind for you,' " Savitch's old friend Mary Manilla said. "But then nothing would happen." Savitch's career was in stall, and she knew it.

Having jettisoned the emotional support of Mel Korn, having only a tenuous connection to reporting, and having had whatever chance she had for the top post evaporate with the arrival of Roger Mudd, Savitch was floundering, both personally and professionally. Although Ron Kershaw was, once again, in her life, he lived in New York and was, once again, busy trying to revive an ailing news operation. But even if he had been on the scene in Washington, their relationship was too rocky, too filled with disputes and brutality, to provide the solace and encouragement she needed now. She wanted someone to hang on to, someone who would offer comfort and security. As can easily be imagined for a pretty woman with a nationally known face, she found someone quickly.

He was Donald Rollie Payne, a gynecologist and obstetrician in Washington. D.C. Savitch had suffered an early miscarriage during her marriage, and had felt poorly for months afterward. After the conventions were over, she consulted Payne, who recommended minor surgery—the same surgery that prompted her to write a will leaving one-third of her estate to Kershaw's kids. When Kershaw and others visited her at Georgetown Hospital, they found Payne at her bedside.

Savitch told friends that she was attracted to the forty-four-year-old Payne in part because he did not know who she was. There were other attractions as well. One of the most important was that Payne, with his air of medical authority and competence, was able to calm Savitch's fears that her miscarriage and subsequent infection might prevent her from ever having children. "When he said he could help her," Mary Manilla recalled, "she invested him with the power of God." A man who seemed to know how to crack a joke and have a good time, he was tall, slim, and handsome; Savitch told Mary Manilla she loved being in bed with someone who had a slender build similar to her own. Although he had been gravely ill with liver ailments a few years earlier, he had apparently recovered. At the time Savitch met him, Payne was a regular squash player and such an avid skier that he had bought a condo in Vail, Colorado, for his own use and one and a half condos in nearby Avon, Colorado, for investment purposes.

Born in Wichita Falls, Texas, and graduated from Rice University and the University of Texas Southwest Medical School, Payne had built up a successful practice in Washington. He was associated with two hospitals, Georgetown and Sibley, and seemed to enjoy his work. He spoke with a slight trace of a southern accent and to his patients had a somewhat paternal manner—"He was charming but chauvinistic," said one, Barbara Fischel, "full of 'Darling, I'm going to take care of you' stuff"—but within the medical establishment he was a progressive figure. He did not bar husbands from the delivery room. One of his trademarks was the humorous posters he put on the ceiling over examining tables so that women who were lying there with their feet in stirrups could look up and have a chuckle. His office waiting room was filled with cartoons and snapshots of babies and proud parents, including Ethel and Robert Kennedy, whose last babies had been delivered by Payne. There were also pictures of his four sons, who had been living with their mother, Dee, since the couple had separated earlier that same year.

Soon Savitch and the doctor were seeing each other frequently. They went roller-skating in Central Park when they were in New York, and when they were in Washington they took long walks in Rock Creek Park and attended dinner parties with Payne's medical colleagues. When Savitch had to be at Nebraska Avenue in the evening to do news updates, Payne came along and read through a stack of medical journals in the waiting room. On weekends, he sat in the visitors' area at the fifth-floor newsroom at 30 Rock. Sometimes, staffers in New York recalled later, Savitch and Payne would spend the two hours between the evening news and the updates in her office with the door locked. "She was really in love," said Ed Fischel, a producer for the local news operation at Nebraska Avenue and Barbara Fischel's husband. "She was acting giddy. She seemed to bounce into work and to be genuinely happy. It was so striking people would talk about it." It was the first time many of her co-workers had seen the exuberant, girlish, high-spirited young woman who had left KYW three long years before. According to Mary Manilla, Savitch's maid, Leila Bright, said that Savitch was having the best sex in her entire life.

Not that all was completely well. Payne's first marriage had been unhappy for years, and there had been ugly stories of loud arguments and physical violence. There had also been talk that Payne was having sexual relationships with men. "It was no great secret among the medical community what his life-style was," said Ann Compton, ABC White House correspondent at the time and the wife of a Washington, D.C., physician associated with Sibley Hospital. "Don was bisexual, if not gay. It was known and accepted—it wasn't any great mystery or source of gossip." After Payne and his first wife, Dee, separated, relations became strained to the point that Dee had him served with divorce papers at his oldest son's high school graduation from St. Alban's, the exclusive boys' prep school associated with the National Cathedral. Payne was so visibly upset that a patient who encountered him at the graduation asked if he was ill.

On November 1, 1980, Payne's divorce from his wife of nineteen years was final. Within days, Mel Korn filed for divorce from Jessica Savitch in Philadelphia. Two weeks later, when Barbara Fischel called Payne in the middle of the night to tell him that she had gone into labor, Payne asked if Savitch could come and watch the delivery. He said that Savitch had never seen a childbirth, an assertion that would doubtless have startled those who had seen Savitch's childbirth series back at KYW. Because Ed Fischel knew Savitch, he and his wife agreed to Payne's request.

"When I had our first baby, Don wanted to watch the football game and kept asking for the score," Barbara Fischel said. "Ed was really mad. But with the second baby, everything was loosey-goosey, like a party." Savitch, outfitted in a green scrub suit, took photographs with Ed Fischel's camera, and Payne's attention did not wander from the business at hand. Two hours after Barbara Fischel checked into the hospital, Robert Wills Fischel was born, and once again, Savitch congratulated the proud parents of a spanking new baby. This time, however, she left the delivery room on the arm of the obstetrician.

As her romance with Payne blossomed, Savitch launched a new initiative to revive her lagging career. While substituting on *Today* for Jane Pauley at the end of January 1981, she interviewed celebrity literary agent Bill Adler about what kind of book deals he expected for the recently released U.S. hostages in Iran. During a commercial break, she told Adler, who had represented dozens of celebrity authors, including Mike Wallace, Howard Cosell, and Phil Donahue, that she was thinking about doing a book herself. Adler was particularly interesting to Savitch because he had been the agent for Dan Rather's bestselling autobiography, *The Camera Never Blinks*. As soon as the show was over, Adler and Savitch repaired to the NBC commissary. Over coffee they came up with a title: *Anchorwoman*. By 5:00 P.M., Adler had sold the book to Putnam editor Phyllis Grann for $50,000; it was, said Harriet Blacker, then publicity director at the same house, "a handsome amount, right on target for those years." When Adler called Savitch in Florida, where she'd gone to make a speech, she was thrilled. "The two most ecstatic reactions I've ever gotten from a woman were from my wife when I proposed and from Jessica Savitch when she got the book deal," he said. "I felt as if I'd saved her life." By June, a contract was signed with a journalist named Barbara King, a former *Town & Country* editor who had collaborated on a book with Dr. Lee Salk, to serve as ghostwriter. In the course of recorded conversations with King, Savitch would describe her rise to the top of her profession, and then King would transcribe the tapes and piece together a book from Savitch's own words.

One of the major reasons for writing the book, Savitch said at the time, was to deal with the double bind in which she now found herself. Unable to get an on-air job in broadcast news only a decade earlier because she was a woman, she now stood accused of being hired only because she was a woman. Although Savitch was not simply a token on-air female, the women's movement, backed by court suits charging stations and networks with discrimination, had played a role in the increasing number of women on air. As was the case for blacks and other minorities, the number of women in television news was still far smaller than their proportionate share of the population, but the sight of a woman with a microphone and a camera crew was no longer so unusual as to seem, as Pauline Frederick once put it, "like an elephant with a hat." As viewers could plainly see, at every local station and on all three networks, women had arrived. What's more, a startling proportion of those women who were now knocking down the doors at local and network had modeled themselves after Jessica Savitch. "For a few years there it seemed like a very large proportion of the tapes I got were Savitch look-alikes," said Alfred Geller, a prominent New York agent. At Savitch's old station in Philadelphia, KYW, management had tried to mold her replacement, Diane Allen, into another Jessica Savitch by tinting her hair the same color, dressing her the same way, and sending her to the same speech coach. A similar process was going on at stations and schools of communication around the country. According to talent scout Don Fitzpatrick, who opened what was to become the nation's largest TV talent bank in San Francisco in 1982, every week he received tape after tape from what he called "Savitch clones," young blond women who dressed in jackets and scarves, looked aggressively but coolly into the camera, and spoke with staccato precision.

In 1981, *Life* magazine commissioned writer Jennifer Allen to do a piece on the blond women of television news. One morning, a number of the medium's most prominent newswomen, including Jessica Savitch, gathered in a huge, empty sound studio on Manhattan's West Side for a session with celebrity photographer Annie Leibowitz. Makeup artists fussed over Lesley Stahl (CBS) and Jane Pauley (NBC). A hairdresser arranged and rearranged the coiffures of Sylvia Chase and Lynn Scherr (both ABC) and Judy Woodruff (NBC). Betsy Aaron (NBC) kept telling the makeup people to tone her makeup down and not to tease her hair. Leibowitz and her assistants bustled about, tinkering with the lights and the camera angle. As the women, several of whom had never met, waited for everyone to be ready, they chatted with each other, trading industry news and small talk. Although being portrayed as one more television blond was not the kind of thing any of the newswomen present liked much—in mock protest, Diane Sawyer, then co-anchor on the *CBS Morning News,* showed up in a cheap black wig—it seemed a reasonably comfortable occasion for everyone.

Everyone, that is, except Savitch. "She was really tense," said Betsy Aaron, a veteran war correspondent in the Mideast who had been brought from CBS to NBC by Bill Small. "She wanted to look not just her best, but *the* best." When her makeup was finally done, Savitch wandered from one small group to another, earnestly telling her peers catch phrases like "The bottom line is gray matter" and "What counts is not what's on your head but what's in your head." To Aaron, Savitch was clearly the odd person out. "She hadn't paid the same [journalistic] dues as the others there," Aaron said. "She was so concerned with what everybody else thought, and nobody else thought anything." Aaron thought Savitch looked pathetic and tried to talk to her, but she found the other woman so tightly wired that it was impossible to have a conversation.

During the same period, journalist Barbara Matusow, who was writing a book on the evolution of the role of the TV news anchor, later published under the title *The Evening Stars,* asked Savitch for an interview. After repeated efforts to pin Savitch down, Matusow was finally able to make an appointment. When she arrived, however, an anxious, nervous Savitch all but ignored her, saying that she had no time. She finally allowed Matusow to interview her briefly while she applied her makeup in the ladies room. Although Savitch had devoted her entire adult life to becoming an anchor, she was too frightened to talk at any length about precisely what that meant to her.

On March 9, Jessica Savitch's divorce from Mel Korn was final. Savitch was pregnant by Don Payne and desperate to have the baby; to do so without risking serious damage to her public image and career, she would have to be married. Payne was reluctant to take on either marriage or another child, but apparently felt he had no choice. After anguished discussions and arguments, they applied for a marriage license and set a date twelve days hence. Not surprisingly, Ron Kershaw was infuriated when Savitch phoned him with the news. He denounced Payne to Savitch as a Georgetown sawbones who was interested in her only for her considerable public-relations value. "Why don't you stub your toe and marry your podiatrist!" he yelled, and slammed down the receiver. They did

281

not have more than the most perfunctory conversation for over a year.

On Saturday, March 21, Savitch and Payne were wed in the National City Christian Church, the main Washington parish of the Christian Church (Disciples of Christ), located downtown on Thomas Circle. Payne and his family had been members back in the 1960s, when it was Lyndon Johnson's church, the scene of Johnson's pre-inauguration service and, eight years later, his funeral. The nuptials were in decided contrast to those at the Plaza just over a year earlier. This time, Savitch wore a high-necked, champagne-colored dress, mid-calf length, and little ribbon streamers in her hair. There were no attendants and only a few dozen guests, including a handful of Savitch's friends and relatives. The atmosphere was hardly celebratory. When Mary Manilla arrived at the large, nearly empty church, she found Savitch utterly despondent. "She looked up at me and said, 'Mary, I've made a terrible mistake,' " Manilla recalled. "I said, 'Just stand up and we'll walk out quietly right now,' but then the music started and it was too late to do anything." The groom, too, looked bad. "Don was glassy-eyed and distant," Manilla said, "and he moved in slow motion. He wasn't focusing on me. I thought the whole thing was very strange." According to Manilla, at the reception, which was held nearby at the Madison Hotel, Payne seemed preoccupied and rude, demanding that Savitch ignore the guests and pay attention only to him.

The marriage began to unravel almost immediately, an unhappy fate that might, perhaps, have been foreseen given the lack of time Savitch and Payne had to recover from their previous matrimonial disasters, in which both had been too obsessed with work to give anything to their partners. Then, on Monday, April 20, just a month after the wedding, Savitch had a bizarre and terrifying experience which further damaged her already shaky new union. Assigned to substitute for Jane Pauley at *Today* for a week, Savitch finished the first program and returned to her desk in the weekend news offices on the fourteenth floor. From Wednesday through Sunday, the area bustled with weekend news preparations, but on Mondays and Tuesdays—the weekend staff's days off—it was deserted. Savitch was standing at a file cabinet in her office when she became aware that a neatly dressed young man was staring at her with what she described later as "a strange, haunted look." As recounted by Savitch in *Anchorwoman,* he said, "Are you Jessica Savitch? I just want to see you. Talk to you . . . touch you." Savitch shoved him out of her office, slammed and locked the door, called security, and crawled under her desk. When NBC officials found her, she was still huddled there, drawn tight in fetal position. She called Payne and asked him to come to New York. He refused, saying that he was too busy.

The next day, Savitch received a letter from the young man which read:

> Crazy what a woman can provoke a man to do, but in my attempt to win your love, I'm going to murder John Swearman in an attempt to get your attention. I realize that as I mull my duty in the luxury of this Hilton hotel room, I only hope my historical deed will win your love and your respect (you might want to rewrite that last sentence).

Enclosed with the letter was a poem entitled "Voices in the Moving Dreams of a Sailor." When authorities traced and arrested the man, Michael Berke, a twenty-two-year-old Nebraska farmer, they found in his car other letters implicitly threatening President Reagan, Vice-President Bush, and Secretary of State Alexander Haig, as well as a photo of the White House (John Swearman was apparently a fictitious name).

Although Savitch was terrified, she refused to cancel the remainder of her week-long stint on *Today*. "She was hysterical, off the wall," said Mary Manilla. "I went with her to the studio every day, and she was glassy-eyed, just a frenzied zombie." One night during that week, Savitch woke up and found her bed covered with blood; she had suffered another miscarriage. On Friday, she returned to Washington and was hospitalized. Again, Payne refused to visit. Andrea Mitchell, by then an NBC correspondent at the White House, stopped by the hospital to see how Savitch was. "The nurse said, 'Thank goodness you're here—she's alone all the time,' " Mitchell recalled.

After the marriage, Savitch bought a new three-story townhouse for her husband and herself a few blocks away from her apartment and NBC. The house was located in the plush

Embassy Park development, which consisted of small groups of brick rowhouses built around shared central courtyards. Savitch moved in, but Payne continued to live at his old house, a four-story Victorian brownstone a block from Dupont Circle. Supposedly Payne was in the process of selling the house, a huge dwelling with five bedrooms and ten fireplaces, and its furnishings, but there was no evidence that any transactions were actually taking place. Savitch told Manilla that Payne had announced to her within a month of their wedding that he was sorry that he'd married her. He also began to hit her. As she had done so many times before, Savitch reacted to rejection by trying that much harder. She tried to entice Payne, the man she had just married, to come to dinner. She became friends with his sister, a psychiatrist in Texas, in hopes that such a tie would ingratiate her with Payne. She obtained passes to sports events for Payne's children. "She was getting increasingly jangled," said Manilla. "Really bonkers. Once when we were walking to the townhouse, she fell on her knees and said she had to find a four-leaf clover, like she used to do with her daddy. She was like Ophelia in *Hamlet,* picking flowers and thyme and rue." Manilla insisted that Savitch see a psychotherapist, which she did, and she began regular sessions with Dr. Brian Doyle.

Then the roof fell in. One day, as Savitch later related the story to Manilla, she was cleaning out Payne's closet at his brownstone and found an enormous bottle of amphetamines. Payne had already been supplying her with them, but, Savitch told Manilla, it was only when she found the bottle that she realized that Payne was addicted himself. She talked to Dr. Doyle and to Payne's family, and then to Payne himself. It turned out that he had been a speed freak for a long time. Together they decided that he should go and stay for a time at the Burke Rehabilitative Center, a discreet private hospital in White Plains, New York. Meanwhile, Savitch told Manilla, she was trying, with the help of her psychiatrist, to break her own dependency on amphetamines.

When Savitch visited Payne at White Plains, which is a half hour from New York City, he told her that she had ruined his life by exposing his drug use and sending him to Burke, and that he feared he would lose his medical license. (His concern about his career was not entirely unfounded. Although it was most improbable that the D.C. board of medical examiners, which had not removed more than a handful of licenses in a decade, would rouse itself to look at Payne's credentials, Sibley Hospital was about to consider reducing Payne's medical duties there in light of his hospitalization.) In between Savitch's frequent visits, Payne would call her office and speak at length to whoever answered the phone; according to one staffer, he often spoke of being depressed and wanting to die. Savitch's explanation of precisely what sort of rehabilitation was involved varied according to the audience. She told some people that Payne had a bad leg, others that he had a back problem, and still others that he still had not recovered from his liver disorder. At lunch with Bill Adler at the Four Seasons, she gave the impression that her husband had cancer and wrapped up a piece of chocolate cake to take to him. "I don't know who this guy [Payne] is anymore," she confided to her old college friend, Judy Girard. "He's like Jekyll and Hyde."

In July Payne was released from Burke and Savitch accompanied him back to her Washington townhouse. She kept close watch on him, but she had to go to New York weekends to do the evening news. On Saturday, August 1, she performed her anchoring duties and the news updates and then went back to her room at the Pierre and called Payne. They had, she later reported, what seemed a normal conversation. The next morning she flew back to Washington and took a taxi to Embassy Park. Inside her house she found Payne hanging from a pipe in the laundry room. Around his neck was the leash of her beloved dog, Chewy. She later told Judy Girard that Payne's tongue was hanging out and bloated, his eyes were popping out of his face, his body had no color, and his hands were swollen. When she ran out into the courtyard and started screaming in horror, neighbors came out and called the police and an ambulance. Within a short time, the press, too, had arrived, and spent the next few days parked on Savitch's doorstep.

The funeral was at St. Columba's Episcopal Church, out Wisconsin Avenue, the parish to which Payne and his first wife, Dee, had belonged in the 1970s. The service, which was arranged by Dee Payne, was held in a small room decorated with children's drawings in bright colors. Judy Girard wondered whether conducting the funeral in what appeared to be a Sunday school room was a judgment of sorts by the church on a member who had taken his own life. The casket was placed in the center of the room and chairs were arranged in several circles around it. Savitch came in last, after Dee Payne and her sons, and was later joined by Mort Crim, then an anchor at WDIV in Detroit. During the service beepers went off, summoning doctors to attend to patients. Afterward funeral-goers went to the home of one of Payne's colleagues, where Savitch secluded herself in a separate room. She later told Judy Girard that she didn't see how she could ever get over her anger at Payne. "She said that he knew she would be the one to find him and that it would be a ghastly sight," Girard said. "She was furious that he would leave her with that memory. She took it as what he did to her—not what he did to himself, but what he did to her, to make her life miserable."

After hiding out for ten days in Mort Crim's guest room in Grosse Pointe, a suburb of Detroit, Savitch took the copy of *When Bad Things Happen to Good People* that Crim had given her and returned to Washington. At her own request, she was then transferred to New York. Friends and colleagues reached out with flowers and letters, but few felt they were able to make any real contact. When Roger Mudd invited her to a party at his Washington home for the *Nightly News* staff, she arrived looking shell-shocked. "I don't think I'd ever seen a person so tightly wound," Mudd said. "She was like a stopwatch, wound up until it just had to break." Betsy Aaron, whose first husband had killed himself because he had terminal lung cancer, wrote a long letter urging Savitch to talk to someone, but received no reply. The Rands did receive a one-sentence reply to their note; the signature was so wobbly as to be almost unreadable.

In New York Savitch sublet a furnished apartment on East 56th Street, but for many nights she and Chewy slept in her office. There she erected a shrine of sorts, a photograph of Payne, surrounded by flowers and clippings and small personal mementos. She sat alone for hours, surrounded by drawings from her nephews and press photos of herself and newspaper articles about herself and the needlepoint pillow with a picture of Chewy that a fan had made for her. On one wall were dozens of snapshots of her on air, photographed and assembled into a crude montage by a loyal viewer. Savitch loved it; the pictures were proofs of affection.

On August 22, three weeks after Payne died, Savitch was once again in front of the camera. That evening she ended the weekend *Nightly News* on a personal note: "My professional relationship with you was overshadowed recently by a personal tragedy. I believe it bears mention here because of the thousands of letters and phone calls and the kind expressions of sympathy which I have received. Please know they are a great comfort, and I sincerely thank you." Her signature smile was subdued, and she bit her lip as the credits rolled over her face in the closing shot.

Eventually Savitch took up residence in her new apartment, and Leila Bright, who had been Savitch's maid in Washington, commuted to New York to work for Savitch there. One day Bright asked Gregg Smith, a teenager who lived in the building, if he would like a job walking Chewy. Soon Savitch became friends with Gregg's mother, Rose, a fashion designer and stylist. Rose Smith had seen Savitch at the salon of their mutual hairdresser, Leslie Blanchard, where Savitch was constantly surrounded by secretaries and piles of paper. At home, she struck her new friend as a frightened, insecure child who needed help with things like shopping for clothes and who would sometimes call up in the middle of the night because she was upset and lonely. When Smith and her son went to 30 Rock to see Savitch deliver the news, Smith was stunned to see a whole other side of her neighbor. "The lights went on, and it was like bingo! Suddenly this needy woman was tough and competent." It seemed to Smith that Savitch was "two different people. It was almost scary because the contrast was so black and white."

Smith arranged for Savitch to meet several different men, including John Coleman, owner of the Ritz-Carlton hotels in Washington and New York and two hotels in Boston. A lavish spender, Coleman dragged Smith along to Bulgari and Van Cleef to buy Savitch presents and flew her around in his private jet, but Savitch hung back from making any strong attachments. Several times Savitch even asked Smith to accompany her on dates. "Whenever a relationship got serious, she'd pull back," Smith said. "She couldn't get involved. Men didn't seem number one on the list—they just weren't a priority." On another occasion, Smith made an appointment for Savitch to meet a producer at ABC; she arrived two hours late and said she had suddenly had to interview Arafat, although in fact the PLO leader was not in New York at the time.

To Rose Smith it seemed that what Savitch craved was a sort of parental affection more than anything romantic. And indeed, she relied more heavily than ever on Sam and Rita Rappaport, visiting them frequently at Bally Heather. After Savitch had an operation to remove an infected ovary, she recuperated at the Rappaport home in Puerto Rico, lying on a chaise lounge next to the pool with a portable telephone in one hand and a copy of her book manuscript in the other. Even more important than the sun was the warm bath of Sam and Rita's concern and generosity.

She also remained in close touch with her mother and her sister, Stephanie. Jessica kept their photos and those of Stephanie's two sons taped to her refrigerator, and they came to visit on weekends and holidays. Her other sister, Lori, did not come to see her. For most of their lives, Jessica had felt more responsible for Lori than for Stephanie and also closer to Lori. She told friends she had contributed to paying for Lori's college education at Miami University in Athens, Ohio, and that she had given talks there when Lori was a student. Lori always saw Jessica on vacations and sometimes made lengthy stays with her oldest sister. But after Lori began following in her sister's footsteps, working at WOND and then going on to pursue a broadcast career, the sisters quarreled. The bad feelings were exacerbated after Jessica helped her sister through a messy divorce and then felt, according to what she told friends, that Lori showed little gratitude and was simply using her. When Don Payne committed suicide, Jessica told Mary Manilla she was furious at Lori's lack of sympathy. Three weeks after Payne died, Jessica set up a trust for Stephanie's children, and four months later, on December 11, 1981, she signed a will in which she left a third of her estate to her mother, a third to Stephanie, and the remaining third to a number of friends. There was no mention of Lori.*

* The beneficiaries included Leila Bright, Mort Crim, Dr. Patricia Payne Mahlstedt (sister of Donald Payne), Mary Manilla, Roberta Spring (a newsroom staffer for NBC Nightly News), Jean Sylvester (wife of a colleague of Don Payne), and Faith Thomas (a childhood friend from Kennett Square).

As it happened, Savitch had a new project to fill her time at NBC. *The Spies Among Us,* a documentary about Russian spies in the United States, was being prepared by producer Bob Rogers. Back in the Kintner days, NBC had turned out documentaries and white papers by the score; now, however, the network's documentary production had slowed to a handful. *Spies* was the first and only time that Savitch, who had made her reputation through her work on special reports for KYW, ever did anything remotely analogous for NBC. Unfortunately, the analogy *was* remote. *Spies* had neither the sort of human-interest material at which Savitch excelled nor any great news value. But even if the program had been made to order for Savitch, she would have been too wobbly to take advantage of the situation. Simply coming back to Washington to work on the piece was difficult. When a driver took her near her house, where Payne had died, she became so distraught she had to delay a scheduled interview with Arkady Shevchenko, the Soviet diplomat who had recently defected from the U.N. Field producer Patricia Creaghan forgave Savitch's conduct; she thought it amazing that Savitch was vertical. On Thanksgiving, the day before *Spies* aired, Savitch was one of a number of guests at Bill Small's large apartment on Central Park West. "She seemed frantic, at loose ends," newscaster Bob Jamieson recalled. "She came in late, talking nonstop, and she left early, still talking a mile a minute. She was rail thin, and she didn't eat a bite."

In the fall of 1981, when Tom Brokaw left *Today* to go to *Nightly News,* Savitch and Jane Pauley made history of sorts by co-anchoring the morning show for several weeks. It was a bold stroke—so bold, in fact, that it took a woman, Jane Pauley, to think of it. "I can still remember the tension in the room when I suggested it," Pauley said. "But I knew it was a good idea, because soon after that I saw it attributed in print to [*Today*'s executive producer] Steve Friedman." Although Pauley admired Savitch's work, she did not find Savitch easy to work with. "You kick back and let your hair down and schmooze at certain points on *Today,*" Pauley said. "But Jessica was never able to relax on air. She was always on." To Pauley, it seemed amazing to see sitting in the next chair a ramrod-stiff woman, tension in every fiber of her body, and then to look over at the monitor and see someone who looked terrific. "It just took your breath away," said Pauley. "She really did have the It, whatever that is, that looked so natural and comfortable."

Steve Friedman, Pauley's producer, was also impressed by Savitch. Unlike the producers of *Nightly News,* he valued her local news skills, her ability to project her involvement in stories and to talk to people live. He also valued her unmistakable star quality on air. Her only problem, he thought, was that she did not have the right vehicle. She could not have *Today,* because Jane Pauley had it, and there was no other such show at NBC. But even if there had been such a slot available, Savitch would have spurned it as too lightweight; like Groucho Marx, she did not seem to be interested in any club—or television show—that was interested in her.

Savitch had always been a needy person, a person whose extraordinary drive and intensity were based in part on her equally extraordinary ability to get others to rescue her from the nagging details of daily life. At this point her neediness escalated sharply. "It wasn't such enormous fun being Jessica's friend anymore," said Mary Manilla. In the past, Manilla said, she and Savitch had shared a certain black humor—Manilla once gave Savitch a buoy that said *SS Titanic*—and a fondness for Evelyn Waugh and Nathanael West, but now their relationship had changed. "Friendship after Don was based on dealing with Jessica's problems. Before that, it was fun and flowers, generosity, specialness, a feeling of optimism and crazy adolescence—we were fourteen-year-olds together and laughed until we couldn't stand up."

Others, including Ida McGuinness, Savitch's longtime agent for speaking engagements, found dealing with her more trouble than they were willing to put up with. Each month Savitch received at least two dozen invitations to speak, of which she accepted eight to ten, at fees ranging from $7,500 to a top of $10,000, making her, in McGuinness's estimation, the top woman speaker in the country. Nonetheless, she was so demanding that McGuinness was forced to sever ties. As McGuinness recollected it, Savitch often changed arrangements a dozen times before an engagement; on the day of a speech, McGuinness said, she had to get up at five in the morning so she could be in the office by seven to phone with the final schedule. Savitch would have McGuinness paged everywhere, including a few times when she was standing in line at the bank; demanded that operators interrupt calls if McGuinness's phone was busy; and acted utterly bereft if McGuinness was not in the audience when she spoke.

As Savitch became ever more in demand as a speaker, she began to refuse invitations that did not include transportation by private charter plane. "Jessica was someone everybody wanted to help," McGuinness said. "You wanted to go out of your way." But ultimately, she said, "I was devoting ninety-eight percent of my time to her, and it was impossible to continue." In McGuinness's view, the fault was really that of fans so devoted that they would pick Savitch up in a fire engine to keep her from getting wet or send a Learjet if the scheduled airlines were inconvenient. "They think they're being nice to a person," McGuinness said, "but then the person just gets used to it." Henceforth, Savitch's speaking was to be handled by a succession of private secretaries who arranged for the private planes and the pampering, but at the cost of further isolating Savitch.

By early 1982, Grant Tinker was persuaded to see things the way Bob Mulholland did—namely, that it would be best for the news division if William J. Small were to go. Immediately. It was, Mulholland told Tinker, time to purge NBC of the interloper from CBS, time to put someone from inside NBC back on top. When Tinker did not disagree, Mulholland called Small into his office and proceeded to do what he had wanted to do for two and a half years. Devastated, Small went straight to Salant's office. At the moment, Salant was meeting with Floyd Abrams, a noted Constitutional lawyer. Small threw the door open and demanded that Salant see him that instant. Salant pointed out that he was in the middle of an important discussion. Small said that he had to talk *right now*. Irritated, Salant stepped into the hall. Speaking in a barely audible voice, Small told him, "I've just been fired by Bob Mulholland." It was all he could say. Later in the week, he moved over to an empty sixth-floor office filled with furniture from the days of Jane Cahill Pfeiffer and began looking for work elsewhere.

(After Small was out of the way, he became friendly with Tinker. Two years later, Tinker pink-slipped Mulholland. According to Dick Salant and others, one reason was that Tinker concluded he'd made a mistake in agreeing to fire Small. As for Small, he was hired to be the new head of United Press International, the ailing news service, and eventually became Larkin Professor of Communications at Fordham University's Graduate School of Business Administration, in New York.)

As word of Small's fate traveled through the halls of 30 Rock, the NBC regulars, seeing themselves abruptly liberated from Small's "reign of terror," broke out the champagne, and started celebrating. In Washington, graffiti appeared on Marvin Kalb's office door and producer Sid Feders, who had come over from CBS with Small, decided he'd better update his résumé. The same evening, Richard Valeriani threw an impromptu party at his house. David Brinkley, who had felt so ill-treated by Small that he had gone to ABC, came by, and the socializing lasted well into the night.

The next morning, NBC News awoke to what was to be the dawn of a new era. The division had been placed in the hands of an old and trusted friend: Reuven Frank, the man whom many considered to have invented television news. Frank had been appointed president of NBC News once before, in 1968, when Bill McAndrew, the longtime and highly regarded news head, died after a nasty fall in the bathtub. Alas, Frank had not had what it took to run the show. He was a dreadful administrator. He hated having to fire people, or shout at people, or sometimes even see people. As president, he still disliked dealing with people, a characteristic that gave rise to jokes about the motto of the Reuven Frank School of Business Management: When in doubt, stay in your office. He wanted his subordinates to get the work done and to leave him alone. A man of the fifth floor at 30 Rock—that is, the newsroom— he had nothing but disgust for procedures of the sixth, or management, floor.

"The organizational disarray was at its worst under Reuven," said Wallace Westfeldt, executive producer of *Nightly News* under Frank the first time around. "Nobody at NBC knew what was going on. There were no beats, no coordination, no overall sense of what was happening. It was a strange, loose thing which I called 'laissez-faire journalism.' " By 1973, Frank was back to his old job as an executive producer, and Richard Wald, the man who seemed to many to be running the show by then anyway, was president of the news.

In the view of John Hart, Frank was like the boy in high school whom nobody will dance with, the kid who vows he will become smarter than all of his enemies, and does. Those kids, Hart said, are always filled with cynical contempt for the crowd, which Hart thought was not a good quality to have if you intended to convey information and make people understand it. One of Frank's favorite programs was a commentary he'd done as executive producer of a magazine show called *Weekend* when it was announced that ABC was hiring Barbara Walters for a million dollars: It consisted simply of still pictures of Walters, Cronkite, Chancellor, and their confreres, together with Dick Powell singing "Thanks a Million and a Million Thanks to You." It was a perfect Frank piece, arch and knowing and accessible only to news junkies; it could easily have been put together by one person in a studio with no help at all.

In March 1982, Frank began his second tour of duty as news president. He still had no appetite for the position, still regarded local news as garbage, still did not want to scream and yell and fire people. Right off the bat, he made Tom Pettit, the correspondent who had stood outside the Senate in the rain and listened to Savitch gripe about hairdressers, his second-in-command. "That," said one senior staffer, "meant you had one bad administrator and one totally inexperienced administrator running the place."

"God, things were a mess then," Frank said afterward. "Why did I ever take that job? Everything was in turmoil, just awful." He assumed the post just six weeks after the network had drawn the worst ratings in the history of the medium, and even the legendary Robert Kintner might have been given pause by the disastrous state of affairs at NBC News. So many key staff members were on the verge of taking up Roone Arledge's tempting offers to come to ABC that most of Frank's first month in office and much of the rest of his first year were devoted to pleading with them to stay.

At the same time, the affiliates were in a state of open revolt. NBC's *Today* had owned the early morning airwaves for years; now, however, under assault from ABC's *Good Morning America*, with David Hartman and Joan Lunden, as well as the successful pairing of Diane Sawyer and Charles Kuralt on *CBS Morning News, Today* was teetering on the brink of third place, a financial disaster for the many local stations who rely heavily on income from selling commercial time in the show to local sponsors. The affiliates were also angry that in spite of all their complaining, *NBC Nightly News,* still with Tom Brokaw and Roger Mudd, had not become more lively. Mudd, a journalist in the Murrow mold, flatly refused to pander to popular taste by nodding or smiling at Brokaw on the air. "I wasn't willing to use the tricks of the trade to make people think we liked each other," he explained later, "although we were and are on good terms." Although white males outside the world of network news had been forced to yield a certain amount of their traditional sway over American society, the NBC newsroom remained the Land of the Gray Suit. Local people knew that female co-anchors, reporter involvement in stories, and friendly remarks between anchor team members, touches that both NBC and CBS persisted in regarding as gimmicks, had paid off in higher ratings, and couldn't believe that the networks still refused to consider such moves.

Just weeks before Frank returned to the president's office, Ted Turner, owner of the then-fledgling Cable News Network, unveiled a second operation, a sort of video wire service that bought and sold news materials directly from local stations on highly favorable terms. All three networks were alarmed that they were about to lose affiliates. Entertainment programs had always been available on the open market; if news could also be obtained outside network channels, local stations might decide there was no longer any compelling reason to remain an affiliate. To prevent them from reaching such a dreadful conclusion, NBC had to do something, and fast.

To certain broadcasters outside of 30 Rock, it made sense for the network to woo its affiliates by featuring one of their favorite newscasters, Jessica Savitch, as prominently as possible. Ever since her arrival at NBC, Savitch had gone to great lengths to maintain good relations with affiliates. She was always ready to go when the network press office asked her to speak at a local event or attend an anniversary celebration, and if she were out in the field doing a story she contacted local news directors and station managers to ask if they wanted her to do anything for them. Between visits, she kept up with affiliate executives on the phone and with Christmas cards. Savitch was a popular speaker during the annual spring meeting with affiliates at the Century Plaza Hotel in Los Angeles, an extravaganza intended to instill fervent devotion in station executives through lavish application of food, liquor, and special performances by top entertainers. Although Savitch's care and feeding of the affiliates did not earn her esteem among the news heavies—"A good anchor doesn't have time to go out on speeches," Dick Salant said dismissively—it did give her a certain clout. Both the sales division, which dealt with the outside world and knew how popular Savitch was because of the constant inquiries about her, and the network honchos on the sixth floor were keenly aware of her usefulness. "Jessica gave great affiliate meeting," said one agent to the superstars. "And the big bosses at the top loved stunning women who knew how to work a room of affiliate general managers."

To Reuven Frank, though, Savitch was anathema. He saw her as ersatz news, bubblehead news, non-journalism, a chatty sex object who was emblematic of the growing trivialization of the great tradition of Edward R. Murrow. In Frank's view, the only people who thought Savitch was a great journalist were the salesmen who ended up being affiliate managers. Frank wanted less Savitch, not more. He wanted to reduce her presence at NBC, not increase it. Although the gossip columns still spoke of Savitch's candidacy for co-anchor of the weeknight *Nightly News,* Frank would have quit if any such step had been taken. Savitch as anchor? That was throwing in the towel to the forces of darkness at local.

Frank had disliked Savitch's work from the start. Four months after she came to NBC, Frank had been looking for an anchor for *Weekend,* his once-a-month, late-night magazine program that was moving to a weekly prime-time slot. Don Meaney insisted that he interview Savitch. Suspicious of what he had heard, Frank was contemptuous of what he found. "As the business moved away from judging competence by competence in journalism, Savitch was able to move in," Frank said later. "She wanted to be famous, [to use anchoring] as a means to that end. But people are in the news business as an end, not a means." After Frank talked to Savitch, items began to appear in newspaper gossip columns to the effect that she was on her way to the program. In late January, after Savitch had turned in her lackluster performance during the live coverage of Hubert Humphrey's body lying in state, Frank returned to Washington to speak with Linda Ellerbee. He told her that although Savitch was still in the lead for *Weekend,* he had talked Les Crystal, who was the president of NBC News at the time, into letting him audition one more person in the interest of fairness. There was to be a contest: Ellerbee and Savitch were each to write and record a script for a story about the teenage model Brooke Shields and her mother, Teri. The job would go to the woman with the best piece. Ellerbee assumed the deal was a setup. What she could not know was that the contest idea had been conceived to cover up the fact that the job was not going to Savitch after all. As it happened, Savitch pulled out of the contest, saving Frank the trouble of dumping her, and the job went to Ellerbee, as he had intended.

Four years later, Frank's opinion of Savitch was unchanged, but he did have the problem of the rebellious affiliates to deal with. After several months, he came up with a number of steps, two of which involved assigning important roles to Savitch. The first step was to expand the affiliate news service, now known as A-News, which forwarded unused network news material to local stations so they could fill their own broadcasts and sell local advertisements therein. More material would be sent more often; in addition, network would supply a three-minute newsbreak every afternoon, with Jessica Savitch at the anchor desk. Frank also decided to make the broadcast day longer by inaugurating a late-night news program, *Overnight,* which would offer an hour of news and commentary by Linda Ellerbee and Lloyd Dobyns. In addition, Frank wanted to expand the broadcast day at the other end with an extra half hour of news. Originally called *Early Today* and later changed to *Sunrise,* it was to be anchored by Jessica Savitch.

Although Frank was not enthusiastic about using Savitch, he did think that anyone getting her salary should be doing more work. "I felt like I was just kind of honor bound [to ask her] before we went outside," Frank said. "And I didn't have anybody else who was free to do it." As he anticipated, Savitch flatly refused the offer to do *Sunrise,* which she considered demeaning, insulting, and more than likely a burial ground, as it would probably eliminate some if not all of her prime-time news updates. According to industry sources, Savitch was so incensed when her agent, Richard Leibner, urged her to consider the idea that she fired him on the spot. "I would guess she was being maybe unconsciously self-protective," Frank said. "She couldn't have handled it. And maybe it was irresponsible of me to have asked it."

He added, "I didn't know her, but she symbolized to me a lot of things that were wrong and that irritated me." What was most wrong, and what was most irritating, although Frank could not acknowledge it, was that Savitch was in some sense one of his creations. It had been Frank who, years before, had underscored the fact that television is not simply radio with pictures but a separate, visual medium. "Let the picture tell the story," he had said. He came to rue some of the effects of the words he had uttered. Over the years the visual eclipsed the words, and the measure of a news program became how it looked and felt and how quickly the images changed. Along the way, the notion that the news was really only someone telling a story got lost. "There's nothing more interesting than the phrase 'Once upon a time,' " Wallace Westfeldt said. "But television never found its equivalent—it just threw up pictures instead."

In 1972, when Westfeldt was executive producer of *NBC Nightly News,* he tried to hold the evening broadcast at nine stories and averaged about a dozen; by 1982, each 22-minute broadcast contained up to twice that many (albeit many were simply the briefest of items). At the networks and every large local station, live remotes and expensive new technology proliferated. Quantel computers blew up, shot down, and rearranged pictures, Chyron machines superimposed text on the screen, and Adda electronic graphics units created new art at the drop of a hat. The product that resulted was far more sophisticated than ever before, but also far more expensive, and news budgets shot up. In turn, the anchors became ever more central, ever more crucial as the one element that differentiated one newscast from another. A quarter century after Frank had uttered his famous dictate, a new role had been created, that of the "communicator"—part journalist, part performer, with the exact proportions depending on the individual—and Jessica Savitch look-alikes were being groomed to fill it. Unfortunately, Savitch herself had been hired by a foundering network, and its president thought her (when he thought of her at all) a Frankenstein monster, a creature of tacky, lower-middle-class mass culture. In her years in the business, her bosses had trained

297

her to become one thing—a news star, a celebrity whose name would dot the popular press, whose public image and life would be of consuming interest to an audience whose choice of channels meant a difference of millions of dollars in income to the networks. But confronted with that thing, her bosses at NBC grew squeamish, and decided that maybe they wanted her to be something else.

Savitch's cause was not helped by the extravagant stories that circulated about her personal life. Her dates with the famous (Warren Beatty and Gary Hart) and the near-famous (John Coleman) were noted by the press in the same breathless manner as Princess Caroline's latest fling. Such treatment might be good for a Hollywood starlet but not for someone seeking approval in the Land of Gray Suits, where nobody had ever heard of John Chancellor going out with anyone but Mrs. Chancellor. Her relationship with Beatty, who had a history of dating television newswomen, seemed particularly titillating. Although Savitch told friends that she refused to sleep with Beatty, broadcast circles buzzed with tales of her transcontinental plane flights to his Hollywood pad, and of the drugs that were consumed to help her over the inevitable jet lag. At NBC, producers and writers and makeup artists talked about the frequent chats with "Warren," who apparently had a habit of phoning just before Savitch was to go on air and continued to call her then even after they had stopped seeing each other.

More lurid was the rumor that she had turned from romantic interludes with men to romantic interludes with women. Even in Houston and Philadelphia, some of her colleagues had been puzzled by her intense attachment to certain women, although these relationships were probably no more than latent, adolescent affairs. Savitch and these earlier friends used private nicknames for each other, wrote girlish notes, called each other on the phone half a dozen times a day, and frequently exchanged gifts, including lacy negligees and panties. The whispers began in earnest when Savitch came to the network and became close friends with another woman newscaster. (This woman, like the others, shall remain anonymous, to protect her career.) She stayed for some weeks at Savitch's apartment, until they had a screaming fight and the other woman left; some versions of the story had Savitch throwing her out in the middle of the night.

Three other women, in Washington and New York, were also said by many to be linked to Savitch. The woman in Washington drove around in a van with chains on the wheels; one of the women in New York was a fierce sports competitor; both were widely thought to be lesbians. The third woman stunned her co-workers by recounting tales of how she and Savitch had stayed in a hotel room when out of town and had diverted themselves by dressing up as twins. Generous but foolish, Savitch seemed to be unaware of what she was letting herself in for by befriending these women. Opinions were divided on just how involved Savitch was with any of them. In fact, the sportswoman denied that Savitch ever had a sexual relationship with a woman. One friend who knew Savitch and the other woman newscaster said that being around them was like being around a man and a woman. "They would be flirting, blushing, and flushing," the friend said. "It made me uncomfortable." Others, such as one producer who worked closely with Savitch at the time, found Savitch so physically and emotionally standoffish and distant that the producer "couldn't imagine her having any sexual relationship with anyone." Whether or not she made love with any of the women, she seemed to act as emotionally manipulative with them as she did with men. At times she would seem to revert back to being an adolescent, brimming over with the same sense of excitement and expectation and enthusiasm she had back in Margate; at other times, she would be driven, intense, and unavailable. Always she was a person who wanted to be taken care of, so unhappy and desperate for reassurance that she would gratefully accept, although not necessarily return, affection from anyone who offered it. Whatever the content of the relationships, the driving force behind them had far more to do with her extreme neediness than her sexual orientation. The important point was that everyone seemed to have an opinion about Savitch. As her news career continued to wind down, she remained present in the business as an enjoyable source of gossip.

Savitch compounded the rumors by retreating into the pathology of stardom. The most visible manifestation was her dependence on the small circle of subordinates, makeup people, hairdressers, wardrobe assistants, and a succession of secretaries who congregated in her office. She added to their number by hiring David Buda, the lover of one of her hairdressers, to work at her apartment and handle her speaking engagements. The secretaries received daily tape cassettes from Savitch, who walked around her apartment late into the night with a recorder, dictating orders. By the time Savitch came in to 30 Rock each day, her secretary had finished the electronic instructions and had on Savitch's desk any important mail, in addition to the usual large stack of books and glossy photos to be signed for fans. In the afternoon, Savitch and her secretary would go over story ideas drawn from a huge file of clips and solemnly discuss what Savitch might do next, for all the world as if she were really reporting stories on a regular basis.

Contractually obligated to do her bidding, the members of her coterie formed a warm, unthreatening, loyal wall between her and the increasingly hostile outside world. Their job was to make her look good and to keep her happy, and they worked well and successfully at it. All attention would focus on Savitch, with total concentration on such matters as new eyeshadow possibilities, a piece of jewelry she might wear on the air, whether her hair needed bleaching. All this was examined and discussed and debated in endless, minute detail. She was extremely particular. The staff had to follow her into the studio when she did the updates, but while there they had to be silent as stone. Savitch enforced a communal attachment to Chewy, asking her little circle to fetch the dog and babysit the dog and walk the dog. In return for their obedience, she was, on the whole, excessively kind. She sent cards, bought wine and presents, dispatched her limo for trips to sick mothers, and often sent out for food for everyone from Hurley's or Hatsuhana, an expensive restaurant on West 49th Street. (Savitch herself barely touched the food.) When one makeup woman got married, Savitch lent her the dress she had worn when she married Donald Payne.

Certain members of the circle appeared to have a particular responsibility: to be sure that Savitch had the recreational chemicals for which she had an increasing appetite. They did their work well, in that they were never found out. Savitch did her part, too; she was rarely directly seen with drugs, and was never caught in the act of using them at NBC. "Drugs were there all along," said one member of the circle. "Jessica would go to the bathroom or for a walk with [one of these people] to do coke. Sometimes I had to take her to the bathroom, but she wouldn't let me go in."

During this time Savitch took a trip on which she was to be joined by a friend a few days later. Just before leaving, the friend, who insisted on complete anonymity, received a phone call from Savitch, who asked if the friend would mind going to Savitch's apartment, where a package was to be waiting. Would the friend bring the package, which contained one of Savitch's favorite garments? The package was not there. Concerned because the errand was making her late for the plane, the friend called the person who was supposed to have sent the package. The person told the friend under no circumstances to deliver anything to Jessica Savitch. Soon afterward the package arrived at the apartment. The friend slit it open. It contained a scrap of cloth and a large sandwich bag full of white powder.

Furious, the friend left a phone message for Savitch: I am coming, but without the package. There's been trouble, the friend said. When the friend arrived, Savitch was in a state, her hair disheveled, her strapless top askew, her heels flapping. The friend explained calmly that the package had arrived, but that it had been ripped, and that inside there was nothing but an old rag, which the friend had left at Savitch's apartment. Relieved, Savitch flew to the phone and called one of her minions. "Everything's all right," she said. "Use what you want, but send some to me by Federal Express." A package arrived the next day.

In the interim, Savitch was without chemical stimulation for twenty-four hours, a situation that at the time she found difficult to withstand. She called a doctor out of the phone book, put on her best anchorwoman voice of authority, and explained that she'd recently had an operation and needed a painkiller. She disappeared for a little while, and came back glassy-eyed and in better spirits. Shortly afterward, the friend ended the acquaintanceship with Savitch. "During the last year I knew her," the friend said later, "she aged so much it was frightening. She had this horrible anorectic body and her skin looked terrible, with these sores that wouldn't heal. The last time I saw her, she didn't look like Jessica Savitch but like a much older relative."

No one in broadcasting could fail to know what an enormous risk drug-taking is to both health and reputation, and yet, between the cocaine and the prescription drugs, Savitch apparently took quite a lot. If the drugs were supposed to make her feel good, they were a resounding failure. Again and again, friends and co-workers spoke of seeing someone who looked as if she rarely if ever felt anything even approaching good. If she took them to stop feeling bad, they were also a failure, as she seemed to feel bad most of the time. What Savitch seemed to feel worst about was that she had lost her lifelong battle to be taken seriously, that she had reached the top only to be dismissed as a bimbo.

At this point, Savitch was seeing a psychoanalyst in New York, John Crow, as well as the shrink she had gone to back in Washington, Brian Doyle. Most of the time she went to Doyle's office in the capital, but at least once he came up to New York for a consultation. "I don't know if they helped her or not," Mary Manilla said. "It seemed to me she was getting too much advice from too many people, including them. I just hoped she wasn't playing them off against each other." Savitch's friends offered different reasons for her unhappiness. "Socially, Jessica is about age twenty-five," Sue Simmons, an anchor at WNBC, told one interviewer. "She's afraid of showing too much of herself. Maybe it's because she has a million guilt buttons and feels that she has to please everybody." Another friend told the same interviewer that she thought Savitch used her work "as an emotional crutch."

It seems clear that much of her distress stemmed from two overwhelming, paradoxical anxieties. The first was the fear of failure; the second, the fear of success. Savitch radiated composure on air, but her co-workers saw someone so fundamentally unsure of herself that it seemed she could never believe that she was a legitimate success, that every accomplishment was not fortuitous and each triumph not illusory. No matter how many times she was profiled in the magazines, or how many bravos greeted her speeches, Savitch always feared that her career might vanish, just as other precious things and people had in the past. No matter how successful she became, every gain served ultimately to remind her only of all she had to lose—she knew full well how fleeting show-biz fame can be. Worse, she was convinced that on some level she deserved to

302

have everything taken away. The scorn she encountered at NBC served to heighten the sense of inauthenticity that permeated her life. She had been told so many times that she was a glossy fraud, a paper-thin construct of blond hair and a toothsome smile, that it is no surprise she came to suspect it might be true.

At first the drugs were a way to forget her fears, to provide a sense of intensity and involvement and engagement that would put the emptiness at bay. And indeed, they did just that, made her feel more whole, more focused, more productive. She didn't take them all that much, and she was very careful not to let them get in the way of her work or with her relationships with the people she cared about and who cared about her, Jessica, the little girl from Margate and Kennett Square, not Jessica, the TV star who might help them get their name in the papers. Behind the drugs she felt better than she had for years, everything humming and going full speed ahead—nearly on top of the world. The inauthenticity wasn't a problem; she was the best, she knew she was the best, and she acted like she was the best, and if certain other people didn't always like it, people who probably didn't like her anyway, that was just too bad.

Now and then she had some problems with the chemicals. They made her feel that things were going too fast, and that she wasn't entirely in charge of everything that was happening inside her head. At times she felt sensations that were not altogether pleasant. Sometimes she wondered if the acclaim and the awards and all the glowing stories in the papers had something to do with the drugs and whether without them she would be in a place that was really bad, much worse than what she had faced before, but she didn't like that way of thinking and most of the time she could get out of it if she just concentrated hard enough. Sometimes, though, those thoughts would take over and pull her down into a vortex and then the only way she could get rid of them was to turn to the drugs a little more.

Success doesn't bring success, Savitch told one interviewer after another. What she didn't say was that success sometimes doesn't even bring itself, that although she seemed to have everything, she couldn't believe that any of it was real, or that it was hers, or that she deserved it. It was a pity, Betsy Aaron said later. Whenever she ran into Savitch at NBC, Savitch seemed so tense and nervous that Aaron was reminded of the old joke about saying hello and having the other person say "What do you mean."

"She could have gotten away with things like a contract calling for a limousine if she believed in herself," Betsy Aaron said later. "If you're an original, you can tell others, 'You're all just jealous. You can stand out and wait for a cab and worry about your hair. I'm going to be a star *and* a reporter.' Other women can carry it off—look at Barbara Walters and Diane Sawyer. But Jessica couldn't, and it was painful to watch."

Instead, Savitch tried, in her own way, to become a Gray Suit. She looked serious on the screen, she talked serious—often to the point of stuffiness—in the scores of interviews she gave, and she tried to think serious. Her co-workers from local news were appalled. "NBC kept formalizing Jessica, making her rich and icy and lacquered, when the value she brought to TV was being warm and friendly and a person," Alan Bell said. "They made her a little newscaster doll you'd wind up." Bell hated the person she became at NBC, and told her so. "The very things she was good at made her embarrassed in front of the heavy newsies at NBC," he said. "NBC took away her trigger finger and worse, she colluded with them [because] she hungered for acceptance as a journalist."

She never received it, in part because in order to ensure that she be given serious attention she also employed the classic tactic of behaving like a star. If she couldn't command attention for her journalism, she could command it by insisting she be treated like a princess, transported by limos and private planes, surrounded by fawning attendants, infinitely indulged no matter how many screaming fits she threw, objects she hurled, outrageous demands she made, preposterous lies she told. One water glass would be indignantly rejected because the bearer's fingers had touched the rim; another would be deemed too warm or not warm enough. Savitch would proclaim to interviewers that she never uttered a word she had not written herself, a claim that her co-workers considered ridiculous. Because of the sheer volume of work, even broadcasters who were gifted writers, such as John Hart, had help with scripts when performing other duties.

Although Savitch's reputation within the network had

plummeted, her popularity outside continued to rise. Requests for interviews and speeches poured in. She gave *Vogue* tips on how to look well-pressed in the midst of a hectic travel schedule. Along with broadcast pioneer Marlene Sanders, PBS correspondent Charlayne Hunter-Gault, and *Good Morning America* co-host Joan Lunden, she modeled executive-style blouses for *Ladies' Home Journal*. *Glamour* photographed the contents of her purse, including raisins for extra energy, eye-drops, and an impressive selection of makeup; missing from the photo were the many bottles of pills co-workers noticed whenever Savitch opened her bag. She told *Redbook* that being a "first" in broadcasting was "crushingly awesome." *People* listed her favorite books and records. Gossip columnists kept readers abreast of the more public details of her life—job switches, marriages, contracts, and Payne's suicide—and continually stoked speculation that someday, soon, any day now, she would become co-anchor of the weeknight *Nightly News*. Any real possibility of this happening had long since evaporated, but Savitch continued to nurse the fantasy that it might somehow occur, if she could just manage to find that elusive edge of credibility within the system.

In the summer of 1982, David Fanning was preparing to launch *Frontline*, the most ambitious documentary series ever done on public television. Beginning in January 1983, *Frontline* would present twenty-six hour-long programs on subjects ranging from a portrait of four women contemplating abortion and an in-depth look at the impact of the defense industry on American society to the role of police informants in the 1980 murder of anti-Klan protesters in Greensboro, North Carolina, and the mysterious death of Vatican banker Roberto Calvi, who was found hanged under a bridge in London in 1981. Fanning, a white South African who had spent years in the United States as a high school student in California and then as a surfer, had already produced *World*, a sort of political travelogue that covered the globe, for public TV station WGBH in Boston. Like most public TV projects, it was a shoe-string operation. Determined to avoid having to nickel-and-dime everything and everyone for *Frontline*, Fanning, who had acquired a considerable reputation as a deal-maker, managed to come up with an unheard-of budget of $6 million through the novel tactic of putting together a consortium of five stations, headed by WGBH.

But now that Fanning had baked the cake, it was time to put on the icing—that is, to sign up a host. He had spent months pursuing Charles Kuralt and Bill Moyers, but they were unavailable. Faced with a deadline of August 31 for submitting a candidate to the consortium's board of directors, Fanning made another unorthodox move. Rather than try for a name that would underscore the program's journalistic weightiness, he would choose a name—and a face—that would pull in an audience. "I wanted someone to get the viewer into the electronic tent," he said. When he called Savitch, she told him she was definitely interested and invited him to come to New York and tell her more. "I told her I wanted her to do the one thing she did best, to look into the camera and say, 'America, pay attention, this is important,' " Fanning said. Savitch said yes on the spot. *Frontline* represented the kind of journalistic credibility Savitch needed; with her contract at NBC coming up for renewal and her book about to be published, Savitch saw the show as opportune indeed.

When Richard Leibner, who was still Savitch's agent at the time, approached Reuven Frank about granting her a partial leave of absence, Frank, too, said yes with alacrity. If it had been Chancellor, Frank would have balked; Savitch was another matter. "They wanted her," he said. "I didn't want her. So why shouldn't I let her do it? I didn't mean to break her rice bowl." The only negative vote was cast by Dick Salant, who in addition to his duties at NBC served as a member of the advisory board for *Frontline*. Horrified at the very thought of using a woman who seemed to him to embody the pernicious influence of news consultants on television journalism, he later cited the hiring of Savitch as one of the main reasons he resigned from the *Frontline* board.

From the fall of 1982 until the spring of 1983, Boston was Savitch's home away from home. *Frontline* rented an apartment at Longwood Towers in the nearby suburb of Brookline. Every Sunday she came up to view programs in rough and fine cuts and go over scripts, reworking them into her own words. "She would ask good Journalism 101 questions," Fanning said later. Savitch, he said, was quick to see the holes in a story. "There would be an enormous panic and everything would be painful and in a rush and Jessica would be pretty wired up, but she could come up with good phrases. She was not an untalented writer for her own voice."

Intending that *Frontline* concentrate on long-term, even philosophic questions, the producers wanted Savitch's introductions to pose those larger issues. Coming out of the breaking-news tradition of local broadcasting, Savitch inevitably pushed for a topical news peg. The producers would have worked for weeks on a story, and then in would come Savitch, the day before the air date, ready to make phone calls for the latest quote. Trying to dissuade her from doing so could be a pain in the neck, particularly since she had been hired for her marquee value rather than her journalism. Nonetheless, Fanning said, "she probably worked more calmly and better with us than in years [at NBC], partly because it was noncompetitive, not like the cynical network environment. The way the staff supported her was very different . . . [and] being here was an escape."

Frontline made its debut on January 17, 1983, with "An Unauthorized History of the NFL," a program investigating associations between organized crime, in the form of big-stakes gamblers, and football professionals, including players and team owners. More than eight million people, watching over one hundred public TV stations, saw Jessica Savitch make stern assertions and, in one of the few on-camera interviews she did for the series, try to nail NFL head Pete Rozelle for negligence in policing his charges. Before the program was broadcast, Savitch had reported receiving death threats and had demanded police protection. Although the *Frontline* staff was skeptical that any such threats had been made, they had to salute her knack for getting plenty of press coverage. After the program aired, critics and football lovers jumped all over Savitch, Fanning, and PBS as pointy-headed intellectuals who probably didn't even know how to throw a football. Fanning was ecstatic. His gamble had worked. For the remainder of the season, *Frontline* was "that show on public TV with Jessica Savitch." It was also "that show on public TV" that people watched.

What brought the audience into the electronic tent, Fanning and Mike Kirk, his senior producer, agreed, was Savitch's phenomenal ability to speak to the viewer. "She said, 'I focus just past the lens,' " Fanning said. " 'There's a person right

307

there and I talk to him. I don't talk to the TelePrompTer but through it.' " To achieve this remarkable focus, Savitch once told Mike Kirk, she had learned how to center herself. She told him that between the bridge of her nose and the back of her head was a spot in her brain on which she would focus all her energy. She would then take that spot and project it through her eyes to a point about a foot and a half on the other side of the lens—that is, to the viewer. "She would send this energy force out through her eyes, like a laser," Kirk said. "You could see it happen. You'd step back and say, 'Christ! What was that!' It would last about forty seconds and then it would be over."

When the laser was operating, Kirk said, no one could do a better job. Unfortunately, it was often on the blink, and nobody, including Jessica Savitch, could predict beforehand whether it would be working. "Sometimes she'd have a whole long string of bad takes," Kirk said. "She would try to burn off the excess energy and get down to what she needed by storming off the set or throwing a tantrum or complaining it was too cold." But the real problem, Kirk thought, was that Savitch simply could not always hit the mark. "Most people who have her particular skill do it on command," he said. "That's the deal you make, why you get all the money and the attention. Some talent played it that they were serious reporters and didn't need to do this performance shit, but she played it as a star, Marilyn Monroe." More than that, Kirk said, Savitch wanted to be Marilyn Monroe *and* a serious journalist, which was a very tough combination to pull off. And when she didn't deliver, she felt everyone's sense of betrayal.

One can only imagine Savitch's distress when the one talent that had never failed her in the past began to flicker, when the red light went on and sometimes she couldn't send the energy force through the lens.

At the beginning, Fanning and Kirk planned to have the host do a live question-and-answer session at the end of the show. They built a set with chairs and tables and couches; Savitch was to spend the last five minutes of every program asking hard-hitting, right-to-the-point questions about whatever issue had just been examined. "She couldn't pull it off," Kirk said. "She wasn't a thinker but a reader. She didn't know how to get to the bottom of something and connect what one guy said to what another guy said. She was really bad at it."

After a few unsuccessful attempts, the idea was scrapped and Savitch's role was limited to one-minute live bits before and after the taped documentary.

To the staff's shock, Savitch was simply unable to do almost anything. When she volunteered to host a staff Christmas party at her Brookline apartment, it quickly became clear that she was completely incapable of doing it. She did not know how to order liquor from a store, or even how to keep track of the cash in her wallet. "She would just sort of stuff bills into her purse," Fanning said. "I think she lost most of it." On New Year's Eve, when David Fanning realized that Savitch had nothing to do, he asked her to join him and several old friends for the evening and she gratefully accepted. Shortly afterward she came running out of her office to tell Fanning that Senator Gary Hart, a great friend of Warren Beatty, had just called and offered to fly across the country to meet her. She spent the evening with Fanning and his friends, and it seemed clear to Fanning that in her humiliating solitude she had simply felt a desperate need to appear desirable.

Although she was extremely thin and looked ill, Savitch talked obsessively about her weight. One day she showed assistant producer Marcia Bemko her "belly bracelet," a thin gold chain that had been soldered around her waist, and said that it was there to warn her if she ever started to put on weight. (The explanation for the chain varied; on another occasion, she told her NBC wardrobe mistress, Susan Erenburg, that she had bought it at Tiffany's to weight down her blouses and keep them neatly tucked inside skirts or pants.) People noticed her nails: They were bitten so badly that the flesh around them looked raw and sore, and she had to wear false fingernails on the air. Sometimes she came up to Boston and stayed by herself at her apartment even when she wasn't working on *Frontline;* on one occasion, she flew back and forth from New York to Boston twice in one day, again by herself. At one point Mike Kirk came into the station to find Savitch lying on the couch in a lounge, her hair matted to her face, her body curled in the fetal position. Between moans, Kirk said, she was trying to eat a piece of dry toast. "She would put it into her mouth and then spit it out into a napkin," Kirk said. "It was basic bag-lady stuff." Eventually she managed to collect herself back into one piece; ninety minutes later, with her hair washed and set and her makeup on and her false fingernails in place, she looked fine. "I don't know if it was drugs or she was just a consummate pro," Kirk said. "I'd think we were screwed, and then she'd come out looking like a million dollars. She could hold it together for about an hour and a half."

Although Kirk never saw Savitch use cocaine, it seemed to him that her behavior was "clearly that of someone on drugs. There were tremendous manic-depressive moments, then an hour later tremendous feelings of power for maybe forty-five minutes, and then extreme paranoia and anger. When I read *Wired* [Bob Woodward's biography of the comic John Belushi, who died of a drug overdose], the whole world of Jessica Savitch came back to me. These were mood swings of a magnitude I'd never seen before."

Occasionally Kirk came to New York to accompany Savitch on outings to raise money for the show. "She'd take me out to some fabulous lunch at Lutèce or La Grenouille with these fifty-five-year-old, pink-fleshed men who wanted to be seen with Jessica Savitch," he said. After the men had eaten and Savitch had pushed her food around her plate, Kirk was supposed to do the pitch. "It was like a Coke date in college," he said. "Nobody ever came through and I knew they wouldn't. Afterward they would drop us off at NBC in their limo and Jessica would sit around in a robe with her hair in curlers and be nervous." A few times Kirk met Savitch at her apartment, the second sublet she had occupied at the building on East 56th Street. She told friends that the new place would be great, but it looked just as impersonal as the first. The furniture was selected by Savitch's private secretary, David Buda, from showroom windows; by all accounts, the apartment looked like a motel, but Savitch didn't seem to care. As in her cold apartment in Washington, the only personal touch was the life-size model of Nipper, which Savitch now claimed was the original RCA dog, straight from the prop room.

Being with Savitch, Kirk said, was "like being her younger brother. We used to spend a lot of time talking about high school." Although Kirk was single at the time, there was, he said, "no boy-girl stuff." Savitch could be nice, especially to Kirk's children, but she was just "too spooky, too raw. You didn't want to get that close to an energy force like that. It was very scary, like a Spielberg horror movie—if you peeled it back, you didn't know what you'd get. There was a feeling like Glenn Close's craziness in *Fatal Attraction*—the same intensity and obsessiveness and feeling of unrequitedness."

At one point, Savitch was asked to give a speech in the Parker Lecture Series, established in the 1960s in memory of George S. Parker, the founder of Parker Brothers, the toy manufacturers, in Salem, Massachusetts, the company base. The program, which sponsored a public address every eighteen months, favored news figures, and Walter Cronkite, Dan Rather, and Eric Sevareid had already appeared there. The first woman so honored, Savitch was to be paid $5,000, in return for which she was to attend a black-tie reception, speak for thirty minutes and answer questions for another thirty minutes, and then go on to a public reception. Before the speech, Savitch waited backstage at Salem High School, nervously folding and unfolding the pages of her speech. David Fanning, who had accompanied her, heard a loud buzz from the other side of the curtain. Peeking out, he saw a stage completely empty except for a small podium with a little light, and over a thousand people waiting for Savitch to appear. It was, Fanning thought, a terrifying prospect: "She was about to have to step out in front of those people and be as wise as Walter Cronkite or what they thought Walter Cronkite should be. To give them wisdom and answer their questions about the world, to be that person she seemed to be on the news every Saturday night." Fanning thought later that her performance was extraordinary. The actual speech had very little content, but her answers to the questions that followed—for example, would Teddy Kennedy run for president in 1984—were deft. "She was making it up as best she could, which people accepted because they needed to accept it. I had real sympathy for her at that moment."

In the fall of 1982, just after Savitch agreed to serve as host for *Frontline,* her autobiography, *Anchorwoman,* was published by Putnam. A short collection of more or less chronological anecdotes of the upbeat variety—one editor at Putnam called it "a sanitized puff piece"—it was a singularly unfortunate document for someone looking to impress her network colleagues, who considered its pages irritating at best and at worst a trove of howlers. Years later, staffers still recalled the astonished delight with which they read the single page on which Savitch explained that "my major task is to answer my mail," and that "nothing I have ever done on-air in either radio or television has been tougher than *Update*." The book had an unhappy prepublication history. Shortly before it came out, Savitch went to Jo Moring, then a senior executive at NBC Radio, and told her that Putnam's fact checkers said that Savitch could not claim to be the first woman anchor in a major market because Moring had been anchoring in Baltimore before Savitch became a weekend anchor in Houston. Would Moring mind terribly, Savitch asked, calling up Putnam and saying that Savitch was first after all? When Moring refused, Savitch pulled out of several joint projects that she and Moring had planned. In addition, Savitch and ghostwriter Barbara King had a falling out, and the press run had to be interrupted at the last moment to remove King's name. Savitch's behavior had not endeared her at Putnam; years later, one executive there still remembered how Savitch called at 3:00 A.M. to announce that she had arrived at the annual American Booksellers Association meeting in Anaheim, California. "It was as if she didn't have any regard for other people's time," the executive said. "All stars are demanding, but she was demanding in a different way. Hers was never the phone call you wanted to take."

Investment banker Richard Wiseman, then a recent acquaintance of Savitch, kicked off the publicity campaign by paying for an extravagant party organized by Savitch's neighbor, Rose Smith, and held at Xenon, a trendy nightclub near Times Square. Invitations went out to over 500 people, ranging from Woody Allen to Ronald Reagan, and Wiseman, a member in good standing of the downtown branch of café society, arranged for Andy Warhol, Cheryl Tiegs, George Steinbrenner, and other column fodder to show up at Xenon. In orthodox starlet fashion, Savitch was over an hour late (according to Rose Smith, Savitch was paralyzed with anxiety and would never have made it to her own party if Smith had not forced her to attend), and the time she did spend there was rigidly scheduled. Disturbed by the number of hangers-on that clustered about Savitch and wondering if she, too, was turning into "just another star-fucker," Mary Manilla cut off contact with Savitch after the party for the next several months. By prearrangement, at midnight Xenon owner Howard Stein let in the public, at the usual cover charge of $10, to mingle with the *Anchorwoman* guests; it was good PR for Xenon and also lowered the tab for the evening.

Other book parties followed at the Rappaports' estate in Philadelphia, and in Houston, Chicago, and Los Angeles. Savitch gave dozens of print interviews, signed hundreds of copies in bookstore promotions, and waved a copy of *Anchorwoman* on what seemed like every television talk show in the land, noting each time that a portion of the proceeds would go to journalism students who had lost financial aid. Although tales filled the Putnam publicity department that Savitch threw tantrums on the road, took drugs on airplane flights, and had to be practically carried to hotels, she never missed a single promotional appearance. Rather to the publisher's surprise, the book appealed to Savitch's many fans, and went into multiple printings. Soon afterwards, paperback rights were sold to Berkley. "Jessica had an incredible following," said a Putnam senior editor who had not expected *Anchorwoman* to be nearly so successful. "The most unlikely people asked for copies. It was really the book that wouldn't die—the book we couldn't kill. No matter what we didn't do for it, it flourished."

The high did not last. In April 1983, while Savitch was still in her first season at *Frontline,* she learned that Connie Chung was coming to NBC to do *Sunrise,* the early morning show that Savitch had turned down. After a brief apprenticeship at a local station in Washington, D.C., Chung had spent five years as a reporter for CBS News, and had then gone on to KNXT (later renamed KCBS), the CBS O&O in Los Angeles, where she had become the highest-paid female anchor in local television. Although it was widely agreed that Chung, like Savitch, jumped out of the screen at viewers, she was dogged and hardworking, a trouper who uncomplainingly did everything that was asked and looked around for more. In marked contrast to Savitch, she was also politic; she was friendly to everyone and never manifested anger or snubbed the help. After nearly six years as the most well-known anchorwoman at NBC, Savitch faced her first real competition, a woman who was a highly successful anchor and had served time in the network trenches as a reporter. It would have been an undesirable situation at any time; now, when Savitch was in negotiations for a new contract, she thought it posed potential disaster.

●

On May 2, the disaster happened. Savitch had flown to Ohio's Cuyahoga Valley to shoot a stand-up for insertion in a *Frontline* program called "For the Good of All," the story of the National Park Service's neglect of a big nature preserve. Between takes, Savitch insisted on being driven to a telephone so that she could call her office. Standing at an outdoor booth, a chilly wind whipping her hair and her scarf, Savitch received some bad news: Connie Chung was taking over Savitch's anchor slot on the weekend *Nightly News*. "This is unfair," Savitch wailed into the receiver. "I've done a good job. What did I do to deserve this?"' Sobbing, she hung up the phone and demanded to be taken for a drink. Production assistant Marcia Bemko pointed out that there was no bar in the middle of the park and the crew was waiting, but Savitch was insistent. Bowing to the inevitable, Bemko drove Savitch and David Buda outside the park to the nearest bar, where a tear-streaked Savitch sat and drank white wine. "It's unfair," she said over and over. "I can't go back."

But she had no choice. She had to go back that night and deal with the newspaper articles that she knew were being written about her loss of the Saturday night anchor chair. One of the first people she talked to was Ed Hookstratten, the agent she had retained to replace Richard Leibner. Known as "the Hook," he was a corpulent super-agent from Los Angeles with a belligerent style. He represented Tom Snyder, Tom Brokaw, and Chris Wallace, and Savitch had been flattered when he had called that spring and asked her to join their company. He told her flatly that he would make her a star. What she needed now, though, was a little help in spin control. Together Hookstratten and Savitch put out the word that she considered herself a free agent. Items appeared in celebrity columns in the *Daily News* and *New York Post* to the effect that she was looking at possibilities in Boston and California.

Savitch and Hookstratten had a drink with Richard Wald, who had moved to ABC, but he said he had no openings. In July, Savitch learned why, when Wald's boss, ABC News president Roone Arledge, was asked in the course of a lengthy *New York* profile whether he would hire Savitch. "I'm not a big fan of hers," Arledge said. "It would depend on what she wanted to do. I wouldn't hire her as an anchor."

Rejected as an anchor by NBC and ABC, Savitch was

frantic, swinging at increasing speed from the imperious persona of an old-time movie star to the terror of a small girl in a roomful of men. Obsessed by the negotiations for her new NBC contract, she was unable to pass by a phone without placing a call to Hookstratten or her lawyer, Donald Hamburg. The worse things went with the Hook's negotiations, the more she was convinced that only he could get her through. Hookstratten, she told friends, was like *that* with Grant Tinker.

In the spring and summer of 1983 Savitch was dating an attorney from out of town who had a house on the Jersey shore. When she stayed there overnight, she couldn't stand waiting to use the phone if someone else was on it. Instead, she rode her bike to the nearest pay phone, where she could check on the contract, which the attorney said seemed "like a knife at her throat." Sometimes she would be optimistic, and fantasize about the million-dollar bonus she would win for putting her name on the dotted line; other times, she would collapse on the sofa, asking whether the attorney thought that anybody would like her when she was no longer on television.

Screw them all, she sometimes told him. I don't need anybody. *TV Guide* says I'm the most trusted anchorperson and my Q-rating is a zillion.

Wait a minute, he replied. We're not talking about the public at large. We're talking about Reuven Frank.

Fuck him, Jessica Savitch said. And then—again and again—she began telling wild tales about how NBC had offered her *Meet the Press* and *Today,* stories that were obviously not true but that equally obviously she believed at the moment. She spun the fantasies out, enjoying them, patting them into shape, putting on the bells and whistles, and then always came out with the crusher. She had turned the offers down, spurned them each and every one.

The attorney wondered if she took a lot of drugs, but he never saw any. He worried about the grasping sycophants who surrounded her and the naïveté that made her unable to size people up. He was distressed by the way she would call him ten times a night if she thought he was annoyed at her. It was too much; everything about her was too excessive and speeded up.

One weekend she went from the attorney's beach house to Chicago for a speech. Returning, she told him she expected

315

him to meet her at the airport in Philadelphia, a fifty-mile ride late in the night. He asked her to take a limousine instead. Savitch blew up. Send me my clothes, she told him. I'm not coming back.

Okay, he said. I'll do it tomorrow.

At one o'clock that morning, Savitch arrived at the beach house in a limousine. Screaming, she threw her clothes into a suitcase and left. An hour later, she was banging at the door again. Still furious, she slept on the sofa in the living room. The next morning, the attorney recalled, Savitch was back to normal. By ten o'clock, she was on the phone to Hookstratten.

A few weeks later, this man spent a weekend with her in New York. She didn't want him to leave on Sunday night. Standing in her bathrobe in the hall, she begged him to stay. She was trembling, the attorney remembered later. He began to drive away, then changed his mind and returned. "She said, 'You came back! You came back! Nobody ever comes back!' It was like she wasn't talking to me, but to everyone she'd ever known. Every good-bye to her was permanent."

On Thursday, July 28, Savitch went with an NBC crew to Saratoga Springs, New York, for a story about Mrs. Cornelius Vanderbilt Whitney and the magnificent ball she held on the eve of the first major horse race of the summer, the Whitney Stakes. As the cameras rolled, Savitch, Mrs. Whitney, and her husband, called "Sonny," sat in white lawn chairs at the Whitney mansion, Cady Hill House, and chatted about Saratoga, racing, and the upcoming social season. Celebrity guests were nothing unusual for the Whitneys, whose guest lists had included Walter Cronkite, Ginger Rogers, and dozens of other well-known figures; nonetheless, Savitch was such a star that when Marylou Whitney's private secretary, June Douglas, learned that Savitch would be there, she asked her employer as a special favor for an introduction.

During her visit, Savitch went to an enclosed arena next to the racetrack for a look at the yearlings that were to be presented at the annual Fasig-Tipton auction. The setting was something like a mini-Astrodome, with circular tiered seats and a large open area in the center in which the horses were shown. That night the place was lively and crowded, with more than two thousand people jostling each other for a better view of the horseflesh on display.

High on the third tier, a tall man wearing aviator glasses and chain-smoking Marlboros surveyed the crowd below. His brown hair was turning gray and his waist had grown a bit thick and he looked preoccupied amid the loud, celebratory atmosphere. It was Ron Kershaw, who had once again brought a faltering news operation to number one but had subsequently been transferred to the network sports division after increasingly erratic behavior that many attributed to an overindulgence in booze and coke. He was currently producer of an NBC program called *Sports Journal,* and had come to Saratoga at the urging of several men friends who told him it was time he got over the sickness that was Jessica. "The women in Saratoga are great," one of the men told him. "You'll see so many beautiful tweeties it'll make your head spin." Hoping that his friend was right, Kershaw had agreed to go. He and his pals walked into the arena, he later recalled, feeling like the guys' night out— hey, we're ready to rock 'n' roll here. Kershaw's friend pointed out pursuable tweeties, but Kershaw wasn't listening. The moment he arrived he had singled out one woman. She was down on the floor, on the other side of the central area, and he slowly began to make his way down to get a better look. "Suddenly her head turned like that, right at me, it's like *boom!*—it's Jessica." Too stunned to speak, Kershaw retreated and headed back to New York. "I was scared to death," he said. "Holy fuck, you know, I'd done it again. I'd gone for the same fucking girl."

On Friday evening, July 29, Savitch, in a mid-calf-length blue-green dress, joined socialite C. Z. Guest, soprano Patrice Munsel, Hollywood producer Ray Stark, and some 275 other guests at the Whitneys' black-tie party, held in Saratoga's nineteenth-century casino. On the front of the oversize invitation to the Whitneys' soiree had been a flower-bedecked horse-drawn carriage, and female guests had been requested to wear something of a floral nature in tribute to the occasion exactly a century earlier when Sonny Whitney's mother, Gertrude Vanderbilt, then age six, had gone to a ball in Saratoga dressed as a rose. For this occasion, her daughter-in-law, Marylou, had a dress with large roses on it, and her guests wore floral prints or pinned blossoms to their gowns. A white gazebo was installed inside the casino and hung with flowers, vases full of flowers were put on every available surface, and nosegays were given out as party favors by young women dressed in Eliza Doolittle costumes.

Just after dawn the next morning, the NBC team was on a plane back to New York. There editors looked at the thousands of feet of videotape that had been shot as Savitch went over her script and then recorded it. Then the vocal track was laid into the final edited footage. A few hours later, anchorwoman Savitch led into the story, which was to be the last one she would do for NBC. "It was a real feature," said Susan Dutcher, the producer on the piece. "There was no sad underside. It was not about poverty or dying children or anything. It was about how the total upper crust spend their time, and it was fun." It was the kind of light women's story that Savitch had spent her entire career trying to avoid. It was very good.

Nine days later, Jessica Savitch checked into the Sonoma Mission Inn, a celebrity health spa located outside San Francisco. For $65 a day, the spa offered a calm, well-regulated day with hiking, exercise classes, rest periods, and healthy food. A refuge for the well-heeled, it was a place to recuperate from exhaustion and stress, to calm down and cool out. Although it was not a treatment center, it offered an opportunity to detox from too many chemicals taken too often. Savitch told friends that Warren Beatty had arranged for her to go there. Whether or not that was true, Sonoma Mission was clearly the sort of place she needed. "I was amazed when I met her," said journalist Kitty Kelley, who was staying there at the same time. "The controlled Jessica Savitch I saw on air was not the soft-spoken hyper Jessica Savitch I met there. She talked so fast I got breathless listening to her."

During a walk with Savitch, Kelley commented on the contrast between Savitch on air and off. Laughing, Savitch told Kelley that her sister had once said that someone could put a spike through her foot on air and she wouldn't say anything. Listening to the other woman run on, Kelley wondered whether Savitch was high; later she joked that the anchorwoman talked like someone who'd just downed five hundred milligrams of Preludin. "It was very tiring to follow someone who sounded like a thirty-three record played on seventy-eight," Kelley said. "By Thursday I was avoiding her."

Even in a place devoted to relaxation, Savitch could not seem to let go. She rarely appeared without full makeup; in

318

exercise classes where everyone else used sweatsuits provided by the spa, Savitch wore a high-fashion metallic green leotard with matching tights. Still in a state about her contract, she phoned Hookstratten throughout her stay. When she moved around the spa, she asked to have a phone plugged in next to her so as not to miss his calls. She did not last the week; two days before the prepaid session was over, she was on her way back to New York to handle the negotiations in person.

At one point, as a prelude to negotiations, Ed Hookstratten had taken Savitch to see another of his clients, Tom Brokaw, at Brokaw's beach house in Southern California. After co-anchoring the nightly news for a year, Brokaw had hit his stride, and in July, NBC management had named him as solo anchor. Brokaw, who had spent the last decade proving that he was a serious newsman, saw Savitch as a performer rather than a journalist and thought that what had happened to her was an example of what was wrong with broadcast news. "The people who brought her in here abandoned her," he said. "They used her for their own purposes, to attract audience and so on, but they never really cared about her career beyond that, never really worked very hard at figuring out where do we go from here." He also had a personal gripe, stemming from when he had been host of *Today* and she had substituted for Jane Pauley for a week. "I busted my fanny to make sure she was happy," Brokaw said. Afterward, he was annoyed to learn that Savitch had complained that as a woman she was always put in the second slot. Still, Brokaw's irritation had not prevented him from telling Hookstratten several times that Savitch was isolated from the rest of the news division, and that this was not helpful to her career. In the end, the Hook had asked Brokaw to speak to Savitch about her attitude.

The day of Savitch's visit, Brokaw recalled, "she was wound just tighter than a two-dollar clock." He and his teenage children had been swimming and were sitting around in wet bathing suits when Savitch arrived, dressed in an expensive white Fila tennis outfit and gold Gucci jewelry, her makeup flawless and her hair carefully sprayed. As Hookstratten had requested, Brokaw drew Savitch aside. "You really have to be part of the group for a while," he later recalled saying. "People just don't have any appreciation of you as a human being, what you're interested in and what you want to do apart from the fact that you want to be a star." That afternoon, Savitch went swimming with Brokaw's kids, who later told their father that they thought Savitch was a troubled person. Brokaw, too, thought she was troubled. He was always struck, he said, by a remark Jane Pauley had once made, that it seemed in a way as if Savitch had made a compact with the devil that in exchange for ten years of stardom she'd do anything, and that now the devil was ready to collect his due.

Finally, at the end of August, the new contract was ready. There was no million-dollar bonus. There was a commitment to making Savitch anchor of the Sunday evening news beginning in January 1984 (when Chris Wallace would leave to cover the presidential campaign), but none to making her an anchor or a substitute anchor on *NBC Nightly News* during the week or the weekend, or of substituting on *Today*. There was mention of, but no commitment to, giving her a "significant assignment" at the 1984 conventions. There were no stipulations regarding reporting duties. There was not even the usual three-year period of employment; the contract was for one year. Instead, there was what Steve Friedman, executive producer of *Today* at the time, considered standard network treatment; because networks are always afraid that someone they let go might do well elsewhere, he said, they hardly ever actually fire anybody, but simply keep paying them more and more to do less and less. Savitch received a 5 percent raise, to $315,000, for what Reuven Frank considered a part-time contract. For the first four months, Savitch would be responsible for a minimum of three evening updates a week (fewer than her 1980 contract); after that, Frank reluctantly allowed her to resume anchoring on Sunday nights. He did not object to her doing the prime-time newsbreaks. Although he was well aware that *NBC News Digest* was the highest-rated news show on the network—"I kept hearing that until I thought I'd throw up," he said later—Frank really didn't care. "Forty-three seconds," he said. "The whole thing is so phony."

There was more bad news waiting for her in the wings. Over the summer, David Fanning and the *Frontline* management decided that Savitch's role in the show's second season would be minimal. She had brought viewers to the show, exactly as Fanning had hoped she would, but the craziness around

320

her was too high to continue using her. Fanning was willing to invest the $90,000 required for Savitch's salary; he wasn't willing to invest the considerable staff time and energy required to prop Savitch up and keep her going, or to absorb the loss of credibility within the journalistic establishment entailed by Savitch's association with the show. "We had hoped she'd accept *Sunrise,*" said Mike Kirk. "We were laboring under Jessica's idea, that NBC really thought a lot of her. But as time went on, we got to know people at NBC and realized they were in the same bind we were. We were all perpetuating something untrue. Nobody wanted to get rid of her, but nobody wanted to give her too much." Larry Grossman, president of the Public Broadcasting System, began sounding out others, including Roger Mudd and journalist and author Richard Reeves, to host the show. Fanning began composing a speech in his head for delivery to Savitch.

On October 3, Fanning flew down to New York to deliver it. They had lunch at the restaurant of her choice, the "21" Club. He was startled to find a very different-looking Savitch sitting at a corner table waiting for him, for on a trip to California in September she had her distinctive Roman nose straightened and her chin tucked. "She said it was the old deviated septum number and that she'd been holed up at Warren Beatty's," Fanning said. "I was transfixed by wanting to say, Jessica, why did you do that. I knew the face, and now it didn't have the right proportions. She had taken the bump out, which was what made the planes of her face work."

As Fanning squirmed uneasily, Savitch chattered away. These phrases shot past him: Things were going to take off . . . Her career was going ahead in a new way . . . She wanted to get perspective on things . . . This contract was not a setback . . . She was thrilled at the opportunity to live a more normal life . . . She was thinking about going back to local TV . . . Maybe she could buy into a local station . . .

It all seemed *off,* Fanning recalled thinking. He listened to her babble about everything being okay, this strange-looking anorectic woman with the new face, and he realized she had stepped farther out, away not only from *Frontline* but from reality. He had the terrible feeling that she had begun to slide, and as she plunged heedlessly on to her rap about how perfect things were, Fanning bit his tongue. He couldn't tell her what he had come to tell her. He had always prided himself on being completely honest with her, but he felt he couldn't do it then.

Shaken, he went back to Boston. He hadn't said a word about her leaving the show.

That evening, at 8:58 P.M., Jessica Savitch did the job for him. In a single *Digest,* forty-three seconds of live television, she destroyed what was left of her career.

10

*N*ew Hope

Just before nine o'clock on the night of October 3, 1983, Sam Donaldson, ABC's White House correspondent, was preparing for an appearance on *Nightline,* the late-night news show. He sat working at the anchor desk, which was located at one end of a big basement studio in Washington, D.C., that was also a working newsroom. As usual, dozens of staffers bustled about readying that night's broadcast. A windowless room, perhaps sixty feet on a side, lined with gigantic maps of the world and scores of television monitors, it had the strange, futuristic *Dr. No* feeling of an underground information bunker. Its location added to the impression: *Nightline* was broadcast just six blocks from the White House. At 8:58 P.M., Donaldson happened to glance at the wall of monitors to his right, and saw them filled with the face of Jessica Savitch doing the *NBC News Digest.* She looked terrible. Shocked, Donaldson pushed a button at his desk to punch up the sound, and what he heard shocked him further. The woman was sloppy, she was slurring her words, she was mumbling. Donaldson thought—he didn't know what he thought. She must be on drugs—in trouble—clearly on some kind of "medication." All these things passed through his mind as he sat there and watched the wall of Jessica

Savitches stumble through the forty-three seconds. By the end of her first headline, everyone in the newsroom was watching, swiveling their heads in astonishment as the *Digest* seemed to go on and on and Savitch's face looked ever more stricken, as though she was just beginning to understand what she was doing to herself. Donaldson didn't know Savitch well. Nonetheless, he knew he was not easily going to forget the sight of her face as she realized that she had just committed the one unforgivable sin of network news. She had lost control on air.

That night, NBC editor and producer Ann Kemp worked on the fourth floor at 30 Rock, where she was editing a story scheduled to air later in the week. She did not see the *Digest,* but she didn't need to. By 9:01, the entire building knew that Jessica Savitch had just freaked out on live TV before millions and millions of couch potatoes. Kemp was not surprised. She had been the *Digest* writer and producer for Savitch every Saturday for the past year. Although Kemp liked Savitch, thinking her both humorous and painfully vulnerable, she also found the anchorwoman an alarmingly undependable performer. One Saturday night several months earlier Savitch had showed up for the run-through with a bottle of champagne and one glass. She had practiced Kemp's script between sips of bubbly. Savitch had then taken a powder for twenty minutes, returning to the anchor chair just two minutes before the newsbreak began. "She was higher than a kite," Kemp said. "She sounded all right on air, but I could hear the difference." Knowing that if there were a disaster, it would be her job, Kemp had been horribly anxious during Savitch's absence, and Kemp was not reassured by Savitch's last-minute reappearance. When the *Digest* was over, Kemp had gone into the bathroom and vomited. Then she had told Savitch that she could never, ever do that again, speaking firmly, as if to a child, to this woman who was a household name, whose salary dwarfed Kemp's, who could have a middle-level producer like Kemp replaced or even fired with a snap of her fingers. "If you talked to her nicely, you didn't get the point across," Kemp said. "She was like a little kid, pushing the limits, wanting to be nailed."

After that performance, Kemp had spoken to Art Kent, the vice-president in charge of affiliate news services who was technically Savitch's direct boss. She asked him whether he would back her up if she ever yanked a drunken or stoned Savitch and put another anchor in her place. He told her he was aware of the problem and that she should keep him posted. He made it clear that he would support Kemp, but he did not—could not—say, Yes, Ann, I will protect you if you kick out the network anchor with the highest Q-rating in America. And Kemp continued to dread that she would be in charge on the night that the inevitable disaster happened. She dreaded it, in fact, until the night the disaster actually did happen, and, mercifully, someone else was on duty.

Art Kent saw the *Digest* at home. As a recently appointed vice-president, he didn't know exactly what a vice-president should do when disaster occurred. Before the *Digest* was over, he phoned the control room. Producer Bill O'Connell told him the place was in a panic. Although the simplest response would have been then and there to order Savitch not to do the next newsbreak, Kent's instinct was to intervene personally. He told O'Connell he was coming, threw on his coat, and raced over in a cab.

A former Middle East correspondent, Kent had been brought back to New York by Tom Pettit in 1982 as part of the endless struggle to regain the affection of the affiliates. Because he was in charge of the afternoon updates, Kent had been working directly with Savitch for the past year and had seen her throwing her weight around. Unlike many at network, however, Kent had a certain sympathy for her, for he had been an anchor at local stations for fifteen years and was well aware of the endless pressure to look good and sound good and at least appear to feel good about being public property.

By the time Kent arrived at 30 Rock, Savitch had fled to her office. He spoke to her there. She was, as Kent put it later, a puddle. He tried to calm her down until Gordon Manning, another vice-president, arrived. Then Manning closeted himself with Savitch and asked her what was going on. Savitch stonewalled. When she was alone, she called Mary Manilla, with whom she had reconciled earlier in the year. In the meantime, Kent crossed his fingers and went downstairs to supervise preparations for the next *Digest*. Savitch seemed calmer, and he thought it was always best to go with what was orginally planned. "Gordon and I thought she was okay," Kent said.

Kent was in the control room when the second *Digest* was done. He then departed, giving Manning a lift home in his taxi, and Savitch left to meet Manilla at Hurley's.

Kent remained disturbed. Over the next few days, he became one of many in the hierarchy who acted as both griller and grillee, quizzing Savitch about what happened, asking members of her little circle what was going on, and, in turn, being asked himself what, if anything, he had noticed when he worked with her. If only he had been involved sooner, he thought, maybe things would be different now.

"We blew it," he said later. "But this is a company, and the bureaucrats will get you every time." Although he did not consider Savitch entirely blameless—"She was a grown-up, in charge of her own life," he said—he thought that management should have stepped in earlier and done more. "We should not let things get to the point where you had to just kind of turn your back and say there's not anything to be done, which is what was happening at the end," he said. "We didn't see the signals that she was getting unraveled, and act sooner. It shouldn't have gotten to the nth hour. There's no excuse."

NBC president Bob Mulholland saw the *Digest* at home and thought, My God, what's going on here? He had never seen anything like that in his life. The woman who had first caught his eye back at KYW and the woman who was there on the *NBC News Digest* that night were two different people, and he wasn't sure he wanted to know the second. The next morning he called Ed Hookstratten and, according to his later recollection, said, "Hey, you know, there's something going on here and we've got to get to the bottom of it." The Hook called Savitch, and she popped into Mulholland's office almost immediately. "What's the fuss?" she said. Mulholland remembered that she told him flatly that she didn't know what he was talking about. There was nothing wrong with her performance the previous evening. Dumbfounded, Mulholland asked her what *she* was talking about. Had she looked at a tape of the broadcast in question? No, Savitch said. She told him that she would do so, and the conversation ended.

Mulholland talked to her again a few days later, and once more after that. Finally she told him that she had been hit in the face in a boating accident in California in September and had been forced to go through reconstructive surgery, and that the combination of the painkillers she had to take and the bright lights in the studio had been too much for her. (Surgery for her *nose*—that was something people at NBC could believe, though they didn't think it was needed because she'd been smacked by a sailboat boom.) Although Mulholland had heard rumors about Savitch's drug use, he said later that he did not ask her about it. "If you asked everybody who's on the air about every rumor that's passed around about them, you'd spend all your life doing it," he said. "Stuff like that—you have to use your common sense." Nor did he suggest that she contact the network's substance abuse program, a well-respected setup that had helped a number of NBC employees to recover from alcohol and drug dependency. "You can only counsel someone who wants to be counseled," he said. "This party was not looking for counseling. A lot of people said, 'Hey, anything we can do to help, any problem, anything going on?' She just said no, no problem at all, nothing."

Even before Mulholland got on the horn with the Hook on Monday morning, Tom Pettit had ordered all extraneous copies of the *Digest* tape destroyed; he did not want them circulating through the bloopers-and-fluffs buffs in the technical divisions, and he especially didn't want copies going to the reporters who kept calling. That day, network and news division brass met to talk over The Savitch Problem. Pettit then called Tom Wolzien, a vice-president, back from a trip to Washington, showed him the tape, and told Wolzien that his new assignment was to hound Savitch until he found out what was going on. Wolzien, who had served in Vietnam as a marine and retained a no-nonsense military demeanor, had been Savitch's producer on the weekend news for a year. There had been a few temper tantrums, but then Wolzien had laid down the law. He had told her that he would take care of the technical end of things and make her look good, and she had begun to relax. "Once we got the ground rules defined—you don't give me bullshit and I don't give you bullshit—everything was okay," he said.

To Wolzien, Savitch was a mixed bag. It seemed to him that she had neither the world's best journalistic judgment nor the worst; when she was in the groove she was great, really remarkable, and when she was off she was still competent. Unlike Mulholland, Wolzien had confronted her many times about drugs in general and cocaine in particular. She had always denied that she had been anywhere near the stuff. When others told him about Savitch and drugs, Wolzien always said that he needed more information. No one would tell him they'd been with her when she was using the stuff, he said later. They were too scared. Instead, people would tell him they'd, uh, *heard* about it. Wolzien would tell them he needed something concrete.

Now Wolzien met with Savitch day after day in her fourteenth-floor office. He kept hammering at her. The *Digest*. What had happened. What was going on. "She looked really worried," he recalled. "She wasn't dressed up like usual. She seemed very tired, and there were lots of tears." At first Savitch told Wolzien, too, that nothing had happened. She was, she insisted, perfectly okay. After a few days, however, it was obvious to Wolzien that she knew she wasn't okay, and that she was watching her career evaporate. Finally she told him she had blown her lines because she had mixed wine and Percodan, a powerful painkiller. "It's not cocaine! It's not cocaine!" she cried, and pulled three bottles bearing prescription labels from her purse.

Savitch talked to Wolzien about quitting, about piling all her stuff in a car and driving west and giving up the whole thing. Wolzien didn't know whether it was possible for her to overcome the *Digest* fiasco; to him, the odds looked pretty bad. He kept asking her about coke, and she continued to deny using it. He told one senior staffer, "NBC should go to Jessica and say we love you and we want you to go away and get taken care of and we'll be here when you come back." But NBC wasn't going to say that, and Wolzien's job was to find out what had happened. He kept at it. On Friday, October 21, two and a half weeks after the *Digest*, Savitch called Wolzien and asked if he and his wife would like to accompany her and a date to the opera. "She'd never invited us to anything," Wolzien said. "She was obviously reaching out. She was ostracized by the world after October 3. It was all over." Wolzien, alas, had a previous engagement, and neither he nor Savitch ended up at Lincoln Center.

•

The day after the *Digest,* Pettit and Manning called in various staffers who had worked with Savitch. "They said, 'What should we do? Send her to a hospital?' " one of those questioned recalled. To that staff member, the questions seemed belated. It seemed that management's lack of interest in Savitch had helped to contribute to her downfall and now they were all trying to cover themselves. Management had helped create a monster and didn't know what to do. People at the top were saying that they cared about Savitch, the staff member thought, but what were they saying behind closed doors?

Wolzien, too, interviewed staffers. According to one interviewee he asked, "What do you think? What do you know? Where does she get drugs? Where does she use them? What kind of drugs?" The interviewee found such concern horribly tardy. It seemed that all these vice-presidents were still at the exploratory stage, not the stage of intervention—that is, of actually doing something.

Others in the network were also busy talking and thinking about The Savitch Problem. Ray Timothy, then president of NBC-TV, was deeply disturbed. Timothy, who had begun his network career as a Rockefeller Center tour guide in the mid-1950s, had risen to the network heights through sales and had a keen appreciation for Savitch's drawing power. To Timothy, Savitch had "a certain Edith Piaf quality, almost a Judy Garland quality, which not every paid reader had." Anytime she was on the air, NBC would get an audience, he said. "And since I'm in the audience-getting business, I was a fan." After October 3, though, Timothy did not know what to think. "We were all concerned," he said. "Meetings were held. We had complaints from the affiliates to deal with. They were all demanding to know what had happened."

Although Bud Rukeyser, who had returned to NBC after Tinker took over the reins, later tended to downplay the significance of the *Digest* screwup, he appeared agitated about it at the time. When a reporter named Laurie Winer came to interview him on an unrelated story for a broadcast trade magazine called *View,* Rukeyser suddenly turned in his chair, popped a tape of the incident—one of the few Pettit had not destroyed—into his office videocassette recorder, and pushed the play button. What, he asked his startled visitor, did she make of *this*? Because October 3 was the only time Savitch had any on-air problems, he said later, there was no easy answer for what NBC should do. He pointed out that unlike alcohol, which can be smelled and causes tipsy behavior, or marijuana, which makes users look and act stoned, cocaine is difficult to detect. "At least in the short term, cocaine can be an enhancer," he said. "Unless we see someone snorting at his or her desk, we can't pin anything down." To give someone a six-week leave of absence on the grounds of rumors of cocaine use seemed to Rukeyser potential grounds for legal action. "I don't claim the institution acted impeccably," he said, "but we didn't ignore it. We did try to do something. But with no evidence and in the face of her denials, I don't know what would have been appropriate."

Reuven Frank's reaction to The Savitch Problem was predictable: He told Pettit to deal with it and then returned to the haven of his office. In Frank's view, his first consideration had to be the health of the news division. He had thought Savitch's anchoring the weekend news was damaging and had therefore stopped her, but he did not think the credibility of NBC News would be damaged by Savitch's continued presence on newsbreaks, which were nothing but glorified commercials anyway. It wasn't worth buying out her contract, he decided, because that was really the equivalent of firing someone. "That's a very public thing to do," he said. "I didn't think she *deserved* that. It wasn't her fault some damn fool hired her. It wasn't a tragic situation, but it was a pathetic one." Perhaps NBC had a certain black eye for having let the situation reach that point, Frank conceded later. Maybe he should have done something, but what he didn't know. "Lower down, people have counseling," he said. "But not a person on her level. She was too high up. There was no available institutional response."

A member of Savitch's coterie, distraught over the drugs in Savitch's office and apartment as well as Savitch's requests that this member obtain more drugs for her, went to a counselor in the personnel division and poured out these concerns. The counselor was bound by company guidelines on confidentiality from saying anything directly to anyone in management. The only person in an official capacity who had been given an account of Savitch's drug problems by an eyewitness, he remained silent. Although those who did speak to Savitch, particularly Wolzien, were direct, they lacked specific information—what might in a court of law be called a smoking gun. And without the smoking gun, they thought they could not confront her with the bottom line, that she would lose her job and her career if she did not stop. Instead, the reality behind the tough talk was that she would still be paid more than $6,000 a week and would still be Jessica Savitch of NBC News. Although officials made their disapproval clear, they did not make clear that even Savitch could not get away with abusing drugs. But in the case of drug addiction, anyplace short of the bottom line is a place that lets the abuser keep using drugs, which is exactly what Jessica Savitch did.

Savitch's newsroom colleagues were also worried. One woman, a successful broadcaster who had worked around Savitch for a number of years, went to Tom Pettit and told him he had to do something. Pettit, who had discussed the rumors of cocaine use with Savitch, told the broadcaster that management was afraid to move from fear that Savitch would kill herself. Another woman, a highly placed producer, went to Tom Wolzien during his investigation and said that she thought Jessica Savitch was flipping out. This producer was anything but a fan of Savitch; on the contrary, she had been dismayed upon meeting Savitch to discover that this woman with the image of intelligent self-confidence was really "an unbearable person who was always in a tizzy." Still, the *Digest* episode upset the producer. When she spoke to Wolzien, he told her that Tom Pettit understood the situation and was very worried, too. "Somebody should have gone and said, 'Jessica, let us help you,' " the producer said. "But nobody seemed to be doing anything." To the producer, it seemed clear that the network heads were busy grooming Connie Chung. "They didn't like Jessica any longer," the producer said, "and they had been making it clear all fall how much they didn't like her."

One of the ways this was made clear was by leaving her out on high-status, select occasions where she would have been prominently featured in the past. At one point, for example, network executives gave a party for Connie Chung on the sixth floor. It was held in a huge reception room filled with bowing Filipino waiters bearing trays of canapés, and Chung, one of only a few women present, was clearly the star. "It was the kind of affair Jessica would have been invited to in the past," one observer said. "Nobody mentioned her name."

On October 14, Savitch did attend a reception at the Plaza Hotel for the NBC press tour, the annual conclave at which the network unveils the next season's shows to TV writers from across the country. It was her first public appearance at such a network event in some time; the previous spring, Savitch had not even been invited to the annual affiliate meetings in Los Angeles. That had been Reuven Frank's decision: The affiliate meeting was a showcase for hot talent and exciting new directions, and to Frank this meant Connie Chung and Willard Scott, the enormously popular weatherman who had come to *Today* a year earlier, not Jessica Savitch. "Why should I [take Jessica]?" Frank said later. "Jessica was nowhere compared to Willard."

At the Plaza reception, Savitch and Chung happened to wear dresses of the same brilliant red hue, an unfortunate coincidence that only highlighted the contrast between the two at the time. Chung was up, on, charming, the captivating focus of attention; after she gave a brief speech, the critics clustered around her for quotes and badgered her for interviews. Standing off to the side, Savitch was anxious, distressed, tense. "She looked like a wounded deer," said Gerry Solomon, who had worked with Savitch back in D.C. and was now executive producer of *Sunrise*. Savitch, the central figure at press tours past, now was yesterday's news, of only passing interest to the critics. The one person really paying attention to her was NBC press official Mary Lou O'Callahan, who seemed to Gerry Solomon to be acting almost like Savitch's keeper. Solomon, who had felt uncomfortable around Savitch ever since he had told a reporter from *Ms.* his frank opinion of Savitch's work, was troubled by what he saw at the Plaza, but felt helpless to do anything about it. "We saw this happening and what did we do to stop it?" he asked later. "Nothing. I saw these terribly destructive things going on, but I had no opportunity to stop them."

A few days later, Don Bowers, the producer assigned to oversee political coverage during the 1984 presidential compaign, received an invitation to dine with Savitch at the "21" Club. A veteran of all three networks, Bowers had gone out on stories with Savitch after she had been pulled from the Senate. He thought that her ideas were cockamamy on the whole, but the two of them had got along reasonably well. In some ways, Bowers thought, she was a producer's dream: "I want a robot, not a thinking person who's going to give me static," he said dryly. He had planned to use her in 1984, figuring that the conventions would have little actual news and it made sense to use someone viewers liked to watch—someone, as he later put it, who had "men all over the country creaming in their pants." After October 3, however, Bowers had to revise his plans. According to Bowers, although Tom Pettit had assured Savitch there would be no penalty for the *Digest,* he and Frank decided that she would not be used for the coming campaign and conventions.

Their reservations at "21" were for after the second *Digest,* and Savitch was prompt. Primly dressed in a suit with a polka-dot blue tie, she looked crisp and attractive, every inch the anchorwoman. Taking the bull by the horns, she told Bowers that she had simply gone blank on October 3 and lost her place. No drugs were involved, she told him firmly. Absolutely none. As they sat there, waiters whisked menus and glasses and plates on and off the small table. Despite the high prices and the fact that the maître d' and the waiters addressed Savitch by name and that there were several celebrities in the room and that a few of them even stopped by their table and said hello, Bowers was not impressed, for the whole place seemed to him lacking in graciousness and any real comfort. He had intended to tell Savitch of the changes mandated from above, but somehow, like David Fanning, the message he actually conveyed was considerably milder. "I didn't tell her absolutely she was cut out of political coverage in 1984," he said. "I just greased the wheels for that message."

Overnight co-anchor Linda Ellerbee was also disturbed by the disintegration she saw taking place in Savitch. In the past, as Ellerbee later frankly confessed, she had been envious of Savitch's meteoric rise and angry at the male executives who were responsible for making her the standard for women on air. "Jessica gave the illusion of being a tough reporter without

333

being a reporter or being tough," she said. "She was the logical extrapolation of all their meanest and smallest hopes for women in television. Looking good wasn't only all they required—it was all they *wanted*."

Recently, however, Savitch had asked Ellerbee to dinner at Hurley's. "Jessica wanted to be one of the guys, to be associated with those of us who did what we were paid to do," Ellerbee said. "She wanted to talk journalism war stories, but hers all had to do with hairdressers and missed planes and missed opportunities." As Ellerbee sat there listening to Savitch, who was talking so loudly that other diners' heads were turning, she felt any remaining envy dissolve into pity for the blond anchorwoman. "NBC was a good place for women to work," Ellerbee said. "We stuck together. But Jessica never got into any of that. She was terrified of being found out, so she never got close to anybody at work. She never trusted any of us."

One of Ellerbee's colleagues, John Hart, shared her concern about Savitch. Hart had been bumped off the weekend news to make room for Savitch and, reasonably enough, had never been one of her fans at NBC. She seemed to him to be performing at all times; even her vulnerability appeared to him fraudulent and calculated. He thought NBC should never have hired her, and certainly should have fired her after discovering she couldn't do the work; he was appalled by what he saw as the network's unprincipled surrender to the commercial advantages of keeping her on the air. Now, however, he saw that there was another, more pressing problem. Whenever he talked to her, she appeared to be in her own world—projecting her own movie, he said. She would begin the conversation in the middle of a story he knew nothing about, or would launch into a spirited defense of some person or act that had nothing to do with him. "The transmitter was going, but not the receiver," Hart said. "I felt there was something really wrong here."

As a recovered alcoholic, Hart was particularly attuned to evidence of substance abuse, and he thought he saw in Savitch a creature like himself. It seemed clear to him that Savitch was on something. He thought management had done Savitch no favor by avoiding the issue, and that senior executives should tell her point-blank that she had to seek help. "But there was something in it for them to keep her on [air] as long as possible," he said. "And executives are not known as courageous."

John Hart's close friend, Pat Trese, was also concerned. Another recovered alcoholic, he, too, thought he recognized Savitch as someone who was hooked. She acted impossible, he thought, because she was in the throes of addiction and was terrified of exposure. "People could see it but they couldn't see it," Trese said. "They couldn't bring themselves to say this woman has a problem. It was easier to say she's a bitch." Trese's own battle with the bottle had come to a head the night of New York City's second big blackout—the same night Jessica Savitch was doing her final audition for NBC—when he was so busy producing a special news report that he didn't have time to get his usual dose of martinis. "I went into the control room stone sober and it was a disaster," he said. When the head of the network's substance abuse center phoned and said, "We've been aware of your pain for some time," Trese went through the NBC treatment program and has been sober ever since.

When Trese spoke to Tom Pettit about Savitch after the October 3 *Digest,* Pettit told him he'd try to think of something to do. Trese wasn't optimistic. He thought about saying something to her himself, but he knew from his own experience that this would have no effect until Savitch was ready to acknowledge that there was something wrong. "It was like standing on the shore and watching someone drown and not being able to do anything," he said.

On Friday, October 21, the night Savitch had invited Wolzien to the opera, Ellerbee, Trese, Hart, and two other staffers convened in one of their offices to talk about The Savitch Problem. It seemed to them that the situation was becoming critical, and that they had no choice but to intervene. Because none of them knew Savitch well, they decided they would go to her together and speak to her as directly as possible. "We wanted to say, 'Jessica, forget your career, your life is in mortal danger,' " Ellerbee said later. " 'Your job will be here when you come back. What can we do to help?' " John Hart suggested that he ask his psychotherapist's advice about how to phrase their remarks, and the group resolved to carry out their plan at the beginning of the next week.

•

Outside the one square block of prime Manhattan real estate occupied by 30 Rock, Jessica Savitch's star appeared to shine as bright as ever. Viewers continued to ask for signed photos, civic groups were delighted to pay her high fees to speak, young women who aspired to broadcast careers spent hours in front of mirrors trying to perfect a Jessica Savitch-style look and delivery, and men fantasized about the woman with the thousand-watt smile. In late September, one such man, a newspaper executive named Martin Fischbein, had his dream come true when a friend wrote a note on his behalf to Savitch and she replied that she'd be delighted to meet him.

Although Savitch could not have known it at the time, she and Fischbein, the vice-president, assistant general manager, and circulation and personnel director of the *New York Post,* had a startling amount in common. He, too, had spent his early years in a middle-class Jewish community, in his case Woodmere, Long Island, and his family had suffered grievous losses (his Polish-born mother was the only member of her family to survive the Holocaust, and two of his siblings had died of Tay-Sachs syndrome, a fatal congenital disorder that afflicts people of Jewish descent). Like Savitch, Fischbein had passed most of his college years off campus, working for Jacob Javits, Nelson Rockefeller, and Daniel Moynihan. Fischbein was thirty-four, and was determined to be the youngest person to achieve his chosen goal, being publisher of a major American newspaper; Savitch, who was thirty-six, had shaved a year off her birthdate in order to make good on a boast that she would get to the networks by the age of thirty, and was thus listed in NBC publicity as only thirty-five. But their most important shared characteristic was that they were both self-made.

While Savitch was sitting in Texas puzzling out how an anchorwoman should look into the camera, Fischbein was in Manhattan studying the careers, connections, and, on occasion, the obituaries of the nation's political and financial big shots in order to plot his own route to the top of the pole. To Fischbein, the key element—the equivalent, in the political and financial realm, of Savitch's on-air presence—was having a personal network of important, accessible contacts, and he proceeded to devote his life to expanding and refining what might be called his own private Rolodex. He cultivated people with a rare skill, listening attentively, putting people in touch with each other, passing along press clippings he knew would be interesting, always remembering birthdays, holidays, and important anniversaries. He had started out working for noted labor negotiator Ted Kheel; after seven years, he'd learned what he could and moved on to become the protégé of Rupert Murdoch. A tall, good-looking man with thick dark hair and wire-rimmed glasses who frequently clamped a Cuban cigar between his teeth even though he didn't smoke, he looked like a charter member of the squash-playing generation then engaged in taking over corporate America. In fact, he had little interest in playing any sports, perhaps because he was oddly graceless, with a ducklike waddle that was incongruous with his well-cut suits and Hermès ties. He had even less interest in that other accompaniment to big-city success, expensive drugs. The kind of guy who'd order a diet Coke in a Japanese restaurant when the rest of the table was having sake, Fischbein rarely touched alcohol and was not known to have even sampled cocaine.

Like Savitch, he had a hard time relaxing and seemed most comfortable, most truly alive, when at work. Like Savitch, he was able to focus intently on someone he had just met in order to make a strong, positive impression. Unlike her, however, Fischbein became a friend to the movers and shakers he angled to do business with, including real estate magnates Mort Zuckerman and Sam LeFrak, broadcast entrepreneur Bob Price, *20/ 20* producer Ave Westin, race-car driver Roger Penske, and the eminent journalist from *Time* Richard Clurman. And although Fischbein, like Savitch, could be distant and demanding with co-workers, no one disputed his ability to deliver the goods. For Murdoch, he produced favorable union contracts and a quiescent work force. At the time he met Savitch, he was well on his way to becoming the publisher of what would be Murdoch's next acquisition, the *Chicago Sun-Times*. Fischbein also had many friends with similarly rising careers, including lawyers, agents, writers, editors, and an NBC documentary producer named Liz Callan.

Like a number of the women in Fischbein's life, Callan was a blind date who quickly turned into a buddy. As she described it later, their first telephone conversation had seemed to her singularly unpromising:

MF: Hello, this is Martin Fischbein. Would you like to get together?
LC: Yes.
MF: Do you have your schedule handy?
LC: No.
MF: No problem, I'm looking at mine. How about three weeks from Tuesday?

When they met for dinner, however, at Mortimer's, a trendy East Side restaurant, Callan found not the Sammy Glick character she expected but a warm, friendly man who seemed genuinely interested in getting to know her. She liked the fact that Fischbein's idea of how to treat a woman seemed to focus more on flowers and good food and a leisurely walk afterward than on how to get his companion into bed; a favorite follow-up was a spoof front page of the *Post* with an eyebrow-raising headline using the woman's name, accompanied by a mock threat to print it if she did not go out with him again soon.

Over the months that followed, Callan learned why Fischbein had so many devoted friends: He would do anything for anyone at any time, usually before they had even thought of what it was they wanted or needed. She, too, received birthday cards and presents on special occasions and useful newspaper clippings. And she, too, came to realize that these things were provided without strings, simply for the pleasure it gave Fischbein to be useful, to put together things—people, deals, stray facts or figures—that might not be together otherwise.

Even then, Fischbein was fixated on Jessica Savitch; one of his first questions was whether Callan knew her. She didn't; nonetheless, they soon developed a running joke about when Liz was going to introduce Marty to Jessica. Savitch was the latest in a series of female broadcasters to catch Fischbein's eye. The first had been Merri Spaeth, a statuesque blond who as a teenager had starred in a movie with Peter Sellers, *The World of Henry Orient,* and had gone on to anchor local news and current-events programs in Columbus, Ohio, and New York City as well as being a free-lance producer for *20/20.* One Sunday morning after they had been together for six years, Fischbein woke up to find Spaeth packing her bags; she had fallen in love with someone else. Devastated, Fischbein spent the next several months trying to figure out what had gone wrong, and then began a search for a replacement. "He was hoping to meet someone dynamic, beautiful, interesting, complex—just like Merri," said Kate White, a close friend who is now the associate editor of *Mademoiselle*. "He didn't want your typical New York woman, one of what he called the Neurotic 400, with her biological clock ticking and her stories of traumas from previous relationships. He wanted a doer."

Fischbein dated Nancy Glass, a Philadelphia newscaster; when she married a dentist, he became close to Anne Garrels, at the time a correspondent for ABC in Washington, and Christy Ferer, who contributed fashion reports to *Today*. But the one who seemed to interest him most was Jessica Savitch. In 1982, he asked reporter Nancy Collins to fix him up with Savitch; eagerly anticipating the occasion, he sent his friend Kate White a copy of *Anchorwoman* and a note saying that he hoped to meet Savitch soon. But then Collins told him she couldn't reach Savitch, and he was back to square one. In the summer of 1983, he mentioned to Garrels that he'd like to meet Jessica Savitch. Then, finally, in September, Callan, who had met Savitch briefly at a Christmas party at Bob Mulholland's apartment in December 1982, told Fischbein she'd send Savitch a note. In the short, typed memo, Callan reminded Savitch that they'd met, then said that she knew this was an unusual thing to do but a young male friend would very much like to meet Savitch. To Callan's amazement, she received a response the next day thanking her for her letter and saying that Savitch would be happy to make Fischbein's acquaintance. Later one of Savitch's staff told Callan that Savitch had been touched by her note. "She thought it was *elegant*," the staffer said.

On their first date, Fischbein pulled out all the stops: limo, orchestra seats to a show, *La Cage Aux Folles,* that had been sold out months in advance, and dinner afterward at what turned out to be the favorite restaurant of both, the "21" Club. For their second date, on Sunday, October 10, Fischbein drove the two of them up along the Hudson River to Hyde Park and West Point. Then they drove across the Bear Mountain Bridge to Boscobel, a Federal-style house open to the public. Built in 1804, it has a magnificent view of the entire Hudson River Valley and thirty acres of beautifully planted grounds. Savitch and Fischbein spent the fall afternoon strolling about the old estate, smelling the fading roses in the formal garden, trying to identify the herbs growing in the little garden off the kitchen, enjoying the tranquillity of this retreat from not just Manhattan but the entire twentieth century. Afterward Fischbein sent Savitch a book of poetry by Amy Lowell; on the flyleaf he wrote,

> For Jessica, with the hope that, when you pick up this volume from time to time, you will remember, among other things, our trip to Boscobel and lovely day in the country (and even, per chance, that you might think of me). With growing respect and affection, love, Martin.

A few days later, Fischbein and Savitch drove to Margate, picked up her two nephews, and took them to a World Series game in Baltimore, where the Orioles beat the Phillies. The kids were delirious with excitement. Afterward, Fischbein told Liz Callan that he understood a lot more about Savitch now. He was struck by the modest circumstances of her background, the little house in Margate and the white-bread culture out of which she had come; it had touched him, he told Callan, that Savitch felt comfortable enough with him to bring him home to meet her family. Savitch, too, was happy with the outing; the next week she wrote a second note to Callan, thanking Callan for introducing her to Fischbein and saying that they simply had to get together soon.

The next week, Fischbein and Savitch had a double date with Fischbein's business partner, Jay Emmett, a film producer, and his wife, Martha, a psychologist and writer. They went to see Anthony Quinn in *Zorba* and then ate at Fischbein's favorite Mexican restaurant. Martha had never met either Fischbein or Savitch, and she liked both immediately. "He was calm and talked slowly and seemed so centered," she said. "In a way they seemed to complement each other perfectly, even in their humor. They were both very funny, but she was whimsical and he was laconic." Martha found Savitch intriguing—"like a nervous colt," she said. "She was so pretty and frail and fearful." Fischbein said that he and Savitch were planning a drive to Pennsylvania on the coming weekend to see the fall foliage and look for antiques and asked the Emmetts to accompany them, but the Emmetts had a previous engagement and wished Fischbein and Savitch a pleasant trip.

For more than a year, Fischbein had wanted to meet Jessica

Savitch, and now he was dating her. But the ghost of Merri Spaeth lingered, and he had no intention of becoming emotionally dependent on Savitch or any other woman, at least not anytime soon. At the same time he was escorting Savitch, he was dating a former model and an investment banker. On Friday, October 21, he told his secretary to have a birthday bouquet delivered the following Monday to yet another romantic interest, a woman in California. Although he was intrigued by Savitch, he was not blind to her problems. He told Callan that Savitch had described the *Digest* fiasco to him and had blamed medication taken after a sailboat accident damaged her nose. He also told Callan that he found Savitch very self-centered. Callan reminded him that Savitch was an on-air talent, a breed known for having major egos; besides, Callan said, Fischbein had a great talent for drawing people out and getting them to talk about themselves. When Callan asked him what would happen to this new romance if he moved to Chicago as publisher of the *Sun-Times,* Fischbein replied, "If it's love, it will work out."

When another friend joked to Fischbein that bad things had happened to people who were involved with Savitch, he simply said that he found Savitch vulnerable and wounded. Because these were characteristics that Fischbein did not ordinarily esteem, the friend assumed he would probably help Savitch as best he could, but would not end up in a long-term relationship with her. Fischbein, who had asked this friend's advice on how to handle a woman whom he once dated who drank too much, never mentioned drugs, from which the friend also assumed that he had no knowledge that drugs were a factor in Savitch's life.

Savitch, too, was interested. She told her makeup and wardrobe and hair people she'd met a great guy. She ran into Bob Sutton, the former program manager at KYW, in the lobby of the *New York Post* and told him she'd met a great guy. She called Mort Crim on Thursday, October 20, and told him, too, that she'd met a great guy. She told one friend that she'd met a great guy—a nice Jewish boy, someone that the friend would approve of.

But Savitch also had other relationships that were not yet over. On Friday, October 21, Ron Kershaw came to see her at her apartment for the first time in many, many months. After he had encountered her at Saratoga, he had sent her a letter declaring that whether or not they ever got back together, he wanted her to know that all the times he said he didn't love her he had been lying. Savitch phoned him and denied having been the woman he saw, but she did agree to let him pay her a visit. He was shocked at what he saw. Although she was tanned and looked well, she seemed to Kershaw to have lost the ambition that had been such an integral part of her personality. Savitch told him that the whole ball of wax just didn't mean anything to her anymore and that she wanted to go back to a local station. Kershaw, who was leaving NBC, tried to talk her into working on some projects together, but was unable to light any spark. "She was empty," he said. "She'd never been empty about anything to do with this business. She'd been all-consumed at times, she'd been disillusioned at times, she'd been pissed at times, but never just empty and not caring."

They talked for hours, laughing and crying about their years together. Kershaw told her that if he could have traded places with her father and let him come and tell her that she was good, that everything was all right, he would have done it in a second. Savitch admitted that she, too, had always loved Kershaw, no matter how often she had told him she hated him. At the end they were totally exhausted and fell asleep on the couch in the living room. Later Kershaw woke up and put his coat on to leave. "Rabbit," Savitch said to him, "I feel like I am dying." When Kershaw told her things would get better, she shrugged. "I just feel like I'm dying," she said again. "You don't need me any more, but please, for me, don't let 'em whip us."

As Kershaw walked down the hall toward the elevator, he was disturbed and distressed. Savitch had always considered herself to be vaguely psychic, and he was afraid she might be right. He knew that she wasn't simply talking about how tired she was, or how discouraged, but that she felt death itself coming on, and she was saying good-bye.

The next night, Savitch went to see Neil Simon's *Brighton Beach Memoirs* with the attorney from out-of-town. At the end of the summer he had gotten back together with his wife and had pulled a disappearing act on Savitch, refusing to answer her phone calls and even going to Europe for a few weeks to avoid her. Now he had come to New York to tell her that their romance was finished but that he was still her friend and would be there for her if she needed him. At dinner after the theater, Savitch told him she'd met a great guy and had visited Hyde Park with him. Although she acted like the attorney didn't matter, that he was just another man she had tired of, it seemed obvious to him that Savitch was trying to develop a sense of competition. Like David Fanning and Don Bowers before him, the attorney did not, in the end, deliver the message he had come to give.

On the morning of October 23, Savitch accompanied Fischbein to the Marble Collegiate Church, on lower Fifth Avenue, to hear Norman Vincent Peale preach. When Spaeth had left him, Fischbein had found consolation in Peale's books and had started to attend his services. This was the second time he had taken Savitch to hear Peale. After church, Savitch returned to her apartment to change for the trip she and Fischbein had planned to New Hope, a small artistic community that had become an elegant tourist trap in Bucks County, Pennsylvania. Fischbein had spent time in the area because Merri Spaeth owned a farm there, and Savitch knew it because it was only a short distance from Kennett Square and was also a favorite retreat for Philadelphians. However, when Mary Manilla stopped by her apartment for a brief chat, Savitch had a change of heart. She told Manilla that what she *really* wanted to do was to send Fischbein away, stay home with Manilla, and send out for pizza. Manilla insisted that Savitch go with Fischbein as planned. She reminded Savitch that this was the first man she'd met that she liked and told her that she could not just stay holed up in her apartment like a mole. Savitch went into the bathroom and threw up. It was, Manilla thought, just another anxious visit with Jessica. Then Savitch put on her raincoat, let Manilla escort her downstairs, and got into the blue Oldsmobile station wagon that Fischbein had requisitioned from the fleet leased for executive use by the *New York Post*. Manilla waved as they left.

That Sunday was full of rain and wind and fog, which ruled out much walking about, but Savitch, Fischbein, and Chewy the dog did manage to view some blazing foliage from the car. In New Hope, they browsed in the little shops that line the main street, then drove along River Road to a restaurant called

Chez Odette, which had been recommended to Fischbein by a friend. Originally a tavern built in 1794 to serve river boatmen on the adjacent Delaware River, it became a barge stop in the 1830s, when the Delaware Canal system was constructed next to the river. The building sat on a small artificial island in the middle of the canal, which there ran parallel to the river and just a few yards away. In 1961 the old, rambling building was bought by a retired Parisian vaudeville star, Odette Myrtil Logan, who gave it the Proustian title "Chez Odette" and lined its fieldstone walls with autographed photographs of her former co-stars, including Maurice Chevalier. In 1977, Odette sold the spot to a man named Frank Csaszar, who kept the decor but brought in a new and not quite so refined chef.

Savitch and Fischbein had reservations under her name for 6:00 P.M. From River Road, they made the hairpin turn over a little bridge into the restaurant parking lot, and stopped the car. Chewy waited in the back seat. Hurrying in from the wet, Savitch and Fischbein sat before the fire in the front room, where the locals ate. Around the corner was the long, low back room, with windows that opened onto the dark river. Because of the bad weather, there were few other clients to stare at the famous anchorwoman eating flounder florentine in the corner of Chez Odette. Savitch and Fischbein drank a little white wine —less than half a glass each. They finished at 7:15. Their waiter kept Savitch's American Express receipt as a souvenir.

Because it was Sunday, there was no valet parking. The weather had got worse, and it was hard to see when Savitch and Fischbein scurried outside to the rented station wagon. Fischbein snapped on his seat belt and started the car. At that point in its course, River Road ran on a rise parallel to the parking lot, which seemed to have two exits but in fact had only one. They had entered from the south, to Fischbein's left. Apparently making the erroneous assumption that the narrow road by which he had entered was one way, Fischbein turned north, or right, into what was in fact a driveway for several houses built on the island. On either side of the driveway were two small, unlit signs, yellow printing on a brown background: MOTOR VEHICLES PROHIBITED. In the rain and the dark, they would have been invisible.

The nearest house had floodlights in front of it, which gave the appearance of an exit; next to it was the unlit canal. Without a fence or any kind of barrier to set it off, it resembled a strip of blacktop. Up ahead, on the far side of the canal, was a blinking yellow light that seemed to indicate that Fischbein could drive out that way. It was an extremely dangerous situation. Over the years, several cars had gone into the canal, and one person had died.

Fischbein drove off the parking lot. About fifty feet up the driveway, the car drove off the stone wall of the canal, flipped over, and fell twelve feet. Although the canal had been dry all summer, it now contained several feet of water on top of four feet of mud. The car sank into the ooze, its top crushed down and stove in like the crease on top of a fedora. All inside were killed almost immediately. Savitch was found in the back seat with her dog.

The accident was not discovered until midnight, when the owners of the house with the floodlights returned from a Philadelphia Flyers game. When the police took the bodies to the morgue, the attendants had to scrape the mud from their faces to establish their identities. Savitch's eyes were still open.

Ron Kershaw covered a football game in Baltimore that night. Early Monday he drove back to New York. He was listening to KYW all-news radio when he heard the latest headline: Jessica Savitch Found Dead. When he reached the exit for New Hope, he turned off and drove to the site of the accident. He was torn by grief. As a reporter will, he sought out the police and learned what he could. He tried unsuccessfully to get Chewy's body so that he could give the dog the decent burial Savitch would have wanted. Walking alongside the canal, he thought about how much Savitch had loved *Wuthering Heights.* For years she had told him to read it. He only got around to it after they split up—actually, he really only watched the movie. But Olivier had made an impression. Walking around that morning, Kershaw kept thinking, Well, I will always be out there on the moors.

Epilogue

Savitch's death made headlines across the country, and obituaries appeared in every major newspaper. All day on October 24, all-news radio stations and Cable News Network repeated the details of the fatal accident. That evening, Tom Brokaw, who occupied the anchor seat that Savitch had wanted all her life, delivered her obituary on *NBC Nightly News*. It was one minute and eight seconds long.

With the stories that had been circulating about Savitch's drug use, many people in the business assumed that cocaine had played some role in her death. But no drugs were found in the car or, according to the coroner's report, in the bodies. It was just as it appeared: a dreadful, unnecessary, tragic accident.

The funeral was held Tuesday, October 25, in a small funeral home at the farthest reaches of Atlantic City. It was at the end of the boardwalk, at a Jewish funeral home in an area of crumbling houses and broken sidewalks. Attendance was by invitation only. Wading through the clutch of photographers in the vacant lot outside were about four dozen people, including Ed Bradley, David Buda, Tony Busch, Mort Crim, David Fanning, Mary Manilla, Martin Rand, the Rappaports, Sue Simmons, and Tom Wolzien—a scattering of people from every part of Savitch's life. Ron Kershaw and Mel Korn were not invited.

It was an awkward, miserable gathering. Although the mourners were confronted by a casket, it was empty. Savitch's body had been cremated with that of Chewy. Crim delivered the eulogy, finishing with the last paragraph of *Charlotte's Web*. After twenty minutes, the owner of the funeral home appeared in a trenchcoat and shooed everybody out with the words, "That's it! That's the end! Please exit by the side door!"

Afterward, they went to Savitch's mother's house. To Fanning, the decaying funeral home had been a surprise; Savitch's mother's modest bungalow was another. He had always seen Savitch in elegant surroundings. There was a disjunction between the food at the "21" Club and the luncheon meat on a platter in the small living room in Margate. It made him sad to think about it. Network was foie gras. But Savitch—Savitch was lunch meat.

For days, the network was deluged with letters and telephone calls expressing sorrow and sympathy over Savitch's death. Even the small-town papers ran stories, and then there were follow-up stories, and notices about a memorial fund at Ithaca College. A week after her death, Savitch was featured for the first time on the cover of *People* magazine. It was, Ron Kershaw thought when he saw it, exactly what she would have wanted. "I was so proud of her," he said. "She'd made it."

Index

213 208 - 1941 - 9413

Noble:
387-
8805

3362
3374
Koll: